Visual Basic Shell Programming

J. P. Hamilton

O'REILLY®

Beijing · Cambridge · Farnham · Köln · Paris · Sebastopol · Taipei · Tokyo

Visual Basic Shell Programming
by J. P. Hamilton

Copyright © 2000 O'Reilly & Associates, Inc. All rights reserved.
Printed in the United States of America.

Published by O'Reilly & Associates, Inc., 101 Morris Street, Sebastopol, CA 95472.

Editor: Ron Petrusha

Production Editor: Jeffrey Holcomb

Cover Designer: Ellie Volckhausen

Printing History:

July 2000:	First Edition.

Library of Congress Cataloging-in-Publication Data

Hamilton, J.P.
    Visual basic shell programming : integrating applications with the Windows shell / J.P.
        Hamilton. p. cm.
      ISBN 1-56592-670-6
       1. Microsoft Visual BASIC. 2. BASIC (Computer program language) 3. Application
    software. I. Title.

QA76.73.B3 H339 2000
005.26'8--dc21   00-033974

ISBN: 1-56592-670-6   [8/00]
[M]

Preface

Some friends and I were talking a few years back about computer books and bookstores in general. At the time, it seemed to us like no one was writing any books for people who already knew how to program. Every book on the shelf was a 900-page behemoth whose first few chapters told you how to turn on your computer, why the particular language was so great, and so on. The last eight chapters were always reference. We were convinced that if you took any one of these two-ton masterpieces and ripped out the irrelevant information, or information that could be found in the documentation, at best you would be left with about 200 pages of pertinence. That was our theory, anyway.

We decided it would be really great if someone would write a book that was *skinny*. These skinny books would contain the juiciest tidbits of programming information—the ripest fruits from the tree of coding knowledge. Anything superfluous would be hacked away and left by the wayside. The skinny book would assume that you already knew why you were using a particular programming language. Therefore, it could forego the first three chapters found in most of the other books. It would be exciting to read cover to cover, because there would be something for everyone in each chapter. And last, but not least, it would serve as a reference that you could come back to again and again.

Now, there are a few such skinny books that I can think of off the top of my head. *The C Programming Language* by Brian W. Kernighan and Dennis M. Ritchie (Prentice Hall) is one of my all-time favorites. Another is *Effective C++* by Scott Meyers (Addison-Wesley). I've had both of these books for years, and they still hold a proud place on my bookshelf. They are *skinny* in the true sense of the word! I say this to prove that such books do exist.

So, what does all this talk about the inherent properties of skinniness mean? Well, I have to say it. The first motivation for writing this book was that I, too, wanted to write a skinny book. But not so fast . . . I am not saying that I place myself in the leagues of the aforementioned authors. You know, and I know, that that would be nothing short of blasphemy. So, make no mistake—I am an everyday programmer, just like you. All I wanted to do was to write a book that would be a good read, cover to cover: a book with good projects and an interesting topic. Really, my true goal was to write a book that I would buy myself. I hope I have done that.

I picked the shell for the topic of the book because, first and foremost, I thought it was really cool. I read an article on browser helper objects (see Chapter 12, *Browser Extensions*) by Scott Roberts in the May 1998 issue of *Microsoft Interactive Developer*. My first thought was, "I wonder if I could pull that off in VB?" (It seems I am always trying to "pull something off" in VB.) Well, I pulled it off. After that I just couldn't get enough of the shell. I wrote a band object (see Chapter 13, *Band Objects*) and then a context menu handler (see Chapter 4, *Context Menu Handlers*). In fact, most of the code for this book was written before I had even started the book.

As I was writing all this code, I realized something. I was working with some really interesting, advanced VB code. I was using pointers like nobody's business, rewriting system-level interfaces, and working with parts of COM that VB tries to hide away. In fact, I learned quite a bit about COM that VB didn't really want me to know. Topics of interest seemed to lead in unexpected directions. For instance, when I was doing the code for Chapter 11, *Namespace Extensions*, I learned how to link lists in VB. That's when I thought to myself that this would make a really great book.

The material in this book pushes the perceived limits of what you can do with Visual Basic. Visual Basic offers a powerful development environment for virtually all types of applications, components, and tools. Yet, much of the time, all that we hear about are Visual Basic's limitations—what you can't do. Each of these "can'ts" is used to prove the inferiority of Visual Basic and the superiority of the critic's favorite development environment or programming language. For instance, Visual Basic is seen as grossly inferior because it can't be used to create standard Windows dynamic link libraries (a contention, by the way, that is completely untrue). Also, how many times have you heard a "real" programmer complain about the absence of pointers in Visual Basic? (This charge, by the way, is also untrue.) Similarly, Visual Basic's strength as an application development package is turned into a weakness by its critics; they argue that, while you can create applications quickly, these applications can't be tightly integrated with the Windows shell, since shell extensions can only be written in C++. Along with most Visual Basic programmers, I accepted that contention for a long time; this book, however, shows that limitation to be false and, in the process, implicitly shows that Visual Basic is a great tool for developing COM components of all kinds.

But I'm not going to lie to you. In order to accomplish some of the things we need to accomplish in this book, we have to take some very, very sneaky steps. But in my opinion, that's what makes VB so much fun. In one sense, this book is for the "hacker," the person who likes to get under the hood and explore the dark catacombs beneath the language. In another sense (hopefully), this book is a testament to just how flexible Visual Basic can be.

So, with that said, I have not tried to write a literary masterpiece. I just wanted to write a really neat book. I hope you enjoy it.

The Book's Audience

You should already be somewhat knowledgeable in Visual Basic. You don't need a black belt in VB kung fu, but you should have already done a few projects in the language. Again, I really need to emphasize that this is not a book for beginners. If you are a beginner, there are many books (big, fat, heavy books) waiting for you. If you know VB but are not really up to speed on COM, that's okay. There is a crash course on COM in Chapter 2, *COM Basics*. We'll take it step by step from there on out.

Developing Your Own Shell Extensions

Have you ever looked at some of the standard features of the Windows family of operating systems and wished that you could take advantage of them in the software that you're developing with Visual Basic? Once you've finished *Visual Basic Shell Programming*, you'll be able to add those standard features successfully to your software as long as they're implemented using shell extensions. Consider the following three examples:

Context-sensitive icons

Have you ever looked at the Recycle Bin icon and thought that you'd like your application icons to behave similarly? For instance, perhaps you'd like one icon to appear if an application data file was backed up successfully and another if it was modified but not backed up. Or perhaps you'd like an icon that reflects the template from which a document was created. For these purposes, you can develop an icon handler. The icon handler developed in this book reads a file and displays an icon based on its content. You can easily extend this to base the displayed icon not only on some aspect of the file's content, but also on some characteristic of the file, such as its creation date and time, its size, or its file attributes.

Browsing namespaces

You've probably noticed that the Windows Explorer, unlike the File Manager of Windows 3.x, does not just display classic filesystem objects. Instead, you can browse such things as printers, Control Panel applets, and computers on the network. Perhaps you'd like to make your application data browsable in the Explorer. By writing a namespace extension, you can do just that. Visual Basic shell programming shows you how to browse namespaces by developing three sample namespace extensions, including one that allows you to browse and navigate the system registry within Explorer.

Customized context menu items

One of the most popular features introduced in Windows 95 was the pop-up menu, the context-sensitive menu that appears when the user right-clicks an item in the list pane of Explorer. In fact, pop-up menus are so popular that users have come to look for them in all applications, and *Visual Basic Shell Programming* will show you how to build them. The context menu handler developed in this book displays particular menu items based on the contents of the selected file. However, the example can be easily extended to display a menu item based on such things as the file's attributes or its creation date. For example, if you were to develop a namespace extension that made your application's database browsable in the Explorer, you'd also want to allow the user to edit the selected record by selecting an option from the context menu if the record was not locked. After reading the chapter on context menu handlers, you'll find building such a shell extension surprisingly easy.

Organization of This Book

This book is loosely divided into four parts. Even though each chapter contains a distinct project, many chapters build on knowledge gained from previous chapters. So, really, the book is best read in the order in which the chapters were written. But don't worry. If you just have to skip ahead to Chapter 10, *InfoTip Handler*, to find out how to write an InfoTip handler, you can do that, too. Any information you might need from previous chapters is referenced. Here's how the book breaks down:

Part I, *Introduction to the Shell and the Basics of COM*

Part I includes Chapters 1, 2, and 3. These chapters are designed to introduce you to the basics of the Windows shell and to provide a jumpstart on the Component Object Model and how it relates to writing in-process components for Visual Basic.

Part II, *Shell Extensions*

Part II includes Chapters 4 through 10. In these seven chapters, we will write seven shell extensions. These chapters are centered around a mythical file type (called a *.rad* file), which contains simple data about animals. Although the focus of these projects centers around a make-believe file type, these chapters are designed to show you the most effective ways to build shell extensions for your own data.

Why an Imaginary File Type?

You may wonder why I've chosen to invent an imaginary file type, rather than showing you how to develop shell extensions that work with an existing file type. The answer is really quite simple: shell extensions change the way a particular feature of Windows works, and I don't feel presumptuous enough to change the way that Windows handles the files you work with day in and day out. However, although the file type is imaginary, the examples are immediately useful. The context menu handler and icon handler examples, for instance, show how to create customized pop-up menu items or to display custom icons based on the contents of the file.

In these chapters we will write the following projects:

Context menu handler

> Context menus are the menus that appear when you right-click on a file. Context menu handlers allow you to add your own items (and the code to carry out the commands) to this menu. Context menu handlers are discussed in Chapter 4.

Drag-and-drop handler

> These are similar to context menu handlers. Drag-and-drop handlers are actually context menus that are displayed when a file is dragged with the right mouse button. Although we won't create any, drag-and-drop handlers are discussed along with context menu handlers in Chapter 4.

Icon handler

> Icon handlers allow files of the same type to have different icons. These icons could indicate the state of the data contained within the files or provide other additional feedback. Creating icon handlers is covered in Chapter 5, *Icon Handlers.*

Property page extension

> The property page dialog appears when you select Properties from a file's context menu. A property page extension allows you to add property tabs to this dialog. This is a convenient way to allow users to access various elements of the data contained within the files without starting up an application. All of Microsoft Office's documents have property page extensions defined for them. Developing property sheet handlers is discussed in Chapter 6, *Property Sheet Handlers.*

Drop handler

> Drop handlers allow your files to become drop targets. This allows files of any type (that you wish) to be dropped on a specified file type. The drop

handler can then perform any processing that you might need on the two files—perhaps a file comparison, for example. Creating drop handlers is covered in Chapter 7, *Drop Handlers*.

Data handler

Data handlers allow you to modify what happens during a copy, cut, or paste operation for a given file type. Developing custom data handlers is discussed in Chapter 8, *Data Handlers*.

Copy hook handler

Copy hook handlers allow you to permit or prevent a given file from being copied or renamed. Developing copy hook handlers is discussed in Chapter 9, *Copy Hook Handlers*.

InfoTip handler

InfoTip handlers provide tool tips for your file. With this tool tip, you can convey information right from the shell about the file in question, such as who wrote it or when it was created. Creating InfoTip handlers is treated in Chapter 10.

Part III, *Namespace Extensions*

Part III contains only Chapter 11, but it's a large chapter indeed. This chapter is designed to introduce you to the very prodigious world of namespace extensions. During the course of this chapter, we will build a simple namespace extension that displays a hierarchy of arbitrary objects. The project is a very simple one that's designed only for the purpose of introducing you to the concepts of namespaces and of developing namespace extensions. However, source code for two real world examples—a registry namespace extension and running object table (ROT) namespace extension—is also provided. By installing the registry namespace extension, for instance, you can view and navigate your system registry just as if it were part of your filesystem.

Part IV, *Browser Extensions*

Part IV includes Chapters 12 through 14. These chapters are concerned with extending the functionality of Internet Explorer, which, as of shell version 4.71 (that is, Internet Explorer 4.0), was basically integrated with the shell. But don't let that fool you. Even though the focus of these chapters is developing for the Internet, these components can be written for Explorer, too. In these three chapters, we will build the following four projects:

Browser helper objects

Browser helper objects (or BHOs) are components that sit between the Internet and the browser. With them, you have access to every HTML tag on every page that you surf. Also, you can capture any event supported by the browser. This means you can use BHOs to perform a wide variety of Internet-related tasks. Developing BHOs is the focus of the first half of Chapter 12.

Browser extensions

> Browser extensions are similar to browser helper objects, but they are only available for Internet Explorer 5.0. Unlike BHOs, browser extensions can have an associated menu item and toolbar button that is available from Internet Explorer. Browser extensions are covered in the second half of Chapter 12.

Band objects

> The Search, History, and Favorites windows that are part of Internet Explorer are actually band objects. Remember the ill-fated Channel window in Windows 98? That was a band object, too. If you have an Internet-related application that needs a user interface, a band object is the way to go. Band objects are discussed in Chapter 13.

Docking windows

> Docking windows are basically toolbars that you can add to Explorer's client area. These can be docked on all four borders of Explorer's client area and can provide a means for components like namespace extensions, browser extensions, and band objects to provide additional user interface capability. Developing docking windows is covered in Chapter 14, *Docking Windows.*

In Parts II through IV, each chapter follows a similar format, which consists of the following four major sections:

How the shell extension works

> This section provides critical background information on the particular shell extension but also can be useful when debugging an application that doesn't behave quite as expected. It covers such topics as how the shell knows that the shell extension exists in the first place and how the shell and the extension communicate with one another.

The interfaces and their methods

> The operation of shell extensions is based on the Windows shell loading the extension and calling methods of its interfaces. This section documents those interfaces and their methods. You can read this section to gain an understanding of what interfaces and which methods are used in a particular kind of shell extension. You can also return to this section when you need a reference source when developing your own shell extensions.

Implementing the extension

> In this section, we develop our example shell extension. Here you can see how a shell extension might be implemented, as well as look at some working Visual Basic code.

Registering the extension

> This final discussion covers the process of installing and registering the shell extension on a particular system. The central part of this section is typically a

.reg file, which registers the extension in the system registry. In most cases, the file need only be slightly modified to work with any shell extension that you might build.

Software Requirements

This book assumes that you are running Windows 95, Windows 98, Windows NT (with service pack 4 or later), or Windows 2000. Basically, I am assuming that you are running Windows. Unless you're running Windows 2000 (where Active Desktop is enabled by default), some of the components also require that you have installed Internet Explorer 4.0 with the Active Desktop option. Unfortunately, by design, Internet Explorer 5.0 does not give you the option to install Active Desktop. To have IE 5.0 install it if it hasn't been installed by IE 4.0, Microsoft's solution is to uninstall Internet Explorer 5.0 and to reinstall Internet Explorer 4.0, selecting Active Desktop. Then once again install Internet Explorer 5.0. It's painful, but some of the really cool examples in this book (in Chapter 13) just won't work without it.

All the code in this book was developed with Visual Basic 6.0. But VB 5.0 will work, too. It might be handy (but not necessary) to have Visual C++ installed as well. A few of the chapters require access to a resource editor, and the one that comes with this product is really good. Also, Visual C++ contains interface definitions and header files that are an invaluable reference when you are working with COM.

Obtaining the Sample Code

All of the sample Visual Basic source code from *Visual Basic Shell Programming* is freely downloadable from the O'Reilly & Associates web site at *http://vb.oreilly.com*. The downloadable content itself falls into three categories:

Sample source code
> Most of the examples developed in this book are intended to illustrate how to build a particular kind of shell extension without providing a real world implementation. In this case, you'll benefit from looking at the code and using it as the basis of the shell extensions that you yourself would like to develop.

Working shell extensions
> Several of the examples developed in this book are complete working extensions that you may want to use. RegSpace, for example, allows you to browse the registry from Explorer without requiring that you open RegEdit or a similar registry browsing tool.

Shell programming type library

Creating a type library that defines the interfaces and methods called by the shell in handling shell extensions is a prerequisite for any serious (and even not so serious) attempt to develop shell extensions. The VB Shell Library, which is described in the following section, is also available both in its source code (IDL) and compiled forms from the O'Reilly Visual Basic web site (*http://vb.oreilly.com*).

The VB Shell Type Library

During the course of this book, we will build a type library that facilitates building shell components. A type library is a language-independent file that contains interface definitions, enumerations, and constants. The type library we build will contain only those definitions that are necessary for programming components for the Windows shell. (Actually, some of the interfaces we use could be used elsewhere.)

Type libraries are built using a scripting language called, simply enough, Interface Definition Language, or IDL. Knowing IDL is not necessary for reading this book. In fact, you can consider this book an IDL boot camp. IDL is actually a rich language, but because of the environment we are in (Visual Basic), many of the more advanced features of the language are beyond our reach. So actually, I will use only the most basic elements of the language in this book.

The type library we will build is specific only with regards to the shell, not the book. Therefore, you will be able to take this library with you for use in your own shell-related projects when you are done. But even though we will focus on the shell, we do so with the idea that you will be able to take the principles learned with you.

Conventions Used in This Book

Throughout this book, I have used the following typographic conventions:

Constant width

Indicates a language construct such as a statement, a constant, an attribute, or an expression. Interface names and lines of code appear in constant width, as do function and method prototypes.

Constant width bold

Indicates a highlighted section of code to be brought to the reader's attention.

Italic

Represents intrinsic and application-defined functions, the names of system elements such as directories and files, and Internet resources such as web documents. New terms are also italicized when they are first introduced.

`Constant width italic`
> Indicates replaceable parameter names in prototypes, command syntax, or body text, and indicates variable and parameter names in body text.

Request for Comments

The information in this book has been tested and verified, but you may find that features have changed (or even find mistakes!). You can send any errors you find, as well as suggestions for future editions, to:

> O'Reilly & Associates, Inc.
> 101 Morris Street
> Sebastopol, CA 95472
> (800) 998-9938 (in the United States or Canada)
> (707) 829-0515 (international/local)
> (707) 829-0104 (fax)

You can also send messages electronically. To be put on the mailing list or request a catalog, send email to:

> *info@oreilly.com*

To ask technical questions or comment on the book, send email to:

> *booktech@oreilly.com*

There is a web site for the book, where examples, errata, and any plans for future editions are listed. You can access this page at:

> *http://www.oreilly.com/catalog/vbshell*

For more information about this book and others, see the O'Reilly web site:

> *http://www.oreilly.com*

For technical information on various aspects of Visual Basic programming, to participate in VB discussion forums, or to acquaint yourself with O'Reilly's line of Visual Basic books, you can access the O'Reilly Visual Basic web site at:

> *http://vb.oreilly.com*

Acknowledgments

When I approached my favorite publishers with the idea for the book, I only included O'Reilly because I thought a rejection email from them would look really great. I had plans to frame it and everything. The fact that I have written a book for the supreme deities of computer publishing still has me in awe. I mean, I have a book with an animal on the cover and everything. All I can do is say "Wow." So first and foremost, I would like to thank Tim O'Reilly for having the faith in me to write this book. I thought it would be a great book; he did too. They call that synergy! But ideas aside, none of this could have happened without the greatest editor in the known Universe. Of course, you all know who it is, but I'll mention his name anyway—Ron Petrusha. For those of you who don't know, editors are the ones who actually know how to write books and spend an awful amount of time trying to teach people like me to do the same. Ron, thank you for convincing me to write this book. I couldn't have done it without you. I think I have mastered the semicolon. Next comes the apostrophe.

I must acknowledge all my friends and family who gave me much support during the course of writing this book. But I would like to give special thanks to Kathy Duval (that's my mom!), Glen Duval, Kara Duval, Chris Mercier (Big Chris), Bill Purvis (The Purvis), and Courtney Lomelo (She Who Must Not Be Named) for being my teachers during this time.

I owe many thanks to my proofreader and technical advisor, Brett Lindsey. When something just doesn't make sense, he is really good at pointing that out. For you, I give you your own paragraph.

There are several people whom I do not know personally, but have my thanks anyway, because without them this book would not have been possible. The first is Matt Curland, the inventor of the vtable swapping trick that makes 99% of this book possible. I learned about this interesting little trick while looking through code for a context menu handler that he had written. (This code still might be available in the VB owner area on Microsoft's web site.) Needless to say, I don't think I ever would have figured that out by myself. This guy is a wicked coder! I also need to mention all the people on the *ATL@DISCUSS.MICROSOFT.COM* listserv. These people really know COM, and sometimes they actually put up with me asking specific questions about VB and COM. When I was looking for technical reviewers, this is where I went looking. A more knowledgeable group of COM commandos does not exist.

Finally, I want to thank Daniel Creeron for his excellent, thorough technical review of the book.

With that said, it is time to explore the shell . . .

Table of Contents

I

Introduction to the Shell and the Basics of COM

1

Introduction

Before I start discussing the shell, it might be a good idea to define what, exactly, the shell is in terms of Windows. Simply put, the shell is a graphical user interface provided by Windows that allows you to access the various components of the operating system. Sounds good, huh? When you think about it, almost everything you do within Windows begins with the shell (unless you do everything from a DOS window or from console mode in Windows NT and Windows 2000). This includes running software, accessing files, configuring your system, and so on.

This shell provided by Windows is contained within the program *Explorer.exe*. For those of you who have been using Windows since the 16-bit days, you might think of Explorer as a glorified version of File Manager, Windows 3.1's utility for accessing the filesystem. This could not be farther from the truth. Explorer is really much more than a file manager. It provides a view of your entire system and the means to interact with it. Not only can you access files and create directories, you can configure your printer, schedule tasks, and even surf the Internet. Throughout the course of this book, we will use the terms shell and Explorer interchangeably. They really are one and the same.

You should also know that Explorer is *always* running. What you think of as Explorer—the browser program that allows you to navigate directories and access your files—is actually a secondary thread in the Explorer process. The primary instance of Explorer is the Desktop. You really are using the shell more than you might think.

COM and the Shell

On the surface, Explorer seems to be the Swiss Army knife of applications—the one application that lets you do everything. But this is not really the case. In actuality,

Explorer is comprised of many different components working together to create the illusion of uniformity.

These components are built using the Component Object Model, or COM. And using this same technology, you can use Visual Basic to write components that fit seamlessly into the heart of Windows using documented interfaces. You actually have the power to extend the functionality of Windows itself.

Programming for the Shell

Suppose that every time you copied a bitmap file, its image was made available on the clipboard. Currently, Windows does not support this functionality. But with a data handler (see Chapter 8, *Data Handlers*) you could easily add this feature yourself. Maybe you would like to navigate into an Access database as if it were just another directory in the filesystem. You could do it with the proper namespace extension (see Chapter 12, *Browser Extensions*). Or you might like to automatically process information on a web page (say, your online brokerage account) every time you navigated to the URL. A browser helper object is the answer (see Chapter 13, *Band Objects*).

These are just a few examples of the many things you can accomplish by programming the shell. But all of these examples, and all shell components in general, share one common attribute: they integrate fully with Explorer. This gives the impression that they are actually a part of the shell itself, and technically, they are. Why is this important? Chances are, the application that is used the most by Windows users world-wide is *Explorer.exe*. It is probably familiar to more people than any other application. This means that, by integrating your application with the shell, you automatically make at least a portion of your application's functionality conveniently and easily available to anyone who is accustomed to working with the shell. An excellent example is the popular WinZip program developed by Niko Mak Computing, Inc: the two most common processes of archive management— adding and extracting files from a *.zip* file—can be accomplished from the shell without directly opening the WinZip program itself.

This shell integration in turn offers a number of advantages:

Greater ease of use
>Because users of your application can work with an interface that's consistent with that of Windows as a whole, they will find your application easier to learn and use. As a result, users will be happy with, rather than frustrated by, your application.

A more professional application
>How many times have you used a "Windows" application that just didn't seem to be written for Windows? Perhaps it had its own printer drivers. Maybe it

deleted files outright rather than moving them to the Recycle Bin. Or possibly its windows just looked funny. In any case, applications that fall into this category for whatever reason are typically perceived as inelegant and amateurish. By integrating your application with the shell, there are fewer surprises for the user, and your application succeeds in conveying your professionalism as a programmer.

Greater programming expertise

As we'll see shortly, the Windows shell is one central area of Windows programming that is very poorly documented. Shell programming also relies heavily on COM, which is cloaked in obscurity for many VB (and even C++) programmers. Hence, when you're programming the Windows shell, you're working on the cutting edge in two areas. For those to whom programming is a passion as well as a profession, shell programming—and the knowledge gained from it—is extremely rewarding.

Clearly there are advantages to developing shell extensions and integrating your applications with Windows Explorer. There are also challenges. Traditionally, developing shell extensions has been seen as a topic for experienced C and C++ programmers only; very few programmers are aware that you can create shell extensions using Visual Basic.

In addition to the fact that few programmers know that VB can be used to create shell extensions, the state of the documentation on programming the Windows shell is perhaps worse than in any other area. Possibly Microsoft felt that, despite the centrality of the Windows shell in the Windows operating system, programming the shell was too complex and too specialized for most programmers. Hence, even for C/C++ programmers, figuring out how to create a particular kind of shell extension and getting it to work is no easy matter.

But we'll surmount the first of these obstacles—the mistaken belief that VB cannot be used for shell programming—by showing you how to develop shell extensions. We'll also help you to surmount the second obstacle by providing the basic documentation on the shell and its COM interfaces that you can use when building your own shell extensions.

Kinds of Shell Extensions

Since our topic is the combination of shell programming and COM, we'll focus on building the following shell extensions, all of which rely on COM interfaces to be loaded and invoked by the shell:

Context menu handlers

A context menu is the pop-up menu that appears when you right-click on an object in Explorer. A context menu handler allows you to customize that menu by adding your own items to it. For instance, if you develop an application that stores thumbnails of graphics files, you might add an "Add to Thumbnail" option to the context menu of any supported graphics file. When the user selects the file, it is automatically added to the application's current thumbnail.

Drag-and-drop handlers

These are specialized context menu handlers; they control the pop-up menu that appears when a shell object is dragged and dropped using the right mouse button.

Icon handlers

Ordinarily, each file type has its own icon. For instance, every Word document is represented by a single icon that serves to identify it. An icon handler, though, allows you to define an icon for an individual instance of that file based on some attribute or condition of the file (its contents, its size, the date it was created, etc.). A classic example is the icon for the Recycle Bin: when it is empty, the Recycle Bin is represented by an empty trash can; when it is not empty, the Recycle Bin is represented by an overflowing trash can.

Property page extension

Every shell object has a Properties dialog that displays one or more property pages when the user selects the Properties menu option for that object. Like many of the features of the shell, the Properties dialog is extensible: you can write property page extensions that add pages to the dialog. An excellent example of this—and itself a powerful feature that can give the user greater control over his documents—is the Custom tab of a Word document's Properties dialog, which allows the user to define custom properties and modify their values.

Drop handler

Drop handlers allow your files to become drop targets. Once again, WinZip provides a good example. Consider what occurs when you drop a file (or files) onto a file object of type *.zip*: after you drop the files, a dialog is displayed that gives you the opportunity to add the files to the *.zip* file. This functionality is achieved through a drop handler.

Data handler

A data handler provides additional clipboard formats for a file object. In layman's terms, this means you can define additional behaviors for a file object during a cut-and-paste operation. There is almost no limit to what you can do with a data handler. When you copy your quarterly financial report (a spreadsheet in Excel), your data handler could place it in the clipboard as a graph. The graph would then be available from any program (via the Paste command) that knows how to deal with bitmaps, such as Microsoft Paint, Adobe Photoshop, Paint Shop Pro, etc.

Copy hook handler

Copy hook handlers are called by the shell before a move, delete, rename, or copy operation. The handler merely approves or disapproves the action. This handler might keep you from accidentally deleting your source code library!

InfoTip handler

InfoTip handlers are a nice touch for any file object. Microsoft Word documents provide a good example. Hold your cursor over any *.doc* file. After a brief moment, a tooltip (or InfoTip) listing the author of the document is displayed.

Namespace extension

My Computer, the Recycle Bin, and Network Neighborhood (to name a few) are all namespace extensions. Namespace extensions allow you to display your hierarchical data as if it were just another folder in the system. Imagine being to able to navigate into an Access database file right from Explorer. Namespace extensions also allow the creation of custom system folders, like the Fonts directory that is found in the Windows folder. This folder contains only fonts and provides additional user interface elements that are specific to fonts, like Print Preview.

Browser helper objects

Browser helper objects, or BHOs, give you access to every running instance of Internet Explorer. Through the Microsoft DHTML object model, a browser helper object also has access to every element of the web page that is currently being displayed. Maybe you would like to automatically convert every web page you view into Spanish. Maybe you need to restrict your customers' browsers to the corporate Intranet. You can do just about anything Internet-related with a browser helper object.

Browser extension

Browser extensions have all the same functionality as browser helper objects, but with two exceptions: they allow you to trigger their functionality via a menu item or toolbar button. For instance, you might write a browser extension that allows you to highlight a company's ticker symbol on any web page. When you press the toolbar button for the extension, the extension could get a real-time stock quote for the symbol and display it in a pop-up. Like browser helper objects, the only limit is your imagination.

Band objects

The Search, History, and Favorites windows that are a part of Internet Explorer are actually band objects. Remember the ill-fated Channel window in Windows 98? That was a band object, too. If you have an Internet-related application that needs a user interface, a band object is the way to go.

Docking Windows

Docking windows are toolbars that can be added to Explorer's client area. They are a great way to provide your other shell components with an additional user interface.

Not every aspect of the Windows shell has something to do with COM. Say, for instance, you want to add your program icon to the system tray. You really only need a few API calls that have nothing to do with COM in order to achieve this. Therefore, I won't discuss tray icons in this book. While this book does deal extensively with the shell, the main purpose of this book is to describe the mechanisms by which we can *extend* the functionality of the Windows operating system by using COM. System tray icons are pretty cool, but they don't really extend the operating system in any way. This is primarily a book on the shell. The secondary focus of the book is writing components with COM.

Conclusion

This book doesn't cover everything; it's really only a starting point. After all, Windows is a big world, especially when you're talking about the shell. And even more so when you bring COM into the picture. But hopefully, by the time you have finished reading this book, you will have learned a little more about both and had some fun in the process. So, now that you know where we are going, it's time to start going. Enjoy.

2

COM Basics

The components that will be developed in this book are in-process COM servers that run in the address space of Explorer, Internet Explorer, or both. Therefore, a discussion of COM, as it relates to the task ahead, is in order. Because the components are in-process, every aspect of COM will not be discussed (e.g., marshalling). The focus is the fundamental principles of COM in Visual Basic terms. And the goal is to present these concepts in a simple and straightforward manner, with the hope that you will understand the components you create in Visual Basic a little better.

What Is COM?

COM is an architecture. It is a standard for developing components that can interact with each other, regardless of the language in which they were written. This means that components that are written in C++, Java, and VB can all work together unaware of the language in which the other was written. This happens because COM is a *binary standard*. Simply put, when a COM component is loaded into memory, it looks a certain way. It's that simple. COM defines the rules that components use to interact with each other and the outside world. It is *not* a language. But any language that can call a function through a pointer can be used to write COM components.

A language like C++ offers a *source code* standard. This allows C++ programmers to reuse code at the source level. In other words, it provides the means for source code reusability. COM, on the other hand, has a much loftier goal. It promises code reuse at the binary level. Unlike C++ source code, a COM component does not need to be recompiled when it is used with a new C++ project. It does not have to be written in C++ either, for that matter. Once that finely tuned sorting algorithm has been placed in a COM server, it is available to any language that supports COM. There is also no need to worry about compiler specifics.

 To avoid any confusion, the terms object, component, and COM component are all used interchangeably. One or more objects can exist in a server, whether that server is a DLL or an EXE. COM servers will also be referred to as ActiveX DLLs.

Interfaces

An interface is the basic mechanism by which a COM component exposes functionality. You can think of an interface as a contract. It describes what a component is supposed to do. How it does it is left up to you as the creator of the interface, to a certain degree. One of the fundamentals of COM is the idea of separating the interface from the implementation.

For instance, Example 2-1 shows an interface created in Visual Basic called Animal.

Recreating the Example

This source code is from a class module, *Animal.cls*, that you should add to a standard VB EXE project named Animals. Set the Instancing property of the class to PublicNotCreatable; this will make the class inaccessible from outside your project and means that the Animal class must be included in the project in which it is being used.

Example 2-1. The Animal Interface

```
'Animal.cls

Private Enum Kingdoms
    Mammal = 1
    Reptile = 2
    Insect = 3
    Bird = 4
    Fish = 5
End Enum

'Returns animal kingdom.
Private Function Kingdom() As Kingdoms
End Function

'Returns the name of an animal in a string.
Private Function Name() As String
End Function
```

Example 2-1. The Animal Interface (continued)

```
'Returns the noise the animal makes in a string.
Private Function Noise() As String
End Function
```

Notice that the functions in the class module *animal.cls* are just empty stubs. C++ programmers would recognize this as an *abstract base class*. This serves only to describe what the Animal interface looks like. By itself this does nothing. The interface must be *implemented* before it becomes useful. This is done in Example 2-2, which creates a Cow class. The Cow class implements and serves as a specific instance of the Animal class.

Example 2-2. Animal Implementation

```
'Cow.cls

Implements Animal

Private Function Animal_Kingdom() As Kingdoms
    Animal_Kingdom = Mammal
End Function

Private Function Animal_Name() As String
    Animal_Name = "Cow"
End Function

Private Function Animal_Noise() As String
    Animal_Noise = "Moo!"
End Function
```

 If you have not done so, now would be a good time to register the copy of *Animals.dll* that is downloadable from the O'Reilly web site (*http://vb.oreilly.com*) using *regsvr32.exe*. This component will serve as a reference for the remainder of the chapter. You can register it from a DOS window using the syntax:

```
regsvr32.exe <path>\animals.dll
```

If you later want to unregister *animals.dll*, you can do it from a DOS window using the following syntax:

```
regsvr32.exe /u <path>\animals.dll
```

The `Animal` interface is specific to a point. `Animal_Kingdom` can't return the string "Mammal." It has to return one of five values defined by the `Kingdoms` enumeration. `Animal_Name` and `Animal_Noise` are little more vague. Theoretically, they could return any string value. Therefore, it's important to remember that the documentation for an interface is a part of the contract, too. The compiler does not enforce these values.

Classes

One of the details VB hides from the programmer is the fact that an interface and a class are two distinct entities. This is easier to visualize once you know what a class really looks like; Figure 2-1 attempts to depict the Cow class graphically. A class is nothing more than a pointer to an array of function pointers (member functions), followed by public and private data. This array of function pointers is called a *virtual function table*, or *vtable*. This arrangement allows multiple instances of a COM component to share the same vtable, which is very efficient in terms of memory. Of course, member variables are not shared. Every instance of a component has its own copy of any public or private member variables. Also, if a class such as Cow had any methods of its own or implemented any additional interfaces, these would be added to the vtable. The order of a vtable is very important, because for all practical purposes the vtable is the physical representation of the interfaces an object has implemented.

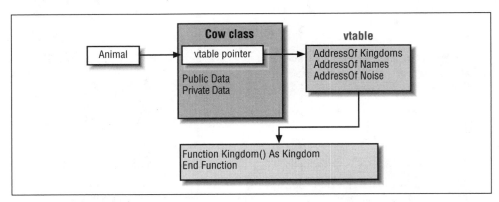

Figure 2-1. The Cow class

Interface Identifiers

The `Animal` and `Cow` interfaces are unique. Behind the scenes, VB has assigned a *globally unique identifier* (GUID) to both of these interfaces. A GUID that names an interface is called an IID. The IID for `Animal` is {101E95AB-018E-11D3-BB7C-444553540000}. Well, actually this is a string representation of an IID. An IID is a unique 128-bit number, and it is this value that is the true name for the `Animal` interface. After all, there's nothing really unique about the name `Animal`. What if another developer on the other side of the world wanted to create an interface named `Animal` with different attributes? GUIDs are how COM guarantees that an interface is unique, and this allows two interfaces with the same name to coexist peacefully on the same machine.

If you register the *Animals.dll* component provided with this chapter, the IID for `Animal` would be 101E95AB-018E-11D3-BB7C-444553540000. If you were to compile the source yourself, without any version compatibility (see the sidebar, "Version Compatibility," later in this chapter), the IID would be something different.

You can find IIDs in the registry under `HKEY_CLASSES_ROOT\Interface`. Figure 2-2 shows the Animal interface in the registry.

Figure 2-2. Registered interface

Because the key name is the IID itself, you will have to do a search on the interface name to find it.

Versions

Once an interface has been published, COM states that the interface is immutable. You never modify an old interface, you just create a new interface. In other words, the IID that is the `Animal` interface should always have three methods: `Kingdom`, `Name`, and `Noise`. These three methods will always be argument free and always return the types Kingdoms, String, and String, respectively. If any aspect of this interface changes, the contract is broken, and clients that relied on that interface will be broken; therefore, old interfaces are never modified.

If it became necessary to add functionality to the `Animal` interface at some future date, the rules of COM state that a new interface should be created (i.e., `Animal2`). This is one of the fundamental tenets of COM: rather than modifying an existing interface, a new interface is created instead. It is important to note that when the new interface is created, the old interface is left in place. Interfaces should never be deleted. This ensures that clients using the original interface will continue to work and that clients that are aware can take advantage of the features the new interface offers.

Class Identifiers

In addition to creating interface definitions, VB generates a *co-class* for `Animal` and `Cow`. A co-class is similar to an interface, but instead of method and property definitions, it contains a list of the interfaces a component supports. It is a component definition. This is what defines the `Animal` and the `Cow` in terms of what interfaces each component supports and the vtable order of those interface methods. Like interfaces, co-classes also have a unique GUID that represents the object. This identifier is called a CLSID. As an IID is the true name for an interface, a CLSID is the true name for the entire component itself. The easiest way to find a CLSID is to first look up the programmatic identifier, or ProgID, of the component. A ProgID is a string that VB creates from the project name and the class name. In the case of our Animals component, the ProgID for Cow would be *Animals.Cow*. The ProgID and the CLSID representing the component can be found in the **HKEY_CLASSES_ROOT** branch of the registry, as shown in Figure 2-3.

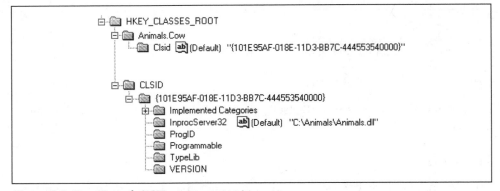

Figure 2-3. ProgID and CLSID registry mappings

Once you have obtained the CLSID for an object, you can find its entry under **HKEY_CLASSES_ROOT**. Notice the **InprocServer32** key. This is how the ProgID, say in a call to the VBA *CreateObject* function, is mapped to the physical location of the component.

Type Libraries

The interface and co-class definitions are stored in a special file called a *type library*. In the case of *Animals.dll*, VB creates the type library automatically and stores it as a resource inside the component. But you can also create your own type libraries. The type libraries that you create can then be referenced from VB. In fact, since VB does not allow us to create type information that is suitable for our needs in developing shell extensions, we're going to have to create our own type library. But before we do that, we will talk about what a type library is and what goes inside of one.

A type library is a language-independent binary file that contains all the information needed to use the component. This includes interface definitions, co-class definitions, structures (UDTs), enumerations, and constants. It is because of type libraries that Visual Basic can implement such great features as Auto List Members (shown in Figure 2-4), Auto Quick Info, and the Object Browser.

Version Compatibility

Specific identifiers are used throughout this book. If you register the components provided with each chapter, your registry settings will mirror the examples used in this book. If you compile the code yourself, the identifiers will be different.

There is a way to enter and compile all the source and have the identifiers match the examples found in this book. You can do this by setting the version compatibility for your projects to Binary Compatibility.

Version compatibility settings are found on the Component tab of the Project Properties dialog. There are three different types of version compatibility that you can specify for your COM projects:

No Compatibility

> When this setting is active, new identifiers are created for every interface and class every time the component is compiled.

Project Compatibility

> Each time you compile a project, all identifiers are kept intact. Interface identifiers are changed only when they are no longer binary-compatible with earlier versions. This setting has changed meaning from VB 5.0 to 6.0. In version 5.0 all identifiers were changed even if only one class was found to be incompatible.

Binary Compatibility

> With binary compatibility set, you can specify an existing component as a template for binary compatibility. Therefore, you can use this setting to specify a DLL provided with this chapter as a reference. When you compile your project, all identifiers from the reference component will be used, and your identifiers will match the examples found in this book.

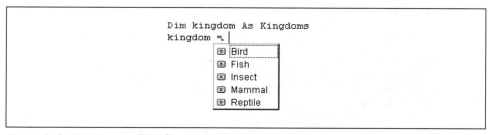

Figure 2-4. Auto List Members from type library

Object Browser is really just a simple type library browser. Although it can provide some very useful information, it does hide a number of things that Microsoft does not want VB programmers to know about. Fortunately, there is a utility called the OLE/COM Object Viewer (usually referred to as OLE View) that will allow us to view the type library generated for *Animals.dll* without hiding a thing. This utility ships with Visual Studio but is also freely available in the downloads section at *http://www.microsoft.com/com.*

Example 2-3 shows the type library listing for *Animals.dll*, which has been generated by OLE View. To view the type library yourself using OLE View, select the View TypeLib option from OLE View's File menu and use the Open dialog to navigate to the *Animals.dll* file.

Example 2-3. Animals Type Library

```
// Generated .IDL file (by the OLE/COM Object Viewer)
//
// typelib filename: Animals.dll

[
  uuid(C6A1FF39-C6B2-11D2-9FCE-00550076E06F),
  version(7.0)
]
library Animals
{
    // TLib :
    // TLib : OLE Automation : {00020430-0000-0000-C000-000000000046}
    importlib("STDOLE2.TLB");

    // Forward declare all types defined in this typelib
    interface _Animal;
    interface _Cow;

    [
      odl,
      uuid(74DAE56B-D1C9-11D2-BB7C-444553540000),
      version(1.0),
      hidden,
      dual,
      nonextensible,
      oleautomation
    ]
    interface _Animal : IDispatch {
        [id(0x60030003)]
        HRESULT Kingdom([out, retval] Kingdoms* );
        [id(0x60030004)]
        HRESULT Name([out, retval] BSTR* );
        [id(0x60030005)]
        HRESULT Noise([out, retval] BSTR* );
    };

    [
      uuid(C6A1FF3B-C6B2-11D2-9FCE-00550076E06F),
      version(1.0),
```

Example 2-3. Animals Type Library (continued)

```
    noncreatable
  ]
  co-class Animal {
      [default] interface _Animal;
  };

  [
    odl,
    uuid(74DAE56C-D1C9-11D2-BB7C-444553540000),
    version(1.0),
    hidden,
    dual,
    nonextensible,
    oleautomation
  ]
  interface _Cow : IDispatch {
  };

  [
    uuid(C6A1FF3E-C6B2-11D2-9FCE-00550076E06F),
    version(1.0)
  ]
  co-class Cow {
      [default] interface _Cow;
      interface _Animal;
  };

  typedef [uuid(74DAE568-D1C9-11D2-BB7C-444553540000), version(1.0)]
  enum {
      Mammal = 1,
      Reptile = 2,
      Insect = 3,
      Bird = 4,
      Fish = 5
  } Kingdoms;
};
```

Example 2-3 is obviously not Visual Basic, and it isn't C or C++ either, so what is it? Example 2-3 is in a language called *IDL*, or *Interface Definition Language*. IDL is compiled using a special compiler, and the result in this case is a type library. This type library has the extension *.tlb* and can be directly referenced from your VB projects.

Interface Definition Language

Just when you thought you had learned enough languages, along comes Interface Definition Language. IDL is the standard language used to define interfaces. If all the attributes (denoted by square brackets in Example 2-3) were removed from the listing, IDL would pretty much look like standard C.

When you create a component in Visual Basic, the type library is automatically compiled and stored in the component. In other environments, type libraries are usually compiled using the Microsoft IDL (or MIDL) compiler. Unfortunately, MIDL does not ship with Visual Basic; it ships with Visual C++. There is a utility that ships with VB, however, that can be used to generate type libraries. This utility is called MKTYPLIB. The difference between the two is that MKTYPLIB is an *ODL* (*Object Definition Language*) compiler. ODL is a subset of IDL, so its feature set is limited in comparison to MIDL. Generally, you want to use MIDL for everything, but our circumstances are a bit different. You see, we are going to be redefining system interfaces so that they are VB-friendly. MIDL would complain that several of these interfaces have already been defined and abort the creation of the type library. MKTYPLIB does not care. Therefore, we will use it instead of MIDL.

If you don't know IDL, don't worry. You will still be able to follow along with the book. When all is said and done, you will probably know more about IDL than you ever wanted to know. But I know some of you are probably thinking, "Why can't we just use VB to generate our interfaces?" If only life were that simple. We can't use VB because VB doesn't generate interfaces that look like the interfaces we need. That's the plain truth. Otherwise we would. We'll discuss this later, so save that thought.

Knowing the general layout of a type library will also help sort out some of the confusion. The layout is fairly simple, as Example 2-4 shows. A type library consists of a variable number of blocks. Each block consists of an attribute section denoted by square brackets ([...]), followed by the block type (`library`, `interface`, `co-class`, etc.), and the body, which is surrounded by curly braces (`{...}`). These blocks can be nested, as is the case with an interface definition inside of a library block. Don't worry about the syntax of interface method definitions right now. You will learn about those as you work through each chapter.

Example 2-4. Type Library Structure

```
[
    // This is the GUID for the library, or LIBID
    uuid(xxxxxxxx-xxxx-xxxx-xxxx-xxxxxxxxxxxx)
]
library Name
{
    // This is an interface block
    [
        // This is the GUID for the interface, or IID
        uuid(xxxxxxxx-xxxx-xxxx-xxxx-xxxxxxxxxxxx)
    ]
    interface XXXX  : base
    {
        //Interface methods
        HRESULT Foo(...);
```

Example 2-4. Type Library Structure (continued)

```
    }

    // This is a co-class block
    [
        // This is the GUID for the co-class, or CLSID
        uuid(xxxxxxxx-xxxx-xxxx-xxxx-xxxxxxxxxxxx)
    ]
    co-class XXXX
    {
        interface XXXX;
    }

}
```

Attributes

Attributes are keywords used to specify the characteristics of an interface. They describe the data itself and how the data is transmitted. Attributes usually appear in square brackets within an IDL file. Table 2-1 contains a list of attributes, or IDL language keywords, that are found in Example 2-3. (Remember, though, that it does not represent every possible attribute recognized by IDL.) Attributes can be applied to interfaces, the methods of an interface, and even the individual parameters of a method. In fact, most elements of an IDL file can be tagged with attributes.

Table 2-1. Interface Attributes in Animal Type Library

Name	Description
default	Indicates that the interface defined inside of a co-class is the default interface. This attribute is for use by macro languages.
dual	Identifies an interface that exposes properties and methods through IDispatch and through the vtable. (See the section "IDispatch" later in this chapter for more information.)
hidden	Indicates that the item exists but should not be displayed. This attribute is for the benefit of programs like Object Browser.
id	Specifies a DISPID for a member function. (See the section "IDispatch" later in this chapter for more information.)
nonextensible	This attribute is only valid if the [dual] and [oleautomation] attributes are present. It specifies that the IDispatch implementation includes only the properties and methods listed in the interface description and cannot be extended with additional members at runtime. (See the section "IDispatch" later in this chapter for more information.) Now, forget about this attribute.
odl	A requirement of MKTYPLIB is that all interfaces have this attribute. It does nothing in and of itself.
oleautomation	Indicates that an interface is compatible with OLE Automation.
uuid	Associates a GUID with an interface.
version	Specifies the version of the type library.

The MIDL Language Reference is part of the Platform SDK (under COM and Active X Object Services) and is available online at *http:// msdn.microsoft.com/library.*

Take note of how settings in VB map to attributes in the type library. For instance, the Instancing property of the Animal class is set to `PublicNotCreatable`, which causes the attribute `[noncreatable]` to be added to the Animal co-class. Don't focus too hard on the `[oleautomation]` and `[dual]` attributes, though. These attributes will be discussed in detail later on.

_Animal

Let's look at the `_Animal` interface in Example 2-3 for a moment. In addition to having the `[hidden]` attribute, an underscore has been added to the interface name, which serves as a signal to Object Browser to keep the interface from being displayed. This is an effort on VB's part to make you believe that an interface and a class are one and the same. It is standard policy to prefix interface names with an I. Had this interface been developed by anything but VB, it most likely would have been called `IAnimal`.

HRESULTs

Consider the definition for the `Noise` method:

```
HRESULT Noise([out, retval] BSTR* );
```

The `[out, retval]` attribute translates into a function in VB that *appears* to return a String:

```
sNoise = Cow1.Noise
```

The actual return value of a method call is an `HRESULT`. An `HRESULT` is an unsigned 32-bit value that is used to return error codes or status information back to the caller. VB manages these values for you, which means you can never get direct access to the `HRESULT` except through the Err object. This is fine if you only need to *look* at an error code. But this can be a problem in situations where the documentation for the interface states that a method needs to return a specific `HRESULT`. VB does not give us the power to return specific `HRESULT`s from an implemented method. Also, using the `Err.Raise` method to generate a specific error condition will not achieve the same result as returning an `HRESULT`.

Unless an error occurs, the actual return value is 0; otherwise, it is a number in the form −214xxxxxxx. Although VB interprets the value to be a negative number, the number is not actually negative; VB does not handle unsigned datatypes (other than Byte). Because of this, large numbers (that is, integer values whose high order bit of their highest order byte is set on) appear to be negative.

As you can see, VB returns HRESULTs through the Err object in decimal format, but the rest of the world uses hexadecimal. So, if you convert the HRESULT codes to hex using the VBA *Hex* function, you should be able to locate most of the standard return codes in *winerror.h*. This file also contains the specific bit mapping for an HRESULT and is a very useful resource when debugging COM servers. Unfortunately, this file is only available with Visual C++.

IUnknown

From looking at the type library, you can see that _Animal is derived from another interface called IDispatch. What is not apparent is that IDispatch is derived from yet another interface called IUnknown. Actually, all interfaces are ultimately derived from IUnknown. This means that all COM components share a dependable commonality.

The IUnknown interface contains three methods:

*   QueryInterface
*   AddRef
*   Release

QueryInterface

The purpose of QueryInterface is to allow clients to discover whether a component supports a given interface. It is also used to navigate between interfaces on a given component. Before returning the requested interface (if it exists), AddRef is called to give the object a reference count.

AddRef and Release

AddRef and Release are used for reference counting. All objects in memory have an associated reference count. Every time an object is created or copied, this count is incremented by one. Every time an object is released, the reference count is decremented by one. When the reference count is zero, the object can safely unload itself. As a VB programmer, you have seen this entire process many times in code fragments like the following, probably without ever realizing precisely what was happening behind the scenes:

```
Dim Cow1 As Animal

'QueryInterface Animal for Cow interface and call AddRef.
'Cow1 now has a reference count of one.
Set Cow1 = New Cow
```

```
Dim Cow2 As Cow

'AddRef is called. Reference count is two.
Set Cow2 = Cow1

'Release Cow1. Reference count is one
Set Cow1 = Nothing

'Release Cow2. Reference count is 0 so component is unloaded.
Set Cow2 = Nothing
```

The VB implementation of **IUnknown** resides in *STDOLE2.TLB* and looks like Example 2-5.

Example 2-5. IUnknown Interface Definition

```
[
  odl,
  uuid(00000000-0000-0000-C000-000000000046),
  hidden
]
interface IUnknown {
    [restricted]
    HRESULT _stdcall QueryInterface(
                    [in] GUID* riid,
                    [out] void** ppvObj);
    [restricted]
    unsigned long _stdcall AddRef();
    [restricted]
    unsigned long _stdcall Release();
};
```

Every method of **IUnknown** has the **[restricted]** attribute. This keeps you, the VB programmer, from calling any of these methods directly. You can try, though. Run the following code fragment:

```
Dim x As IUnknown
x.AddRef
```

When you declare the **IUnknown** variable, it will not be displayed in the Auto Quick Info drop-down. This is because the interface is marked with the **[hidden]** attribute. If you enter all the code in lowercase, VB will adjust the case for your entry. So we know that VB knows about this interface; it's just not talking. But you won't be able to compile this fragment, and if you try to run the code from the IDE, you will get a nasty message like the one shown in Figure 2-5. Fortunately, we can work around this limitation, but we'll discuss that later.

Refer to Example 2-3 for a moment. Find the first line of IDL inside the library block that is not a comment. It looks like this:

```
importlib("STDOLE2.TLB");
```

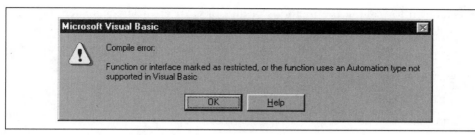

Figure 2-5. Calling IUnknown methods is not allowed

This line of IDL causes the Animals type library to contain all of the definitions found in *stdole2.tlb*. Incidentally, *stdole2.tlb* contains the definition of IUnknown (among other things) that is used by VB. If you are interested, you can use OLE View to examine this type library. The type library is called OLE Automation (Version 2.0).

IDispatch

As mentioned previously, _Animal is directly derived from an interface called IDispatch. Interfaces derived from IDispatch often have the [dual] attribute and appropriately are called *dual interfaces*. This is because the interface supports vtable binding (binding at compile time) and late binding (binding at runtime). The methods that comprise IDispatch facilitate the process known as late binding, which results from code like that shown in Example 2-6.

Example 2-6. Late Binding

```
'Late binding Cow

Dim cow1 As Object
Set cow1 = CreateObject("Animals.Cow")

MsgBox cow1.Noise
```

CreateObject uses the ProgID for the component and maps it to a CLSID. This allows an instance of the component to be created. Internally, this is done by calling the *CoCreateInstanceEx* API. Once the component is loaded, a call to QueryInterface is made and a pointer to an IDispatch interface is returned. The generic Object datatype really means IDispatch. Then late binding is used to make the call to the Noise method.

Late binding is generally avoided whenever possible for reasons of efficiency (it's extremely slow). But in scripting languages like VBScript and JavaScript, late binding is the only choice available. This is because type information is used at *compile time* to bind method calls to the object. Code run in a scripting environment is not compiled. It is interpreted at runtime, line by line. Therefore, there needs to be a mechanism for calling the methods of an object in environments such as these. This is where IDispatch comes in. The four methods of IDispatch are:

- GetTypeInfoCount
- GetTypeInfo
- GetIDsOfNames
- Invoke

GetTypeInfoCount

GetTypeInfoCount returns either a 0 or a 1, depending on the availability of type information. Since we know the Animals component contains type information, an implementation of GetTypeInfoCount written in Visual Basic might be as simple as this:

```
Private Sub GetTypeInfoCount() As Long
    GetTypeInfoCount = 1
End Sub
```

GetTypeInfo

GetTypeInfo returns an ITypeInfo interface pointer, which provides the means for accessing information in a type library. ITypeInfo is useful when no prior knowledge of a component is available. Utilities such as Object Browser and OLE View use IDispatch::GetTypeInfo to get information about a component from a type library. Typically, you are familiar with the components you use in your day to day development efforts. Therefore, this method is rarely used.

GetIDsOfNames

Refer back to the _Animal interface for a moment and look at the [id] attribute that accompanies each method in the interface. This ID is called a *dispatch identifier*, or DISPID. This is the value that is returned by GetIDsOfNames. Without going into detail, GetIDsOfNames basically takes the method name (like Noise) as an argument and returns the DISPID associated with that method. It is this number that is used in place of the function name to make a method invocation at runtime. This is for efficiency reasons. Remember, some COM components are out-of-process servers that might be running on another machine. Passing an integer across a network is more efficient than passing a string.

Invoke

Invoke is the heart of the IDispatch interface. This method is responsible for making the late binding call to a method or property. Invoke indirectly calls a method or property using the DISPID returned by GetIDsOfNames. The return value, if there is one, is packed into a VARIANT structure and returned to the caller.

Now that we have discussed IUnknown and IDispatch, you should have a better idea of what is going on internally in a component written in Visual Basic. We now know that there is a little more going on in the _Animal interface than was initially apparent. Figure 2-6 shows a graphic depiction of the _Animal interface.

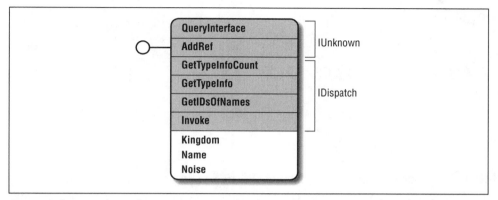

Figure 2-6. Animal interface

And with this last piece of information, the question "Why can't we use VB to generate the interfaces we need?" can finally be answered. The answer is very simple. We can't use VB because the interfaces we will need must be derived directly from IUnknown. How do we know that they must be derived directly from IUnknown? Because that's what the Platform SDK says they are derived from. Remember, we have contracts to abide by here!

Conclusion

You should have a basic understanding of the components you are creating with Visual Basic. This chapter, far from being a comprehensive treatise on COM, is merely meant to introduce some of the fundamental concepts that we will be dealing with throughout the remainder of this book. It does not represent the extent of the book. Many new concepts will be discussed as the need arises. For now, you should have a basic understanding of COM, the architecture used by Visual Basic for creating component-based software. These components expose their functionality through interfaces. Interface definitions are stored in a type library, which provides information to clients that wish to use the object. Interface definitions are written in IDL, which is the standard language for defining interfaces, and compiled with the MIDL compiler or MKTYPLIB. The fundamental interface that all objects have in common is IUnknown. IUnknown contains methods that allow for interface discovery and reference counting. The interfaces of objects created with Visual Basic are derived from IDispatch, making the process of runtime binding possible.

3

Shell Extensions

Everything that can be viewed within the tree view of Windows Explorer represents what is called a *namespace*. This namespace not only represents files and directories, but also entities such as drives, printers, and network resources. The shell presents these items in a singular hierarchy with the desktop at the root. Objects in the namespace fall into two categories: folders and file objects.

Folders and File Objects

Folders represent collections within the namespace. Many folders represent actual directories in the filesystem, but some folders are virtual. These virtual folders include Desktop, My Computer, Recycle Bin, Control Panel, Dial-up Networking, and Fonts. Virtual folders are not part of the native filesystem and often are referred to as system folders. Many of these virtual folders can only contain a specific type of file or object. For instance, the Control Panel can only contain Control Panel applications, and the Printer folder can only contain printers.

All folders, whether virtual or not, share the same fundamental properties. Folders are file objects that can contain other file objects. What are file objects? For the most part, file objects represent actual files, but they can include other resources like printers and drives, as well as other folders. The use of the word "file" is somewhat of a misnomer here, because a file object is really any object that is part of the shell namespace. And if an item is part of the shell namespace, a shell extension can be written for it.

Shell Extensions

Every file object visible in the shell is a member of a *file class* and can be programmatically extended by a shell extension. There are certain predefined actions that determine which shell extensions will be invoked. These actions include things like right-clicking, copying, moving, dragging, cutting, pasting, and even displaying an icon for a file. Shell extension handlers are in-process COM servers that implement a variety of interfaces, depending on the type of handler being implemented. There are five handlers that perform actions based on a specific file type:

- Context menu handlers
- Icon handlers
- Property sheet handlers
- Drop handlers
- Data handlers

There are also two types of handlers that are associated with file operations like copying, moving, renaming, and deleting:

- Copy hook handlers
- Drag-and-drop handlers

Context Menu Handler

A *context menu* is the menu that appears when a file is right-clicked. A sample context menu is shown in Figure 3-1. Every item in the shell has an associated context menu. This menu provides the means to perform generic operations such as copying, moving, deleting, and renaming file objects.

A *context menu handler* allows items to be added to this menu for a specific file object. This allows custom processing to be performed on the file object via the menu selection.

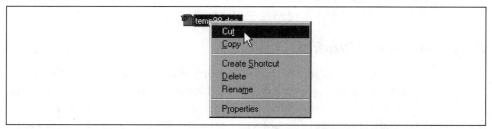

Figure 3-1. Context menus provide a means for additional file processing from within the shell

Context menu items can be defined quite easily in the registry without writing any code whatsoever. But there are situations where you may need to display a different menu for file objects of the *same* type. This is where context menu handlers come into play. For example, you might want to add a Backup option to a context menu for a file whose archive bit is set. Or you might want to determine whether a file's size exceeds a floppy drive's free space before displaying a Copy to Floppy menu option.

Icon Handler

Every file object has an associated icon. Icons for a given file object are specified in the registry by a subkey called `DefaultIcon` under the object's application identifier key. You could, for example, change the icon the shell displays for your hard drives by changing the default value of the key shown in Figure 3-2. The number 8 in Figure 3-2 refers to the index of the icon that is contained in *shell32.dll.*

Figure 3-2. Default icon location

Icon handlers provide a way to display different icons for the same file objects on a per instance basis. These icons can be used to provide additional state information for a file or resource. For instance, a *.rad* file (this is a made-up file type that we will use to discuss handlers) could display an icon representing the type of animal specified by the file, as Figure 3-3 shows.

Name	Size	Type	Modified
dog.rad	1KB	Shell Extension File	02/11/99 11:39 AM
cat.rad	1KB	Shell Extension File	03/15/99 10:51 AM

Figure 3-3. Icon handlers provide per-instance icon support

Property Sheet Handler

Property sheet handlers add pages to the property dialog for a specific file object. These additional property pages allow for additional file processing in much the same manner as a context menu handler. These pages can be specific to a class of file objects or to an individual file object, depending on the needed functionality. For example, Figure 3-4 shows the default property sheet for a text file.

The Microsoft Word *.doc* file Properties dialog provides a good example of property sheet handlers. The property sheet extension adds not one, but four pages in addition to the default property sheet, as illustrated in Figure 3-5. A wide variety of document attributes can then be changed right from the shell without the need to open Word.

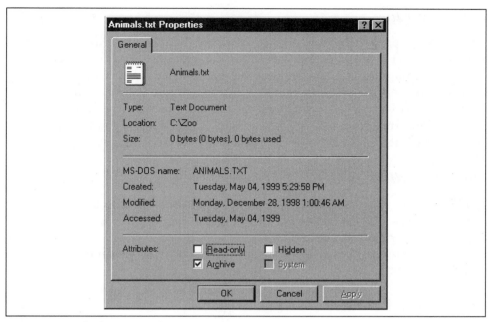

Figure 3-4. Default property sheet

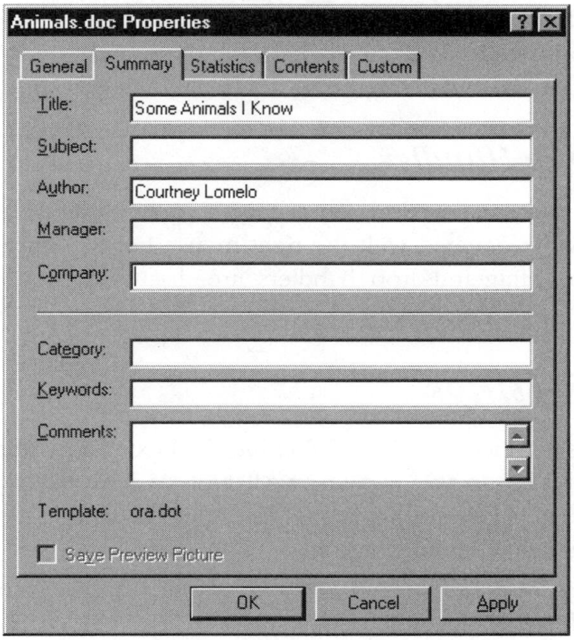

Figure 3-5. .doc file property sheets

Data Handler

Data handlers provide custom clipboard formats that are made available whenever a file object is dragged from the shell or copied to the clipboard. They can be used to alter the default copy-and-paste behavior implemented by the shell. Consider a *.bmp* file for a moment. Suppose that when you copied the file from the shell, you also wanted the image that the file represented to be made available from the clipboard. A custom *.bmp* data handler would allow you to copy image data right from the shell into another program such as Adobe Photoshop.

Drop Handler

A drop handler allows a file of a specific class to become a drop target. Consider one of the most popular shareware programs around, WinZip. WinZip defines a drop handler for files of type *.zip*. When files are dropped onto a *.zip* file, a drop handler processes the files and add them to the archive. Drop handlers allow you to define such behaviors for your own file types.

Copy Hook Handler

Copy hook handlers are associated with folder objects (they are valid for folder objects only and do not pertain to files) and are called before a folder is copied, moved, renamed, or deleted. They do not perform the task, but rather they approve or disapprove the task. Copy hook handlers could be used to keep your favorite source code directory from being accidentally deleted or moved.

Drag-and-Drop Handler

A drag-and-drop handler is nothing more than a context menu handler that is displayed when a file is dragged with the right mouse button. Since they are similar to context menus, drag-and-drop handlers are discussed in Chapter 4, *Context Menu Handlers*.

Registry Settings

The registry plays a critical role in defining the shell extensions available for particular filesystem objects. In this section, we'll look at how the registry is used to define the shell extensions for particular file types, as well as how it determines the scope of a particular shell extension.

File Associations

There are two entries in the registry that are associated with files of a specific type: the file association key and the application identifier key. For example, in

Figure 3-6, `HKEY_CLASSES_ROOT\.rad` is a file association key. The file association key merely points to the application identifier key; that is, its default value
contains the name of the application identifier key, which in the case of Figure 3-6
is `HKEY_CLASSES_ROOT\radfile`. The application identifier key contains the
`shellex` subkey (`shellex` stands for "shell extension"), which defines the specific handler types and the CLSIDs of the objects designated to handle them. Some
handlers, like context menu handlers and property page handlers, require a named
value that points to the proper CLSID. This can be any name, but it must be
unique at the level in which it resides.

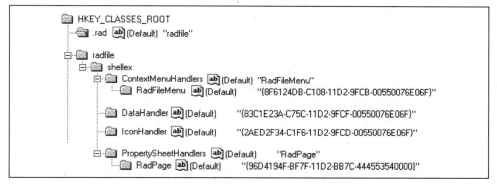

Figure 3-6. Registry settings for shell extensions of a specific file type

Once Explorer has the CLSID for the component that is implementing a particular
shell extension, it can find the physical location of the component by going to the
`HKEY_CLASSES_ROOT\CLSID` key and finding the matching CLSID. A subkey of
the CLSID key called `InProcServer32` contains the physical location of the component. Explorer can then load the component and call methods on the appropriate interfaces. Figure 3-7 shows the mapping from a CLSID to a physical location.

```
    HKEY_CLASSES_ROOT
    CLSID
        {2AED2F34-C1F6-11D2-9FCD-00550076E06F}
            InprocServer32  D:\Animals\Animals.dll
```

Figure 3-7. How an icon handler is mapped to a physical location

When Explorer loads our component, it gets a pointer to its **IUnknown** interface.
Explorer can then call all of the methods that we have implemented for a given
shell extension.

Scope

All file objects can have handlers associated with them. The scope is determined
by where the handlers are registered in the registry. All of these locations are

direct subkeys of HKEY_CLASSES_ROOT and themselves contain subkeys similar to those found in Figure 3-6. These include:

*   This key can be used to register context menu handlers, property sheet handlers, and copy hook handlers that apply to all registered file objects. For example, WinZip uses a subkey of this key to define a context menu handler that examines the type of filesystem object and, if it is either a file or a folder, adds an "Add to Zip" context menu item.

Drive

This key is used to register shell extensions for all drives. For example, a property sheet handler defined by a subkey of the Drive key displays information on the free and used space available on the designated drive.

Folder

All handlers that are registered by HKEY_CLASSES_ROOT* can also be registered here, with the addition of drag-and-drop handlers. These handlers apply to all folders in the system. For example, a subkey of HKEY_CLASSES_ROOT\Folder defines a Sharing option for a folder's context menu.

Printers

Handlers for all system printers are registered here. The type of handlers that are allowed for this key are the same as Folders, but additional extensions are provided to handle adding and removing printers and setting the default printer.

Directory

The Directory key has the same configuration as the Folders key, but is only used for filesystem folders. Examples of system folders include *History*, *Favorites*, *Downloaded Program Files*, and *Offline Web Pages*. These folders can usually be found under your Windows directory.

Directory/Background

This subkey is used to create context menu handlers that are not associated with any particular file object, but rather with the empty area of a system folder. This can be demonstrated with the *History* system folder, which is located under the Windows directory. This folder does not contain files. It contains browsing histories. Right-clicking in this folder supplies a context menu specific to the objects contained in the folder. It is a slightly different context menu than you would find in a folder containing files.

AllFileSystemObjects

This key contains the same entries as Folder and pertains to all filesystem objects. It is used to define a handler that determines whether a Send To option appears on the object's context menu.

The .rad File

The shell extensions discussed throughout this book will be developed for the mythical *.rad* file, which is just an imaginary file type I've used to demonstrate the concepts presented in the book. An existing file type could have been used instead, but by using a made-up type, we get to build everything from the ground up. If I had used an existing file type, many of the needed registry entries would already be in place, diminishing the "hands on" approach of the book. Changing registry settings for existing file types also has a tendency to change the way that Windows handles your applications, something you're not likely to appreciate. Also, chances are that you will be writing these extensions for your own file types, not for someone else's.

The format of a *.rad* file is exactly the same as an *.ini* file and looks like this:

```
[Animal]
Type = (dog, cat, fish, snake, cow, or armadillo)
Gender = (M or F)
Color = (Black, White, Gray, Brown, or Green)
Age = (positive integer)
Weight = (positive integer)
```

You can think of a *.rad* file as an *.ini* file with a specific format. The animal types and file format have been purposefully simplified to keep the focus away from the file itself and on the shell extensions. It's not because of laziness . . . Anyway, if you suddenly find yourself with large amounts of free time that just can't be used productively anywhere else, by all means extend the file in any way you wish.

Registering the .rad File

The file association key and the application identifier key must be added to the registry for the *.rad* file. You can use *rad.reg*, which is included with the book's code (downloadable from *http://vb.oreilly.com*), or add it by hand. The keys are as follows:

HKEY_CLASSES_ROOT\.rad = radfile
> This notation signifies that the default value for .rad is radfile. This is the file association key; it only serves as a pointer to radfile.

HKEY_CLASSES_ROOT\radfile = Rudimentary Animal Data
> This is the root key for all shell extensions. The default value contains the description of the file type that will be displayed in Explorer.

HKEY_CLASSES_ROOT\radfile\shellex
> All shell extensions for the *.rad* file will be listed under this key. This is where all of the action takes place.

The Shell Extension Project

All of the handlers that we will implement will be contained in a single ActiveX DLL project called *RadEx*. A stub project with the appropriate settings is included with the book's downloadable code for this chapter. The project is an ActiveX DLL project set for Apartment threading (see Appendix A, *VBShell Library Listing*), which is a requirement for shell extensions. The component will not load if this is not set. That's all there is to it; there is nothing more to the project.

Registering Components the Easy Way

The easiest way to register components is to associate DLL files with *regsvr32.exe*. This simplifies component registration to a double click.

If the *.dll* file type is currently not associated with any program, you can make this association yourself by simply double-clicking on any *.dll* file in the shell. This action displays the Open With dialog box, which will allow you to select a program for association. Just navigate to *regsvr32.exe*, which is located in your system directory.

If you want to be really hard-core about it, you can add the keys for the association yourself into the registry. This information is placed under the application identifier for *.dll* files, which happens to be called `dllfile`, as illustrated in Figure 3-8.

Of course, the path to *regsvr.exe* might be different on your machine. Notice the `%1` on the command line. This will be replaced by the name of the DLL that is being registered.

The source code that is provided with this chapter in the book's sample code serves as a template for future chapters. As the book progresses, the downloadable code for each subsequent chapter will contain source for the extensions created up to that point and an accompanying DLL. This is only to provide Binary Compatibility and keep the GUIDs referred to in this book the same as the GUIDs on your system. Remember, since each chapter contains a new component, it will have to be registered.

A type library containing all the interfaces you will need is included with the source code for the book, which is available for download from *http://vb.oreilly. com*. It will be necessary to add a reference to this library for each of the projects we will build in the book. The complete listing for this type library is also provided in Appendix A.

Figure 3-8. Associating regsvr32.exe with the dllfile file type

Unfortunately, MKTYPLIB does not allow IDL files to be included within other IDL files. Therefore, all our interfaces are defined within one file, called *vbshell.idl*. This makes for one really gigantic file, but the interfaces will be listed in alphabetical order. It should be fairly simple to navigate the file to examine its contents.

Incidentally, since *vbshell.idl* defines all of the interfaces used in building shell extensions, it will remain a valuable resource long after you've finished reading this book. You can continue to use it to access information about interfaces and their methods from Visual Basic for all of the shell extensions you build.

Restarting the Shell

Before you test any of the components that we will build throughout the course of this book, it will be necessary to restart the shell. Restarting the shell does not mean shutting down every instance of Explorer you have running because, even after you have done that, there is still one more instance running: the Desktop. That's right, the Desktop is the first instance of Explorer. You will need to restart everything. The obvious method is to just reboot. While this works, it is a little time consuming. There are other ways to restart the shell without shutting down.

If you are developing under Windows NT, you can simply bring up the Task Manager and kill the Explorer process. You can then start a fresh instance by running Explorer from the Run menu.

If you are running Windows 98, restarting the shell is not as straightforward. First, you need to bring up the Task Manager by pressing Ctrl-Alt-Del. Select the Explorer process and then click the End Task button. The Shut Down Windows dialog will appear. This is the same dialog that appears when you select Shut Down from the Start menu. Now this is important: *do not press OK*. Press Cancel instead. Wait a few moments. Windows will then display a dialog box prompting you to end the task.

When the Shell Crashes

Under NT, shell crashes are not really a problem. You can access the Run command from the Task Manager and start up another instance of *Explorer.exe*.

Under Windows 98, there is no Run command that is available from the Task Manager. When developing for the shell, you can save yourself countless headaches by keeping a simple program running at all times during your development. This program can have a form with one command button that executes the following line of code:

```
Shell "Explorer.exe"
```

II

Shell Extensions

4

Context Menu Handlers

The shell displays a context menu for a file object when it is clicked with the right mouse button. This context menu allows various operations to be performed on the file object from within the shell, like printing it or opening it with another program. For example, Figure 4-1 shows the context menu that's displayed when the user clicks on a file in Windows Explorer.

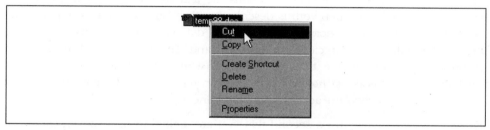

Figure 4-1. A context menu

The items on context menus fall into two categories: *static* and *dynamic*. Static context menu items are always the same for every file object of a given type. They can be associated with a file object with just a few registry entries and require no shell extension handlers. The "handler" in this circumstance—that is, the object that performs some action on the file object when that particular context menu item is selected—is usually a normal executable that is passed the name of the file as a command-line parameter. Dynamic context menus, on the other hand, are created with the help of a shell extension handler, which, as we discussed earlier, is a COM component that runs in-process to Explorer. This handler provides the means to display different context menu items for file objects of the same type. The exact appearance of the context menu typically is determined by some state internal to the file itself. Static menus warrant a brief discussion, but the main focus of this chapter will be on dynamic context menus.

Static Context Menus

Static context menu items are listed under the application identifier key under a subkey called `shell` (as opposed to the `shellex` key). These entries remain constant for every instance of the file object and require no implementation code.

Figure 4-2 illustrates how to add an Open context menu item to the *.rad* file. The subkey of `shell` (in this case `open`) is the verb value for the command. There are seven verbs, called *canonical verbs*, whose meaning is automatically recognized by the shell: `open`, `find`, `explore`, `print`, `printto`, `openas`, and `properties`. (The `printto` key is never shown in a context menu, but allows a file to be dragged to a printer object for printing.)

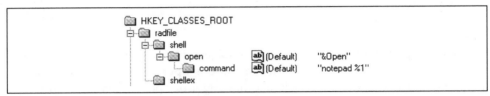

Figure 4-2. Registry entry for static "Open" context menu

The default value of the verb key contains the text for the context menu; in the case of Figure 4-2, the open verb is described in the context menu as "Open." The verb key's subkey is the `command` key, whose default value contains the path of the file that will be used to carry out the command. The `%1` portion of this string in Figure 4-2 denotes the file that was selected within the shell. Whatever file is selected will be passed to *notepad.exe* on the command line. Of course, this only works because *notepad.exe* accepts command-line arguments.

However, don't believe for a second that you are limited to these seven canonical verbs. You can actually add you own commands to the context menu and call them anything you want. For example, let's add Register and Unregister commands to the context menu for DLLs. This will provide us with a convenient way to register and unregister components.

To accomplish this, we need to locate the application identifier key for a DLL, which happens to be `dllfile`. Then, under the `shell` subkey, we add two other keys: `Register` and `Unregister`. Figure 4-3 shows how the relevant portion of the registry should appear in order to support these two static commands.

As you can see from Figure 4-2, we must also add an additional subkey named `command`. The default value for this key will contain the command that we actually want to execute. The following script, *DLLRegister.reg*, will do everything for you:

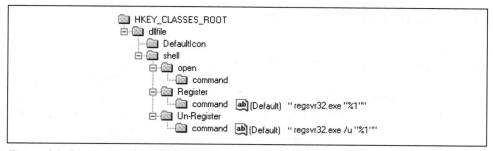

Figure 4-3. Static menu handlers to register and unregister DLLs

```
REGEDIT4

[HKEY_CLASSES_ROOT\dllfile\shell\Unregister\command]
@="regsvr32.exe /u %1"

[HKEY_CLASSES_ROOT\dllfile\shell\Register\command]
@="regsvr32.exe %1"
```

Static Context Menus in IE 5.0

With the release of Internet Explorer 5.0, Microsoft has made it possible for you to define your own static context menu items. It's as simple as adding a new registry key at the following location:

```
HKEY_CURRENT_USER
    SOFTWARE
        Microsoft
            Internet Explorer
                MenuExt
```

The default value for the key can be either a URL or a program. An additional key called **contexts** must also be present. This key contains a binary value that determines to which context menu (Internet Explorer provides several, depending on the circumstances) you want to add the new menu item. The values are:

Context Menu	Value
Default	0x01
Image	0x02
ActiveX Control	0x04
Table	0x08
Selected Text	0x10
Hyperlink	0x20

Dynamic Context Menus

Static context menus are limited because they are the same for every file object of a given type. Also, the number of files that can be processed through a static menu is limited by the program that is used to carry out the command. What if you need to process 20 files? What if you need different processing options based on the state of the file itself? There are also situations where you might need one context menu for a group of files and another for a single file. This is where dynamic context menus come into play.

A context menu handler is an ActiveX DLL that implements two interfaces: `IShellExtInit` and `IContextMenu`. A third interface, `IDataObject`, is required to implement `IShellExtInit`. It is not implemented by the object itself but exists as a method parameter in `IShellExtInit`. We'll explore these interfaces in greater depth after we examine how the shell uses a context menu handler to assemble a context menu.

The process begins when one or more files is right-clicked in Explorer. When this occurs, the shell checks the `shellex` key under the application identifier key to see if a context menu handler has been defined for the selected file type. In the case of the *.rad* file, the shell would look under the following key:

```
HKEY_CLASSES_ROOT/
    radfile/
        shellex/
            ContextMenuHandlers/
```

If you select 15 files that are of all different types, there is still only one file with active focus: the last file selected in the group. It is this file for which the shell attempts to find an associated context menu handler.

If a context menu handler exists, the shell loads the handler and calls `IShellExtInit::Initialize`. One of the parameters of `Initialize` is a reference to `IDataObject`. The shell uses `IDataObject` to tell us how many files are selected and what their names happen to be. This gives us the opportunity (as the implementors of `IShellExtInit`) to save the filenames and the number of selected files for later use. This information can be stored in private member variables within the class. Later, when a command is actually selected from the context menu, the array of files can be referenced and processing decisions can be made.

Next, the shell calls `IContextMenu::QueryContextMenu`. This method is responsible for adding items to the context menu. The shell passes into the method a handle to the context menu, called an `HMENU`. An index representing a valid insertion point for the menu item is also passed in. Adding the menu item is simply a matter of calling the *InsertMenu* API.

You might want different menu items displayed based on whether one or multiple files have been selected. Since the number of files selected can be determined in `IShellExtInit::Initialize`, this becomes a trivial matter. You also have the ability to base the menu item on the file itself. In addition to the number of files selected, you would also already know the filenames in question. This means you could open the file, retrieve information, and base the menu item on actual data. Or you could examine some other attribute of the file (such as its creation date, its size, or its read-only status) and base the menu item on that information as well.

At this point, the shell displays the context menu with the additional menu items. Once the context menu is displayed, the shell attempts to call `IContextMenu::GetCommandString` whenever the mouse is moved over the new context menu item. This allows you to provide a help string that will be displayed in the status bar of Explorer when the context menu item is highlighted.

When the command is actually selected, the shell calls `IContextMenu::InvokeCommand` on the handler. The method allows you to determine which context menu item has been selected, and as a result your handler can carry out the appropriate actions.

Context Menu Handler Interfaces

The components we will write in this book will all implement any given number of system interfaces. "System" in this context (no pun intended) means that these interfaces have already been defined by Microsoft. They are documented, and you can read all about them in the Platform SDK (though the details may be a little murky sometimes).

You can think of an interface as a defined functionality. When a component *implements* an interface, it is really saying, "I support this functionality!" Consider a Triangle component. It implements the interface `Shape`. `Shape` defines two methods: `Draw` and `Color`. Therefore, you could expect to access the following functionality through Triangle:

```
Triangle.Draw
Triangle.Color
```

Because the Circle, Square, and Trapezoid components *also* implement `Shape`, you would expect these objects to have the same functionality as well. This is what it means to implement an interface.

The components in this book all implement some functionality that is required by the shell. This means that when the shell loads our components, it will be able to gain access to our component through a defined mechanism: an interface.

With that said, let's talk about the interfaces a context menu handler component needs to implement before it can be loaded by the shell.

IShellExtInit

IShellExtInit contains one method (besides the IUnknown portion of the interface), Initialize, as shown in Table 4-1.

Table 4-1. IShellExtInit

Method	Description
Initialize	Initializes the shell extension

IShellExtInit::Initialize is the first method called by the shell after it loads the context menu handler; it is the context menu handler's equivalent of a class constructor in C++ programming or the Class_Initialize event procedure of a class in VB. Typically, this method is used by the context menu handler to determine which file objects are currently selected within Explorer. Initialize is defined as follows:

```
HRESULT Initialize(LPCITEMIDLIST pidlFolder,
                   IDataObject *lpdobj,
                   HKEY hkeyProgID );
```

All three arguments are provided by the shell and passed to the context menu handler when it is invoked, which is indicated by the [in] notation in the following argument list. The three arguments are:

pidlFolder

[in] A pointer to an ITEMIDLIST structure (commonly referred to in shell parlance as a PIDL) with information about the folder containing the selected objects. If you want more information on PIDLs and what you can do with them, see Chapter 12, *Browser Extensions*. We are not going to use this member, and we are not even going to discuss it (yet), because the topic of PIDLs is a universe unto itself. All you need to know is that a PIDL provides a location of something (such as the path of a file or folder object) within the Windows namespace.

lpdobj

[in] A pointer to an IDataObject interface that provides information about the selected objects. The IDataObject interface is discussed in the following section.

hKeyProgID

[in] The handle of the registry key containing the programmatic identifier of the selected file. For instance, if a Word *.doc* file was right-clicked, *hKeyProgID* would be a handle to the HKEY_CLASSES_ROOT\Word.Document.8 key on

systems with Office 2000 installed. Once the handle to this key is available, it is a trivial matter to find the host application that is responsible for dealing with this file type, which in the case of our example happens to be Microsoft Word. The context menu handler can then defer any operations to the host application, if necessary.

The only parameter in which we are interested is the second, *lpdobj*, which is a pointer to an `IDataObject` interface. Like the first parameter, `IDataObject` is also a world unto itself. Fortunately for us, we don't need to know too much about the interface at this juncture. In Chapter 8, *Data Handlers*, when we create a data handler, we will put this interface under the knife, so to speak, but until then let's just cover what we need to know. The shell uses this interface to communicate to us the files that were clicked on in Explorer. We'll see how this works momentarily.

Now that we know a little bit about this interface, let's get on to how we are actually going to implement it. There are some problems ahead.

`IShellExtInit`, like most of the interfaces in this book, is a VB-*unfriendly* interface. An unfriendly interface contains datatypes that are not automation compatible. You can think of an automation-compatible type as basically anything that will fit into a `Variant`. Table 4-2 lists all of the datatypes that are considered OLE automation compatible.

Table 4-2. OLE Automation-Compatible Types

Datatype	Description
boolean	Corresponds to the VB Boolean type
unsigned char	8-bit unsigned data item
double	64-bit IEEE floating-point number
float	32-bit IEEE floating-point number
int	Signed integer whose size is system-dependent
long	32-bit signed integer
short	16-bit signed integer
BSTR	Length-prefixed string; this is the String datatype in VB
CURRENCY	8-byte, fixed-point number
DATE	64-bit, floating-point fractional number of days since December 31, 1899
SCODE	Error code for 16-bit systems
Typedef enum *myenum*	Signed integer whose size is system-dependent
Interface IDispatch *	Pointer to the `IDispatch` interface
Interface IUnknown *	Any interface pointer that directly derives from `IUnknown`
dispinterface *Typename* *	Pointer to an interface derived from `IDispatch`

Table 4-2. OLE Automation-Compatible Types (continued)

Datatype	Description
Co-class *Typename* *	Pointer to a co-class name
[oleautomation] interface *Typename* *	Pointer to an interface that derives from `IUnknown`
SAFEARRAY(*TypeName*)	Array of any of the preceding types
*TypeName**	Pointer to any of the preceding types
Decimal	96-bit unsigned binary integer scaled by a variable power of 10 that provides a size and scale for a number (as in coordinates)

Now, to implement `IShellExtInit` successfully, the interface will have to be redefined with automation-compatible types and made available through a type library. This interface contains one method, `Initialize`. Let's tear it apart to see what we need to do in order to make this interface work for us.

Consider the first parameter of the `Initialize` method, which is an `LPCITEMIDLIST`. The documentation for the interface states that this is an address of an `ITEMIDLIST`. (We'll talk about `ITEMIDLIST` in Chapter 11, *Namespace Extensions*.) The structure is defined like this:

```
typedef struct _ITEMIDLIST {
        SHITEMID mkid;
    } ITEMIDLIST;
```

As you can see, the one and only member of this structure is another structure called `SHITEMID`, which is not an automation-compatible type. This means we cannot define this parameter as a pointer to an `ITEMIDLIST` when we define the `IShellExtInit` interface. What can we do? Well, a pointer is four bytes wide, so the automation-compatible type that can be used in place of `LPCITEMIDLIST` is a `long`. When we create our type library, we will just redefine `LPCITEMIDLIST` to mean a `long`, like so:

```
typedef [public] long LPCITEMIDLIST;
```

When we actually define the `Initialize` method (see Example 4-1), we can still use `LPCITEMIDLIST` for the datatype of the first parameter. Then, when VB displays the parameters for the method via `IntelliSense`, rather than seeing `long`, we will see `LPCITEMIDLIST`. This acts as a reminder of what the original definition is supposed to be.

We'll do the same thing for the third parameter, which is an `HKEY`. An `HKEY` is a handle to a registry key. Handles to anything are four bytes, so a `long` works in this case, too:

```
typedef [public] long HKEY;
```

We don't have to redefine anything as far as the second parameter goes. It's an `IDataObject` interface pointer. And interface pointers that are derived from `IUnknown` or `IDispatch` are automation compatible, so this portion of the definition is fine as is.

Let's talk about these parameters we have redefined for a moment. As it turns out, we will not need the first or the third parameters of this method in order to implement a context menu handler. But what if we did? After all, these types have been redefined as long values. Well, an `HKEY` is really a void pointer—that is, a pointer that does not point to any specific datatype. As a `long`, you can use this value as is with any of the registry API functions that take `HKEY`s.

How do we access the pointer to the ITEMIDLIST when all we have is a long value? We can use the *RtlMoveMemory* API (a.k.a. *CopyMemory*) to make a local copy of the UDT. This API call is defined like so:

```
Public Declare Sub CopyMemory Lib "kernel32" _
    Alias "RtlMoveMemory" (pDest As Any, _
                           pSource As Any, _
                           ByVal ByteLen As Long)
```

The code on the VB side would then look something like the following:

```
Private Sub IShellExtInit_Initialize(_
    ByVal pidlFolder As VBShellLib.LPCITEMIDLIST, _
    ByVal pDataObj As VBShellLib.IDataObject, _
    ByVal hKeyProgID As VBShellLib.HKEY)

    Dim idlist As ITEMIDLIST

    CopyMemory idlist, ByVal pidlFolder, len(idlist)
```

Notice, though, that the second parameter to *CopyMemory* (our `ITEMIDLIST` that has been redefined as a long) is passed to the function `ByVal`. This is because this long value represents a raw address. We'll talk more about this later, since we will use techniques similar to this throughout the course of this book.

Example 4-1 shows the modified definition for the `IShellExtInit` interface as it exists in our type library.

Example 4-1. IShellExtInit Interface

```
typedef [public] long HKEY;
typedef [public] long LPCITEMIDLIST;

[
    uuid(000214E8-0000-0000-C000-000000000046),
    helpstring("IShellExtInit Interface"),
    odl
]
```

Example 4-1. IShellExtInit Interface (continued)

```
interface IShellExtInit : IUnknown
{
    [helpstring("Initialize")]
    HRESULT Initialize([in] LPCITEMIDLIST pidlFolder,
                       [in] IDataObject  *pDataObj,
                       [in] HKEY         hKeyProgID);
}
```

Structures and IDL

We had to redefine the `ITEMIDLIST` pointer for the `IShellExtInit::Initialize` method because the structure contained a non-automation-compatible type. However, there are some circumstances in which we'll deal with pointers to structures that contain types whose members are *all* automation compatible. In situations like these, we don't have to redefine the pointer to the structure as a `long` like we had to for `ITEMIDLIST`.

Consider the `POINT` structure, which is defined as follows:

```
typedef struct {
    long x;
    long y;
} POINT;
```

This structure's members are all automation compatible.

Let's assume we have an interface (this is hypothetical, of course) that contains a `GetCoordinate` method. This method returns a pointer to `POINT` that specifies the location of some object. In IDL, its definition looks like this:

```
HRESULT GetCoordinate([in] POINT *location)
```

If we were to implement this method in VB, we could do the following:

```
Private Sub IBattleShip_GetCoordinate(_
    location As POINT)

    location.x = 10
    location.y = 20

End Sub
```

Instead of having to use *CopyMemory* to create a local copy of `POINT`, we can access the structure directly.

The `[public]` attribute used in Example 4-1 makes the `typedef` values available through the type library; otherwise, they would just be available for use inside of the library itself.

The [odl] attribute is required for all interfaces compiled with MKTYPLIB. MIDL supports this attribute as well, but only for the sake of backward compatibility. The attribute itself does absolutely nothing.

The [helpstring] attribute, as you can probably guess, denotes the text that will be displayed for a library or an interface from within Object Browser or the Project/References dialog.

The [in] attribute is known as a directional attribute. This indicates that the parameter is passed from the caller to the COM component. (In the case of our context menu handler, it indicates that the shell is passing our COM component a parameter.) Another attribute, [out], specifies the exact opposite, which is a parameter that is passed from the component to the caller. All parameters to a method have a directional attribute. This is either [in], [out], or [in, out]. But VB cannot handle [out]-only parameters. Parameters designated as [out] usually require the caller to free memory. VB likes to shield responsibility from the programmer whenever possible, especially when it comes to memory management.

Look at the GUID for IShellExtInit, (000214E8-0000-0000-C000-000000000046). This GUID comes straight from the registry. It has been defined by Microsoft as the GUID for IShellExtInit. It is important that you use the correct GUID for interfaces already defined by the system, because, after all, that is their true name. The GUID for the library block (see Appendix A, *VBShell Library Listing*), on the other hand, can be anything since it's being defined by us—but not anything you can think of off the top of your head. Whenever you need to define your own GUID, you should use GUIDGEN (see Figure 4-4). GUIDGEN is a program used for generating GUIDs that guarantees them to be unique (theoretically) and copies them to the clipboard. GUIDGEN ships with Visual Studio, but if you don't have it, you can always make your own, as Example 4-2 demonstrates.

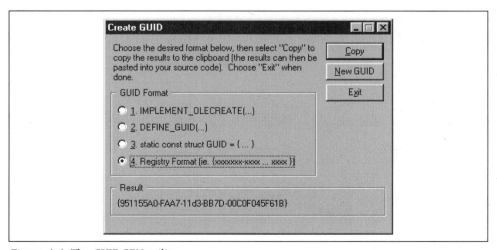

Figure 4-4. The GUIDGEN utility

Example 4-2. Source Code for a Self-Created GUIDGEN Utility

```
Option Explicit

Private Type GUID
    Data1 As Long
    Data2 As Integer
    Data3 As Integer
    Data4(7) As Byte
End Type

Private Declare Function CoCreateGuid Lib "ole32.dll" _
    (g As GUID) As Long
Private Declare Sub CopyMemory Lib "kernel32" Alias _
    "RtlMoveMemory" (pDst As Any, pSrc As Any, _
    ByVal ByteLen As Long)
Private Declare Function StringFromCLSID Lib "ole32.dll" _
    (pClsid As GUID, lpszProgID As Long) As Long

Private Sub StrFromPtrW(pOLESTR As Long, strOut As String)

    Dim ByteArray(255) As Byte
    Dim intTemp As Integer
    Dim intCount As Integer
    Dim i As Integer

    intTemp = 1

    'Walk the string and retrieve the first byte of each WORD.
    While intTemp <> 0
        CopyMemory intTemp, ByVal pOLESTR + i, 2
        ByteArray(intCount) = intTemp
        intCount = intCount + 1
        i = i + 2
    Wend

    'Copy the byte array to our string.
    CopyMemory ByVal strOut, ByteArray(0), intCount

End Sub

Private Sub Command1_Click()

    Dim g As GUID
    Dim lsGuid As Long
    Dim sGuid As String * 40

    If CoCreateGuid(g) = 0 Then
        StringFromCLSID g, lsGuid
        StrFromPtrW lsGuid, sGuid
    End If

    InputBox "This is your GUID!", "GUID", sGuid

End Sub
```

Figuring out the details of this code is an exercise for you. However, this will be much easier to do after you have finished this book, since we will discuss all of the functions in this listing extensively.

IDataObject

IDataObject is not implemented by the context menu handler directly, but rather, it is a parameter to IShellExtInit::Initialize. Therefore, it has to be defined in the type library. IDataObject provides the means to determine which files have been right-clicked within the shell. IDataObject is a fairly complex interface that contains nine methods: GetData, GetDataHere, QueryData, GetCanonicalFormat, SetData, EnumFormatEtc, DAdvise, DUnadvise, and EnumDAdvise. This interface is the soul of OLE data transfers.

In regards to context menu handlers, there is only one method, GetData, that we will use to implement the extension. Its syntax is:

```
HRESULT GetData(FORMATETC * pFormatetc, STGMEDIUM * pmedium);
```

Its parameters are:

pFormatetc

[in] Pointer to a FORMATETC structure. The FORMATETC structure represents a generalized clipboard format. It's defined like this:

```
typedef struct {
        long  cfFormat;
        long  ptd;
        DWORD dwAspect;
        long  lindex;
        TYMED tymed;
    } FORMATETC;
```

pmedium

[in] Pointer to a STGMEDIUM structure. STGMEDIUM is a generalized global-memory handle used for data-transfer operations. It is defined like this:

```
typedef struct tagSTGMEDIUM {
    DWORD tymed;
    union {
        HBITMAP hBitmap;
        HMETAFILEPICT hMetaFilePict;
        HENHMETAFILE hEnhMetaFile;
        HGLOBAL hGlobal;
        LPWSTR lpszFileName;
        IStream *pstm;
        IStorage *pstg;
    };
    IUnknown *pUnkForRelease;
}STGMEDIUM;
```

Because VB does not support unions, our type library will contain a more generalized definition of this structure:

```
typedef struct {
        TYMED     tymed;
        long      pData;
        IUnknown *pUnkForRelease;
   } STGMEDIUM;
```

Admittedly, the discussion of FORMATETC and STGMEDIUM is rather cryptic here. This is intentional. When we implement IShellExtInit later in the chapter, just understand that the shell is using IDataObject to transfer a list of files to us. IDataObject is the primary interface involved in OLE data transfers. That's about all you need to know right now. We will learn much more about this interface in Chapter 8.

IContextMenu

As Table 4-3 shows, IContextMenu contains three methods: GetCommandString, InvokeCommand, and QueryContextMenu. This is the core of the context menu handler. The methods of this interface provide the means to add items to a file object's context menu, display help text in Explorer's status bar, and execute the selected command, respectively. We'll discuss each of these methods in turn.

Table 4-3. IContextMenu

Method	Description
GetCommandString	Returns the help string that Explorer will display in the status bar.
InvokeCommand	Implements menu commands when the menu items are selected.
QueryContextMenu	Adds items to the context menu.

GetCommandString

GetCommandString allows the handler to specify the text that will be displayed in the status bar of Explorer. This occurs when a particular context menu item is selected. Its syntax is:

```
HRESULT GetCommandString(
    UINT idCmd,
    UINT uFlags,
    UINT *pwReserved,
    LPSTR pszName,
    UINT cchMax
    );
```

Its parameters are:

idCmd

The ordinal position of the selected menu item.

uFlags

A flag specifying the information to return.

pwReserved

Unused; handlers must ignore this parameter, which should be set to NULL.

pszName

A pointer to the string buffer that holds the null-terminated string to be displayed.

cchMax

Size of the buffer defined by *pszName*.

When the method is invoked by the shell, the shell passes the following items of information to the GetCommandString method:

- The *idCmd* argument to indicate which menu item is selected.

- The *uFlags* argument to indicate what string the method is expected to return. This can be one of the following values:

Constant	Description
GCS_HELPTEXT	Returns the Help text for the context menu item.
GCS_VALIDATE	Validates that the menu item exists.
GCS_VERB	Returns the language-independent command name for the menu item.

- The *cchMax* argument to indicate how many bytes of memory have been allocated for the string that the method is to pass back to the shell.

The method can then place the desired string in the *pszName* buffer. As a general rule, the string should be 40 characters or less and should not exceed *cchMax*.

InvokeCommand

The shell calls this method to execute the command selected in the context menu. Its syntax is:

```
HRESULT InvokeCommand(LPCMINVOKECOMMANDINFO lpici);
```

with the following parameter:

lpici

A pointer to a CMINVOKECOMMANDINFO structure that contains information about the command to execute when the menu item is selected.

The CMINVOKECOMMANDINFO structure is defined in the Platform SDK as follows:

```
typedef struct _CMInvokeCommandInfo{
    DWORD cbSize;
    DWORD fMask;
    HWND hwnd;
    LPCSTR lpVerb;
```

```
    LPCSTR lpParameters;
    LPCSTR lpDirectory;
    int nShow;
    DWORD dwHotKey;
    HANDLE hIcon;
} CMINVOKECOMMANDINFO, *LPCMINVOKECOMMANDINFO;
```

Its members are:

cbSize

The size of the structure in bytes.

fMask

Zero, or one of the following values:

Constant	Description
CMIC_MASK_HOTKEY	The *dwHotKey* member is valid.
CMIC_MASK_ICON	The *hIcon* member is valid.
CMIC_MASK_FLAG_NO_UI	Tells the system to refrain from displaying user-interface elements, like error messages, while carrying out a command.

hwnd

The handle of the window that owns the context menu.

lpVerb

Contains the zero-based menu item offset in the low-order word.

lpParameters

Not used for shell extensions.

lpDirectory

Not used for shell extensions.

nShow

If the command opens a window, specifies whether it should be visible or not visible. Can be either SW_SHOW or SW_HIDE.

dwHotKey

fMask must contain CMIC_MASK_HOTKEY for this value to be valid. It contains an optional hot key to assign to the command.

hIcon

Icon to use for any application activated by the command.

QueryContextMenu

This method is called by the shell to allow the handler to add items to the context menu. Its syntax is:

```
HRESULT QueryContextMenu(
    HMENU hmenu,
    UINT indexMenu,
    UINT idCmdFirst,
    UINT idCmdLast,
    UINT uFlags
    );
```

with the following parameters:

hmenu

Handle of the menu.

indexMenu

Zero-based position at which to insert the first menu item.

iCmdFirst

Minimum value that the handler can use for a menu-item identifier.

iCmdLast

Maximum value that the handler can use for a menu-item identifier.

uFlags

Flags specifying how the context menu can be changed. These flags are discussed later in this chapter.

In invoking the method, the shell provides the context menu handler with all of the information needed to customize the context menu. The `QueryContextMenu` method can then use this information when calling the Win32 *InsertMenu* function to modify the context menu.

The documentation for the interface states that `QueryContextMenu` should return the menu identifier of the last menu item added, plus one. This presents an interesting problem, because VB does not allow access to the `HRESULT`. Fortunately, there is a workaround. We will discuss this in detail when we actually implement the interface. The complete IDL listing for IContextMenu is shown in Example 4-3.

Example 4-3. IContextMenu

```
typedef [public] long HMENU;
typedef [public] long LPCMINVOKECOMMANDINFO;
typedef [public] long LPSTRVB;
typedef [public] long UINT;

[
    uuid(000214e4-0000-0000-c000-000000000046),
    helpstring("IContextMenu Interface"),
    odl
]
interface IContextMenu : IUnknown
{
    HRESULT QueryContextMenu([in] HMENU hmenu,
```

Example 4-3. IContextMenu (continued)

```
                              [in] UINT indexMenu,
                              [in] UINT idCmdFirst,
                              [in] UINT idCmdLast,
                              [in] QueryContextMenuFlags uFlags);

    HRESULT InvokeCommand([in] LPCMINVOKECOMMANDINFO lpcmi);

    HRESULT GetCommandString([in] UINT     idCmd,
                             [in] UINT     uType,
                             [in] UINT     pwReserved,
                             [in] LPSTRVB  pszName,
                             [in] UINT     cchMax);
}
```

Notice the last parameter of **QueryContextMenu**, which takes a type of **QueryContextMenuFlags**. This is actually an enumeration defined within the type library. Enumerations are a good way to restrict the range of values that can be accepted as a method parameter. We will define many such enumerations throughout the course of this book. This provides some type safety for this method, though not much. The enum does not require an attributes block, although you could add one if you wanted. **QueryContextMenuFlags** is defined as follows:

```
typedef enum {
    CMF_NORMAL        = 0x00000000,
    CMF_DEFAULTONLY   = 0x00000001,
    CMF_VERBSONLY     = 0x00000002,
    CMF_EXPLORE       = 0x00000004,
    CMF_NOVERBS       = 0x00000008,
    CMF_CANRENAME     = 0x00000010,
    CMF_NODEFAULT     = 0x00000020,
    CMF_INCLUDESTATIC = 0x00000040,
    CMF_RESERVED      = 0xffff0000
} QueryContextMenuFlags;
```

Creating a Context Menu Handler

Let's put all of this into action and actually implement a context menu handler for the *.rad* file. We'll add a context menu item that displays the noise an animal makes in a message box. The menu item itself will be displayed in the format (*Animal Name*) Noise. *Animal Name* will be determined from the *.rad* file in question. Let's begin.

Type Library

The first step to creating the *.rad* file context menu handler is to compile the type library containing the interface definitions and constants that will be needed from VB. Constants and UDTs will also be put into the type library with their associated interfaces. But only the groups of constants that are needed will be put in the library. For instance, we need the menu constants **MF_BYPOSITION**, **MF_STRING**, and **MF_SEPARATOR**. Therefore, the library will contain all of the **MF_** constants. We *don't* need any of the menu state constants (**MFS_**), so they will not be included with the library.

The complete listing for the type library that will be used throughout the course of this book can be found in Appendix A. To compile the library, you need to have MKTYPLIB in your path. MKTYPLIB takes one argument on the command line, the name of the *ODL* file containing the type library definition. To compile, simply type:

```
mktyplib vbshell.odl
```

from the command line. If everything is in order, this should produce a file named *vbshell.tlb*. This is the type library.

To use this library from Visual Basic, you should select Project → References . . . from the main menu. You should then browse to the location of the *.tlb* file and select it. This will do two things. First, it will register the type library at that location; second, it will make it available to the References dialog for all future projects.

The Project

The context menu handler begins life as an ActiveX DLL project called RadEx. Our first step is to register the type library so that interface definitions are available for us to implement. That is done by selecting Project → References from VB and then Browse (the library is not registered, so it will not be in the list). Navigate to the library that is associated with this chapter and add the reference. The library will be available in the References list box from this point on.

Next, add the class that will implement the handler to the project. Call this class clsContextMenu. With the class added to the project, **IShellExtInit** and **IContextMenu** can be implemented as follows:

```
Option Explicit

Implements IContextMenu
Implements IShellExtInit
```

Implementing IShellExtInit

Let's implement **IShellExtInit::Initialize** first. Notice that, in the code shell that Visual Basic creates for the **Initialize** method, the parameters are prefixed with the name of the library in which their definitions are located:

```
Private Sub IShellExtInit_Initialize( _
   ByVal pidlFolder As VBShellLib.LPCITEMIDLIST, _
```

```
        ByVal pDataObj As VBShellLib.IDataObject, _
        ByVal hKeyProgID As VBShellLib.HKEY)
```

In some cases, you might want to add a private variable to your class to hold the
IDataObject reference passed in by the shell, since from it you can determine
how many files are selected in the user interface and what the names of those files
happen to be. We will use **IDataObject** to get the selected files from
IShellExtInit::Initialize immediately, but it may be preferable to wait until
a menu item is actually selected before the selected files are determined (possibly
for performance reasons). In this particular case, saving the **IDataObject** reference is not necessary. Rather than hold a reference to **IDataObject**, we will use
pDataObj directly and build an array containing the names of the selected files.
This array will be kept as private data. The entire listing for the **Initialize**
method is shown in Example 4-4.

Example 4-4. Implementing IShellExtInit::Initialize

```
'handler.bas

Public Declare Function DragQueryFile Lib "shell32.dll" _
    Alias "DragQueryFileA" (ByVal HDROP As Long, _
    ByVal pUINT As Long, ByVal lpStr As String, _
    ByVal ch As Long) As Long

Public Declare Function ReleaseStgMedium Lib "ole32.dll" _
    (pMedium As STGMEDIUM) As Long


'clsContextMenu.cls

Option Explicit

Implements IContextMenu
Implements IShellExtInit

Private m_sFiles() As String
Public m_nFiles As Byte

Private Sub IShellExtInit_Initialize( _
    ByVal pidlFolder As VBShellLib.LPCITEMIDLIST, _
    ByVal pDataObj As VBShellLib.IDataObject, _
    ByVal hKeyProgID As VBShellLib.HKEY)

    Dim FmtEtc As FORMATETC
    Dim pMedium As STGMEDIUM
    Dim i As Long
    Dim lresult As Long
    Dim sTemp As String

    With FmtEtc
        .cfFormat = CF_HDROP
        .ptd = 0
```

Example 4-4. Implementing IShellExtInit::Initialize (continued)

```
        .dwAspect = DVASPECT_CONTENT
        .lindex = -1
        .TYMED = TYMED_HGLOBAL
    End With

    pDataObj.GetData FmtEtc, pMedium

    m_nFiles = DragQueryFile(pMedium.pData, &HFFFFFFFF, _
            vbNullString, 0)

    ReDim m_sFiles(m_nFiles - 1)

    For i = 0 To (m_nFiles - 1)
        sTemp = String(1024, 0)
        lresult = DragQueryFile(pMedium.pData, i, sTemp, _
                        Len(sTemp))
        If (lresult > 0) Then
            m_sFiles(i) = Left$(sTemp, lresult)
        End If
    Next

    ReleaseStgMedium pMedium

End Sub
```

There's quite a bit going here, so let's just take it from the top, starting with the call to GetData. GetData takes two parameters: an [in] parameter containing a pointer to a **FORMATETC** structure, and an [in, out] parameter that returns a pointer to a **STGMEDIUM** structure. The function is called like so:

```
    pDataObj.GetData FmtEtc, pMedium
```

The parameters are as follows:

FORMATETC

FORMATETC is a generalized clipboard format used by OLE wherever data format information is required. The structure contains the clipboard format, a pointer to a target device, the view of the data, how much of the data should be transferred, and the medium used to transfer the data. The members of the structure are assigned values in the following code fragment from Example 4-4:

```
    With FmtEtc
        .cfFormat = CF_HDROP
        .ptd = 0
        .dwAspect = DVASPECT_CONTENT
        .lindex = -1
        .TYMED = TYMED_HGLOBAL
    End With
```

Pointers

There are three undocumented functions that allow the use of pointers from Visual Basic. These functions are *VarPtr*, *StrPtr*, and *ObjPtr*. *VarPtr* will return the address of all VB datatypes (even UDTs), except for Strings. *StrPtr* is used to get the address of a String. *ObjPtr* is used to get the address of an Object. Internally, these three functions are all mapped to one function, *VarPtr*. But use these functions with caution. *StrPtr* and *VarPtr* will not return the same value for a String. *StrPtr* returns a pointer to the Unicode string value, and *VarPtr* returns the address where VB stores the pointer to the Unicode BSTR. For more information on VB's undocumented pointer functions, see Appendix B, *Pointers*.

In this case, the data transferred will be a handle to a drop structure (our list of files) specified by `CF_HDROP`. The target device (specified by `ptd`) is 0, because we don't care about its value; it's actually device-independent. `DVASPECT_CONTENT` means we want the actual data. A clipboard format can support more than one aspect or view. Here, we don't need a view, we just need the data. `lindex` is unimportant to the discussion. Last is the `TYMED_HGLOBAL` flag, which means the transfer will take place using global memory (as opposed to a file or structured storage objects). The `TYMED` member specifies which member of the `STGMEDIUM` union will be valid.

STGMEDIUM

The second parameter to GetData is a pointer to a `STGMEDIUM` union. The union is based on the type of medium, which in this case is `TYMED_HGLOBAL` (specified by `FORMATETC`). Therefore, under normal circumstances, the union member `hGlobal` would contain the handle to the drop structure. However, since this structure has been redefined, the `pData` member will always point to the data. This handle can be passed directly to the Win32 *DragQueryFile* function, which then allows us to find out how many files have been selected:

```
nFiles = DragQueryFile(pMedium.pData, &HFFFFFFFF, vbNullString, 0)
```

Passing *DragQueryFile* the value `&HFFFFFFFF` tells it that we want the number of files selected. We can also pass it a number between 0 and the total number of files selected to get the name of the file itself.

The value for `nFiles` allows us to redimension our file array. *DragQueryFile* can then be called in a loop with the index of the requested file supplied as the second argument to the function. The filename (which is written to the buffer that passed as the third argument to the function) is retrieved and stored in the file array. If multiple files of different types are selected and the file with primary focus is a *.rad* file, our handler will still be called. But we have to filter these extraneous types if necessary. To do this, we can have

`IContextMenu::InvokeCommand` loop through this array and process the context menu command for every valid file that is selected.

Here's one last detail: the `STGMEDIUM` structure has been allocated by the call to GetData. It is common to see this structure populated by a "provider" outside of the code in which it is being used, as is the case in Example 4-4. This means freeing the memory is our responsibility, and that is what the final call to *ReleaseStgMedium* (a routine found in *Ole32.dll*) is doing.

Implementing IContextMenu

The `IContextMenu` interface is responsible for displaying the text of the menu item, for showing help text associated with the menu item, and for defining the action to be performed if the menu item is selected. In this section, we'll examine the code for the methods responsible for those operations.

GetCommandString

The source code for the `GetCommandString` method is shown in Example 4-5. `GetCommandString` is called by the shell for the purpose of retrieving help text for a context menu item. This help text is then displayed in the status bar. This method is notable in that this is the first time we have to worry about implementing a method that will run under both Windows 98 and Windows NT. As you might guess, this has to do with how both platforms deal with strings. Windows 98 uses ANSI strings internally; Windows NT uses Unicode. VB uses Unicode strings internally, regardless of what platform is being used. Confusing, to say the least.

The menu item in question is determined by the *idCmd* parameter passed in by the shell. *uType* indicates the flags that inform us of the information being requested. We will return the same string regardless of these flags. The only distinction we are interested in is whether the values should be ANSI or Unicode. (There are separate ANSI and Unicode versions of each constant stored to *uType*.) A buffer for the help string is provided through the *pszName* parameter. *cchMax* is the size of this buffer.

The ANSI portion of the listing uses *StrConv* to convert the string from Unicode to ANSI. From this point forward, a common tactic is used. The string is copied into a byte array, and its starting address is copied to the memory location provided by the shell.

Example 4-5. GetCommandString Listing

```
Private Sub IContextMenu_GetCommandString( _
    ByVal idCmd As VBShellLib.UINT, _
    ByVal uType As VBShellLib.UINT, _
    ByVal pwReserved As VBShellLib.UINT, _
    ByVal pszName As VBShellLib.LPSTRVB, _
```

Example 4-5. GetCommandString Listing (continued)

```
    ByVal cchMax As VBShellLib.UINT)

    Dim szName As String
    Dim bszName() As Byte

    Dim sMenuHelp As String

    Select Case idCmd
        Case 0 'Noise
            szName = "Display Animal Noise"

        'Other menu items would be added like so:

        'Case 1 'Menu item 2
        '    szName = "Menu Item 2"

        'Case 2 'Menu item 3
        '    szName = "Menu Item 3"
    End Select

    szName = Left$(szName, cchMax) & vbNullChar

    Select Case uType
        Case GCS_VERBA, GCS_HELPTEXTA, GCS_VALIDATEA
            If (szName <> "") Then
                bszName = StrConv(szName, vbFromUnicode)
                CopyMemory ByVal pszName, _
                            bszName(0), _
                            UBound(bszName) + 1
            End If
        Case GCS_VERBW, GCS_HELPTEXTW, GCS_VALIDATEW
            If (szName <> "") Then
                bszName = szName
                CopyMemory ByVal pszName, _
                            bszName(0), _
                            UBound(bszName) + 1
            End If
    End Select

End Sub
```

InvokeCommand

InvokeCommand is called when the shell is ready to execute the context menu command. Its source code is shown in Example 4-6. The implementation of this method is fairly straightforward. Of interest is the pointer to the CMINVOKECOMMANDINFO structure that is passed in by the shell. CMINVOKECOMMANDINFO is one of those structures that mean something different depending on the context in which it is used. Check the Platform SDK for full details on this one.

This structure, while weighty as far as information goes, contains only one member that is of interest to us: *lpVerb*. The low-order word of *lpVerb* contains the menu identifier of the command being invoked.

By the time the shell calls **InvokeCommand**, we already have an array of the selected files stored as private data within our component. This allows us to grab every file in a loop, to find out the animal type of the file with a call to *GetPrivateProfileString*, and to display the appropriate information.

Example 4-6. InvokeCommand Listing

```
Private Sub IContextMenu_InvokeCommand(ByVal lpcmi As VBShellLib. _
LPCMINVOKECOMMANDINFO)

    Dim cmi As CMINVOKECOMMANDINFO
    CopyMemory cmi, ByVal lpcmi, Len(cmi)

    Dim i As Long
    Dim sNoise As String
    sNoise = Space(255)

    If LOWORD(cmi.lpVerb) = 0 Then
        For i = 0 To m_nFiles - 1

            GetPrivateProfileString "Animal", _
                                    "Noise", _
                                    "Unknown", _
                                    sNoise, _
                                    Len(sNoise), _
                                    m_sFiles(i)

            MsgBox Trim(sNoise), vbOKOnly, "Animal Noise"

        Next i
    End If

End Sub
```

The *LOWORD* function is defined in *handler.bas*. There is also a *HIWORD* function thrown in for good measure. The two functions look like this:

```
Public Function LOWORD(ByVal lVal As Long) As Integer
    LOWORD = lVal And &HFFFF&
End Function

Public Function HIWORD(ByVal lVal As Long) As Integer
    HIWORD = 0
    If lVal Then
        HIWORD = lVal \ &H10000 And &HFFFF&
    End If
End Function
```

QueryContextMenu

QueryContextMenu is used to add menu items to a file object's context menu. Implementing IContextMenu::QueryContextMenu is going to be a tricky process. The Platform SDK states that this method must return a positive integer representing the menu identifier of the last menu item added plus one. You might have noticed that these interface methods are implemented as subs, not functions. Even though we are dealing with a sub, VB still returns a value for each of these methods: a 0 if everything is okay or an error code that is available through the Err object. We have no direct access to the value returned from these methods.

There is a solution to this dilemma. We will write a replacement function for QueryContextMenu and put it in a code module located in the project. Then we will find the vtable entry for QueryContextMenu in our object (see Chapter 1, *Introduction*). We will use the AddressOf operator, in conjunction with *CopyMemory*, and swap the two addresses. Our new function, *QueryContextMenuVB*, will be called instead of the class implementation. Of course, *QueryContextMenuVB* will be a function, and we can return any value we want. When the object is released, the two addresses will be swapped back for posterity's sake. Our troubles are solved.

The addresses of the two functions need to be swapped as quickly as possible. Therefore, the Initialize and Terminate events (which are shown in Example 4-7 and Example 4-9, respectively) of the context menu handler class are used for this purpose.

Example 4-7. Swapping vtable Entries

```
Private m_pOldQueryCtxMenu As Long

Private Sub Class_Initialize()

    Dim pVtable As IContextMenu
    Set pVtable = Me

    m_pOldQueryCtxMenu = SwapVtableEntry(ObjPtr(pVtable), _
        4, AddressOf QueryContextMenuVB)

End Sub
```

A variable of type IContextMenu is set to Me. This gives us a pointer to the IContextMenu portion of the vtable. This memory location is copied into *pVtable*, effectively giving us a pointer to the IContextMenu portion of our object's vtable. Then, *SwapVtableEntry* (shown in Example 4-8) is called with the address of the first method of IContextMenu (this is the portion of the vtable where IContextMenu begins), the relative position in the vtable of the method we want to replace (in this case, 4—we'll see why in a few moments), and the address of the new function. One thing of interest in *SwapVtableEntry* is the call to *VirtualProtect*. VB has marked the object memory as protected. This call changes the access permissions, allowing us to swap the addresses.

Example 4-8. SwapVtableEntry Listing

```
Public Function SwapVtableEntry(pObj As Long, _
    EntryNumber As Integer, _
    ByVal lpfn As Long) As Long

    Dim lOldAddr As Long
    Dim lpVtableHead As Long
    Dim lpfnAddr As Long
    Dim lOldProtect As Long

    CopyMemory lpVtableHead, ByVal pObj, 4
    lpfnAddr = lpVtableHead + (EntryNumber - 1) * 4
    CopyMemory lOldAddr, ByVal lpfnAddr, 4

    Call VirtualProtect(lpfnAddr, 4, _
                        PAGE_EXECUTE_READWRITE, _
                        lOldProtect)

    CopyMemory ByVal lpfnAddr, lpfn, 4
    Call VirtualProtect(lpfnAddr, 4, lOldProtect, lOldProtect)

    SwapVtableEntry = lOldAddr

End Function
```

How do we know where `QueryContextMenu` is located in relation to this address? Well, we can't look at our class file for clues, because VB just displays all of the implemented methods in alphabetical order. This is not an accurate representation of our object.

To determine the vtable order of the method in question, look at the ODL listing. The methods are listed in the order in which they appear in the vtable. You can also use OLE View to get this information (should ODL be unavailable). Object Browser, however, does not provide it; it just lists the methods in alphabetical order. If you examine the `IContextMenu` interface definition in this manner, you will see that `QueryContextMenu` is the first method listed in the interface. Taking into consideration that the interface is derived from `IUnknown`, which contains three methods, `QueryContextMenu` is the fourth method. Thus, we pass 4 to *SwapVtableEntry*.

When the object terminates, the addresses can be switched back in the same manner, as shown in the class Terminate event handler in Example 4-9.

Example 4-9. Restoring vtable Entries

```
Private Sub Class_Terminate()
    Dim pVtable As IContextMenu
    Set pVtable = Me
    m_pOldQueryCtxMenu = SwapVtableEntry(ObjPtr(pVtable), _
        4, m_pOldQueryCtxMenu)
End Sub
```

QueryContextMenuVB

`QueryContextMenuVB` gives us some insight into just how a class works. We already know that a class keeps track of its member functions with the vtable. But once we are inside one of those member functions, how is it that we can have access back to the class? To the other methods? To Private and Public data members? Well, when a member function is called, a pointer to the class is also passed with the parameters to the function. VB (also C++) handles this behind the scenes, making everything look nice and smooth. C++ programmers refer to the parameter as the **this** pointer. VB can use this pointer to resolve all references back to the object.

`QueryContextMenuVB` must make allowances for this parameter, because it is not a part of a class; it is a function defined in a code module. This means we have to add our own **this** pointer to the parameter list. Example 4-10 shows how we can then define a local copy of clsContextMenu and use the this pointer to get a reference back to our class. This is really cool, because we don't have to use a global variable to get at our class now.

Example 4-10. QueryContextMenuVB Implementation

```
'ContextMenu.bas

Public Function QueryContextMenuVB (ByVal this As IContextMenu, _
    ByVal hMenu As Long, _
    ByVal indexMenu As Long, _
    ByVal idCmdFirst As Long, _
    ByVal idCmdLast As Long, _
    ByVal uFlags As Long) As Long

    Dim ctxMenu As clsContextMenu
    Set ctxMenu = this
```

The main task of **QueryContextMenuVB** (which we seem to have ignored for a while) is to add menu items to the context menu. First, the circumstance in which the context menu is activated needs to be determined. This is accomplished with the *uFlags* parameter that is passed in by the shell. The following code fragment shows the various situations in which the context menu can be activated. The flag we are primarily interested in is **CMF_EXPLORE**:

```
    If (uFlags And &HF) = CMF_NORMAL Then

        'Implement this for Drag-and-Drop handler.
```

```
    ElseIf (uFlags And CMF_VERBSONLY) Then

        'This is a context menu for a shortcut item.

    ElseIf (uFlags And CMF_EXPLORE) Then

        'Right-click on file in Explorer.
        'This is what we are interested in for our context
        'menu.

    ElseIf (uFlags And CMF_DEFAULTONLY) Then

        'Indicates a default action is being performed (typically a
        'user is double-clicking on the file).

    End If
```

Once it has been determined that files have been right-clicked in Explorer, the context menu item can be added accordingly. The menu item added is based on the number of files selected and the type of animal represented by the file. The animal type is determined with a call to *GetPrivateProfileString*:

```
    ElseIf (uFlags And CMF_EXPLORE) Then

        'Right-click on file in Explorer

        If ctxMenu.FileCount > 1 Then
            sMenuItem = "Bunches o' Animal noises"
        Else
            GetPrivateProfileString "Animal", _
                                    "Type", _
                                    "Unknown", _
                                    sAnimal, _
                                    Len(sAnimal), _
                                    ctxMenu.FileName

            sAnimal = Trim(sAnimal)
            sAnimal = Left$(sAnimal, Len(sAnimal) - 1)

            sMenuItem = sAnimal & "Noise"

        End If

        Call InsertMenu(hMenu, _
                        indexMenu, _
                        MF_STRING Or MF_BYPOSITION, _
                        idCmd, _
                        sMenuItem)

        idCmd = idCmd + 1
        indexMenu = indexMenu + 1

        'If you want to add another item just repeat the following code.
        '
```

```
'sMenuItem = "Animal Name"
'Call InsertMenu(hMenu, _
'                indexMenu, _
'                MF_STRING Or MF_BYPOSITION, _
'                idCmd, _
'                sMenuItem)
'
'idCmd = idCmd + 1
'indexMenu = indexMenu + 1

'etc. , etc., etc.
'
'Do not increment idCmd for separators!
'IndexMenu is always incremented.

Set ctxMenu = Nothing

'Lastly, the number of menu items added + 1 is returned.
QueryContextMenuVB = indexMenu
```

Drag-and-Drop Handlers

Drag-and-drop handlers are displayed when a user drags a file with the right mouse button. They are really just specialized context menu handlers; therefore, they don't get a chapter of their own.

To implement one, you would need to insert menu items based on the context menu flag being equal to CMF_NORMAL, and only equal to CMF_NORMAL. It cannot be ANDed with any other value. In addition, you would have to add the handler to the registry as shown in Figure 4-5.

The handler is also added to the approved shell extensions list in the registry (see Chapter 2, *COM Basics*).

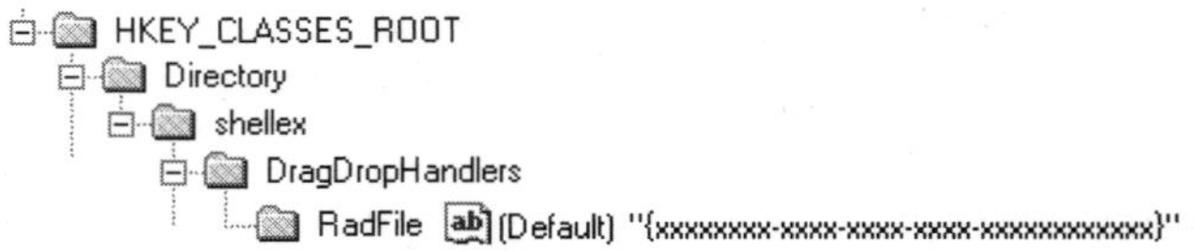

Figure 4-5. Defining a drag-and-drop handler in the registry

Registration and Operation

Last but not least, the handler needs to be registered. As always, the file *rad.reg* that is included with this chapter's downloadable code contains the appropriate registry entries. Example 4-11 contains the entire listing. Note that items in square brackets must exist on the same line (the listing is formatted to fit on the page).

Example 4-11. rad.reg

```
REGEDIT4

[HKEY_CLASSES_ROOT\.rad]
@ = "radfile"

[HKEY_CLASSES_ROOT\radfile]

[HKEY_CLASSES_ROOT\radfile]
@ = "Rudimentary Animal Data"

[HKEY_CLASSES_ROOT\radfile\shellex]

[HKEY_CLASSES_ROOT\radfile\shellex\ContextMenuHandlers]
@ = "RadFileMenu"

[HKEY_CLASSES_ROOT\radfile\shellex\ContextMenuHandlers\RadFileMenu]
@ = "{D4F9CECF-E84E-11D2-BB7C-444553540000}"

[HKEY_LOCAL_MACHINE\Software\Microsoft\Windows\CurrentVersion\Shell Extensions\
Approved]
"{D4F9CECF-E84E-11D2-BB7C-444553540000}" = "RAD file context menu extension"
```

These are the same entries that were discussed in Chapter 3, *Shell Extensions*. Review the entries until you become familiar with them. It shouldn't take too long. If you want to register the extension by hand, you will need to find the CLSID for the object. The easiest way to do that is to search under **HKEY_CLASSES_ROOT** for the *programmatic identifier*, or ProgID, of the extension object. The ProgID is formed by appending the class name to the project name with a period in the middle. So look for "RadEx.clsContextMenu," and there should be a CLSID subkey with the needed value.

After you have registered the handler, kill off any instances of Explorer you might have running. The handler, which is shown in Figure 4-6, will be available with the next instance you run. There are sample *.rad* files included with the source of this book that you can use to test the handler.

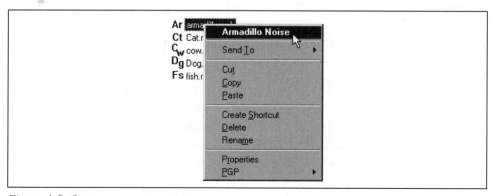

Figure 4-6. Context menu in action

5

Icon Handlers

Icons are defined for a particular file class by adding a `DefaultIcon` key under the files association key in the registry. `DefaultIcon` is then set to a path containing the *.exe* or *.dll* that contains the icon to be displayed and the zero-based index of that icon within the file, if multiple icons are present. Figure 5-1, for example, shows the relevant registry keys for our example *.rad* file type, which is configured to use the second icon in *notepad.exe*. Every icon for the file class in question will have the same icon when this key is registered.

Figure 5-1. Registering the default icon for a file class

Icon handlers allow file objects of the same type to display different icons on a per-instance basis. This means that such things as the value of particular file attributes or state information internal to the file can be conveyed to the user through the shell. Take the *.rad* file, for instance. Using an icon handler, we could display a picture of the animal represented by the file (for a limited number of animals, of course), the age of the animal, the gender, or whatever.

How Icon Handlers Work

Icon handlers are required to implement two interfaces: `IPersistFile` and `IExtractIcon`. These interfaces are interesting from a programmatic standpoint for several reasons. `IPersistFile` is not directly derived from `IUnknown`; it's derived from `IPersist`. And as luck would have it, VB doesn't like to implement interfaces that are not directly derived from `IUnknown` or `IDispatch`.

`IExtractIcon` is the general name given to one of two interfaces: `IExtractIconA` or `IExtractIconW`. These interfaces contain the ANSI and Unicode versions, respectively, of `IExtractIcon`. As fate would have it, we will have to implement both of them. The interfaces are defined almost the same (typedefs aside). The only difference is how the methods will be implemented. Also, one of the methods, `IExtractIcon::Extract`, has to return the value `S_FALSE` (1). In other words, a vtable swap is in order.

Here's how custom icon handlers work. When the shell is about to display an icon for a file object (for the first time), it checks for the following registry key to determine if there is an icon handler for that particular type:

```
HKEY_CLASSES_ROOT\
    radfile\
        shellex\
            IconHandler
```

If an icon handler is present, the shell loads it and attempts to call `IPersistFile::Load`. One of the parameters to the `Load` method is a pointer to the name of the file whose icon the shell is requesting. Typically, an implementor of `IPersistFile` would store the name of the file object in a private member variable for later use. The other five methods of `IPersistFile` are ignored.

The shell then calls `IExtractIcon::GetIconLocation` to get the icon for the file object in question. If `GetIconLocation` fails, the shell will use the icon specified by the `DefaultIcon` registry key. If it succeeds, then the shell examines the *pwFlags* parameter of `GetIconLocation` to determine if the `GIL_NOTFILENAME` bit is turned on. If it is, the shell assumes that the icon handler wants to extract its own icon and calls `IExtractIcon::Extract`.

Basically, if the icon to be displayed resides in a file, `GetIconLocation` can provide all the necessary details for displaying the icon. If the icons exist in an image list control or you want to handle loading the icons yourself, `Extract` is used for this purpose. `Extract` provides the icons for Explorer in the form of two handles, or `HICON`s. One handle is the small icon (16×16). The other is for the normal-sized icon (32×32).

Icon Handler Interfaces

Now that you know how an icon handler works, let's discuss the interfaces involved in a little more detail.

IPersistFile

`IPersistFile` inherits one method, `GetClassID`, from `IPersist`. `IPersistFile` contains an additional five methods (see Table 5-1): `IsDirty`, `Load`,

`Save`, `SaveCompleted`, and `GetCurFile`. Typically, `IPersistFile` is implemented when you want to read or write information from a file. There are many more scenarios. You are encouraged to learn more about this interface, because in the world of COM, this interface gets some major game time. In our case, however, we are only interested in one method, and that's `Load`.

We do have a small problem with `IPersistFile`. It's derived from `IPersist`, and VB does not like interfaces that are derived from anything other than `IUnknown` or `IDispatch`. This is because Microsoft believes that Visual Basic objects should always support late binding and, hence, should always be derived from `IDispatch`. So what do we do? Before addressing this question, let's look at the IDL in Example 5-1, which shows that `IPersistFile` is derived from `IPersist`. `IPersistFile` has inherited the `IPersist` method `GetClassID`.

Example 5-1. VB Will Not Accept This Definition of IPersistFile

```
[
    uuid(0000010c-0000-0000-C000-000000000046),
    helpstring("IPersist Interface"),
    odl
]
interface IPersist : IUnknown
{
    HRESULT GetClassID([in, out] CLSID *lpClassID);
}


[
    uuid(0000010b-0000-0000-C000-000000000046),
    helpstring("IPersistFile Interface"),
    odl
]
interface IPersistFile : IPersist
{

    HRESULT IsDirty();

    HRESULT Load([in] LPCOLESTR pszFileName,
                 [in] DWORD dwMode);

    HRESULT Save([in] LPCOLESTR pszFileName,
                 [in] BOOL fRemember);

    HRESULT SaveCompleted([in] LPCOLESTR pszFileName);

    HRESULT GetCurFile([in, out] LPOLESTR *ppszFileName);

}
```

Fortunately, the solution to this problem is very easy. We will simulate the inheritance by deriving `IPersistFile` from `IUnknown`. Then we add the method from

`IPersist` that would have been a part of the interface via inheritance directly to the definition listing for `IPersistFile`. In other words, we remove the inheritance. The resulting IDL file is shown in Example 5-2.

Example 5-2. IPersist Is Added to IPersistFile to Simulate Inheritance

```
[
    uuid(0000010b-0000-0000-C000-000000000046),
    helpstring("IPersistFile Interface"),
    odl
]

// original - interface IPersistFile : IPersist

interface IPersistFile : IUnknown
{

    // IPersist is added to IPersistFile definition
    HRESULT GetClassID([in, out] CLSID *lpClassID);

    //IPersistFile starts here
    HRESULT IsDirty();

    HRESULT Load([in] LPCOLESTR pszFileName,
                 [in] DWORD dwMode);

    HRESULT Save([in] LPCOLESTR pszFileName,
                 [in] BOOL fRemember);

    HRESULT SaveCompleted([in] LPCOLESTR pszFileName);

    HRESULT GetCurFile([in, out] LPOLESTR *ppszFileName);

}
```

Table 5-1 shows the methods supported by `IPersistFile`. We'll look at only one of these, the `Load` method, in detail, since it's the only method that we'll actually have to write any code for.

Table 5-1. IPersistFile

Method	Description
GetClassID	This method is inherited from `IPersist`. It should return the CLSID of an object.
IsDirty	Checks an object for changes since it was last saved.
Load	Opens the selected file and initializes the object.
Save	Saves the object into the selected file.
SaveCompleted	Notifies the object that it can write to its file.
GetCurFile	Gets the name of the file that is currently associated with the object.

Load

The `Load` method is invoked by the shell immediately after the icon handler is loaded. The `Load` method is responsible for providing the icon handler with the name of the file that is to be displayed.

The documentation for the `Load` method states that its purpose is to open a specified file and initialize an object from the file contents. This is an important distinction to remember. `Load` does not load a file. It loads an object based on the contents of a file. The how and the why is left to the implementor. This function is only used for initialization. It does not return the object to the caller. Its syntax is as follows:

```
HRESULT Load(LPCOLESTR pszFileName, DWORD dwMode);
```

Its parameters are:

pszFileName
A pointer to the name of the file for which the shell is requesting an icon to display.

dwMode
The access mode (which is ignored in the case of icon handlers).

Because the first parameter actually comes to us as a 4-byte address, we will have to use the *CopyMemory* API and the undocumented *StrPtr* function to retrieve the actual string value of the filename. This will be discussed in more detail in the implementation section of this chapter.

IExtractIcon

`IExtractIcon` is actually `IExtractIconA` or `IExtractIconW`, depending upon the circumstance. The original definition of this interface is found in a header file named *shlobj.h*. For those of you with Visual C++ installations, take a look at the file. It contains most of the interfaces used by the shell with liberal commenting, making it a really good source of information. It also will show you how to define an interface in straight C++. That's right; there's no IDL in this file.

Preprocessor definitions in the file are used to determine whether `IExtractIcon` is being compiled for Windows 9x or Windows NT and Windows 2000. The appropriate interface, `IExtractIconA` or `IExtractIconW`, is then used. Typically, interface names ending in "A" denote the Windows 9x version and the interface names ending in "W" are for Windows NT and Windows 2000. We do not have the luxury of a preprocessor in VB. We will have to define both interfaces (each has a distinct GUID) and implement both interfaces, as well. The complete listing for `IExtractIcon` is shown in Example 5-3.

Example 5-3. IExtractIconA and IExtractIconW

```
typedef [public] long HICON;
typedef [public] long LPSTRVB;
typedef [public] long UINT;

typedef enum {
    GIL_SIMULATEDOC   = 0x0001,
    GIL_PERINSTANCE   = 0x0002,
    GIL_PERCLASS      = 0x0004,
    GIL_NOTFILENAME   = 0x0008,
    GIL_DONTCACHE     = 0x0010
} GETICONLOCATIONRETURN;

[
    uuid(000214eb-0000-0000-c000-000000000046),
    helpstring("IExtractIconA Interface"),
    odl
]
interface IExtractIconA : IUnknown
{
    HRESULT GetIconLocation([in] UINT uFlags,
                            [in] LPSTRVB szIconFile,
                            [in] UINT cchMax,
                            [in,out] long *piIndex,
                            [in,out] GETICONLOCATIONRETURN *pwFlags);


    HRESULT Extract([in] LPCSTRVB pszFile,
                    [in] UINT nIconIndex,
                    [in,out] HICON *phiconLarge,
                    [in,out] HICON *phiconSmall,
                    [in] UINT nIconSize);
}


[
    uuid(000214fa-0000-0000-c000-000000000046),
    helpstring("IExtractIconW"),
    odl
]
interface IExtractIconW : IUnknown
{
    HRESULT GetIconLocation([in] UINT uFlags,
                            [in] LPWSTRVB szIconFile,
                            [in] UINT cchMax,
                            [in,out] long *piIndex,
                            [in,out] GETICONLOCATIONRETURN *pwFlags);

    HRESULT Extract([in] LPWSTRVB pszFile,
                    [in] long nIconIndex,
                    [in,out] HICON *phiconLarge,
                    [in,out] HICON *phiconSmall,
                    [in] UINT nIconSize);
}
```

As its name indicates, `IExtractIcon` is concerned with retrieving the icon to be displayed by the context icon handler. The methods of this interface are shown in Table 5-2.

Table 5-2. IExtractIcon

Method	Description
Extract	Specifies the location of an icon.
GetIconLocation	Retrieves the location and index of an icon.

GetIconLocation

`GetIconLocation` is used by the shell to retrieve the location and index of an icon from the icon handler. If the icon is in a DLL or EXE, then `GetIconLocation` returns the filename and the index of the icon as it resides in the resource section of that file; otherwise, the method returns a value of `GIL_NOTFILENAME` in the *pwFlags* parameter. Its syntax is:

```
HRESULT GetIconLocation(UINT uFlags, LPSTR szIconFile, INT cchMax,
LPINT piIndex, UINT *pwFlags );
```

Its parameters are the following:

uFlags

> [in] Icon state flags. This value is supplied by the shell.

szIconFile

> [in, out] The address that receives the name and location of the icon file from the icon handler. This is a null-terminated string.

cchMax

> [in] Size of the buffer that receives the icon location. This is usually set to the value of `MAX_PATH` and defines the total number of characters that the icon handler can write to *szIconFile*.

piIndex

> [in, out] The zero-based ordinal position of the icon in the file whose path and name are written to the *szIconFile* buffer. The icon handler provides the shell with this value if the icon is to be extracted from a file.

pwFlags

> [in, out] A value from the `GETICONLOCATIONRETURN` enumeration. This parameter tells the shell how it should handle the icon file that is returned.

The first parameter, *uFlags*, is of no concern to us, so we can skip it for now. It will come into play later when we create namespace extensions (see Chapter 12, *Browser Extensions*).

The second parameter, *szIconFile*, is a pointer. If the icon handler uses `GetIconLocation` (as opposed to `Extract`) to provide the icon file, *szIconFile* should point to a buffer that contains a valid filename upon successful completion. This is a long value. We can't assign a string directly to *szIconFile*. You should start getting used to the idea of using pointers now. Out of necessity, we will be using pointers to strings, rather than the strings themselves, for most of the book.

The third parameter, *cchMax*, is merely the size of the buffer that contains the icon filename.

Upon successful completion, the fourth parameter contains the index of the icon to be displayed. This is the index of the icon as it appears in the resource section of the file specified by *szIconFile*.

The icon handler should assign the fifth parameter one or more of the values from the GETICONLOCATIONRETURN enumeration defined in Table 5-3. These can be ORed together.

Table 5-3. The GETICONLOCATIONRETURN Enumeration

Constant	Description
GIL_DONTCACHE	The physical image bits of the icon should not be cached by the caller.
GIL_NOTFILENAME	The location of the icon is not a filename/index pair. If this flag is set when the method returns, the shell will then call the Extract method for the icon location.
GIL_PERCLASS	All objects of this class have the same icon. There is no need to use this flag, since it defeats the purpose of an icon handler.
GIL_PERINSTANCE	Each object of this class has its own icon.
GIL_SIMULATEDOC	The icon is the one registered for the file object's document type.

Extract

Extract is called by the shell after the icon handler supplies a value of GIL_NOTFILENAME for the *pwFlags* parameter of the GetIconLocation method and is used to provide the location of an icon (or the handle to an icon) that does not reside as a resource in a file. There are various reasons for returning a handle rather than the filename and index at which the icon can be found. For example, in Chapter 12, when we implement a namespace extension, the icons used will reside in an image list. This is for reasons of speed. Repeatedly opening and closing a file to retrieve an icon is very slow. If you have to access a file a few hundred times just to get an icon, you might consider using the Extract method instead. The syntax for Extract is as follows:

```
HRESULT Extract( LPCSTR pszFile, UINT nIconIndex, HICON *phiconLarge, HICON
*phiconSmall, UINT nIconSize );
```

Its parameters are:

pszFile

[in] The icon filename. This is the same value returned by the
GetIconLocation method.

nIconIndex

[in] The icon's index. This is the same value returned by the
GetIconLocation method.

phiconLarge

[in, out] Handle to the large icon.

phiconSmall

[in, out] Handle to the small icon.

nIconSize

[in] Size of the icon being requested by the shell. Icons are always square,
so only one dimension needs to be specified.

pszFile and *nIconIndex* are the same values returned by GetIconLocation. If
Extract returns S_FALSE (an OLE-defined error), then these values must contain a
valid filename/index pair. Otherwise, *phiconLarge* and *phiconSmall* should
contain valid handles to icons, such as from a call to the Win32 *LoadIcon* function
or the *ImageList_GetIcon* function in *COMCTL32.DLL*.

Creating an Icon Handler

Our icon handler is going to be very impractical, but it is going to be a great
example. We are going to create icons for several animal types, including dogs,
cats, fish, cows, and armadillos. There will also be an icon representing an
unknown animal. Our icon handler will allow us to determine which animal we
are dealing with and display the appropriate icon in the shell. The icons will be
stored in a resource file that we will include in the server. Each animal will have a
16×16 icon that will be displayed by the shell for the file object and a 32×32 icon
that is used by the Property Page for the file. We have a little bit of work to do, so
let's get started.

We aren't going to create a new project for the icon handler (although you may if
you wish). We are simply going to continue with the project we started in
Chapter 4, *Context Menu Handlers*. This brings up an interesting point. Our server
can contain as many objects as we wish. There doesn't have to be a one-to-one
relationship between the COM server and the server object (in this case a shell
extension). In fact, every shell extension we create in the book will reside in one
COM server. Each shell extension in the book will have its own class. But you
don't have to implement separate classes, either. You could have just one class

with all the appropriate interfaces implemented inside of it to support multiple shell extensions. It would be gargantuan and hard to get around in, but you could do it!

Let's begin the project by adding a new class module called clsExtractIcon. clsExtractIcon will implement three interfaces: `IPersistFile`, `IExtractIconA`, and `IExtractIconW`, as follows:

```
Option Explicit

Implements IPersistFile
Implements IExtractIconA
Implements IExtractIconW
```

Implementing IPersistFile

`IPersistFile` represents one of the few breaks we're going to get throughout the course of this book. First of all, `IPersistFile` contains five methods, but we only have to implement one of them, **Load**. Second, the implementation is the same every time we use it. Third, it's only two lines of code. It will not get this easy again! Example 5-4 contains the full listing for **Load**.

Example 5-4. Load Implementation

```
Private m_sFile As String

Private Sub IPersistFile_Load( _
    ByVal pszFileName As VBShellLib.LPCOLESTR, _
    ByVal dwMode As VBShellLib.DWORD)

    m_sFile = Space(255)
    CopyMemory ByVal StrPtr(m_sFile), _
            ByVal pszFileName, _
            Len(m_sFile)

End Sub
```

As stated earlier, *pszFileName* is a pointer. It contains an address of a filename. This is a Long value, not a String. We can't just assign *pszFileName* to *m_sFile*. That's a type mismatch. We need to copy the string from the location pointed to by *pszFileName* into our private variable, *m_sFile*. We can do that with a call to *CopyMemory* (See Appendix B, *Pointers*). *StrPtr* is used to provide the address of our target, *m_sFile*. Notice that *m_sFile* has been preallocated with 255 spaces. Pointers to any local memory that are passed to *CopyMemory* must be preallocated. You cannot pass a pointer to a string that has no size. The shell will crash.

m_sFile will be used later by `IExtractIcon::GetIconLocation` to determine the icon that needs to be displayed for the given file. That's all there is to this method.

There is one more thing we need to do to finish our `IPersistFile` implementation. Remember, every method in an interface needs to be implemented even if the methods are not used. Fortunately for us, all we need to do is add one line of code to the remaining methods of `IPersistFile`:

```
Err.Raise E_NOTIMPL
```

Should the method be called (in our situation, it will not), the client will be informed that the method has not been implemented.

 We can return OLE Automation error codes that begin with `E_` in this manner, but this will not work for codes beginning with `S_`, such as `S_FALSE`. Codes beginning with `E_` specify an error condition. Therefore, raising an error would be valid in this circumstance. Codes beginning with `S_` mean that the method was successful, but that the desired result was not achieved. To return `SCODE` values, we need to swap the function address of the desired method in the vtable with our own implementation.

Implementing IExtractIcon

`IExtractIcon` will provide the shell with the location of an icon to display for a single instance of a *.rad* file object. The icons that we use reside inside of our server in a resource file. `GetIconLocation` will provide the shell with all the information necessary to display our icons. Even so, the shell will still call `Extract`. `Extract` must return `S_FALSE` to indicate that it already has enough information to display the icon (as a result of the previous call to `GetIconLocation`). We cannot directly return the `HRESULT S_FALSE` from `Extract`, so we will swap the class implementation with our own. (See the discussion of swapping routines in "Implementing IContextMenu" in Chapter 4.)

Our icon handler will implement the following methods of `IExtractIcon`:

GetIconLocation
> The source for `GetIconLocationW` (NT Version) is shown in Example 5-5, and the source for `GetIconLocationA` (ANSI version) is shown in Example 5-6. These functions are almost identical. The differences will be noted in the listing. Basically, the string representing the pathname to the icon file must be converted from Unicode to ANSI in `GetIconLocationA`. This is similar to what we had to do with the `IContextMenu::GetCommandString` method (see Chapter 4). The string just needs to be converted from Unicode in the ANSI version. The difference between these two listings is only one line of code.

Here's how it works. The full path to the icon file (our server) will be built using the App object and our filename. This path is copied to the address pointed to by *szIconFile*, and the index of the icon is assigned to *piIndex*. The icons used for the handler will reside in a resource file in the server. The index passed back to the shell is the zero-based position of the icon in this resource file. *pwFlags* is used to tell the shell that each file of this type has its own icon (GIL_PERINSTANCE) and that it should not cache the icons (GIL_DONTCACHE).

Example 5-5. GetIconLocationW Listing

```
Private Sub IExtractIconW_GetIconLocation( _
    ByVal uFlags As VBShellLib.UINT, _
    ByVal szIconFile As VBShellLib.LPWSTRVB, _
    ByVal cchMax As VBShellLib.UINT, _
    piIndex As Long, pwFlags As VBShellLib.GETICONLOCATIONRETURN)

    Dim szName As String
    Dim szType As String
    Dim sType As String
    Dim bszName() As Byte

    szName = App.Path & "\" & App.Title & ".dll"
    szName = Left$(szName, cchMax) & vbNullChar
    bszName = szName
    CopyMemory ByVal szIconFile, ByVal StrPtr(szName), _
            UBound(bszName) + 1

    szType = Space(255)

    GetPrivateProfileString "Animal", _
                            "Type", _
                            "Unknown", _
                            szType, _
                            Len(szType), _
                            m_sFile

    sType = Trim(LCase(szType))
    sType = Left(sType, Len(sType) - 1)

    If sType = "armadillo" Then
        piIndex = 0
    ElseIf sType = "cat" Then
        piIndex = 1
    ElseIf sType = "cow" Then
        piIndex = 2
    ElseIf sType = "dog" Then
        piIndex = 3
    ElseIf sType = "fish" Then
        piIndex = 4
    Else
        piIndex = 5 'Unknown
```

Example 5-5. GetIconLocationW Listing (continued)

```
    End If

    pwFlags = pwFlags Or GIL_PERINSTANCE Or GIL_DONTCACHE

End Sub
```

Example 5-6. GetIconLocationA Listing

```
Private Sub IExtractIconA_GetIconLocation( _
    ByVal uFlags As VBShellLib.UINT, _
    ByVal szIconFile As VBShellLib.LPSTRVB, _
    ByVal cchMax As VBShellLib.UINT, _
    piIndex As Long, pwFlags As VBShellLib.GETICONLOCATIONRETURN)

    Dim szName As String
    Dim szType As String
    Dim sType As String
    Dim bszName() As Byte

    szName = App.Path & "\" & App.Title & ".dll"
    szName = Left$(szName, cchMax)
    bszName = StrConv(szName, vbFromUnicode) & vbNullChar
    CopyMemory ByVal szIconFile, bszName(0), UBound(bszName) + 1

    szType = Space(255)

    GetPrivateProfileString "Animal", _
                            "Type", _
                            "Unknown", _
                            szType, _
                            Len(szType), _
                            m_sFile

    sType = Trim(LCase(szType))
    sType = Left(sType, Len(sType) - 1)

    If sType = "armadillo" Then
        piIndex = 0
    ElseIf sType = "cat" Then
        piIndex = 1
    ElseIf sType = "cow" Then
        piIndex = 2
    ElseIf sType = "dog" Then
        piIndex = 3
    ElseIf sType = "fish" Then
        piIndex = 4
    Else
        piIndex = 5 'Unknown
    End If

    pwFlags = pwFlags Or GIL_PERINSTANCE Or GIL_DONTCACHE

End Sub
```

Extract

Extract provides the shell with a means to get an icon from an alternate location, say an image list or perhaps a call to the Win32 *LoadIcon* function. Since a location has been provided by **GetIconLocation**, this method is simply supposed to return **S_FALSE** (1). Here we run into the problem of not being able to specify an **HRESULT** to return. So, once again, a vtable entry must be swapped (see the discussion in "Implementing IContextMenu" in Chapter 4). We swap the vtable for both the ANSI and Unicode version of the interface. Since both versions of **Extract** just return **S_FALSE**, we can swap both versions of **Extract** with the same function. This is done in the icon handler's Class_Initialize event procedure, as Example 5-7 shows.

Example 5-7. The Class_Initialize Event Procedure

```
Private Sub Class_Initialize()

    Dim pVtable1 As IExtractIconA
    Set pVtable1 = Me
    m_pOldExtractA = SwapVtableEntry(ObjPtr(pVtable1), 5, _
                                AddressOf ExtractVB)

    Dim pVtable2 As IExtractIconW
    Set pVtable2 = Me
    m_pOldExtractW = SwapVtableEntry(ObjPtr(pVtable2), 5, _
                                AddressOf ExtractVB)

End Sub
```

The value 5 is passed to *SwapVtableEntry* because **Extract** is the second method defined in the interface (**IUnknown** [3] + Extract [2] = 5). This can be verified by looking directly at the IDL listing for **IExtractIcon** or using OLE View.

Class_Terminate merely swaps the function addresses back in a similar fashion (see "Implementing IContextMenu" in Chapter 4). *ExtractVB*, which is shown in Example 5-8, simply returns **S_FALSE**.

Example 5-8. ExtractVB

```
Public Function ExtractVB(ByVal this As IExtractIconA, _
    ByVal pszFile As LPCSTRVB, _
    ByVal nIconIndex As UINT, _
    phiconLarge As HICON, _
    phiconSmall As HICON, _
    ByVal nIconSize As UINT) As Long

    ExtractVB = S_FALSE

End Function
```

Notice that the `this` pointer is of type `IExtractIconA`. Since it is not being used, we can get away with using this function for both versions of the interface. If we did need to use it, however, we would have to write two separate functions.

[in, out] parameters

If you look at the listing for `IExtractIcon` (see Example 5-3), you will notice that several method parameters have been marked as `[in, out]`. The `[in]` attribute means that the parameter is being passed from the client (the shell, in the case of a shell extension) to the called method. The `[out]` attribute says that the parameter is a pointer and that the client (our server) should use this pointer to return any values. Basically, it gives us the power to use the parameter directly and not have to mess around with *CopyMemory*. The *pwFlags* and *piIndex* parameters in `GetIconLocation` (see Examples 5-5 and 5-6) are good examples of this technique. We use it just as we would a parameter passed `ByRef`. Consider the following code fragment. *piIndex* and *pwFlags* are defined as `[in, out]` parameters in the `IExtractIcon` IDL. You can think of this as being equivalent to the shell passing us an argument `ByRef`. We can use these values directly to return information back to the shell:

```
Private Sub IExtractIconW_GetIconLocation(
    ByVal uFlags As VBShellLib.UINT, _
    ByVal szIconFile As VBShellLib.LPWSTRVB, _
    ByVal cchMax As VBShellLib.UINT, _
    piIndex As Long, _
    pwFlags As VBShellLib.GETICONLOCATIONRETURN)
    .
    .
    .
    pwIndex = 5
    pwFlags = pwFlags Or GIL_PERINSTANCE Or GIL_DONTCACHE

End Sub
```

Stubs

Every method of an interface *must* be implemented. The server will not compile otherwise. In this book, all methods not implemented will be marked as such with a comment:

```
Private Sub IPersistFile_GetClassID(lpClassID As VBShellLib.CLSID)
'Not implemented
End Sub
```

VB automatically returns an `HRESULT` of `S_OK` (0) in instances such as these. In COM programming (in C++), it is common to see methods like this return `E_NOTIMPL` (&H80004001), `S_FALSE` (1), or `E_FAIL` (&H80004005)—in other words, some indicator that the method is not actually implemented. Returning `S_OK` for an empty method (like we will be doing) is somewhat misleading. Someone calling the method may wonder why it is returning successfully when nothing is happening! Returning S_OK is not entirely clear, but swapping vtable entries for every function that we do not implement is simply too much work. So, we will take the easy way out and let VB do its thing.

Registration

The icon handler is a little easier to register because there can be only one per file type (as opposed to context menu handlers). Add an **IconHandler** key under the **shellex** key and assign its default value the CLSID of the component. Remember, the CLSID for the component can be found under its ProgID, RadEx.clsIconHandler:

```
HKEY_CLASSES_ROOT
    radfile
        shellex
            IconHandler = {B3213FAC-EB84-11D2-9FD9-00550076E06F}
```

Of course, the icon handler's CLSID must also be added to the list of approved shell extensions. That key is as follows:

```
HKEY_LOCAL_MACHINE
    Software
        Microsoft
            Windows
                CurrentVersion
                    Shell Extensions
                        Approved
```

After the component is registered, the icons for the individual *.rad* files will be displayed, as Figure 5-2 illustrates. You might need to refresh the shell's display by pressing F5, but other than that, everything is ready to go.

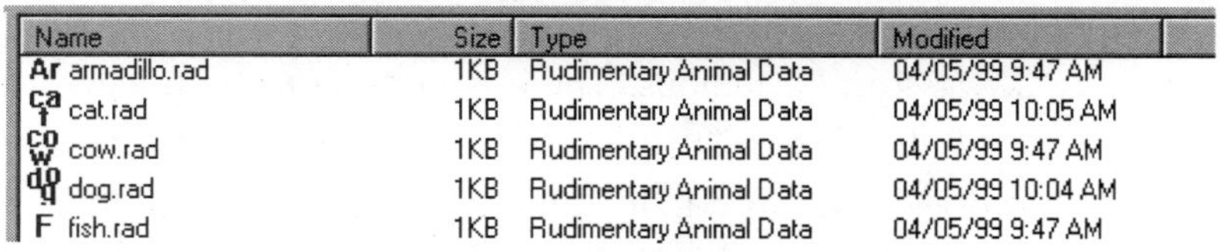

Name	Size	Type	Modified
Ar armadillo.rad	1KB	Rudimentary Animal Data	04/05/99 9:47 AM
ca cat.rad	1KB	Rudimentary Animal Data	04/05/99 10:05 AM
co cow.rad	1KB	Rudimentary Animal Data	04/05/99 9:47 AM
do dog.rad	1KB	Rudimentary Animal Data	04/05/99 10:04 AM
F fish.rad	1KB	Rudimentary Animal Data	04/05/99 9:47 AM

Figure 5-2. Each .rad file displays a different icon

The following script registers the component that is included with this chapter:

```
REGEDIT4

[HKEY_CLASSES_ROOT\.rad]
@ = "radfile"

[HKEY_CLASSES_ROOT\radfile]
```

```
[HKEY_CLASSES_ROOT\radfile]
@ = "Rudimentary Animal Data"

[HKEY_CLASSES_ROOT\radfile\shellex]

 [HKEY_CLASSES_ROOT\radfile\shellex\IconHandler]
@ = "{B3213FAC-EB84-11D2-9FD9-00550076E06F}"

 [HKEY_LOCAL_MACHINE\Software\Microsoft\Windows\CurrentVersion\Shell Extensions\
Approved]
"{61E9A1D1-5985-11D3-BB7C-444553540000}" = "RAD file icon handler"
```

Resource Files

The resource file in this book was created with Visual C++ and compiled using the resource compiler, *RC.EXE*. If you do not have a resource editor such as the one that is part of Visual C++, you can create these files by hand. *RC.EXE* does ship with Visual Basic, so compiling resource scripts should not be a problem. The resource script for the icon handler is very simple:

```
#define IDI_ARMADILLO          101
#define IDI_CAT                102
#define IDI_COW                103
#define IDI_DOG                104
#define IDI_FISH               105
#define IDI_UNKNOWN            106


IDI_ARMADILLO ICON DISCARDABLE "armadill.ico"
IDI_CAT       ICON DISCARDABLE "cat.ico"
IDI_COW       ICON DISCARDABLE "cow.ico"
IDI_DOG       ICON DISCARDABLE "dog.ico"
IDI_FISH      ICON DISCARDABLE "fish.ico"
IDI_UNKNOWN   ICON DISCARDABLE "unknown.ico"
```

Every resource is assigned a unique identifier, and this identifier is then mapped to the actual file containing the icon. Using the Visual C++ resource editor is the best option, because it will do everything for you. Writing your own resource scripts can be tedious. There is nothing to be ashamed of by using a tool to do it for you.

Visual Basic 6.0 does have an add-in called the VB Resource Editor. It will allow you to create a resource file of icons that can be used in this chapter. What it will *not* do is allow you to create dialog box templates. Dialog box templates will be necessary when we create property page extensions in the next chapter.

Your options are limited to getting a resource editor or coding the script by hand. Writing your own resource script is a little trickier where dialogs are concerned, but it is not out of the question. As you can see, the script for icons is very straightforward.

6

Property Sheet Handlers

A standard set of properties is available for every file object via the Properties context menu or by selecting File → Properties from Explorer's main menu. These properties include things like file attributes, size, location, date created, and so on. The information is made available in a tabbed dialog, as shown in Figure 6-1, providing the user with an opportunity to change a file's attributes (in the most generic implementation). Property sheet handlers permit additional pages to be added to this dialog, allowing the possibility of additional file processing.

Microsoft Word is a good example of this functionality in action, as it adds four additional property pages to the standard dialog for its *.doc* file type. These additional property pages allow users to modify *.doc* file attributes like title, author, and subject of a document without having to start Microsoft Word. Figure 6-2, for instance, shows the Summary property sheet of a Microsoft Word *.doc* file, an interface element added by Word's property sheet handler.

How Property Sheet Handlers Work

Property sheet handlers are required to implement two interfaces: `IShellExtInit` and `IShellPropSheetExt`. You are already familiar with `IShellExtInit` (see Chapter 4, *Context Menu Handlers*). `IShellPropSheetExt` contains only two methods: `AddPages`, which is called to add a page to a property dialog, and `ReplacePage`, which, as you might guess, replaces an existing property page. A property sheet handler implements `AddPages` only. `ReplacePage` is not implemented, since it applies only to Control Panel objects.

When the Properties menu item is selected for a file object, Explorer initializes the handler by calling `IShellExtInit::Initialize`. The selected file is passed to the handler via an `IDataObject` interface. Typically, the property sheet handler would save the name of the file in a private member variable for later use.

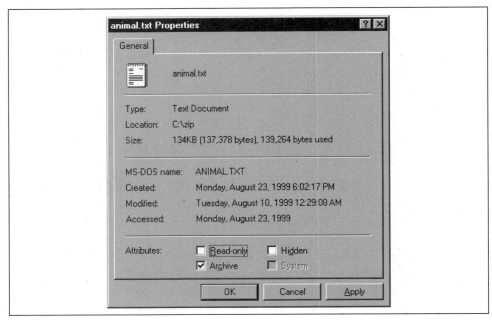

Figure 6-1. Property page dialog

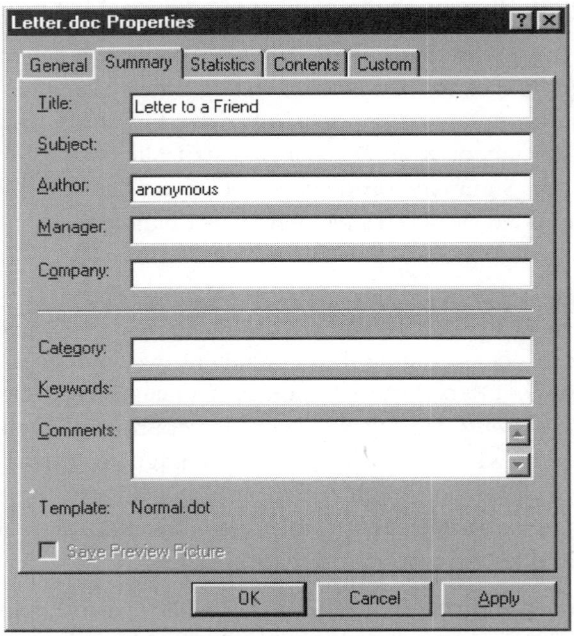

Figure 6-2. Word Summary property sheet

Then the shell calls `IShellPropSheetExt::AddPages`. The implementor of `AddPages` is required to fill out a `PROPSHEETPAGE` structure that contains information about the new property page. The structure is then passed to the *CreatePropertySheetPage* API, and a handle to the newly created property page is returned if the call was successful.

One of the parameters passed in by the shell to `AddPages` is a function address. The function specified by this address must then be called with the handle to the newly created page as its only parameter. If you are confused, don't worry. We'll go over this in detail when we implement `IShellPropSheetExt`.

Property Sheet Handler Interface

Now that you know how a property sheet handler works, let's discuss the interfaces involved in a little more detail.

IShellExtInit

The implementation of `IShellExtInit` is exactly the same as it was in Chapter 4. (For the details of the `IShellExtInit` interface, see "Context Menu Handler Interfaces" in Chapter 4.) Well, almost. The functionality provided by `IShellExtInit`—which is used to determine which files are selected in the Explorer—is generic enough to be wrapped in a class. All future extensions that must implement `IShellExtInit` in this book will use this class. The class is called clsDropFiles, and the complete class listing is shown in Example 6-1.

Example 6-1. clsDropFiles Class

```
Option Explicit

Private m_nFiles As Long
Private m_sDropFiles() As String

Public Sub GetDropFiles(pDataObj As IDataObject, _
                 ByVal sExtension As String)

    Dim FmtEtc As FORMATETC
    Dim pMedium As STGMEDIUM
    Dim i As Long
    Dim lresult As Long
    Dim sTemp As String
    Dim lIndex As Long

    With FmtEtc
        .cfFormat = CF_HDROP
        .ptd = 0
        .dwAspect = DVASPECT_CONTENT
        .lIndex = -1
```

Example 6-1. clsDropFiles Class (continued)

```
        .TYMED = TYMED_HGLOBAL
    End With

    pDataObj.GetData FmtEtc, pMedium
    m_nFiles = DragQueryFile(pMedium.pData, &HFFFFFFFF, _
                             vbNullString, 0)

    lIndex = 0
    For i = 0 To m_nFiles - 1
        sTemp = Space(255)
        lresult = DragQueryFile(pMedium.pData, i, sTemp, Len(sTemp))
        If (lresult > 0) Then
            sTemp = Left$(sTemp, lresult)
            If LCase(Right(sTemp, 4)) = sExtension Then
                ReDim Preserve m_sDropFiles(lIndex + 1)
                m_sDropFiles(lIndex) = sTemp
                lIndex = lIndex + 1
            End If
        End If
    Next i

    m_nFiles = lIndex

    ReleaseStgMedium pMedium

End Sub

Public Property Get Count() As Integer
    Count = m_nFiles
End Property

Public Property Get Files(nIndex As Integer) As String

    Files = ""

    If (m_nFiles) Then
        If (nIndex >= 0) And (nIndex < m_nFiles) Then
            Files = m_sDropFiles(nIndex)
        End If
    End If

End Property

Public Property Get SelectedFile() As String

    SelectedFile = ""

    If (m_nFiles) Then
        SelectedFile = m_sDropFiles(0)
    End If

End Property
```

Now that we have a class that handles the extraction of filenames from `IDataObject`, implementing `IShellExtInit` becomes a little easier. The complete listing for `IShellExtInit::Initialize` is shown in Example 6-2.

Example 6-2. New Initialize Implementation

```
Private m_clsDropFiles As clsDropFiles

Private Sub IShellExtInit_Initialize( _
            ByVal pidlFolder As VBShellLib.LPCITEMIDLIST, _
            ByVal pDataObj As VBShellLib.IDataObject, _
            ByVal hKeyProgID As VBShellLib.HKEY)

    Set m_clsDropFiles = New clsDropFiles
    m_clsDropFiles.GetDropFiles pDataObj, ".rad"

End Sub
```

All `IShellExtInit::Initialize` needs to do is declare an instance of clsDrop-Files and call the member function, `GetDropFiles`. `GetDropFiles` takes as parameters an `IDataObject` reference and a file filter and creates an internal array holding all of the filenames contained within the data object that have the extension *.rad.*

IShellPropSheetExt

`IShellPropSheetExt` contains two methods, `AddPages` and `ReplacePage`, for adding and replacing property sheets (see Table 6-1). There is really nothing unusual about this interface; we don't have to do anything crazy like vtable swapping! The implementation of this interface, on the other hand, is a wild ride, to say the least. But we'll talk about that later. For now, let's familiarize ourselves with the interface and the methods it contains.

Table 6-1. IShellPropSheetExt

Method	Description
AddPages	Adds a page(s) to a property sheet for a file object.
ReplacePage	Replaces a page in a property sheet for a Control Panel applet. Not used for shell property sheet extensions.

AddPages

`AddPages` is the method responsible for adding a property sheet to an existing property page dialog. When a property sheet is about to be displayed, the shell calls `AddPages` for each handler registered to the selected file type. Its syntax is as follows:

```
HRESULT STDMETHODCALLTYPE AddPages(
    LPFNADDPROPSHEETPAGE lpfnAddPage,
```

```
        LPARAM lParam
    );
```

The parameters are as follows:

lpfnAddPage

> [in] The address of a function that the property sheet extension must call to
> display a property page.

lParam

> [in] Parameter to pass to the function specified by *lpfnAddPage*.

ReplacePage

ReplacePage is used to replace property sheet pages for a Control Panel object. It
is not used for property sheet handlers. Its syntax is as follows:

```
HRESULT STDMETHODCALLTYPE ReplacePage(UINT uPageID,
        LPFNADDPROPSHEETPAGE lpfnReplacePage,
        LPARAM lParam );
```

The parameters to ReplacePage are the same as AddPages, with the exception of
one parameter:

uPageID

> This is the identifier of the page to replace. Since ReplacePage is used exclu-
> sively with Control Panel applets, the valid values for this parameter can be
> found in the *Cplext.h* header file in the Platform SDK.

Implementing IShellPropSheetExt

The IDL listing for IShellPropSheetExt is shown in Example 6-3.

Example 6-3. IShellPropSheetExt Interface Listing

```
typedef struct {
        long x;
        long y;
    } POINT;

typedef struct MSG {
    HWND    hwnd;
    UINT    message;
    WPARAM wParam;
    LPARAM lParam;
    DWORD   time;
    POINT   pt;
} MSG;

typedef struct {
    HWND hwndFrom;
    UINT idFrom;
    UINT code;
```

Example 6-3. IShellPropSheetExt Interface Listing (continued)

```
} NMHDR;

typedef enum {
    PSPCB_RELEASE = 1,
    PSPCB_CREATE  = 2
} PROPSHEETCALLBACKMSG;

typedef enum {
    PSP_DEFAULT            = 0x00000000,
    PSP_DLGINDIRECT        = 0x00000001,
    PSP_USEHICON           = 0x00000002,
    PSP_USEICONID          = 0x00000004,
    PSP_USETITLE           = 0x00000008,
    PSP_RTLREADING   = 0x00000010,
    PSP_HASHELP   = 0x00000020,
    PSP_USEREFPARENT   = 0x00000040,
    PSP_USECALLBACK   = 0x00000080,
    PSP_PREMATURE   = 0x00000400,
    PSP_HIDEHEADER         = 0x00000800,
    PSP_USEHEADERTITLE     = 0x00001000,
    PSP_USEHEADERSUBTITLE = 0x00002000
} PROPERTYSHEETFLAG;

typedef enum {
    PSN_SETACTIVE   = -200,
    PSN_KILLACTIVE = -201,
    PSN_APPLY = -202,
    PSN_RESET = -203,
    PSN_QUERYCANCEL = -209
} PROPSHEETNOTIFYMSG;

typedef struct {
    DWORD dwSize;
    DWORD dwFlags;
    HINSTANCE hInstance;
    LPCSTRVB pszTemplate;
    HICON hIcon;
    LPCSTRVB pszTitle;
    DLGPROC pfnDlgProc;
    LPARAM lParam;
    LPFNPSPCALLBACK pfnCallback;
    long pcRefParent;
    LPCTSTRVB pszHeaderTitle;
    LPCTSTRVB pszHeaderSubTitle;
} PROPSHEETPAGE;


[
    uuid(000214e9-0000-0000-c000-000000000046),
    helpstring("IShellPropSheetExt Interface"),
    odl
]
```

Example 6-3. IShellPropSheetExt Interface Listing (continued)

```
interface IShellPropSheetExt : IUnknown
{
    HRESULT AddPages([in] LPFNADDPROPSHEETPAGE lpfnAddPage,
                     [in] LPARAM lParam);

    HRESULT ReplacePage([in] UINT uPageID,
                        [in] LPFNADDPROPSHEETPAGE lpfnReplaceWith,
                        [in] LPARAM lParam);
}
```

Creating a Property Sheet Handler

In this chapter, we will create a property sheet extension that will allow us to modify every aspect of a *.rad* file: animal type, gender, color, age, weight, and noise. The property sheet we will create is shown in Figure 6-3.

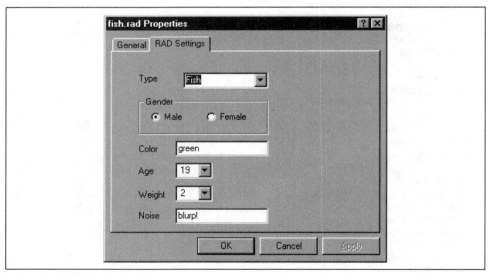

Figure 6-3. RAD property sheet

Implementing IShellExtInit

We will continue to use the RadEx project. But the first thing we need to do is to add the clsDropFiles class to the project (See Example 6-1). This class will handle the implementation of **IShellExtInit**. If you look at the class listing, you will see that it contains the code that was used previously in our implementation of **IShellExtInit** (see Chapter 4). The code is very generic. In fact, we will reuse the clsDropFiles class when we discuss drop handlers in Chapter 8, *Data Handlers*.

After clsDropFiles has been included in the project, we need to add another class to the project called clsPropSheet. This class will contain everything necessary to implement a property sheet handler. Once this has been done, we can implement `IShellExtInit` in the clsPropSheet class module as follows:

```
'clsPropSheet

Option Explicit

Implements IShellExtInit
Implements IShellPropSheetExt

Private m_clsDropFiles As clsDropFiles

Private Sub IShellExtInit_Initialize( _
        ByVal pidlFolder As VBShellLib.LPCITEMIDLIST, _
        ByVal pDataObj As VBShellLib.IDataObject, _
        ByVal hKeyProgID As VBShellLib.HKEY)

    Set m_clsDropFiles = New clsDropFiles
    m_clsDropFiles.GetDropFiles pDataObj, ".rad"

End Sub
```

Creating a Dialog Resource

Before we actually implement `IShellPropSheetExt`, we need to add a resource file to the project that contains the dialog that will be our property sheet. People who program Windows in C/C++ do this every day. To a VB programmer, this might be a new experience.

The property sheet dialog will be defined as a resource that will be stored in our COM server along with the icons that were used for the icon handler. The resource file created for this book was done with the editor in Visual C++ shown in Figure 6-4, but feel free to use any tool you wish if you plan to create your own resource file. Be warned, coding dialog resources by hand is tedious, because you have to enter in the position of all the dialog items yourself, which is a guessing game at best. If you don't have Visual C++, find another resource editor. They are out there.

For the masochists out there, Example 6-4 is the complete listing for *handler.rc*, the resource file used for this chapter. It can be compiled into an *.res* file by using a program called *RC.EXE*. This program ships with Visual Basic. You can compile from the command line (provided *RC.EXE* is in your path) as follows:

```
C:\>rc handler.rc
```

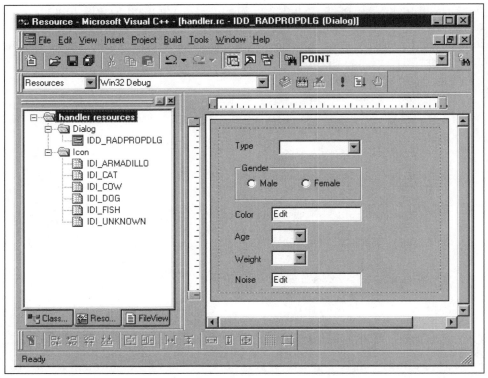

Figure 6-4. Creating a dialog template with Visual C++ resource editor

 handler.rc makes reference to the icons used for our icon hander (see Chapter 5, *Icon Handlers*). These files need to be in the directory where the resource file is being compiled.

Example 6-4. Handler.rc Listing

```
//Microsoft Developer Studio generated resource script.
//
#include "resource.h"

#define APSTUDIO_READONLY_SYMBOLS
/////////////////////////////////////////////////////////////////////////////
//
// Generated from the TEXTINCLUDE 2 resource.
//
#include "afxres.h"

/////////////////////////////////////////////////////////////////////////////
#undef APSTUDIO_READONLY_SYMBOLS
```

Example 6-4. Handler.rc Listing (continued)

```
/////////////////////////////////////////////////////////////////////////
// English (U.S.) resources

#if !defined(AFX_RESOURCE_DLL) || defined(AFX_TARG_ENU)
#ifdef _WIN32
LANGUAGE LANG_ENGLISH, SUBLANG_ENGLISH_US
#pragma code_page(1252)
#endif //_WIN32


/////////////////////////////////////////////////////////////////////////
//
// Icon
//

// Icon with lowest ID value placed first to ensure application icon
// remains consistent on all systems.
IDI_ARMADILLO           ICON    DISCARDABLE     "armadill.ico"
IDI_CAT                 ICON    DISCARDABLE     "cat.ico"
IDI_COW                 ICON    DISCARDABLE     "cow.ico"
IDI_DOG                 ICON    DISCARDABLE     "dog.ico"
IDI_FISH                ICON    DISCARDABLE     "fish.ico"
IDI_UNKNOWN             ICON    DISCARDABLE     "unknown.ico"

#ifdef APSTUDIO_INVOKED
/////////////////////////////////////////////////////////////////////////
//
// TEXTINCLUDE
//

1 TEXTINCLUDE DISCARDABLE
BEGIN
    "resource.h\0"
END

2 TEXTINCLUDE DISCARDABLE
BEGIN
    "#include ""afxres.h""\r\n"
    "\0"
END

3 TEXTINCLUDE DISCARDABLE
BEGIN
    "\r\n"
    "\0"
END

#endif    // APSTUDIO_INVOKED


/////////////////////////////////////////////////////////////////////////
//
// Dialog
```

Example 6-4. Handler.rc Listing (continued)

```
//

IDD_RADPROPDLG DIALOG DISCARDABLE  0, 0, 210, 154
STYLE WS_CHILD | WS_VISIBLE | WS_BORDER
FONT 8, "MS Sans Serif"
BEGIN
    LTEXT           "Type",IDC_STATIC,21,18,20,10
    LTEXT           "Color",IDC_STATIC,21,76,22,8
    LTEXT           "Age",IDC_STATIC,21,95,18,9
    LTEXT           "Weight",IDC_STATIC,21,114,25,8
    LTEXT           "Noise",IDC_STATIC,21,131,32,8
    COMBOBOX        IDC_TYPE,60,17,73,69,CBS_DROPDOWN | CBS_HASSTRINGS |
                    WS_TABSTOP
    GROUPBOX        "Gender",IDC_STATIC,21,37,112,32,WS_GROUP
    CONTROL         "Male",IDC_MALE,"Button",BS_AUTORADIOBUTTON,31,50,32,9
    CONTROL         "Female",IDC_FEMALE,"Button",BS_AUTORADIOBUTTON,79,50,40,
                    9
    EDITTEXT        IDC_COLOR,53,74,80,13,ES_AUTOHSCROLL
    COMBOBOX        IDC_AGE,53,92,32,55,CBS_DROPDOWN | WS_VSCROLL |
                    WS_TABSTOP
    COMBOBOX        IDC_WEIGHT,53,111,32,55,CBS_DROPDOWN | WS_VSCROLL |
                    WS_TABSTOP
    EDITTEXT        IDC_NOISE,53,129,80,13,ES_AUTOHSCROLL
END


/////////////////////////////////////////////////////////////////////////
//
// DESIGNINFO
//

#ifdef APSTUDIO_INVOKED
GUIDELINES DESIGNINFO DISCARDABLE
BEGIN
    IDD_RADPROPDLG, DIALOG
    BEGIN
        LEFTMARGIN, 7
        RIGHTMARGIN, 203
        TOPMARGIN, 7
        BOTTOMMARGIN, 147
    END
END
#endif    // APSTUDIO_INVOKED


/////////////////////////////////////////////////////////////////////////
//
// Dialog Info
//

IDD_RADPROPDLG DLGINIT
BEGIN
```

Example 6-4. Handler.rc Listing (continued)

```
    IDC_TYPE, 0x403, 10, 0
0x7241, 0x616d, 0x6964, 0x6c6c, 0x006f,
    IDC_TYPE, 0x403, 4, 0
0x6143, 0x0074,
    IDC_TYPE, 0x403, 4, 0
0x6f43, 0x0077,
    IDC_TYPE, 0x403, 4, 0
0x6f44, 0x0067,
    IDC_TYPE, 0x403, 5, 0
0x6946, 0x6873, "\000"
    0
END


#endif    // English (U.S.) resources
/////////////////////////////////////////////////////////////////////////


#ifndef APSTUDIO_INVOKED
/////////////////////////////////////////////////////////////////////////
//
// Generated from the TEXTINCLUDE 3 resource.
//


/////////////////////////////////////////////////////////////////////////
#endif    // not APSTUDIO_INVOKED
```

After you have *handler.res* in your possession (hopefully you just used the copy provided), include it in the project.

Implementing IShellPropSheetExt

IShellPropSheetExt contains two methods named **AddPages** and **ReplacePage**, as Table 6-1 shows. **ReplacePage** functions similarly to **AddPages**, but we will not write any code for this method; we'll just have the method return **E_NOTIMPL**. This is because **ReplacePage** is used to replace property sheet pages in Control Panel applications, not shell extensions. That leaves us with one method, and implementing it is no walk in the park, because we have to handle all the messages for the property sheet through a dialog procedure. This means that we have to deal with raw window messages. No events here. Tedious, to say the least. But we'll talk about this later.

AddPages

The implementation for this method is fairly involved, so let's slow way down. The first thing we need to do is populate a **PROPSHEETPAGE** structure that will describe our property sheet. Other than the specifics of this structure, **AddPages** is almost always implemented the same. This is handy to know should you want to come

up with a more generic implementation later. The `PROPSHEETPAGE` is defined as
follows in the Platform SDK:

```
typedef struct _PROPSHEETPAGE {
    DWORD dwSize;
    DWORD dwFlags;
    HINSTANCE hInstance;
    union {
        LPCSTR pszTemplate;
        LPCDLGTEMPLATE pResource;
        };
    union {
        HICON hIcon;
        LPCSTR pszIcon;
        };
    LPCSTR pszTitle;
    DLGPROC pfnDlgProc;
    LPARAM lParam;
    LPFNPSPCALLBACK pfnCallback;
    UINT FAR * pcRefParent;

#if (_WIN32_IE >= 0x0400)
    LPCTSTR pszHeaderTitle;
    LPCTSTR pszHeaderSubTitle;
#endif
} PROPSHEETPAGE, FAR *LPPROPSHEETPAGE;
```

Notice the two union blocks in the structure. As VB programmers, many of you
probably have never seen a union before. In C/C++, they are quite common. A
union is simply two or more members of a structure that occupy the same address
in memory. VB does not have the concept of a union, but there is a simple solution to this problem (in this case). We can just flatten out the structure. This means
that we keep the member of the union that we need and toss out the rest. This is
easy to do here; actually, it doesn't matter which member we keep, because both
unions contain members that are of the same datatype (as far as we are concerned)—pointers. The final IDL version of this structure (from Example 6-3) looks
like this:

```
typedef struct {
    DWORD dwSize;
    DWORD dwFlags;
    HINSTANCE hInstance;
    LPCSTRVB pszTemplate;      // from union
    HICON hIcon;               // from union
    LPCSTRVB pszTitle;
    DLGPROC pfnDlgProc;
    LPARAM lParam;
    LPFNPSPCALLBACK pfnCallback;
    long pcRefParent;
    LPCTSTRVB pszHeaderTitle;
    LPCTSTRVB pszHeaderSubTitle;
} PROPSHEETPAGE;
```

Table 6-2 provides information on the members of this structure. Before we continue, familiarize yourself with the structure (see also Table 6-3). If you are also a C/C++ programmer, you can probably tell what most of the parameters are just by looking at them. If not, don't worry. We'll discuss each member in detail during the implementation of AddPages.

Table 6-2. PROPSHEETPAGE Structure

Member	Description
dwSize	Size of this structure.
dwFlags	Option flags used when creating a property sheet page. (See Table 6-3.) These values may be Ored together.
hInstance	Instance handle from which to load the icon or title string resource.
pszTemplate	Dialog box template used to create the property sheet. This can be a resource ID or the address of a string that points to the name of the template.
hIcon	If the PSP_USEHICON flag is specified, this should contain the handle of an icon to use in the property sheet. If PSP_USEICONID is specified, then this should be the resource ID of an icon to use in the property sheet.
pszTitle	Title of the property sheet.
pfnDlgProc	Address of the dialog procedure for the property sheet.
lParam	Application-defined data that will be passed to the dialog procedure.
pfnCallback	Address of an application-defined callback function that is called when the page is created and when it is about to be destroyed.
pcRefParent	Address of the reference count value. This value is ignored if the PSP_USEPARENT flag is not specified.
pszHeaderTitle	Title of the header area.
pszHeaderSubTitle	Subtitle of the header area.

Table 6-3. dwFlags for PROPSHEETPAGE

Flag	Description
PSP_DEFAULT	The default meaning is used for all structure members.
PSP_DLGINDIRECT	Creates the page from the dialog box template in memory pointed to by *pResource*. *pResource* is actually *pszTemplate* in the VB version of PROPSHEETPAGE.
PSP_HASHELP	Enables the property sheet help button.
PSP_HIDEHEADER	Causes the header area to be hidden in a wizard property sheet.
PSP_PREMATURE	Causes the page to be created when the property sheet is created. Otherwise, the page will not be created until it is selected the first time.

Table 6-3. dwFlags for PROPSHEETPAGE (continued)

Flag	Description
PSP_RTLREADING	Causes the property sheet to display *pszTitle* using right-to-left reading order on Hebrew or Arabic systems.
PSP_USECALLBACK	Calls the function specified by *pfnCallback* when creating or destroying the property sheet page.
PSP_USEHEADERSUBTITLE	Displays the text in *pszHeaderSubTitle* as the subtitle of the header area.
PSP_USEHEADERTITLE	Displays the text in *pszHeaderTitle* as the title of the header area.
PSP_USEICONID	Uses *pszIcon* as the name of the icon resource to load and use as the small icon on the tab for the page.
PSP_USEREFPARENT	Maintains the reference count specified by *pcRefParent* for the lifetime of the property sheet page.
PSP_USETITLE	Uses *pszTitle* as the title of the property sheet dialog box instead of the title stored in the dialog box template.

Now that you are somewhat familiar with **PROPSHEETPAGE**, let's implement **AddPages**. The first thing we need to do is populate a **PROPSHEETPAGE** structure and define the behavior of our property sheet. Example 6-5 starts us off.

Example 6-5. AddPages

```
Private Sub IShellPropSheetExt_AddPages( _
            ByVal lpfnAddPage As VBShellLib.LPFNADDPROPSHEETPAGE, _
            ByVal lParam As VBShellLib.lParam)

    Dim psp As PROPSHEETPAGE
    Dim sTitle As String
    Dim lAddPage As Long

    sTitle = StrConv("RAD Settings", vbFromUnicode)

    With psp
        .dwSize = Len(psp)
        .dwFlags = PSP_USECALLBACK Or PSP_USETITLE
        .hInstance = App.hInstance
        .lParam = ObjPtr(Me)
        .pfnDlgProc = GetAddress(AddressOf PropSheetDlgProc)
        .pfnCallback = GetAddress(AddressOf PropSheetCallbackProc)
        .pszTemplate = IDD_RADPROPDLG
        .pszTitle = StrPtr(sTitle)
    End With
```

There is quite a bit more going on here than you might realize. Let's examine the *pfnDlgProc* and *pfnCallback* members of the PROPSHEETPAGE structure more closely. See the call to *GetAddress*? This is a simple function that exists just to work around the fact that *AddressOf* cannot be used in an assignment. *GetAddress* is a simple hack and looks like this:

```
'Called like this:
'lpAddr = GetAddress(AddressOf SomeFunc)

Public Function GetAddress(ByVal lpfn As Long)
    GetAddress = lpfn
End Function
```

In direct terms, *GetAddress* provides the address of a function for the right-hand side of an assignment. So, referring to Example 6-5, *pfnDlgProc* and *pfnCallback* are assigned the addresses of two functions: *PropSheetDlgProc* and *PropSheetCallbackProc*. These two functions are known as *callback* functions.

This is where things get tricky. In the world of VB, forms are created just by adding a form object to your project. Predefined events are provided for. Everything is nice and simple. All you need to do is add code for a specific event and *presto*, when you click on a command button your code is executed. If you have never programmed Windows in C, you probably don't realize how incredibly easy VB makes your life. You are about to get a glimpse of what it is like to program Windows in another language. We'll be using VB, of course, but the code will look more like something that is found in a C program. Why?

Remember, we have added a dialog template to the project that will be our property sheet. It would have been nice to use a VB form, but we just can't do that. We are restricted by the **PROPSHEETPAGE** structure, which requires us to provide a resource identifier to a dialog template. Because of this, we don't have access to the event procedures VB normally provides for us when we use forms. In order for this to work, we will have to handle event processing for the property sheet ourselves, without the benefit of VB events. This is where the two functions *PropSheetDlgProc* and *PropSheetCallbackProc* come in. (We'll discuss these two functions in detail in a moment.) All events for the dialog will be processed by these two functions. So, looking back at Example 6-5, the assignment to *pfnDlgProc* indicates that the function called *PropSheetDlgProc* will handle all the events for the dialog.

Let's get back to the **PROPSHEETPAGE** structure.

dwSize is set to the size of the structure itself. *hInstance* is set to the instance handle provided by the App object. *dwFlags* is set to PSP_USECALLBACK and PSP_USETITLE. This means the callback function specified by the *pfnCallback* member will be called twice, once when the page is created and once when it is destroyed. This also means that the string pointed to by the *pszTitle* member should be used as the title for the property sheet. Notice that the string is converted from Unicode to ANSI before the assignment.

lParam is an interesting member because it functions like the Tag property on many VB controls. It can hold any long value that we wish or none at all. We can do whatever we want with this parameter. In our case, it is assigned a pointer to

our object. This is very fortunate for us, because once the property sheet is created, the events will be handled by our two callback procedures,
PropSheetDlgProc and *PropSheetCallbackProc*. These two functions exist in a code
module outside of our class. By assigning a pointer to our object to `lParam`, we
can get a reference back to our object (should we actually need to) once the property sheet is up and running. This will become more evident when we actually
code these two functions.

`pszTemplate` is assigned to `IDD_RADPROPDLG`, a constant that equals 106. Why
106? 106 just happens to be the resource identifier for the dialog template. If you
were to open the copy of *handler.rc* provided with the book's downloadable
source in the Visual C++ IDE, you would see that the value corresponds to the
dialog. In any event, this value should represent the resource identifier of the dialog being used as the property sheet.

That's it for `PROPSHEETPAGE`. The next thing we need to do is to call `AddRef` on
our property sheet handler. We do this to counteract a call to `Release` that the
shell will call on our object. If we don't increase the reference count of our object,
it will be destroyed before we ever even see the property sheet. Presumably, the
shell does this so that the handler can be unloaded if the creation of the property
sheet fails. Regardless, the burden is on us to keep our component alive.

Remember, though, that the methods of `IUnknown` are restricted. We can't simply
call `AddRef` directly. One way around this problem is to declare a private member variable of type clsPropSheet. Then we could do something like this:

```
Private m_refObject As clsPropSheet

Private Sub IShellPropSheetExt_AddPages( _
        ByVal lpfnAddPage As VBShellLib.LPFNADDPROPSHEETPAGE, _
        ByVal lParam As VBShellLib.lParam)
    .
    .
    .

    Set m_refObject = Me
```

This will add a reference to our object. But this is not too clear. We can do things
the right way with a little workaround. What we need to do is to add our own version of `IUnknown` to the type library. This version of `IUnknown`, which we'll call
`IUnknownVB`, will be used any time we need to call `IUnknown` methods on our
objects.

This brings up an interesting point. One of the reasons we are using the older
MKTYPLIB to compile our type library is that we can have duplicate entries like
this in the type library. Since `IUnknown` is already defined in the type library with
the inclusion of *stdole2.tlb* (see Appendix A, *VBShell Library Listing*), MIDL will

complain that the interface is already defined. MKTYPLIB will not. Thus, we use MKTYPLIB. The listing for **IUnknownVB** is shown in Example 6-6.

Example 6-6. IUnknownVB Interface

```
[
    uuid(00000000-0000-0000-C000-000000000046),
    helpstring("IUnknownVB Interface"),
    odl
]
interface IUnknownVB
{
    HRESULT QueryInterface([in] REFIID priid,
                           [in, out] VOID *ppvObject);

    long AddRef();
    long Release();
};
```

Now that we have an **IUnknown** that we can use, calling **AddRef** on our object is a trivial matter. It's also a little clearer than the first method. This is shown in Example 6-7, which is the continuation of our **AddPages** implementation.

Example 6-7. AddPages, Continued

```
'AddRef
Dim pUnk As IUnknownVB
Set pUnk = Me
pUnk.AddRef
```

Okay, now we are ready to create the property sheet. We do this by calling the Win32 function *CreatePropertySheetPage*, which is found in *comctl32.dll*. The function is declared as follows:

```
Public Declare Function CreatePropertySheetPage _
    Lib "comctl32.dll" Alias "CreatePropertySheetPageA" _
    (p As PROPSHEETPAGE) As Long
```

The *CreatePropertySheetPage* function takes the **PROPSHEETPAGE** structure we have just finished populating as its only parameter. Upon successful completion of the call, we are returned a handle to the newly created property sheet, as Example 6-8 demonstrates.

We now have a handle to our newly created property sheet, if all has gone well.

Now things get strange. Look at the first parameter to **AddPages**, *lpfnAddPage*. This is a *pointer* to a function that we are supposed to call with *hPage*. There is no way to call a function through a pointer in VB. This function, which is pointed to by *lpfnAddPage,* actually displays the property sheet.

Moving API Declarations to a Type Library

Although it is not done in this book, it is possible to declare API functions in a type library. Consider *GetWindowText* and *SetWindowText*. Both of these functions are defined in *user32.dll*. Their IDL definitions might look like this:

```
[
    dllname("user32.dll")
]
module User32
{
    [entry("GetWindowTextA")]
    int _stdcall GetWindowText(
        [in] long hwnd,
        [in,out] LPSTR lpsz,
        [in] int cbMax
    );

    [entry("SetWindowTextA")]
        void _stdcall SetWindowText(
        [in] long hwnd,
        [in, out] LPSTR lpsz
    );

}
```

The listing is fairly self explanatory. The [**dllname**] attribute defines the location of the exported functions listed in the module block. This is nice, because you only have to define this location once, unlike using **Declare** statements in a module.

The [**entry**] attribute is analogous to the **Alias** keyword in Visual Basic. If you happen to have the ordinal of the exported function, you can use that in place of the string value.

The functions are defined exactly as they have been listed in the Platform SDK. Be careful if you are reverse-engineering definitions from your module files. Remember, an **int** here is 4 bytes, unlike VB, in which it is 2 bytes (for backward compatibility). Also, notice how Strings are declared as **LPSTR**. That's a pointer, hence the [**out**] attribute.

Using this paradigm, you could also define module blocks for the GDI and Kernel functions as well. It was not done in this book because we wanted to keep the type library as simple as possible and to leave the focus on the interfaces being defined.

Although there is no way to call a function through a pointer in VB, it can be done in C++, and that is what we will do.

Example 6-8. AddPages, Continued

```
Dim hPage As Long
hPage = CreatePropertySheetPage(psp)

If hPage Then
    lAddPage = AddPropertyPage(lpfnAddPage, hPage, lParam)

    If lAddPage = 0 Then
        DestroyPropertySheetPage hPage
    End If
End If
```

```
End Sub
```

There is a DLL included with the source in this chapter called *propext.dll*. You need to be move this to your system directory in order for the property sheet handler to function properly. This DLL contains one exported function, *AddPropertyPage* (shown in Example 6-9), that will allow us to call the function given to us by the shell. The code for *AddPropertyPage* is shown in Example 6-6.

Example 6-9. AddPropertyPage (in C++)

```
BOOL WINAPI AddPropertyPage(LPFNADDPROPSHEETPAGE lpfnAddPage,
                            HPROPSHEETPAGE hPage,
                            LPARAM lParam)
{
    // In C++ you can call a function through
    // an address.
    return(lpfnAddPage(hPage, lParam));
}
```

If a nonzero result is returned, *DestroyPropertySheetPage* is called to free memory associated with the property sheet.

PropSheetCallbackProc

This function is called once when the property sheet is being created and once right before it is to be destroyed. It is not called by us, but by Explorer. It is defined as follows:

```
UINT CALLBACK PropSheetPageProc(HWND hwnd,
                                UINT uMsg,
                                LPPROPSHEETPAGE ppsp );
```

with the following parameters:

hwnd

This parameter is reserved. It should be NULL.

uMsg
> This is the action flag. It will be equal to one of two values: PSPCB_CREATE (2) upon creation of the property sheet or PSPCB_RELEASE (1) when the property sheet is being destroyed.

ppsp
> This is a pointer to the PROPSHEETPAGE structure used to create the property sheet.

The implementation of this function is fairly simple. We do not need to process any messages in this function. It will be used only to get a reference to the property sheet object over to the module file. What does this mean exactly? Well, once the property sheet is up and running, we will not have access to the property sheet handler object anymore. This is because the two callback functions that handle all of the property sheet messages are located in a code module outside of the class.

Remember the *lParam* member of our PROPSHEETPAGE structure (see Example 6-5)? It's a pointer to our object. The *ppsp* parameter of *PropSheetPageProc* is a pointer to our original PROPSHEETPAGE structure. Therefore, we have access back to our object through this parameter. This is good because it keeps us from having to resort to a global variable. It also provides a good opportunity to show you how to copy an object without incrementing its reference count. These are good tricks to know if you find yourself doing any advanced COM programming in the future. Example 6-10 details *PropSheetCallbackProc*, which is located in a code module called *PropSheet.bas*. All of the items specific to our property sheet implementation will be located in this file.

Example 6-10. The PropSheetCallbackProc Function

```
'Property Sheet object reference
Private m_pPropSheet As clsPropSheet

Public Function PropSheetCallbackProc(ByVal hwnd As hwnd, _
                            uMsg As MSG, _
                            ByVal ppsp As Long) As Long

    Dim psp As PROPSHEETPAGE
    CopyMemory psp, ByVal ppsp, Len(psp)

    'Get reference to object. No AddRef!!!!!
    CopyMemory m_pPropSheet, psp.lParam, 4


    Select Case uMsg

        Case PSPCB_CREATE
            'Return non-zero to create page. 0 prevents it.
```

Example 6-10. The PropSheetCallbackProc Function (continued)

```
    Case PSPCB_RELEASE:
        'Page is being destroyed. Return value is ignored.

End Select


    PropSheetCallbackProc = 1

End Function
```

We are given a pointer to a PROPSHEETPAGE structure, *ppsp*, as a parameter to the callback. This pointer is copied to a local instance of PROPSHEETPAGE using *CopyMemory*. This technique should be very familiar to you now. Once we have a local copy of PROPSHEETPAGE, we can get access to the lParam member of the structure. The lParam member of *ppsp* contains a pointer to our property sheet extension. This pointer can be used to create a *copy* of our object. There will be no call to AddRef. We have a copy of the object, and its reference count is one. This is a very important distinction. Because we have a copy of the object itself, we cannot set the object equal to Nothing when we are done with it. I will talk about how to free this copy when I discuss *PropSheetDlgProc*, the second callback function, later in the chapter.

The rest of this function is very straightforward. There are only two messages this callback will receive: PSPCB_CREATE and PSPCB_RELEASE. This callback is called only twice, once for each message. These messages are not important to us, since VB provides us with Initialize and Terminate events to handle startup and shutdown operations. In addition to those two events, we also have access to the Window procedure for the dialog box itself, which means we can process WM_INITDIALOG and WM_DESTROY messages ourselves.

PropSheetDlgProc

This function is responsible for processing all of the events for the property sheet. It is known as a DLGPROC, and its syntax is as follows:

```
    BOOL CALLBACK DialogProc(HWND hwndDlg,
                             UINT uMsg,
                             WPARAM wParam,
                             LPARAM lParam);
```

DialogProc is just a generic name for a dialog procedure. When you create your own dialog procedures, you can name them whatever you want (i.e., *PropSheetDlgProc*).

The parameters to the *DialogProc* function are:

hwndDlg
>   Handle of the property sheet.

uMsg
>   The message being received by the property sheet.

wParam
>   Additional message-specific information.

lParam
>   Additional message-specific information.

The real action for the property sheet extension happens in *PropSheetDlgProc*, which is the message handler for the entire dialog box. This function is more complex than *PropSheetCallbackProc* only in that we are dealing with a few more Windows messages. We are not dealing with events here, but rather with raw Windows messages. These messages are passed in to us and processed by a `Select` statement, as Example 6-11 illustrates. Windows programs written in C process messages in this exact way. They are notorious for having gigantic `switch` (the C version of `Select Case`) statements—sometimes hundreds of lines long. Fortunately for us, there are only three messages we are interested in: `WM_INITDIALOG` (sent when the property page is created), `WM_NOTIFY` (sent for all control events), and `WM_DESTROY` (sent when the property sheet is destroyed). This makes our life somewhat easier.

Example 6-11. Dialog Procedure for Property Sheet

```
Public Function PropSheetDlgProc(ByVal hwndDlg As hwnd, _
    ByVal uMsg As UINT, _
    ByVal wParam As wParam, _
    ByVal lParam As lParam) As BOOL

    Select Case uMsg

        Case WM_INITDIALOG
            InitDialog hwndDlg

        Case WM_NOTIFY
            Notify hwndDlg, lParam

        Case WM_DESTROY
            'DO NOT DO THIS: Set m_pPropSheet = Nothing.
            CopyMemory m_pPropSheet, 0&, 4

    End Select

    PropSheetDlgProc = 0

End Function
```

Let's discuss the messages we are processing. Notice how these messages correspond to VB events. This is no coincidence. Under the hood, VB traps these same messages and provides events for you. It probably works something like this (ignoring the fact that VB is not actually coded in VB):

```
Select Case uMsg

        Case WM_INITDIALOG
            Call Form_Load
    .
    .
    .
```

WM_INITDIALOG

The first message we will process is **WM_INITDIALOG**, which is analogous to the Form_Load event. We use this opportunity to populate drop-down lists with their appropriate values, read Animal data, and configure the dialog so that it displays the information found in the currently selected *.rad* file. As you can see, the handler for the message has been farmed out to a helper function called *InitDialog*. By creating helper functions to handle the messages, the dialog procedure remains less cluttered and is easier to work with (should we want to handle additional messages).

Let's take a peek at *InitDialog*, which is shown in Example 6-12. It's pretty tedious and repetitive, but it should make you more than a little grateful that you don't have to code your dialogs like this every day (unlike you C/C++ programmers out there). Take note of the *SendDlgItemMessage* and *SetWindowText* calls. These two API functions are the workhorses of *InitDialog*.

SendDlgItemMessage is how we send messages to "windows" (as opposed to Windows sending messages to us). Functions like *SendDlgItemMessage* and *SendMessage* are how the various "properties" of controls and windows get set. Even though many of these controls are COM objects themselves, under the covers, the work gets done by a call to *SendMessage* somewhere. This function is responsible for things like adding items to list boxes or combo boxes, removing items from list boxes or combo boxes, and setting and clearing checkboxes and radio buttons. The list goes on and on. There are literally hundreds of messages that various controls can receive. It is definitely the Swiss Army knife of the API world. For our property sheet, *SendDlgItemMessage* will be used to populate the Animal, age, and weight drop-downs.

SetWindowText does just what it says. Whenever you set the caption of a form, a label, button, or text box, you can bet that a call to this function is being made somewhere. *SetWindowText* will be used to populate all of the textboxes on our property sheet.

Because the *.rad* file mimics the format of an *.ini* file, retrieving data from the file is as simple as using a call to *GetPrivateProfileString*.

Example 6-12. WM_INITDIALOG Handler

```
Public Sub InitDialog(ByVal hwndDlg As hwnd)

    Dim c As Byte
    Dim sz As String
    Dim hwnd As hwnd

    'Populate Animal type dropdown
    sz = StrConv("Armadillo", vbFromUnicode)
    SendDlgItemMessage hwndDlg, IDC_TYPE, CB_ADDSTRING, 0, StrPtr(sz)
    sz = StrConv("Cat", vbFromUnicode)
    SendDlgItemMessage hwndDlg, IDC_TYPE, CB_ADDSTRING, 0, StrPtr(sz)
    sz = StrConv("Cow", vbFromUnicode)
    SendDlgItemMessage hwndDlg, IDC_TYPE, CB_ADDSTRING, 0, StrPtr(sz)
    sz = StrConv("Dog", vbFromUnicode)
    SendDlgItemMessage hwndDlg, IDC_TYPE, CB_ADDSTRING, 0, StrPtr(sz)
    sz = StrConv("Fish", vbFromUnicode)
    SendDlgItemMessage hwndDlg, IDC_TYPE, CB_ADDSTRING, 0, StrPtr(sz)
    sz = StrConv("Unknown", vbFromUnicode)
    SendDlgItemMessage hwndDlg, IDC_TYPE, CB_ADDSTRING, 0, StrPtr(sz)

    'Populate Age dropdown
    For c = 1 To 20
        sz = StrConv(str(c), vbFromUnicode)
        SendDlgItemMessage hwndDlg, IDC_AGE, CB_ADDSTRING, 0, StrPtr(sz)
    Next c

    'Populate Weight dropdown
    For c = 1 To 200
        sz = StrConv(Str(c), vbFromUnicode)
        SendDlgItemMessage hwndDlg, IDC_WEIGHT, CB_ADDSTRING, _
            0, StrPtr(sz)
    Next c

    'Set Animal type
    sz = Space(255)
    GetPrivateProfileString "Animal", "Type", "Unknown", sz, _
        Len(sz), m_pPropSheet.SelectedFile
    sz = TrimNull(sz) 'chop off NULL and convert to ANSI

    hwnd = GetDlgItem(hwndDlg, IDC_TYPE)
    SetWindowText hwnd, sz

    'Set Animal Age
    sz = Space(255)
    GetPrivateProfileString "Animal", "Age", "1", sz, _
        Len(sz), m_pPropSheet.SelectedFile

    'Set combo = animal age
    SendDlgItemMessage hwndDlg, IDC_AGE, CB_SETCURSEL, _
```

Example 6-12. WM_INITDIALOG Handler (continued)

```
        Int(sz) - 1, 0

    'Set Animal Weight
    sz = Space(255)
    GetPrivateProfileString "Animal", "Weight", "1", sz, _
        Len(sz), m_pPropSheet.SelectedFile

    'Set combo = animal weight
    SendDlgItemMessage hwndDlg, IDC_WEIGHT, CB_SETCURSEL, _
        Int(sz) - 1, 0

    'Set Animal gender
    sz = Space(255)
    GetPrivateProfileString "Animal", "Gender", "M", sz, _
        Len(sz), m_pPropSheet.SelectedFile
    If UCase(Left(sz, 1)) = "M" Then
        SendDlgItemMessage hwndDlg, IDC_MALE, BM_SETCHECK, 1, 0
    Else
        SendDlgItemMessage hwndDlg, IDC_FEMALE, BM_SETCHECK, 1, 0
    End If

    'Get Animal color
    sz = Space(255)
    GetPrivateProfileString "Animal", "color", "unknown", sz, _
        Len(sz), m_pPropSheet.SelectedFile
    sz = LCase(TrimNull(sz))

    hwnd = GetDlgItem(hwndDlg, IDC_COLOR)
    SetWindowText hwnd, sz

    'Set Animal noise
    sz = Space(255)
    GetPrivateProfileString "Animal", "Noise", "unknown", sz, _
        Len(sz), m_pPropSheet.SelectedFile
    sz = LCase(TrimNull(sz))

    hwnd = GetDlgItem(hwndDlg, IDC_NOISE)
    SetWindowText hwnd, sz

End Sub
```

WM_NOTIFY

Notification messages are sent by controls to the parent window for a variety of reasons. When the property sheet is selected, a notification is sent. When it is deselected, a notification is sent. Notifications are also sent when OK, Cancel, and Apply are pressed. And finally, a notification is sent right before the property sheet is about to be destroyed. Basically, a WM_NOTIFY message is sent whenever the control needs to notify its parent (our property sheet) of an event.

When a `WM_NOTIFY` message is sent, *lParam* contains a pointer to an `NMHDR` structure. *CopyMemory* can then be used to copy this address into a local instance of
`NMHDR`. The structure is defined as follows:

```
typedef struct {
    HWND hwndFrom;
    UINT idFrom;
    UINT code;
} NMHDR;
```

with the following members:

hwndFrom

The Windows handle of the control sending the message.

idFrom

The ID of the control.

code

The message being sent.

We will ignore every member except for *code* in our `WM_NOTIFY` event handler,
which is shown in Example 6-13.

Example 6-13. WM_NOTIFY Handler

```
Public Sub Notify(ByVal hwndDlg As hwnd, ByVal lParam As lParam)

    Dim nh As NMHDR

    CopyMemory nh, ByVal lParam, Len(nh)

    Select Case nh.code
        Case PSN_APPLY
            'OK and Apply
            SaveProperties hwndDlg

        Case PSN_QUERYCANCEL
            'Cancel has been clicked. Return 1 to prevent. 0 to allow.

        Case PSN_SETACTIVE
            'sent when property tab is selected for first time

        Case PSN_KILLACTIVE
            'sent when another property tab is selected

        Case PSN_RESET
            'Cancel has been allowed. About to be destroyed

    End Select

End Sub
```

The various messages that will be processed are listed with comments about their meaning, but the only message we are interested in is **PSN_APPLY**. This message is sent when OK or Apply has been pressed. We are not implementing Apply, so this distinction is not important. When OK is pressed, *SaveProperties* is called, and all the information from the dialog is written back into the *.rad* file.

SaveProperties, which is shown in Example 6-14, is very similar to *InitDialog*. In fact, it is almost its inverse. Where we used *SetWindowText* before, now we use *GetWindowText*. *WritePrivateProfileString* (alias *WPPString*) handles writing the information back to the *.rad* file.

Example 6-14. SaveProperties

```
Public Sub SaveProperties(ByVal hwndDlg As hwnd)

    Dim lret As Long
    Dim sz As String
    Dim hwnd As hwnd

    'Save animal type
    sz = Space(255)
    hwnd = GetDlgItem(hwndDlg, IDC_TYPE)
    GetWindowText hwnd, sz, Len(sz)
    sz = Trim(sz)
    'WritePrivateProfileString
    WPPString "Animal", "Type", sz, m_pPropSheet.SelectedFile

    'Save gender
    lret = SendDlgItemMessage(hwndDlg, IDC_MALE, BM_GETCHECK, 0, 0)
    If lret Then
        WPPString "Animal", "Gender", "M", m_pPropSheet.SelectedFile
    Else
        WPPString "Animal", "Gender", "F", m_pPropSheet.SelectedFile
    End If

    'Save color
    sz = Space(255)
    hwnd = GetDlgItem(hwndDlg, IDC_COLOR)
    GetWindowText hwnd, sz, Len(sz)
    sz = Trim(sz)
    WPPString "Animal", "Color", sz, m_pPropSheet.SelectedFile

    'Save age
    lret = SendDlgItemMessage(hwndDlg, IDC_AGE, CB_GETCURSEL, 0, 0)
    sz = str(lret + 1)
    WPPString "Animal", "Age", sz, m_pPropSheet.SelectedFile

    'Save weight
    lret = SendDlgItemMessage(hwndDlg, IDC_WEIGHT, CB_GETCURSEL, 0, 0)
    sz = str(lret + 1)
    WPPString "Animal", "Weight", sz, m_pPropSheet.SelectedFile
```

Example 6-14. SaveProperties (continued)

```
'Save noise
sz = Space(255)
hwnd = GetDlgItem(hwndDlg, IDC_NOISE)
GetWindowText hwnd, sz, Len(sz)
sz = Trim(sz)
WPPString "Animal", "Noise", sz, m_pPropSheet.SelectedFile

End Sub
```

WM_DESTROY

The last message we are interested in is **WM_DESTROY**, which provides us with an opportunity to free the reference to our object. But remember, we are dealing with a copy of the object (see Example 6-7). It has a reference count of 1. Explorer has a valid reference to the property sheet extension. When Explorer is shut down, it will try to call **IUnknown::Release** to free the reference it is holding. If we set *m_pPropSheet* equal to **Nothing**, it will be released from memory, and the reference held by Explorer will no longer be valid. This translates into a crash the next time Explorer is closed. Instead of setting *m_pPropSheet* equal to **Nothing**, 0 will be copied to its address to mark the memory as free. This is demonstrated in Example 6-8.

Registering the Property Sheet Handler

Property sheet extensions are registered in the same manner as context menus. The shell allows multiple property sheets to be defined for any given file class. These property sheets can exist in one server or across multiple servers. It's up to you. The default property sheet is determined by setting the default value for the **PropertySheetHandlers** key, as shown in Figure 6-5. Additional property sheets do not need to be defined in this manner. They can just be added under **PropertySheetHandlers**.

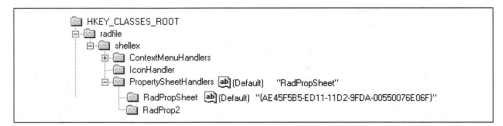

Figure 6-5. Property sheet handlers in the registry

After you add the property sheet to the approved extension section of the registry, the property sheet can be accessed by right-clicking on a *.rad* file. When the property sheet appears, it should contain a RAD Settings dialog like the one shown in Figure 6-6.

Don't forget to copy *propext.dll* to your system directory!

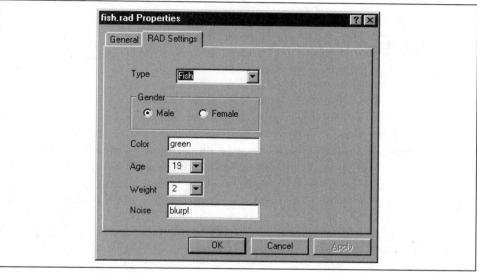

Figure 6-6. RAD property sheet allows every property of the file to be modified

With the property sheet extension in place, you can now change every attribute of the file. When you change the animal type, notice how our icon handler updates the shell to display the new icon for the animal. The shell extensions work together well.

7

Drop Handlers

Drop handlers allow file objects to become drop targets—that is, to define a custom behavior when one or more files are dropped on them. When a file is dropped on another file, the handler is provided with the names of both the target and source file(s). The files can then be processed in any manner appropriate to the situation. Consider the popular WinZip archive program. When a file is dropped onto an existing .*zip* file, it is added to the archive. This behavior is accomplished with the help of a drop handler.

Drop handlers are easy to implement. They implement two interfaces (`IDropTarget` and `IPersistFile`), one of which is already familiar to us.

The drop handler we will implement in this chapter offers no practical functionality other than to show you how one works. It will allow you to drop one or more files onto a .*rad* file object. The drop handler will report the names of the source file(s), the target file, and keyboard/mouse states.

How Drop Handlers Work

When one file (the source file) is dragged over another file (the target file), the shell checks under the target file's application identifier key to see if a drop handler has been registered for that particular file class. This key is in the following location (assuming we are talking about .*rad* files):

```
HKEY_CLASSES_ROOT\
    radfile\
        shellex\
            DropHandler = {CLSID}
```

As you can see from the registry setting, there can be only one drop handler registered for a file class.

If a drop handler for the target file exists, the shell will load it and pass it the name of the target file through `IPersistFile::Load`. Once this occurs, the shell will start calling methods on the `IDropTarget` portion of the handler object.

The drop handler will be notified via `IDropTarget` several times during the drag-and-drop operation: once when the files enter the target area (`IDropTarget::DragEnter`), once when the files exit the target area (`IDropTarget::DragLeave`), and every time the mouse is moved within the target area (`IDropTarget::DragOver`). There is also a notification when the files are dropped (`IDropTarget::Drop`).

As the drop operations occur, the handler is given the opportunity to notify the shell of the drop operation status. This allows the shell to visually notify the user of what is happening by changing the cursor. For instance, if our drop handler only accepts *.txt* files and we drag a *.zip* file over the target, the drop handler can tell the shell that the operation will not work. The shell can then display the No Drop cursor (see Figure 7-1) to inform the user that files of type *.zip* are not acceptable for this particular drop target.

When a successful drop operation occurs, the shell will pass the name of the source files via an `IDataObject` interface to the drop handler. As you saw in Chapter 5, *Icon Handlers*, it's a simple matter to extract the names of the files from the data object and process the files in a manner befitting the situation.

Drop Handler Interfaces

Now that you know how a drop handler works, let's discuss the interfaces involved in a little more detail.

IDropTarget

As Table 7-1 shows, `IDropTarget` contains four methods: `DragEnter`, `DragOver`, `DragLeave`, and `Drop`.

Table 7-1. IDropTarget

Method	Description
DragEnter	Determines whether a drop is valid.
DragOver	Provides drop information as object is dragged over the target.
DragLeave	Called when object leaves drop target.
Drop	Called when object is dropped on the target.

DragEnter

`DragEnter` is used to determine whether a drop is acceptable. For instance, if the file being dropped is not of a particular type, the operation could be cancelled (we will not do this here). This method also provides us with some minimal keyboard state information, such as whether the Alt, Shift, or Ctrl keys were pressed during the drop. Left- and right-mouse button states are also provided.

The syntax of the `DragEnter` method is as follows:

```
HRESULT DragEnter(IDataObject *pDataObj,
                  DWORD grfKeyState,
                  POINTL pt,
                  DWORD *pdwEffect);
```

The method's parameters are:

pDataObj

> [in] A pointer to an `IDataObject` interface on a data object. This object contains the data being transferred via the drag-and-drop operation.

grfKeyState

> [in] The current state of the keyboard. It can contain one or more of the following values:

Constant	Description
MK_LBUTTON	Left mouse button is pressed.
MK_RBUTTON	Right mouse button is pressed.
MK_SHIFT	Shift key is pressed.
MK_CONTROL	Ctrl key is pressed.
MK_MBUTTON	Middle mouse button is pressed.
MK_ALT	Alt key is pressed.

You should never compare *grfKeyState* for equality with one of these KEYSTATES values, as in the following code fragment:

```
'Do not check for equality
If grfKeyState = MK_CONTROL Then
 .
 .
 .
```

Always mask for the desired values using the **And** operator, as follows:

```
'This is the proper way to determine mouse/key state
If grfKeyState And MK_CONTROL Then
 .
 .
 .
```

pt

> [in] The current cursor coordinates. This a POINTL structure that is defined as follows (it's really the same as the POINTAPI structure):

```
typedef struct _POINTL {
    long x;
    long y;
} POINTL;
```

pdwEffect

> [in, out] Upon return, this parameter should contain one or more of the following values from the DROPEFFECT enumeration:

```
typedef enum tagDROPEFFECT {
    DROPEFFECT_NONE = 0,
    DROPEFFECT_COPY = 1,
    DROPEFFECT_MOVE = 2,
    DROPEFFECT_LINK = 4,
    DROPEFFECT_SCROLL = 0x80000000
}DROPEFFECT;
```

> These values have the following meaning:

Constant	Description
DROPEFFECT_NONE	Drop target cannot accept the data.
DROPEFFECT_COPY	Drop results in a copy. Original data is unmodified.
DROPEFFECT_MOVE	Drag source should remove the data.
DROPEFFECT_LINK	Drag source should create a link to the original data.
DROPEFFECT_ SCROLL	Scrolling is about to start or is currently occurring at the target. This value is used in addition to the other values.

> As with the *grfKeyState* parameter, these values should never be checked for equality. Mask the values using the And operator.

DragOver

DragOver is implemented in a similar manner to DragEnter. It is called whenever a drag occurs over a respective target, not just upon entry. We will not implement this method, since DragEnter provides all the functionality that we will need. The syntax of DragOver is:

```
HRESULT DragOver(
    DWORD grfKeyState,
    POINTL pt,
    DWORD * pdwEffect
);
```

The parameters to this method are the same as those for DragEnter.

DragLeave

DragLeave provides a means to free any references to **IDataObject** that were possibly held as a result of a **DragEnter** or **DragOver** call. We do not store any references to **IDataObject**; therefore, this method is not necessary for our drop handler to function properly. Its syntax is:

```
HRESULT DragLeave(void);
```

Drop

This method is where the actual drop takes place. Its syntax is as follows:

```
HRESULT Drop(
   IDataObject * pDataObject,
   DWORD grfKeyState,
   POINTL pt,
   DWORD * pdwEffect
);
```

The parameters for this method are exactly the same as **DragEnter**.

IPersistFile

IPersistFile is used to get the target file of the drop. It is implemented exactly as it was in our icon handler. **Load** is the only method that is implemented. The name of the target file is stored in a private data member, which allows it to be accessed from **Drop**. See Chapter 5 for an explanation of this interface.

Creating a Drop Handler

We need to add a new class to the RadEx project that will implement **IPersistFile** and **IDropTarget**. Call the file *clsDropHandler.cls*. Its declarations section begins as follows:

```
'clsDropHandler.cls

Implements IDropTarget
Implements IPersistFile
```

Implementing IPersistFile

The only method that we need to implement on this interface is **Load**. The code is the same as the code we used to create the icon handler back in Chapter 5. Example 7-1 contains the implementation.

Example 7-1. IPersistFile::Load Implementation

```
'clsDropHandler.cls

Private m_sTargetFile As String

Private Sub IPersistFile_Load(
    ByVal pszFileName As VBShellLib.LPCOLESTR, _
    ByVal dwMode As VBShellLib.DWORD)

    m_sTargetFile = Space(255)
    CopyMemory ByVal StrPtr(m_sTargetFile), _
            ByVal pszFileName, _
            Len(m_sTargetFile)

End Sub
```

Implementing IDropTarget

The most interesting aspect of implementing the `IDropTarget` interface (and, in particular, its `DragEnter` method) concerns the `POINTL` parameter to the `DragEnter` method. Notice from our earlier presentation of the method's syntax that it is an `[in]` parameter; therefore, it is not a pointer. We have a slight problem here, because Visual Basic does not allow UDTs to be passed `ByVal`, which is what is going on here. `POINTL` is a structure that contains the location of the mouse in the drop area. It is defined like this:

```
typedef struct _POINTL {
    LONG x;
    LONG y;
} POINTL;
```

Fortunately, we do not need this point information, so there is a simple workaround. Instead of passing a point, we can use two Longs, which will occupy the same space on the stack as a `POINTL` structure. The final definition for `DragEnter` looks like this:

```
HRESULT DragEnter
(
    [in] IDataObject *pDataObj,
    [in] KEYSTATES grfKeyState,
    [in] long x,
    [in] long y,
    [in, out] DROPEFFECT *pdwEffect
);
```

DragOver and Drop will also use two Long values in place of POINTL.

DragEnter

With that said, let's get on to the actual implementation of **IDropTarget**. We only
need to implement two methods (**DragEnter** and **Drop**) to satisfy our needs. Let's
look at the **DragEnter** implementation, which is shown in Example 7-2, and then
we'll discuss how it works.

Example 7-2. DragEnter Implementation

```
Private m_dwDropKey As KEYSTATES
Private m_dwMouseKey As KEYSTATES

Private Sub IDropTarget_DragEnter( _
    ByVal pDataObj As VBShellLib.IDataObject, _
    ByVal grfKeyState As VBShellLib.KEYSTATES, _
    ByVal x As Long, _
    ByVal y As Long, _
    pdwEffect As VBShellLib.DROPEFFECT)


    pdwEffect = DROPEFFECT_COPY

    'Get keyboard state

    'Does NOT take into account multiple keys being held down

    If grfKeyState And MK_CONTROL Then
        m_dwDropKey = MK_CONTROL
    ElseIf grfKeyState And MK_SHIFT Then
        m_dwDropKey = MK_SHIFT
    ElseIf grfKeyState And MK_ALT Then
        m_dwDropKey = MK_ALT
    Else
        m_dwDropKey = 0
    End If

    'Get mouse state
    If grfKeyState And MK_LBUTTON Then
        m_dwMouseKey = MK_LBUTTON
    ElseIf grfKeyState And MK_RBUTTON Then
        m_dwMouseKey = MK_RBUTTON
    End If

End Sub
```

The first parameter given to us by the shell is an **IDataObject** reference. Remember clsDropFiles? This is the class we used in Chapter 6, *Property Sheet Handlers*,
to implement **IShellExtInit::Initialize**. We could pass this **IDataObject**
reference to an instance of clsDropFiles to get a list of all the source filenames for
our **Drop** implementation. But we won't, because in this instance it would be a little slow. It would be called every time we enter the drop target, which is way too

often. Instead, we'll wait until `Drop` is actually called to get a list of the source file-names. So, for now, we can ignore the *pDataObj* parameter. The parameters we are really interested in are *pdwEffect* and *grfKeyState*.

The *pdwEffect* parameter is set to one of the DROPEFFECT enumeration values and is used to visually indicate what the result of a drop operation would be. The shell conveys this by changing the cursor to one of the shapes shown in Figure 7-1. As the cursor moves over a drop target, the shell changes the cursor to visually show what type of drop operation is occurring. To cancel a drop operation, *pdwEffect* is set to DROPEFFECT_NONE.

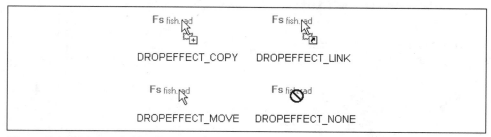

Figure 7-1. DROPEFFECT operations

The *grfKeyState* parameter contains keyboard- and mouse-state information.

Our implementation sets *pdwEffect* to DROPEFFECT_COPY regardless of the keys pressed. This will cause the cursor to change (as shown in Figure 7-1), giving us a visual cue that the files can be dropped. Keyboard and mouse states are stored in two separate private data members. These values will be used when we implement `Drop`.

Drop

`Drop` is where all the action takes place. This is the method that is called when a file is dropped on a drop target. Our implementation, which is shown in Example 7-3, is fairly straightforward. Let's take a look.

Example 7-3. Drop Implementation

```
Private Sub IDropTarget_Drop( _
    ByVal pDataObj As VBShellLib.IDataObject, _
    ByVal grfKeyState As VBShellLib.KEYSTATES, _
    ByVal x As Long, _
    ByVal y As Long, _
    pdwEffect As VBShellLib.DROPEFFECT)

    Dim i As Integer
    Dim sMsg As String

    Set m_clsDropFiles = New clsDropFiles
```

Example 7-3. Drop Implementation (continued)

```
    m_clsDropFiles.GetDropFiles pDataObj, ".rad"

    If (m_clsDropFiles.Count = 0) Then
        MsgBox "Only RAD files can be dropped here!", _
            vbOKOnly, _
            "RAD Drop Handler"
        Exit Sub
    End If


    If m_dwMouseKey = MK_LBUTTON Then
        sMsg = "MK_LBUTTON" & vbCrLf
    End If

    If m_dwMouseKey = MK_RBUTTON Then
        sMsg = "MK_RBUTTON" & vbCrLf
    End If

    Select Case m_dwDropKey
        Case MK_CONTROL
            sMsg = sMsg & "Drop + CTRL"
        Case MK_SHIFT
            sMsg = sMsg & "Drop + SHIFT"
        Case MK_ALT
            sMsg = sMsg & "Drop + ALT"
        Case Else
            sMsg = sMsg & "Normal Drop"
    End Select

    sMsg = sMsg & vbCrLf & vbCrLf
    sMsg = sMsg & "Drop File(s):" & vbCrLf

    For i = 0 To m_clsDropFiles.Count - 1
        sMsg = sMsg & m_clsDropFiles.Files(i) & vbCrLf
    Next i

    sMsg = sMsg & vbCrLf
    sMsg = sMsg & "Target File: " & m_sTargetFile

    MsgBox sMsg, vbOKOnly, "RAD Drop Handler"

End Sub
```

The shell passes in a reference to **IDataObject**, which we in turn pass on to an instance of clsDropFiles (see Chapter 5). If our file count is 0 at this point, we know that the files dropped were not *.rad* files, and we can display an error message. Otherwise, a list of the target files, the name of the drop file, and the keyboard and mouse states are displayed in a message box like the one shown in Figure 7-2.

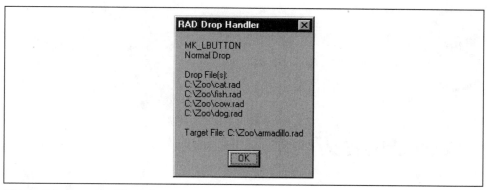

Figure 7-2. Drop handler info

Registering the Drop Handler

There can be only one drop handler for a file type; therefore, drop handlers are registered in a similar manner to icon handlers, as Figure 7-3 illustrates. The default value points to the CLSID of the drop handler, and the CLSID is added to the approved extensions list.

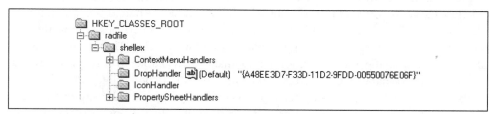

Figure 7-3. Registering a drop handler in the registry

The following registry script will properly register the example for this chapter. As always, lines contained within square brackets must be on the same line:

```
REGEDIT4

[HKEY_CLASSES_ROOT\.rad]
@ = "radfile"

[HKEY_CLASSES_ROOT\radfile]

[HKEY_CLASSES_ROOT\radfile]
@ = "Rudimentary Animal Data"

[HKEY_CLASSES_ROOT\radfile\shellex]

[HKEY_CLASSES_ROOT\radfile\shellex\DropHandler]
@ = "{A48EE3D7-F33D-11D2-9FDD-00550076E06F}"

[HKEY_LOCAL_MACHINE\Software\Microsoft\Windows\CurrentVersion\Shell Extensions\
Approved]
"{A48EE3D7-F33D-11D2-9FDD-00550076E06F}" = "RAD drop handler"
```

8

Data Handlers

Data handlers allow you to define custom handling for copy-and-paste operations involving files of a given type. Normally, when you select a file and press Ctrl-C or select Copy from the Explorer menu, the shell copies the name of the file using the `CF_HDROP` format. This is evident in the clsDropFiles class that we used to implement the `IShellExtInit::Initialize` and `IDropTarget::Drop` methods in Chapter 7, *Drop Handlers*. But what if we want to change this behavior for our file type? Take a bitmap file for instance. What if, instead of copying the file, we want to copy the actual image contained within the file? Then you would be able to highlight the file in Explorer and make it available to any program that knows how to handle `CF_BITMAP` information (Microsoft Paint, Adobe Photoshop, etc.). Or what if we want to copy information from the file, say in `CF_TEXT` format, to the clipboard? We might want to copy its dimensions, for example, or the color depth of the file. This would allow us to select a file in the shell, press Ctrl-C, and copy pertinent information directly from the file into other programs like Microsoft Word or Excel.

Data handlers are required to implement two interfaces. These interfaces are `IPersistFile` and `IDataObject`. The `IPersistFile` implementation serves the same purpose it did for our icon handler and drop handler. We will just implement `Load` to get the name of the file in question.

We have *used* `IDataObject` before, but we have never implemented it. Admittedly, when `IDataObject` was last discussed (see Chapter 4, *Context Menu Handlers*), all you got was a really glossed overview of the interface. In this chapter, we will talk more about this interface and get a little better idea of how it works. But by no means will the discussion be complete. To write a data handler, we need to implement only three of nine available methods. But after we implement these methods, you should be able to explore the rest of `IDataObject` with better understanding.

Our data handler will be fairly simple, although the implementation is somewhat involved. When a *.rad* file is copied in the shell, the data handler will determine the type of animal represented by the file and build the string "The (*animal name*) is on the clipboard." This string is then made available to any program that allows for text transfers (**CF_TEXT** format) over the clipboard via the Paste command. Figure 8-1, for example, shows a string generated by the data handler for *.rad* files that has been pasted into Notepad.

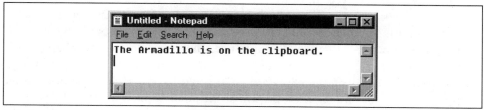

Figure 8-1. Accessing the .rad file data handler from Notepad

How Data Handlers Work

Data handlers are activated when a file is copied in the shell. Selecting Copy from Explorer's File menu, selecting Copy from the context menu of the file object itself, pressing Ctrl-C, or pressing Ctrl-Insert will all initiate a registered data handler if one exists. To do this, the shell looks under the following key:

```
HKEY_CLASSES_ROOT\
     {application identifier}\
          shellex\
               DataHandler
```

Once loaded, the shell passes the name of the file being copied to the data handler via the **IPersistFile::Load** method. We've seen this functionality a few times already (icon handlers and drop handlers). Nothing's different here. Like before, the filename can be stored in a private class member until it is needed at a later time.

The shell then calls **IDataObject::QueryGetData** repeatedly in an attempt to figure out all of the formats a data handler can use. Each time **QueryGetData** is called, a pointer to a **FORMATETC** structure is passed in by the shell. The **FORMATETC** structure describes the format of the data that will be involved in the data transfer: text, bitmaps, metafiles, etc. We'll talk about this structure later.

Every time the shell calls **QueryGetData**, it is saying, "If I call **GetData** with this format, will the call be successful?" In other words, will **GetData** be able to provide me the data described by this **FORMATETC** structure? The **QueryGetData** method is provided by data objects (objects that implement **IDataObject**) as a way for the caller to determine what formats the data object can provide. However, the fact that the shell calls this method seems a little odd, because `IDataObject` has another method called `EnumFormatEtc`.

`EnumFormatEtc` provides a way for the shell to retrieve all of the formats that are supported by the data handler. In fact, it is this method that the shell calls right after `QueryGetData`. This is strange behavior because, rather than ask what formats a data object supports, the shell could just ask for the formats.

After the shell has received all of the valid formats that the data object supports, it will then call `IDataObject::GetData` to retrieve the data. Whatever this "data" happens to be is completely arbitrary. The data handler can provide whatever it wants when `GetData` is called. For instance, the example for the chapter will retrieve the name of the animal inside of a *.rad* file and create a string that says "The (*animal name*) is on the clipboard." We could have just as easily provided a bitmap of the animal or a short biography of the animal's life thus far. The point is that whatever you want to provide is up to you, and `GetData` is where the work gets done.

So after `GetData` has been called, the handler is out of the picture. But the show is not over . . .

At this point (with regard to our chapter example), the Paste menu of any program supporting `text` (`CF_TEXT`) clipboard transfers will be active. Programs supporting `CF_TEXT` include Notepad and Microsoft Word. When Paste is selected from the menu of one of these programs or a similar program, the contents of the clipboard are transferred to the application.

Programs supporting formats other than `CF_TEXT`, such as Microsoft Paint, would display a grayed out Paste menu.

Data Handler Interfaces

Data handlers implement two interfaces: `IPersistFile` and `IDataObject`. Everything that needs to be said about `IPersistFile` has already been said (see the "IPersistFile" section in Chapter 5, *Icon Handlers*). Conversely, we know almost nothing about `IDataObject`. And even when we are done with this chapter, there will still be much that has not been said about this interface. The world of `IDataObject` is huge. It is one of the fundamental interfaces involved in OLE data transfers.

IDataObject

Table 8-1 shows all nine methods of `IDataObject`, but only three are required when writing data handlers in Visual Basic: `QueryGetData`, `EnumFormatEtc`, and `GetData`.

Table 8-1. The IDataObject Interface

Method	Description
GetData	Retrieves data from a data object, as defined by a FORMATETC structure. The data is then transferred through a STGMEDIUM structure.
GetDataHere	Similar to GetData except the caller is responsible for allocating and freeing all memory associated with FORMATETC and STGMEDIUM.
QueryGetData	Given a FORMATETC structure, this method determines if a resulting call to GetData will be successful.
GetCanonicalFormatEtc	Determines if two different FORMATETC structures would produce the same data, providing a means to eliminate a second call to GetData.
SetData	Allows another object to send data to the data object.
EnumFormatEtc	Provides a means to enumerate all the ways a data object can describe data in a FORMATETC structure.
DAdvise	Creates an event sink between the caller and the data object, allowing the data object to be notified when data changes.
DUnadvise	Releases the event sink created by DAdvise.
EnumDAdvise	Enumerates the active event sinks between the caller and the data object.

QueryGetData

This method determines whether the data handler is capable of providing data in the format that is being requested by the shell. This method has the following syntax:

```
HRESULT QueryGetData(FORMATETC *pFormatEtc);
```

When a data handler is first loaded, the shell calls **QueryGetData** several times in order to determine what formats the handler can provide. You can picture the shell asking the handler, "Do you support text? Do you support bitmaps? Do you support wave files?" The query comes in the form of a FORMATETC structure. This structure is used to describe data that will be involved in a transfer. It is defined like this:

```
typedef struct tagFORMATETC {
    CLIPFORMAT cfFormat;
    DVTARGETDEVICE *ptd;
    DWORD dwAspect;
    LONG lindex;
    DWORD tymed;
}FORMATETC, *LPFORMATETC;
```

Its members are as follows:

cfFormat

Contains the particular clipboard format of interest. This can be one of the following values in the **CLIPFORMAT** enumeration (this is defined in *vbshell.odl*):

```
typedef enum {
        CF_TEXT              = 1,     'Text format
        CF_BITMAP            = 2,     'Handle to a bitmap
        CF_METAFILEPICT      = 3,     'Handle to a metafile picture format
        CF_SYLK              = 4,     'Microsoft Symbolic Link format
        CF_DIF               = 5,     'Software Art's data interchange format
        CF_TIFF              = 6,     'Tagged-image file format
        CF_OEMTEXT           = 7,     'Text format in OEM character set
        CF_DIB               = 8,     'Memory object containing BITMAPINFO
        CF_PALETTE           = 9,     'Handle to a color palette
        CF_PENDATA           = 10,    'Data for pen extensions
        CF_RIFF              = 11,    'Audio data
        CF_WAVE              = 12,    'Audio data in WAV format
        CF_UNICODETEXT       = 13,    'Unicode text format
        CF_ENHMETAFILE       = 14,    'Handle to enhanced metafile
        CF_HDROP             = 15,    'Handle that identifies list of files
        CF_LOCALE            = 16,    'Handle to locale identifier
        CF_MAX               = 17,    'Undocumented????
        CF_OWNERDISPLAY      = 0x0080, 'Owner display format
        CF_DSPTEXT           = 0x0081, 'Text in private format
        CF_DSPBITMAP         = 0x0082, 'Bitmap display in private format
        CF_DSPMETAFILEPICT   = 0x0083, 'Metafile in private format
        CF_DSPENHMETAFILE    = 0x008E  'Enhanced metafile in private format
    } CLIPFORMAT;
```

ptd

This member is a pointer to a **DVTARGETDEVICE** structure that contains information about the target device for which the data is being readied. We will not discuss this parameter for two reasons. First, it would really complicate our discussion. If you need to write a data handler that dumps data to a printer, then you would need this parameter (see the documentation for the Platform SDK). Second, the data handler we will write (and most of the ones you will probably write) are device-independent, so this parameter is meaningless. It will most likely always be 0.

dwAspect

This member can be *one* of the following values from the **DVASPECT** enumeration, which is defined like so:

```
typedef enum tagDVASPECT {
    DVASPECT_CONTENT = 1,
    DVASPECT_THUMBNAIL = 2,
    DVASPECT_ICON = 4,
    DVASPECT_DOCPRINT = 8
} DVASPECT;
```

A single clipboard format can support multiple views, or aspects. Think about Explorer when the view is configured as "View as Web Page." If you select a graphics file in the shell, a thumbnail image is shown to the left of the files listing. The data handler involved in this process most likely received a request for the data with this parameter set to DVASPECT_THUMBNAIL.

The members of this enumeration have the following meaning:

Constant	Description
DVASPECT_CONTENT	Returns the data in a format that is ready for the screen or the printer.
DVASPECT_THUMBNAIL	Presents the data in a 120×120, 16-color, device-independent bitmap.
DVASPECT_ICON	Provides an iconic representation of the data.
DVASPECT_DOCPRINT	Provides a view of the data on the screen as though it were printed on a printer using the File → Print command. The data might represent a series of pages.

lindex

Part of the aspect when the data is split across page boundaries. The most common value is −1, which identifies all of the data. For the aspects DVASPECT_THUMBNAIL and DVASPECT_ICON, this value is ignored.

tymed

One of the TYMED enumeration constants used to indicate the type of storage medium being used to facilitate a data transfer. The enumeration is defined like so:

```
typedef enum tagTYMED {
    TYMED_HGLOBAL = 1,
    TYMED_FILE = 2,
    TYMED_ISTREAM = 4,
    TYMED_ISTORAGE = 8,
    TYMED_GDI = 16,
    TYMED_MFPICT = 32,
    TYMED_ENHMF = 64,
    TYMED_NULL = 0 }
TYMED;
```

We will use the value TYMED_HGLOBAL to tell the shell that our data transfers will take place via global memory. But as you can see, there are many more options.

EnumFormatEtc

Before the shell can get data from the data object, it must retrieve the formats that the object supports. It does this by calling IDataObject::EnumFormatEtc. This method has the following definition:

```
HRESULT EnumFormatEtc(DWORD dwDirection,
                      IEnumFORMATETC ** ppenumFormatetc);
```

Its parameters are:

dwDirection

> This is a value from the following enumeration:

```
typedef enum tagDATADIR {DATADIR_GET = 1,
                         DATADIR_SET = 2,
    } DATADIR;
```

> If the value of *dwDirection* is DATADIR_GET, the shell is asking the data handler to supply all of the formats that can be passed to GetData successfully. Conversely, if *dwDirection* equals DATADIR_SET, then the shell wants to know which formats will work with a call to SetData. A data handler will not be asked for SetData formats.

ppenumFormatetc

> This is an IEnumFORMATETC reference provided by the data object that the shell will use to enumerate all of the formats that the object supports.

GetData

Called when the client (Explorer) is ready to receive the data. The function is defined as:

```
HRESULT GetData(FORMATETC * pFormatetc, STGMEDIUM * pmedium);
```

GetData returns the data in the format described by *pFormatetc* and transfers this data through *pmedium*.

FORMATETC should already be familiar to you from the discussion of the IDataObject interface's QueryGetData method. STGMEDIUM, however, requires some explanation. The structure looks like this:

```
typedef struct tagSTGMEDIUM {
    DWORD tymed;
    union {
        HBITMAP hBitmap;
        HMETAFILEPICT hMetaFilePict;
        HENHMETAFILE hEnhMetaFile;
        HGLOBAL hGlobal;
        LPWSTR lpszFileName;
        IStream *pstm;
        IStorage *pstg;
    };
    IUnknown *pUnkForRelease;
}STGMEDIUM;
```

Here's how the structure works: the *tymed* member contains a value from the TYMED enumeration, which has already been seen in our discussion of QueryGetData. This value determines which value of the union is valid. So if *tymed* is equal to TYMED_HGLOBAL, the hGlobal member of the union should contain the data for the transfer. If *tymed* is equal to `TYMED_ISTREAM`, the data should be made available through the `IStream *` member of the structure.

There is a problem with this structure, however: VB does not support unions. Remember, though, that members of a union occupy the same physical address in memory, so a workaround is fairly simple. We can define the structure like this:

```
typedef struct {
    TYMED    tymed;
    long pData;
    IUnknown *pUnkForRelease;
} STGMEDIUM;
```

This works because, naturally, every member of the union is essentially a 4-byte value (a pointer or a handle).

The last member of this structure that needs to be discussed is *pUnkForRelease*. Remember the *ReleaseStgMedium* function (see Chapter 4, *Context Menu Handlers*)? This function is called to free the storage allocated by `STGMEDIUM`. Well, if *pUnkForRelease* is `NULL`, then *ReleaseStgMedium* uses its default methods to release this memory. If it's not `NULL`, then *ReleaseStgMedium* uses the `IUnknown` pointer specified by this member to free the storage. It does this by calling `IUnknown::Release`.

The IDL listing for `IDataObject` is shown in Example 8-1.

Example 8-1. IDataObject IDL Definition

```
//-----------------------------------------------------------
// IDataObject
//-----------------------------------------------------------
typedef enum {
    DV_E_FORMATETC            = 0x80040064,
    DV_E_DVTARGETDEVICE       = 0x80040065,
    DV_E_STGMEDIUM            = 0x80040066,
    DV_E_STATDATA             = 0x80040067,
    DV_E_LINDEX               = 0x80040068,
    DV_E_TYMED                = 0x80040069,
    DV_E_CLIPFORMAT           = 0x8004006A,
    DV_E_DVASPECT             = 0x8004006B,
    DV_E_DVTARGETDEVICE_SIZE  = 0x8004006C,
    DV_E_NOIVIEWOBJECT        = 0x8004006D
} DV_ERROR;

typedef enum tagDATADIR
{
    DATADIR_GET = 1,
    DATADIR_SET = 2
} DATADIR;

[
```

Example 8-1. IDataObject IDL Definition (continued)

```
    uuid(0000010e-0000-0000-C000-000000000046),
    helpstring("IDataObject Interface"),
    odl
]
interface IDataObject : IUnknown
{
    HRESULT GetData(
                [in] FORMATETC *pformatetcIn,
                [in,out] STGMEDIUM *pmedium);

    HRESULT GetDataHere(
                [in] FORMATETC *pformatetc,
                [in,out] STGMEDIUM *pmedium);

    HRESULT QueryGetData(
                [in] FORMATETC *pformatetc);

    HRESULT GetCanonicalFormatEtc(
                [in] FORMATETC *pformatectIn,
                [in,out] FORMATETC *pformatetcOut);

    HRESULT SetData(
                [in] FORMATETC *pformatetc,
                [in] STGMEDIUM *pmedium,
                [in] BOOL fRelease);

    HRESULT EnumFormatEtc(
                [in] long dwDirection,
                [in,out] IEnumFORMATETC **ppenumFormatEtc);

    HRESULT DAdvise(
                [in] FORMATETC *pformatetc,
                [in] long advf,
                [in] long pAdvSink,
                [in] long pdwConnection);

    HRESULT DUnadvise(
                [in] long dwConnection);

    HRESULT EnumDAdvise(
                [in] long ppenumAdvise);
}
```

 Notice that throughout the IDL listing for IDataObject, explicit pointers to FORMATETC and STGMEDIUM are used as parameters to several of the methods. This is possible because the members of both of these structures are all automation compatible.

Creating a Data Handler

We begin the data handler by adding a new class module to the RadEx Project called clsDataHandler. The handler will implement IDataObject and IPersistFile, which have already been defined in the type library from previous chapters. We should add the following code to the general declarations section of clsDataHandler:

```
'clsDataHandler.cls

Implements IDataObject
Implements IPersistFile
```

Implementing IPersistFile

The first thing we want to do is implement IPersistFile. Although IPersistFile supports a number of methods (GetCurFile, IsDirty, Load, Save, and SaveCompleted), there is only one method with which we are concerned, Load.

Load

The Load method is implemented exactly as it was in Chapter 5. All we are doing is getting the name of the file being copied, which is passed to the Load method as its *pszFileName* argument. Example 8-2 shows the code to do this.

Example 8-2. The IPersistFile_Load Method

```
'clsDataHandler.cls

Implements IDataObject
Implements IPersistFile

Private m_sFile As String

Private Sub IPersistFile_Load(ByVal pszFileName As LPCOLESTR, _
    ByVal dwMode As DWORD)

    m_sFile = Space(255)
    CopyMemory ByVal StrPtr(m_sFile), ByVal pszFileName, Len(m_sFile)

End Sub
```

Implementing IDataObject

With that out of the way, we can focus on our IDataObject implementation. Of the nine methods supported by IDataObject, we need to implement just three: QueryGetData, EnumFormatEtc, and GetData.

QueryGetData

The first method we are concerned with is `QueryGetData`. Remember, the shell calls `QueryGetData` and passes in a pointer to a `FORMATETC` structure. `QueryGetData` must determine if the format indicated by the `FORMATETC` structure is valid for the data handler. If it is, `QueryGetData` returns `S_OK`; otherwise, it returns `DV_E_FORMATETC`, which signals an invalid format.

Because we are dealing with `HRESULT`s in this function, we will need to replace the `QueryGetData` method in clsDataHandler with our own implementation, *QueryGetDataVB*. Swapping vtable entries (see Chapter 4) should be familiar to you by now. Just so you know, we'll have to swap the vtable entries for every method we implement for `IDataObject`, so get ready. The code to swap the `QueryGetData` method with the *QueryGetDataVB* function is as follows:

```
'clsDataHandler.cls

Implements IDataObject
Implements IPersistFile

Private m_sFile As String

Private m_pOldQueryGetData As Long

Private Sub Class_Initialize()

    Dim pVtable As IDataObject
    Set pVtable = Me

    'QueryGetData is method 6 in the vtable.
    m_pOldQueryGetData = SwapVtableEntry(ObjPtr(pVtable), _
                                6, _
                                AddressOf QueryGetDataVB)

End Sub
```

QueryGetDataVB, which resides in *handler.bas* and is shown in Example 8-3, is a very simple function. It just checks the members of `FORMATETC` and returns `S_OK` if they match our data format. Otherwise, it returns `DV_E_FORMATETC`.

Example 8-3. QueryGetDataVB

```
'handler.bas

Public Function QueryGetDataVB(ByVal this As IDataObject, _
 pformatetc As FORMATETC) As Long

    'Default return value
    QueryGetDataVB = DV_E_FORMATETC

    'Text format
    If (fmtEtc.cfFormat And CF_TEXT) And _
```

Example 8-3. QueryGetDataVB (continued)

```
        (fmtEtc.dwAspect = DVASPECT_CONTENT) And _
        (fmtEtc.tymed = TYMED_HGLOBAL) And _

        QueryGetDataVB = S_OK

    End If

End Function
```

As you can see, only three members of the structure participate in this interchange. The *cfFormat* member can contain more than one format; therefore, we need to use the **And** operator to determine if the format we are looking for is being described. Don't check for equality here. The shell will always group together several formats with **Or**. *dwAspect* and *tymed*, however, must be explicit values.

EnumFormatEtc

EnumFormatEtc will need to return **HRESULT**s back to the shell. Therefore, we will swap this method with the *EnumFormatEtcVB* function, which lives in *DataHandler.bas*. We will add the code to achieve the swap to our **Class_ Initialize** function:

```
    Private m_pOldQueryGetData As Long
    Private m_pOldEnumFormatEtc As Long

    Private Sub Class_Initialize()

        Dim pVtable As IDataObject
        Set pVtable = Me

        m_pOldQueryGetData = SwapVtableEntry(ObjPtr(pVtable), _
                                    6, _
                                    AddressOf QueryGetDataVB)

        m_pOldEnumFormatEtc = SwapVtableEntry(ObjPtr(pVtable), _
                                    9, _
                                    AddressOf EnumFormatEtcVB)
    End Sub
```

Remember, the shell calls this method in order to retrieve all of the formats that are supported by the data object. The request is fulfilled by providing the shell with another object that supports the **IEnumFORMATETC** interface. We will not discuss this interface in detail here. All you need to know is that this interface supports four methods: **Next**, **Reset**, **Skip**, and **Clone**. Once the enumerator has been given to the shell, the **Next** method will be called repeatedly. This is Explorer's way of saying, "Next format, please." The data object must provide the shell with a new format every time this method is called. Once all the formats have been provided, the method must return **S_FALSE**.

Fortunately for us, we don't have to create an enumeration object. As it turns out, we can register all the formats our object supports in the registry. Then we can call *OleRegEnumFormatEtc*. *OleRegEnumFormatEtc* returns a reference to an `IEnumFORMATETC` interface that is implemented somewhere deep in the bowels of *ole32.dll*. After we pass this interface pointer back to the shell, the shell will use it to enumerate all of the formats that have been stored in the registry. Example 8-4 demonstrates the process.

Example 8-4. EnumFormatEtcVB

```
'handler.bas
Public Declare Function OleRegEnumFormatEtc Lib "ole32.dll" ( _
        refclsid As GUID, _
        ByVal dwDirection As DATADIR, _
        lpEnumFormatEtc As IEnumFORMATETC) As Long
'DataHandler.bas
Public Function EnumFormatEtcVB(_
    ByVal this As IDataObject, _
    ByVal dwDirection As Long, _
    ppenumFormatEtc As IEnumFORMATETC) As Long

    Dim clsid As GUID
    CLSIDFromProgID ByVal StrPtr("RadEx.clsDataHandler"), clsid

    EnumFormatEtcVB = OleRegEnumFormatEtc(clsid, _
        DATADIR_GET Or DATADIR_SET, ppenumFormatEtc)

End Function
```

The first parameter to *OleRegEnumFormatEtc* is a `REFCLSID`, or a reference to a class identifier. This is a fancy way of saying a pointer to a GUID. We need an actual GUID here, and since there is no datatype that is 128 bits wide, we make our own. GUID is defined in *handler.bas*, not the type library, for reasons of automation compatibility. (It contains an array of bytes which is incompatible.) The definition looks like this:

```
'handler.bas

Public Type GUID
    Data1 As Long
    Data2 As Integer
    Data3 As Integer
    Data4(7) As Byte
End Type
```

OleRegEnumFormatEtc is expecting a reference to our data handler's CLSID. The easiest way to get this value is by calling *CLSIDFromProgID*, which will populate the GUID structure we need when passed the programmatic identifier of our data handler, which is `Radex.clsDataHandler`. *CLSIDFromProgID* is found in *ole32.dll* and is declared as follows:

```
Public Declare Function CLSIDFromProgID Lib "ole32.dll" _
    (ByVal lpszProgID As Long, pCLSID As GUID) As Long
```

The second parameter can be either DATADIR_GET or DATADIR_SET or both. DATADIR_GET causes the function to enumerate all of the formats that can be passed to IDataObject::GetData; DATADIR_SET enumerates the formats that could be passed to IDataObject::SetData.

Make Your Own Enumerator

You can create a class that implements IEnumFORMATETC yourself, if you want to provide your own enumerator. The implementation must be separate from the data object. For more details, see the discussion of IEnumIDList in Chapter 11, *Namespace Extensions*. (All of the IEnumXXXX interfaces contain the same methods and implement the same behavior. Chapter 11 should provide you with enough details.) The IEnumFORMATETC definition is included in the type library for this purpose. Once you have created your own enumerator, implementing EnumFormatEtc would simply be a matter of passing your own enumerator back to the shell:

```
Public Function EnumFormatEtcVB(_
    ByVal this As IDataObject, _
    ByVal dwDirection As Long, _
    ppenumFormatEtc As IEnumFORMATETC) As Long

    Dim ef As clsEnumFormatEtc 'Your enumerator
    Set ef = New clsEnumFormatEtc

    Set ppenumFormatEtc = ef

End Function
```

The third parameter is a pointer to a pointer to an IEnumFORMATETC interface. Conveniently, we can just pass in the value provided to us by Explorer.

The last thing we need to do to make sure that EnumFormatEtc will work properly is to actually register the data format(s) that we can provide, in our case CF_TEXT. The data format is registered under the CLSID of our data handler as shown in Figure 8-2.

The string "1,1,1,3" is the format itself and corresponds to the values *<format, aspect, medium, direction>*. In our case CF_TEXT = 1, DVASPECT_CONTENT = 1, and TYMED_HGLOBAL = 1. The direction value comes from the DATADIR enumeration, which is simply defined as:

```
typedef enum tagDATADIR {
    DATADIR_GET = 1,
```

Figure 8-2. Data format registry settings

```
    DATADIR_SET = 2
} DATADIR;
```

Therefore, (DATADIR_GET Or DATADIR_SET) = 3. This value implies that the format is valid for get and set operations.

GetData

GetData is a little more complex than QueryGetData, but basically here's how it works: the shell passes in a pointer to a FORMATETC structure and a pointer to a STGMEDIUM structure. If the FORMATETC structure describes the format that we can provide, then the STGMEDIUM structure can be populated with a pointer to the data we want to make available—in our case, a string describing the Animal type contained in the *.rad* file. As is the case with QueryGetData, if the format queried is invalid, we return DV_E_FORMATETC. This means we need to swap the GetData in clsDataHandler with our own function so we can return HRESULTs. The Class_Initialize event for clsDataHandler does this, as the following code shows:

```
'clsDataHandler.cls

Private m_pOldGetData As Long
Private m_pOldQueryGetData As Long
Private m_pOldEnumFormatEtc As Long

Private Sub Class_Initialize()

    Dim pVtable As IDataObject
    Set pVtable = Me

    m_pOldQueryGetData = SwapVtableEntry(ObjPtr(pVtable), _
                                6, _
                                AddressOf QueryGetDataVB)

    m_pOldEnumFormatEtc = SwapVtableEntry(ObjPtr(pVtable), _
                                9, _
                                AddressOf EnumFormatEtcVB)

    m_pOldGetData = SwapVtableEntry(ObjPtr(pVtable), _
                                4, _
                                AddressOf GetDataVB)

    'AddRef
```

```
        Dim pUnk As IUnknownVB
        Set pUnk = Me
        pUnk.AddRef

    End Sub
```

Take note that the data handler needs to make a call to **AddRef**; otherwise, the handler will terminate before the data can be transferred.

Now, let's break down *GetDataVB*, the first portion of which is shown in the following code fragment:

```
'handler.bas

Public Function GetDataVB(ByVal this As IDataObject, _
                pformatetcIn As FORMATETC, _
                pmedium As STGMEDIUM) As Long

    GetDataVB = DV_E_FORMATETC

    Dim b() As Byte
    Dim dataObj As clsDataHandler
    Dim hGlobalMem As HGLOBAL
    Dim pGlobalMem As Long
    Dim szType As String
    Dim szMsg As String

    Set dataObj = this

    If (pformatetcIn.cfFormat = CF_TEXT) And _
       (pformatetcIn.dwAspect = DVASPECT_CONTENT) And _
       (pformatetcIn.tymed = TYMED_HGLOBAL) Then _
```

The first thing we will do is get a reference to our class object. By setting *dataObj* equal to **this**, we are calling **QueryInterface** on our object. This returns a reference back to our object (an **IDispatch** pointer) that we can use from *handler.bas*. This alleviates the need for a global variable.

We then compare the *cfFormat*, *dwAspect*, and *tymed* members of the **FORMATETC** structure to make sure it is the format we are looking to provide data for. If it is, we are good to go. Since we have a reference back to clsDataHandler that allows us to easily retrieve the name of our *.rad* file, we can then use *GetPrivateProfileString* to get the animal type from the selected file, as the next fragment from the *GetDataVB* method shows:

```
'Get Animal type
szType = Space(255)
GetPrivateProfileString "Animal", _
                    "Type", _
                    "Unknown", _
                    szType, _
                    Len(szType), _
                    dataObj.FileName
```

We have the animal type, so now what? Remember that the shell is expecting the format of text being transferred in global memory. What we need to do is copy the string into global memory. Before we do that, we actually need to lay our hands on some global memory. We can do that by calling *GlobalAlloc*, which is defined like this:

```
Public Declare Function GlobalAlloc Lib "kernel32" _
    (ByVal wFlags As Long, ByVal dwBytes As Long) As Long
```

Using the `HGLOBAL` (handle to global memory) returned to us by *GlobalAlloc*, we can get a pointer to global memory itself and copy our string into that location. This is accomplished using *GlobalLock*, *CopyMemory*, and *GlobalUnlock*, as the next code fragment from the `GetDataVB` method shows:

```
'Allocate global memory.
hGlobalMem = GlobalAlloc(GMEM_MOVEABLE, 1024)

'Get a pointer to the global memory.
pGlobalMem = GlobalLock(hGlobalMem)

'Copy Animal type into global memory.
szType = TrimNull(szType)
szMsg = "The " & szType & " is on the clipboard." & vbCrLf
b = StrConv(szMsg, vbFromUnicode) & vbNullChar
CopyMemory ByVal pGlobalMem, b(0), UBound(b) + 1

'Unlock global memory.
GlobalUnlock hGlobalMem
```

We are not quite done yet. Now that the global memory we have allocated contains our string, we need to make it available to the clipboard. We do this by populating a `STGMEDIUM` structure and copying it to the location passed in by the shell:

```
stgMed.pData = hGlobalMem
stgMed.TYMED = TYMED_HGLOBAL
Set stgMed.pUnkForRelease = this
GetDataVB = S_OK
```

Registration and Operation

Lastly, we have to register the data handler (and make sure the data format is registered, too). There can be only one data handler per file object, so registration is fairly simple (see Figure 8-3).

Don't forget to add the CLSID to the approved shell extensions section!

If the data handler is not working at this point, try restarting the shell. Data handlers can be really picky!

Figure 8-3. Data handler registry settings

The following registry script will handle registering this chapter's example. Note that statements appearing inside of square brackets must reside on the same line:

```
REGEDIT4

[HKEY_CLASSES_ROOT\radfile\shellex\DataHandler]
@ = "{5BE98B48-FD84-11D2-9FE5-00550076E06F}"

[HKEY_CLASSES_ROOT\CLSID\{5BE98B48-FD84-11D2-9FE5-00550076E06F}\DataFormats\
GetSet\0]
@ = "1,1,1,3"

[HKEY_CLASSES_ROOT\CLSID\{5BE98B48-FD84-11D2-9FE5-00550076E06F}\DataFormats\
GetSet\1]
@ = "2,1,16,3"

[HKEY_LOCAL_MACHINE\Software\Microsoft\Windows\CurrentVersion\Shell Extensions\
Approved]
"{5BE98B48-FD84-11D2-9FE5-00550076E06F}" = "RAD data handler"
```

Select a *.rad* file and select the Copy command from Explorer's Edit menu. The clipboard now contains our string. Open up Notepad or Word. The Paste command should be available because both of these programs support the **CF_TEXT** format. Microsoft Paint, on the other hand, cannot get the data because it wants **CF_BITMAP**.

As an exercise, you might want to modify the data handler to copy a picture of the animal to the clipboard using **CF_BITMAP**. Instead of **TYMED_HGLOBAL**, specify **TYMED_GDI**. The **FORMATETC** structure you are interested in looks like this:

```
FORMATETC

cfFormat = CF_BITMAP
ptd = 0
dwAspect = DVASPECT_CONTENT
lIndex = -1
TYMED = TYMED_GDI
```

The bitmaps for the various animals could be stored in a resource file. You don't have to mess around with *GlobalAlloc*, because you only need a handle to a bitmap, which is easily attained by calling the *LoadIcon* API.

Adding Additional Formats

Since it sounds so easy to add support for bitmaps, let's go ahead and do it. The first thing we want to do is add the bitmap format to the registry. The previous script already has the entry we need:

```
[HKEY_CLASSES_ROOT\CLSID\{5BE98B48-FD84-11D2-9FE5-00550076E06F}\DataFormats\
GetSet\1]
@ = "2,1,16,3"
```

As stated earlier, these values correspond to *<format, aspect, medium, direction>*, in this case CF_BITMAP, DVASPEC

T_CONTENT, TYMED_GDI, and DATADIR_GET ORed with DATADIR_SET.

Next, we need to modify QueryGetData in order to recognize the new format. When the shell asks if we can provide bitmaps, we need to be able to tell it "yes." Example 8-5 contains the modified version of the method.

Example 8-5. QueryGetData with Bitmap Format Added

```
Public Function QueryGetDataVB(ByVal this As IDataObject, _
                              pformatetc As FORMATETC) As Long

    QueryGetDataVB = DV_E_FORMATETC

    'Text
    If (pformatetc.cfFormat And CF_TEXT) And _
        (pformatetc.dwAspect = DVASPECT_CONTENT) And _
        (pformatetc.TYMED = TYMED_HGLOBAL) Then

        QueryGetDataVB = S_OK

    End If

    'Bitmap
    If (pformatetc.cfFormat And CF_BITMAP) And _
        (pformatetc.dwAspect = DVASPECT_CONTENT) And _
        (pformatetc.TYMED = TYMED_GDI) Then

        QueryGetDataVB = S_OK

    End If

End Function
```

Good news: we don't have to do a thing with EnumFormatEtc. Everything there is already in place.

This leaves us with GetData. Since we are providing data in two formats now, it might be a good idea to clean up our implementation somewhat. We can move all of the code that deals with the text format into a Private method called GetText.

All the code for bitmaps can go into `GetBitmap`. Now our `GetData` implementation, which is shown in Example 8-6, is a little more streamlined. We can now add formats without getting in the way of the implementation.

Example 8-6. GetData with Bitmap Support

```
Public Function GetDataVB(ByVal this As IDataObject, _
                          pformatetcIn As FORMATETC, _
                          pmedium As STGMEDIUM) As Long

    GetDataVB = DV_E_FORMATETC

    If (pformatetcIn.cfFormat And CF_TEXT) And _
       (pformatetcIn.dwAspect = DVASPECT_CONTENT) And _
       (pformatetcIn.TYMED = TYMED_HGLOBAL) Then

        GetDataVB = GetText(this, pmedium)

    End If

    If (pformatetcIn.cfFormat And CF_BITMAP) And _
       (pformatetcIn.dwAspect = DVASPECT_CONTENT) And _
       (pformatetcIn.TYMED = TYMED_GDI) Then

        GetDataVB = GetBitmap(this, pmedium)

    End If

End Function
```

Of course, now we have to actually provide the data for both of our formats. We'll look at `GetText` first (see Example 8-7), simply because it makes the chapter more suspenseful that way. Anyway, we have already discussed this code. There is nothing new, other than the fact that its implementation has been moved outside of `GetData`.

Example 8-7. GetText

```
Private Function GetText(ByVal pDataObject As IDataObject, _
                         pmedium As STGMEDIUM) As Long

    GetText = DV_E_FORMATETC

    Dim b() As Byte
    Dim dataObj As clsDataHandler
    Dim hGlobalMem As HGLOBAL
    Dim pGlobalMem As Long
    Dim szType As String
    Dim szMsg As String

    Set dataObj = pDataObject
```

Example 8-7. GetText (continued)

```
'Get Animal type.
szType = Space(255)
GetPrivateProfileString "Animal", _
                        "Type", _
                        "Unknown", _
                        szType, _
                        Len(szType), _
                        dataObj.FileName

'Allocate global memory.
hGlobalMem = GlobalAlloc(GMEM_MOVEABLE, 1024)

'Get a pointer to the global memory.
pGlobalMem = GlobalLock(hGlobalMem)

'Copy Animal type into global memory.
szType = TrimNull(szType)
szMsg = "The " & szType & " is on the clipboard." & vbCrLf

b = StrConv(szMsg, vbFromUnicode) & vbNullChar
CopyMemory ByVal pGlobalMem, b(0), UBound(b) + 1

'Unlock global memory.
GlobalUnlock hGlobalMem

pmedium.pData = hGlobalMem
pmedium.TYMED = TYMED_HGLOBAL
Set pmedium.pUnkForRelease = pDataObject

Set dataObj = Nothing

GetText = S_OK

End Function
```

Now, the moment we have all been waiting for. Inside of the resource file that contains the icons for our icon handler (Chapter 5) and the dialog for our property sheet extension (Chapter 6, *Property Sheet Handlers*), there are five bitmaps. These bitmaps are all pictures of O'Reilly books that have animals on the cover matching our *.rad* file animal types. The resource identifiers are defined like so:

```
Private Const IDB_ARMADILLO = 101
Private Const IDB_CAT = 102
Private Const IDB_COW = 103
Private Const IDB_DOG = 104
Private Const IDB_FISH = 105
```

Now that you have this bit of background information, we can look at the **GetBitmap** function. Don't get excited, though. The function is so simple it's almost anti-climatic. Example 8-8 contains the listing.

Example 8-8. GetBitmap

```
Private Declare Function LoadBitmap Lib "user32" Alias _
    "LoadBitmapA" (ByVal hInstance As Long, _
    ByVal lpBitmapName As Long) As Long

Private Function GetBitmap(ByVal pDataObject As IDataObject, _
                            pmedium As STGMEDIUM) As Long

    GetPicture = DV_E_FORMATETC

    Dim dataObj As clsDataHandler
    Dim szType As String
    Dim lBitmap As Long

    Set dataObj = pDataObject

    'Get Animal type.
    szType = Space(255)
    GetPrivateProfileString "Animal", _
                            "Type", _
                            "Unknown", _
                            szType, _
                            Len(szType), _
                            dataObj.FileName

    szType = TrimNull(szType)

    Select Case UCase$(szType)
        Case "ARMADILLO"
            lBitmap = IDB_ARMADILLO
        Case "CAT"
            lBitmap = IDB_CAT
        Case "COW"
            lBitmap = IDB_COW
        Case "DOG"
            lBitmap = IDB_DOG
        Case "FISH"
            lBitmap = IDB_FISH
        Case Else
            Exit Function
    End Select

    pmedium.pData = LoadBitmap(App.hInstance, lBitmap)
    pmedium.tymed = TYMED_GDI
    Set pmedium.pUnkForRelease = pDataObject

    Set dataObj = Nothing

    GetPicture = S_OK

End Function
```

`GetBitmap`'s first duty is to retrieve a reference back to our data object and get the name of the *.rad* file that has just been copied. Then, based on the type of animal, the local variable *lBitmap* is assigned to one of the resource identifiers representing the picture of an animal.

Providing the bitmap to the shell is as simple as calling *LoadBitmap* with the resource identifier of the animal that we want.

It should be mentioned that the declaration of *LoadBitmap* has been modified somewhat. The datatype of the last parameter has been changed from String to Long in order to allow us to pass the resource identifier to the function. We're not going to talk about why this works. Just know that it does.

Lastly, the *tymed* member of the `STGMEDIUM` structure needs to be set to `TYMED_GDI` in order to inform the shell that the data is a GDI component—in other words, a handle to a bitmap.

Now, we have two formats available for one copy operation. The original text string will be available to any program that can handle `CF_TEXT` data, and, as Figure 8-4 illustrates, programs that can manipulate `CF_BITMAP` data are provided for as well.

Figure 8-4. Armadillo data in CF_BITMAP format

9

Copy Hook Handlers

Copy hook handlers are invoked every time a shell folder or printer object is moved, deleted, copied, or renamed. Their sole purpose is either to approve or to disapprove the operation in question. They take no part in the operations themselves, and they don't care about the results. When one of the aforementioned processes is initiated, the shell provides the name of the source object, the name of the destination object, and the action being performed to the copy hook handler. The handler merely says, "Yeah, go ahead," or "Stop right there!" That's it. In fact, the copy hook handler is not even notified of whether the action was successful. It is merely a sentry that stands guard over a particular folder or printer.

Copy hook handlers are a little different from the other shell extensions we have discussed. First and foremost, they are not associated with file types, but rather with shell folders and printer objects. Second, they implement only one interface, `ICopyHook`. If you remember, the previous shell extensions were first initialized either through `IShellExtInit` or `IPersistFile`. In contrast, copy hook handlers depend on neither interface. `ICopyHook` contains one method, `CopyCallback`, that provides everything the handler will need, initialization and all. There is another major difference, but we'll need to look at the definition for `ICopyHook::CopyCallback` to see it:

```
UINT CopyCallback(
    HWND hwnd,
    UINT wFunc,
    UINT wFlags,
    LPCSTR pszSrcFile,
    DWORD dwSrcAttribs,
    LPCSTR pszDestFile,
    DWORD dwDestAttribs
    );
```

Notice that `CopyCallback` returns a `UINT` instead of an `HRESULT`. All interface methods, by convention, are supposed to return an `HRESULT`. Who knows what the designers of this interface were thinking? One thing is certain, there is definitely something suspicious going on here. This is going to cause us a problem later when we try to implement the interface because VB will not accept a method definition that does not return an `HRESULT`. Of course, by now you can probably guess that we will redefine the interface to return an `HRESULT` instead of a `UINT`. Each is 4 bytes wide, so this is feasible, but not without problems. But we'll cross that bridge when we get to it.

Before we can add an interface definition to the type library, we'll need its IID. Herein lies a problem. If you search the Platform SDK for `ICopyHook`, you will find a description of the interface, a short discourse on copy hook handlers, and so on. But if you search for `ICopyHook` in the registry (or with OLE View), you *will not* find it. It seems we have a little bit of a mystery going on here.

Let's search for the interface in *shlobj.h*. If you don't remember, this is the C/C++ header file that contains most of the interface definitions used by the shell. In this file, you will find references to both `ICopyHookA` and `ICopyHookW`. As you should know by now, these represent the ANSI and wide versions of the interface, respectively. Now we're on to something. But we still need the IID.

Most of the IIDs for the shell interfaces are found in a file called *shlguid.h*. But if you do a search for `ICopyHookA` or `ICopyHookW`, you won't find a thing. What is going on here? There's nothing in OLE View either! Apparently, what we have found is a lack of consistency.

Maybe if we search for `CopyHook`, we will have some luck. Sure enough, if you inspect *shlguid.h* closely, you will find references to `IShellCopyHookA` and `IShellCopyHookW`, along with the IIDs. Whew!

 I refer to the interface as `ICopyHook` throughout the remainder of this chapter. I only distinguish between `ICopyHookA` and `ICopyHookW` when necessary.

How Copy Hook Handlers Work

A copy hook handler is a system-wide component. Whenever a folder or printer is about to be moved, copied, deleted, or renamed, Explorer looks under the following keys in the registry for any copy hook handlers:

```
HKEY_CLASSES_ROOT\
    Directory\
        shellex\
            CopyHookHandlers\
```

and:

```
HKEY_CLASSES_ROOT\
    Printers\
        shellex\
            CopyHookHandlers\
```

All registered handlers are called one after the other until every handler has been called or until one of the handlers cancels the operation being performed. The shell loads the component directly and calls `ICopyHook::CopyCallback`, passing in all the values the handler will need in order to make a decision about the operation in question. These values include such things as the source of the operation (a pathname or printer name), the destination (where the object is being moved, what it is being renamed, etc.), and the type of operation being performed (moving, deleting, copying, or renaming).

The copy hook handler takes all of these values into consideration and returns one of three values. It will return `IDYES` if the operation is allowed, `IDNO` if it is not allowed, or `IDCANCEL` to prevent the current operation and cancel any remaining operations.

Because a copy hook handler is global, a few things must be taken into consideration. First, a copy hook handler cannot be associated with a specific folder or printer. It is up to the handler to determine if the operation taking place is of any interest. Second, it is possible to write a copy hook handler that conflicts with another handler. For instance, Handler A tells the shell to ignore the delete operation on the folder *c:\source_code*. Handler B says that it is okay. Guess who wins? The answer is Handler A. Once an operation has been disallowed, subsequent return values are ignored by the shell.

Copy Hook Handler Interface: ICopyHook

Now that we are somewhat familiar with copy hook handlers, let's talk about `ICopyHook`. This interface is the only interface a copy hook handler needs to implement. It contains one method, `CopyCallback`. Don't let the simplicity fool you, though. Implementing a copy hook handler is much more difficult than it seems at first glance (as you will soon see). As Table 9-1 shows, `ICopyHook` contains one method called `CopyCallback`. This is the only method ever called on a copy hook handler.

Table 9-1. ICopyHook

Method	Description
CopyCallback	Determines whether the shell will be allowed to move, copy, delete, or rename a folder or printer object.

The syntax of the **CopyCallback** method is as follows:

```
UINT CopyCallback(
    HWND hwnd,
    UINT wFunc,
    UINT wFlags,
    LPCSTR pszSrcFile,
    DWORD dwSrcAttribs,
    LPCSTR pszDestFile,
    DWORD dwDestAttribs
    );
```

Table 9-2 lists the parameters that the shell passes to the copy hook handler and their meaning.

Table 9-2. CopyCallback Parameters

Parameter	Datatype	Description
hwnd	HWND	Handle to a window that the copy hook handler should use to display any user-interface elements.
wFunc	UINT	Operation to be performed (see Table 9-3).
wFlags	UINT	This value can be ignored for copy hook handlers.
pszSrcFile	LPCSTR/ LPCWSTR	Address of a string that contains the name of the source folder or printer.
dwSrcAttribs	DWORD	Attributes of the source folder or printer (see Table 9-3).
pszDestFile	LPCSTR/ LPCWSTR	Address of a string that contains the name of the destination folder or printer.
dwDestAttribs	DWORD	Attributes of the source folder or printer. These can be any of the file attribute flags that begin with FILE_ ATTRIBUTE_* and are available from the API Viewer.

Table 9-3. wFunc Values

Name	Description
FO_COPY	Copy
FO_MOVE	Move
FO_DELETE	Delete
FO_RENAME	Rename

CopyCallback can return one of three values:

IDYES

>   The operation is allowed.

IDNO

>   Prevents the operation on this folder. The shell can continue with any other operations that are pending.

IDCANCEL

>   Prevents the current operation and cancels all pending operations.

The IDL listing for both ICopyHookA and ICopyHookW is shown in Example 9-1.

Example 9-1. ICopyHook Interface

```
typedef enum {
    FO_MOVE   = 0x0001,
    FO_COPY   = 0x0002,
    FO_DELETE = 0x0003,
    FO_RENAME = 0x0004
} FO;

[
    uuid(000214EF-0000-0000-C000-000000000046),
    helpstring("ICopyHookA Interface"),
    odl
]
interface ICopyHookA : IUnknown
{
    HRESULT CopyCallback([in] HWND hwnd,
                         [in] UINT wFunc,
                         [in] UINT wFlags,
                         [in] LPCSTRVB pszSrcFile,
                         [in] DWORD dwSrcAttribs,
                         [in] LPCSTRVB pszDestFile,
                         [in] DWORD dwDestAttribs);
}


[
    uuid(000214FC-0000-0000-C000-000000000046),
    helpstring("ICopyHookW Interface"),
    odl
]
interface ICopyHookW : IUnknown
{
    HRESULT CopyCallback([in] HWND hwnd,
                         [in] UINT wFunc,
                         [in] UINT wFlags,
                         [in] LPCWSTRVB pszSrcFile,
                    [in] DWORD dwSrcAttribs,
                         [in] LPCWSTRVB pszDestFile,
                         [in] DWORD dwDestAttribs);
}
```

Implementing ICopyHook

Before we begin implementation of ICopyHook, we need to add a new class to the RadEx project called *clsCopyHook*. The class needs to implement both ICopyHookA and ICopyHookW:

```
'clsCopyHook.cls

Implements ICopyHookA
Implements ICopyHookW
```

Also, the address of CopyCallback for both versions of ICopyHook will need to be swapped out in the vtable. We have to do this because CopyCallback will need to return one of three values: IDYES, IDNO, or IDCANCEL. This code, which should be very familiar to you by now, is shown in Example 9-2.

Example 9-2. Class_Initialize Event for Copy Hook Handler

```
'clsCopyHook.cls

Private m_pOldCopyCallbackA As Long
Private m_pOldCopyCallbackW As Long

Private Sub Class_Initialize()

    Dim pCopyHookA As ICopyHookA
    Set pCopyHookA = Me

    m_pOldCopyCallbackA = SwapVtableEntry( _
                    ObjPtr(pCopyHookA), _
                    4, _
                    AddressOf CopyCallbackA)

    Dim pCopyHookW As ICopyHookW
    Set pCopyHookW = Me

    m_pOldCopyCallbackW = SwapVtableEntry( _
                    ObjPtr(pCopyHookW), _
                    4, _
                    AddressOf CopyCallbackW)
End Sub
```

The preceding code is something we've seen before.

All that remains now (this is a lie, of course) is to implement CopyCallbackA and CopyCallbackW. For now, our copy hook handler will do nothing but display a message box that says "Access Denied" and then it will return IDNO. Later, we will reimplement the function to display all of the parameters passed in by the shell.

Example 9-3 shows our implementation of CopyCallback. The code is self-explanatory. All it does is display a message and return IDNO. All of the parameters to the method are ignored (for now).

Example 9-3. CopyCallback Implementation

```
Public Const IDCANCEL = 2
Public Const IDYES = 6
Public Const IDNO = 7

Public Function CopyCallbackA(ByVal this As ICopyHookA, _
                              ByVal hwnd As hwnd, _
                              ByVal wFunc As UINT, _
                              ByVal wFlags As UINT, _
                              ByVal pszSrcFile As LPCSTRVB, _
                              ByVal dwSrcAttribs As DWORD, _
                              ByVal pszDestFile As LPCSTRVB, _
                              ByVal dwDestAttribs As DWORD) As Long

    MsgBox "Access Denied", vbOKOnly, "CopyCallbackA"
    CopyCallbackA = IDNO

End Function

Public Function CopyCallbackW(ByVal this As ICopyHookW, _
                              ByVal hwnd As hwnd, _
                              ByVal wFunc As UINT, _
                              ByVal wFlags As UINT, _
                              ByVal pszSrcFile As LPCWSTRVB, _
                              ByVal dwSrcAttribs As DWORD, _
                              ByVal pszDestFile As LPCWSTRVB, _
                              ByVal dwDestAttribs As DWORD) As Long

    MsgBox "Access Denied", vbOKOnly, "CopyCallbackW"
    CopyCallbackW = IDNO

End Function
```

We are ready to compile the component. After you finish compiling, all that is left to do is to register the component.

Registering Copy Hook Handlers

Copy hook handlers are registered in two locations, depending on whether they are for shell folders or printer objects.

If the handler is for a shell folder, it is registered like so:

```
HKEY_CLASSES_ROOT\
    Directory\
        shellex\
            CopyHookHandlers\
                {Copy Hook Name} = {CSLID}
```

If the handler is for a printer object, it is registered in the following location:

```
HKEY_CLASSES_ROOT\
    Printers\
```

```
shellex\
     CopyHookHandlers\
          {Copy Hook Name} = {CSLID}
```

{*Copy Hook Name*} can be any name that you wish, and {*CLSID*} is, of course, the class identifier of the copy hook handler.

Also, both types of copy hook handlers need to be registered as approved shell extensions at the following location:

```
HKEY_LOCAL_MACHINE\
     Software\
          Microsoft\
               Windows\
                    CurrentVersion\
                         Shell Extensions\
                              Approved = {CLSID}
```

Example 9-3 contains the registry script that will register the copy hook handler developed in this chapter under the **Directory** key. Remember, when entering registry scripts, lines enclosed in square brackets must be on one line:

```
REGEDIT4

[HKEY_CLASSES_ROOT\Directory\shellex\CopyHookHandlers\RadCopyHook]
@ = "{FAE14EFA-03DA-11D3-BB7C-444553540000}"

[HKEY_LOCAL_MACHINE\Software\Microsoft\Windows\CurrentVersion\Shell Extensions\
Approved]
"{FAE14EFA-03DA-11D3-BB7C-444553540000}" = "RAD Copy Hook"
```

Testing the Handler

We're going to do something a little different in this chapter. We're going to test the handler we have just created. Why? Because it doesn't work. Oh, we wrote it correctly; it just doesn't work. And it's not even our fault. Let's take a look.

First, restart the shell. Now, move a folder somewhere on your system. You should see the dialog shown in Figure 9-1.

Figure 9-1. The first attempt to move a folder

Everything looks good so far. "So what's the problem?" you ask. Move the folder back to its original location, and then you'll see.

Boom!

As you can see from Figure 9-2, the component crashes the shell the second time around.

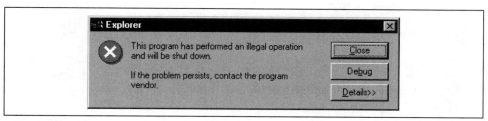

Figure 9-2. A second, unsuccessful attempt to move a folder

If you have compiled RadEx with symbolic debugging info and you have Visual C++ installed on your machine, Windows will give you the option to debug the component. Looking at a bunch of assembly code won't really do the average programmer any good, but the debugger does give you the option to look at the call stack. The call stack will show you where the crash occurred and what functions were called before it. Typically, when the copy hook handler we have created crashes, the call stack looks something like this:

```
0045fe24()
SHELL32! 7fd1f771()
SHELL32! 7fd1cdd9()
SHELL32! 7fd1de1a()
SHELL32! 7fd1ec79()
```

The function specified by address `0045fe24()` is located in Explorer. You know this because the debugger will tell you that the exception occurred in Explorer when it loaded. As you can see, the previous four functions are somewhere in *shell32.dll*. What this means is that the crash occurred nowhere near our code. But that still doesn't mean it's not our fault. Let's examine one more thing before we jump to any conclusions.

Let's look at some of the values the shell passes in to the copy hook handler on the first pass (when the crash doesn't happen). This will require a small rewrite of `CopyCallbackA`. It should now look as follows:

```
Public Function CopyCallbackA(ByVal this As ICopyHookA, _
                    ByVal hwnd As hwnd, _
                    ByVal wFunc As UINT, _
                    ByVal wFlags As UINT, _
                    ByVal pszSrcFile As LPCSTRVB, _
                    ByVal dwSrcAttribs As DWORD, _
                    ByVal pszDestFile As LPCSTRVB, _
                    ByVal dwDestAttribs As DWORD) As Long
```

```
Dim strOut As String * 255

StrFromPtrA pszSrcFile, strOut
MsgBox strOut

CopyCallbackA = IDNO

End Function
```

If you are testing under Windows NT or Windows 2000, change *StrFromPtrA* to *StrFromPtrW*.

After you compile this code, restart the shell, and move a folder somewhere on your system. You should see a message box like the one in Figure 9-3 that displays the name of the folder you just attempted to move.

Figure 9-3. Displaying the name of the folder to be moved

The *pszSrcFile* parameter is pointing to valid data. Also, if you were to check the *hwnd* parameter, you would also find that it is equal to the handle assigned to Explorer. This is easily verified by running Spy++, a utility that ships with Visual Studio. Another clue is that there is still a reference count on the component. This is easily determined by putting a **MsgBox** statement in the Class_Terminate event of the handler. It will not be displayed, meaning the component is still loaded in memory.

What does this all mean? For one thing it means that our component is getting called at least one time with valid data. What is happening after the first call to the handler is anyone's guess.

The short of it is that there is nothing wrong with the component itself, but there seems to be some erroneous handling of the **ICopyHook** interface pointer after the first call.

The Workaround

Fortunately, there is a workaround, and we don't have to modify any of the code we have just written. Unfortunately, we will have to use an additional component written in C++ to accomplish the task. This certainly doesn't look good, seeing that this is a VB book, but at this point, we are out of options (several more bizarre attempts to handle this error were made before this chapter was written, but nothing else seemed to work).

The saving grace is that the component can be used with any copy hook handler that you write. It's completely generic. This component is called CopyHook.Factory, and it lives in *copyhook.dll.*

 For those of you who are familiar with C++, the code for this DLL is included with the source for this chapter and can be downloaded from *http://vb.oreilly.com.*

Here's how it works: CopyHook.Factory implements both `ICopyHookA` and `ICopyHookW`. It, and not VB, will be responsible for loading our copy hook handler. The shell will load CopyHook.Factory and call `CopyCallback`. CopyHook. Factory's implementation of `CopyCallback` will load our component and call `CopyCallback` on our implementation, passing it whatever parameters the shell passed it. CopyHook.Factory will simply return whatever value our `CopyCallback` implementation returns. Basically, CopyHook.Factory is a wrapper around our component.

Instead of adding the CLSID of our copy hook handler under the **Directory** or **Printers** key in the registry, we will add the CLSID of CopyHook.Factory, regardless of how many copy hook handlers we have installed:

```
HKEY_CLASSES_ROOT\
    Directory\
        shellex\
            CopyHookHandlers\
              CopyHook_1 = {CLSID-CopyHook.Factory}
                                  CopyHook_2 = {CLSID-CopyHook.Factory}
                                  CopyHook_3 = {CLSID-CopyHook.Factory}
```

As you can see, every copy hook handler registered here is pointing to the same component, CopyHook.Factory.

When CopyHook.Factory is loaded the first time (in this example, when the shell calls CopyHook_1), it looks under the following key for the available copy hook handlers:

```
HKEY_CLASSES_ROOT\
    CopyHook.Factory\
        CopyHookHandlers\
            {CLSID-CopyHook_1}
            {CLSID-CopyHook_2}
            {CLSID-CopyHook_3}
```

These are the CLSID identifiers of the copy hook handlers that have been written in VB. (Actually, they could be written in anything. It doesn't matter.)

It will then enumerate all of the CLSIDs it finds under this key and store the list internally in a linked list. As the shell calls each copy hook handler (CopyHook_2, CopyHook_3, etc.), CopyHook.Factory will load the component next in its internal list and pass the parameters that were given to it by the shell.

Revisiting CopyCallback

Now that our problem has been solved, let's implement `CopyCallback` for real this time (see Example 9-4). This implementation will merely display a message box that contains all of the parameters involved in the operation. Not quite practical, but a good example nonetheless.

Example 9-4. Final Implementation of CopyCallback

```
Public Function CopyCallbackA(ByVal this As ICopyHookA, _
                              ByVal hwnd As hwnd, _
                              ByVal wFunc As UINT, _
                              ByVal wFlags As UINT, _
                              ByVal pszSrcFile As LPCSTRVB, _
                              ByVal dwSrcAttribs As DWORD, _
                              ByVal pszDestFile As LPCSTRVB, _
                              ByVal dwDestAttribs As DWORD) As Long

    Dim strMsg As String
    Dim sTemp As String * MAX_PATH
    Dim sOut As String

    strMsg = "HWND: " & hwnd & vbCrLf
    strMsg = strMsg & "wFunc: " & wFunc & vbCrLf
    strMsg = strMsg & "wFlags: " & wFlags & vbCrLf
    strMsg = strMsg & "wFunc: " & wFunc & vbCrLf

    StrFromPtrA pszSrcFile, sTemp
    sOut = Left(sTemp, InStr(sTemp, vbNullChar) - 1)

    strMsg = strMsg & "Source: " & sOut & vbCrLf
    strMsg = strMsg & "Source Attributes: " & dwSrcAttribs & vbCrLf

    StrFromPtrA pszDestFile, sTemp
    sOut = Left(sTemp, InStr(sTemp, vbNullChar) - 1)

    strMsg = strMsg & "Destination: " & sOut & vbCrLf

    strMsg = strMsg & "Dest Attributes: " & dwDestAttribs & vbCrLf

    MsgBox strMsg

    CopyCallbackA = IDYES
```

Example 9-4. Final Implementation of CopyCallback (continued)

```
End Function

Public Function CopyCallbackW(ByVal this As ICopyHookW, _
                             ByVal hwnd As hwnd, _
                             ByVal wFunc As UINT, _
                             ByVal wFlags As UINT, _
                             ByVal pszSrcFile As LPCWSTRVB, _
                             ByVal dwSrcAttribs As DWORD, _
                             ByVal pszDestFile As LPCWSTRVB, _
                             ByVal dwDestAttribs As DWORD) As Long

    Dim strMsg As String
    Dim sTemp As String * MAX_PATH
    Dim sOut As String

    strMsg = "HWND: " & hwnd & vbCrLf
    strMsg = strMsg & "wFunc: " & wFunc & vbCrLf
    strMsg = strMsg & "wFlags: " & wFlags & vbCrLf
    strMsg = strMsg & "wFunc: " & wFunc & vbCrLf

    StrFromPtrW pszSrcFile, sTemp
    sOut = Left(sTemp, InStr(sTemp, vbNullChar) - 1)

    strMsg = strMsg & "Source: " & sOut & vbCrLf
    strMsg = strMsg & "Source Attributes: " & dwSrcAttribs & vbCrLf

    StrFromPtrW pszDestFile, sTemp
    sOut = Left(sTemp, InStr(sTemp, vbNullChar) - 1)

    strMsg = strMsg & "Destination: " & sOut & vbCrLf

    strMsg = strMsg & "Dest Attributes: " & dwDestAttribs & vbCrLf

    MsgBox strMsg

    CopyCallbackW = IDYES

End Function
```

Reregister Everything

To finish things up, we need to make sure everything is properly registered. So, in the registry, remove all the entries you previously made under the **Directory** key when we first registered the component. You can also remove the entry under the approved shell extensions key as well.

Next, register *copyhook.dll*. When this component is registered, one entry for CopyHook.Factory is added under the **Directory** key, and one entry is added to the **Printers** key. If you require more copy handlers in the future, you can add additional references to CopyHook.Factory under either key.

Now, the only thing left to do is to add the CLSID for our VB component at the following location:

```
HKEY_CLASSES_ROOT\
    CopyHook.Factory\
        CopyHookHandlers\
            {FAE14EFA-03DA-11D3-BB7C-444553540000}
```

If you wish, you can run the following registry script, which will handle this task for you:

```
REGEDIT4

[HKEY_CLASSES_ROOT\CopyHook.Factory\CopyHookHandlers\{FAE14EFA-03DA-11D3-BB7C-
444553540000}]
@ = "Rad Copy Hook"
```

Restart the shell, and you are all set.

10

InfoTip Handler

InfoTip handlers display tool tips, or "info" tips, for a file object on a per-instance basis. You can view this behavior for yourself if you have Microsoft Word installed on your machine. Find a *.doc* file and select it. Hold the cursor over the file and an InfoTip displaying the author of the document should appear momentarily. Figure 10-1 demonstrates the InfoTip in action.

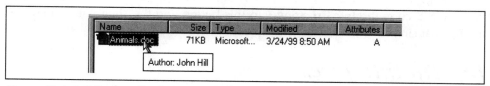

Figure 10-1. InfoTip handler for Microsoft Word

InfoTip handlers are usually not considered shell extensions (the Platform SDK says nothing about them), but they are, in fact, just that. They are also very easy to implement.

InfoTip handlers implement `IPersistFile` (we only have to implement the `Load` method) and `IQueryInfo`. `IQueryInfo` has two methods, but we need to implement only one of them. There are no hoops to jump through this time around. Everything is very straightforward. What a nice change! This chapter will also end our discussion of shell extensions and the RadEx project on which we have been working in the last seven chapters. So let's get on with it! The InfoTip handler we create will display the animal type associated with the *.rad* file in the format "Type: (Animal Type)."

How InfoTip Handlers Work

When the cursor is placed over a file object in Explorer, the shell checks the registry under the following key to see if there are any registered InfoTip handlers for that particular file object:

```
HKEY_CLASSES_ROOT\
    .rad\
        shellex\
            {00021500-0000-0000-C000-000000000046}
```

The *.rad* key is replaceable with the file object of your choice, of course. But notice the CLSID. This key will be the same for every InfoTip handler that you write. It is the GUID of `IQueryInfo`, the primary interface that is implemented by all InfoTip handlers. Also, notice that unlike the other shell extensions, this handler is registered under the file association key, as opposed to the application identifier.

If a handler exists, the shell passes the name of the file object to the handler via `IPersistFile::Load`. This allows the InfoTip handler to examine the contents of the file, extract pertinent information, and construct a meaningful InfoTip for the shell to display.

After `Load`, the shell calls `IQueryInfo::GetInfoTip`, passing in a buffer. The handler will copy the InfoTip string into this buffer, and the shell will display the tip. It's that simple.

InfoTip Interfaces

InfoTip handlers implement two interfaces: `IPersistFile` and `IQueryInfo`. We have discussed `IPersistFile` several times already, most notably in Chapter 5, *Icon Handlers*, so we will jump straight into `IQueryInfo`. Let's examine the interface definition, which is shown in Example 10-1. Table 10-1 gives a brief description of each of the methods.

Example 10-1. IQueryInfo

```
//------------------------------------------------------
// IQueryInfo
//------------------------------------------------------
    [
        uuid(00021500-0000-0000-C000-000000000046),
        helpstring("IQueryInfo Interface"),
        odl
    ]
    interface IQueryInfo : IUnknown
    {
        HRESULT GetInfoTip([in] DWORD dwFlags,
```

Example 10-1. IQueryInfo (continued)

```
                         [in,out] LPWSTRVB *ppwszTip);

        HRESULT GetInfoFlags([in,out] DWORD *pdwFlags);
    }
```

Table 10-1. IQueryInfo

Method	Description
GetInfoFlags[a]	Retrieves the information flags for an item.
GetInfoTip	Gets the InfoTip text for the file object.

[a] This method is not currently used—not here, and according to the Platform SDK, not anywhere.

`IQueryInfo` is a very basic interface that contains two methods: `GetInfoTip` and `GetInfoFlags`. `GetInfoFlags` is not currently used by the shell, so it will not be discussed. That leaves `GetInfoTip`.

GetInfoTip

`GetInfoTip` is called by the shell to request an InfoTip string from the handler. Its syntax is:

```
    HRESULT GetInfoTip( DWORD dwFlags, LPWSTR *ppwszTip );
```

with the following parameters:

dwFlags

> [in] This parameter is not used currently by the shell.

ppwszTip

> [in, out] The address of a wide-character string that will receive the pointer to the InfoTip string.

If you haven't figured it out yet, this is the simplest interface in the book. All we need to worry about is one method and one parameter. The shell is basically giving us a buffer and saying, "Put a string in here!" That's all that is happening.

The Project

We start by adding a class called clsQueryInfo to the RadEx project. The class implements `IQueryInfo` and `IPersistFile`. Example 10-2 is the project listing. It's really short, so let's walk through the whole thing.

Example 10-2. Project Listing

```
'clsQueryInfo.cls

Implements IPersistFile
```

Example 10-2. Project Listing (continued)

```
Implements IQueryInfo

Private m_sFile As String

Private Sub IPersistFile_Load(
    ByVal pszFileName As VBShellLib.LPCOLESTR, _
    ByVal dwMode As VBShellLib.DWORD)

    m_sFile = Space(255)
    CopyMemory ByVal StrPtr(m_sFile), ByVal pszFileName, Len(m_sFile)

End Sub

Private Sub IQueryInfo_GetInfoTip(
    ByVal dwFlags As VBShellLib.DWORD, _
    ppwszTip As VBShellLib.LPWSTRVB)

    Dim b() As Byte

    Dim sTemp As String
    sTemp = Space(255)

    Dim sMsg As String

    GetPrivateProfileString "Animal", _
                            "Type", _
                            "Unknown", _
                            sTemp, _
                            Len(sTemp), _
                            m_sFile


    sMsg = "Type: " & sTemp & vbCrLf

    ppwszTip = StrPtr(sMsg)

End Sub
```

First, let's get `IPersistFile::Load` out of the way. This should be very familiar
to you, since we have already implemented `Load` for icon handlers, drop handlers, and data handlers. InfoTip handlers are no different: we simply copy the
name of the selected file, which is passed to the `Load` method in the
pszFileName argument, to a local variable, *m_sFile*.

To complete the implementation of `IPersistFile`, you can just add the following line of code for the remainder of the methods:

```
Err.Raise E_NOTIMPL
```

After you have implemented the remaining methods of `IPersistFile`, we can
begin implementing `IQueryInfo`. And for once, we can breathe easy, because

`IQueryInfo` could not be simpler to implement. Here's what happens: the shell calls `GetInfoTip` and passes us a pointer to a buffer that we can copy the InfoTip into.

The pointer to the tool tip function is declared with the [`in, out`] attribute, so we can just assign the pointer to our InfoTip right to ***ppwszTip***. We don't have to use *CopyMemory*. That's all there is to it.

Registration and Operation

Well, we actually have to register the handler, and that's done a little bit differently than in previous chapters. The handler is registered under the file association key, not the application identifier. Also, the handler is not named. It uses the CLSID for `IQueryInfo` as the key name. The default value of this key points to our InfoTip handler. Figure 10-2 shows the appropriate entries.

```
HKEY_CLASSES_ROOT
└── .rad
    └── ShellEx
        └── {00021500-0000-0000-C000-000000000046}
            (Default)    "{1CBC449C-065A-11D3-BB7C-444553540000}"
```

Figure 10-2. Registering InfoTip handler

This is the only entry that needs to be made for the InfoTip handler. It does not have to be added to the approved shell extensions list. The following registry script will register the example for this chapter:

```
REGEDIT4

[HKEY_CLASSES_ROOT\.rad]
@ = "radfile"

[HKEY_CLASSES_ROOT\.rad\shellex\
{00021500-0000-0000-C000-000000000046}]
@ = "{1CBC449C-065A-11D3-BB7C-444553540000}"
```

For some strange reason, the InfoTip handler will not be displayed if the shell is in web view. But have no fear, the tip is displayed in the lefthand portion of the view.

Before trying out the handler, you should restart the shell.

III

Namespace Extensions

11

Namespace Extensions

The Windows namespace is similar to the directory structure of a filesystem, but in addition to files, it also contains other objects, like printers, storage devices, and network resources. As Figure 11-1 shows, this namespace is a single hierarchy that begins with the Desktop and contains everything that is visible within Explorer. Namespace extensions provide the means for you to insert your own objects into this hierarchy. This allows you to browse your data as if it were just another object in the system, but it also provides the means for you to manipulate that data in a manner that is specific to your needs.

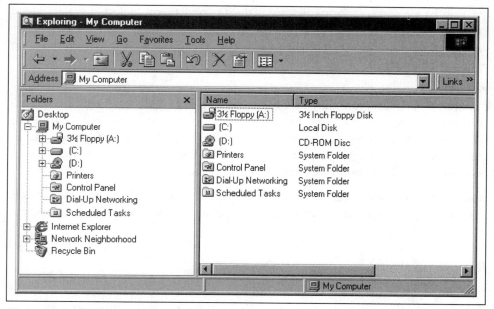

Figure 11-1. The namespace

Consider the desktop for a moment (see Figure 11-1). The Desktop contains My Computer, Network Neighborhood, My Briefcase, and the Recycle Bin. My Computer in turn contains Printers, Control Panel, and Dial-Up Networking. If you examine the registry's `HKEY_CLASSES_ROOT\CLSID` key for each of these objects, you will see that each of them is mapped to *shell32.dll*. In other words, these are all namespace extensions. Actually, everything you can see that is displayed in Explorer is being handled by a namespace extension—even the directories and files. Nothing is built-in. Explorer is literally a shell that's a namespace browser.

Namespace Fundamentals

The topic of namespaces is monumental, to say the least. This chapter is the longest in the book; even so, consider this a crash course. But before we dive in and start discussing how namespace extensions work, let's spend some more time discussing some of the fundamentals.

Rooted vs. Non-rooted

There are two types of namespace extensions: rooted and non-rooted. There is no difference code-wise between these two types. The difference is just how they are used.

A *rooted extension* has its own root. In other words, you can't navigate to a level above it, and only its branches are available. For an example of this, right-click on the task bar and select Properties from the Context menu. Select the Start Menu Programs tab and then press Advanced. A rooted view of the Start menu will be displayed with the Start menu selected (see Figure 11-2). Notice that the level-up button on the tool bar is disabled.

Probably everything you can find discussing rooted extensions uses this same example. That's how rare they are. But to be fair, a rooted view might be good if you are creating a namespace extension that allows you to navigate into a file (such as a *.zip* file or an Access database), and "upward" navigation from it makes little sense. But then again, even this is arguable. A rooted namespace should only be used if your data really does need to stand alone.

Non-rooted extensions, on the other hand, are aware of the entire namespace. Their root is the desktop. You can freely navigate to other parts of the namespace in a non-rooted view.

Junction Points

A namespace extension for all intents and purposes is a folder. Therefore, it needs to have a specific location in the shell. This location is called a *junction point*.

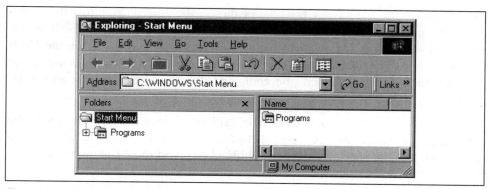

Figure 11-2. Rooted view of Start menu

There are four ways to create a junction point:

- Associate the namespace extension with a file type.

- Use *desktop.ini* in a directory.

- Use a directory with a CLSID.

- Associate a folder with an existing namespace.

I'll now talk about each of these methods in detail.

Using a file type

Suppose you want to create a namespace extension that allows you to actually navigate into the contents of a file. Several file types that could take advantage of this come to mind—*.zip*, *.cab*, *.ini*, and *.mdb* files, to name just a few. These files contain data that exists in a format that could easily be viewed hierarchically within the namespace.

Associating a namespace extension with a file involves making a few entries in the registry under the file's application identifier key. Let's pretend we are associating a namespace extension with the *.rad* file type. The registry entries involved would look like this:

```
HKEY_CLASSES_ROOT\
    \radfile
        \shell
            \{verb}
                \command = "explorer /root, {CLSID}, %1"
```

The value **verb** can be any thing we want. You might choose "Browse," "Navigate," or something similar. Whatever you choose, this value will be displayed in the context menu for the file object. But the system defines seven of these as canonical verbs: **open**, **find**, **explore**, **print**, **printto**, **openas**, and **properties**. Each of these verbs, except for **printto**, corresponds to a context menu item for the file. (The advantage of these canonical verbs is that they automatically appear in mixed case and in the default language used on the host system.) You can also define the verb that is automatically executed when the file is double-clicked. The default value of the **shell** key is where this done. If no default value has been defined, the command defined by the verb **open** will be executed.

The **/root** command line parameter tells Explorer to use a rooted view with the namespace extension as the root. *{CLSID}*, of course, is the CLSID of the namespace that the shell will use for the file object, and the **%1** is merely a placeholder for the filename Explorer will pass to the namespace extension.

Using a directory desktop.ini

Namespace extensions can be associated with a physical directory in the filesystem. You probably have seen this before without realizing that it was being done by a namespace extension. Consider the following folders: *Fonts*, *Downloaded Program Files*, and *History* (each of these is a subdirectory under Windows). Each of the folders has a physical location in the filesystem. But instead of containing a standard file list like a normal directory, they contain a custom view that is handled by a namespace extension.

There are two ways to associate a namespace extension with a physical directory in the filesystem—that is, to have a designated namespace extension (rather than the default one) handle the display of filesystem information. The first technique involves creating the directory and placing a hidden file in the directory called *desktop.ini*. The basic format of the file is as follows:

```
[.ShellClassInfo]
CLSID={CLSID}
```

The display name of this folder can be set by changing the default value of the following key:

```
HKEY_CLASSES_ROOT
    \CLSID
        \{CLSID} = "Folder Name"
```

Additionally, you can specify the default icon for this folder with the following key:

```
HKEY_CLASSES_ROOT
    \CLSID
        \{CLSID}
            \DefaultIcon = "filename, icon index"
```

where *icon index* is the zero-based position of the icon in the file named *filename*.

Consider the folder called *My Documents*; it contains a *desktop.ini* file that looks like the following:

```
[.ShellClassInfo]
CLSID={450d8fba-ad25-11d0-98a8-0800361b1103}
InfoTip=Stores your documents, graphics, and other files.
```

The `[.ShellClassInfo]` section can also contain the following additional entries:

ConfirmFileOp

When this value is set to 0, the "You Are Deleting a System Folder" message will not be displayed when you attempt to delete or move the folder.

NoSharing

Setting this value to 1 prevents the folder from being shared.

IconFile

This is the name of the custom icon file for the folder. Files with the *.ico* and *.bmp* extensions are acceptable. It is also possible to specify an *.exe* or a *.dll*. For the latter option, it is necessary to use the `IconIndex` setting as well.

IconIndex

The zero-based index of an icon if it is contained in a *.dll* or *.exe* (which is specified by `IconFile`).

InfoTip

Allows you to create an InfoTip for the folder.

Using a directory and the CLSID

The second method involving associating a directory with a namespace is very simple and requires no registry settings. You merely create a folder with the following naming convention:

```
FolderName.{CLSID}
```

The CLSID portion of this name will be invisible once the folder is created.

Here's a neat trick that demonstrates this idea. Right-click on the Start button in the task bar and select Explore. Create a folder with the following name:

```
Control Panel.{21EC2020-3AEA-1069-A2DD-08002B30309D}
```

This will add the Control Panel to your Start menu, as Figure 11-3 demonstrates.

Using an existing namespace

The last method for creating a junction point involves inserting the extension into an existing namespace—into Desktop, My Computer, Network Neighborhood, or Internet Explorer.

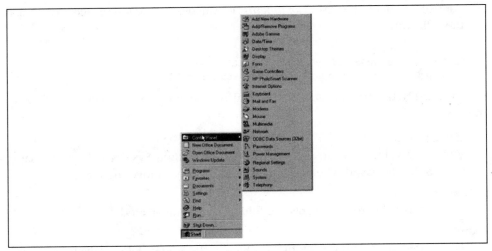

Figure 11-3. Control Panel namespace from Start menu

To insert a namespace extension in one of these locations, you need to find the following key:

```
HKEY_LOCAL_MACHINE\
    \Software
        \Microsoft
            \Windows
                \CurrentVersion
                    \Explorer
                        \Namespace
                            \Namespace
                                \{CLSID} = "Folder Name"
```

The value *Namespace* (the key that's a direct subkey of **Explorer**) should be replaced with one of the following values: **Desktop**, **MyComputer**, **NetworkNeighborhood**, **ControlPanel**, **RemoteComputer**, or **Internet**. *{CLSID}*, of course, should be replaced with the CLSID of your component that is implementing the namespace extension.

Explorer Architecture

As Figure 11-4 illustrates, there are five distinct parts to Explorer: the menu, the toolbar, the tree view, the content pane (or view), and the status bar.

When Explorer finds a namespace extension at a junction point (as defined in any of the four ways discussed in the "Junction Points" section earlier in this chapter), it loads the extension and queries for **IShellFolder**. This interface represents the folder in the tree view and basically acts as a liaison to the rest of the namespace extension. Everything a namespace extension needs is generated through this interface.

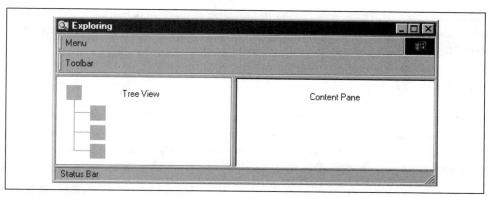

Figure 11-4. Explorer architecture

Explorer then asks the extension for an ISHellView interface. This interface is provided by ISHellFolder and is responsible for creating the view window in the content pane. The view in turn is responsible for displaying the data. Something that might not be so obvious is that Explorer *does not* provide the list view that is usually found in the content pane. It is the responsibility of the object implementing ISHellView to create this window. Also, it must be noted that a namespace extension must be prepared to create multiple views. For example, Explorer provides five views: Large Icons, Small Icons, Details, List, and View as Web Page. But you can also provide custom views. Consider the Fonts namespace extension. It provides a view called List Fonts by Similarity that allows you to see groups of fonts that are similar in appearance. Because several views are possible, the object implementing ISHellFolder is distinct from the object implementing ISHellView. This is a one-to-many relationship.

Explorer provides the object implementing ISHellView with a reference to an interface called ISHellBrowser. This interface can be used by the view object to manipulate the menu, toolbar, and status bar of Explorer to add new menu items and toolbar buttons, and to manage text in the status bar.

Once the content pane has been made ready to receive data, the shell asks the namespace extension to enumerate the contents of the folder. This is handled by a third object that implements the IEnumIDList interface. This object is separate from ISHellFolder because, like ISHellView, it must be called multiple times throughout the lifetime of the extension.

Every time a branch of the extension is opened, an instance of IEnumIDList is created. In the tree view, the enumerated items that have the "folder" attribute are displayed. If these folders have the "has subfolders" attribute, a "+" node is displayed. The "+" nodes, of course, can be opened, and the entire process begins again.

`IShellFolder` provides services to handle the display text for each item. Additional user interface elements such as icons, context menus, and InfoTips are provided for as well.

The PIDL

Explorer needs a way to uniquely identify each item in the namespace unambiguously in relation to other items in the namespace. It must be able to enumerate these items in a consistent, generic manner, even though these items represent a wide variety of data. It does this with a PIDL.

A PIDL is a pointer to an item identifier list, or `ITEMIDLIST`. An `ITEMIDLIST` is an array of shell item IDs. Each one of these identifiers is an array of bytes that contains information that is specific to the namespace extension using it.

How can Explorer use PIDLs if they are different in respect to every extension? Well, as it turns out PIDLs are pretty simple creatures. Let's look at how a PIDL is defined, and you'll be able to see this for yourself. Here is what an `ITEMIDLIST` (just remember a PIDL is a pointer to one of these) looks like, as defined by the Platform SDK:

```
typedef struct _ITEMIDLIST {
    SHITEMID mkid;
} ITEMIDLIST, * LPITEMIDLIST;
```

As you can see, an `ITEMIDLIST` is nothing more than a structure that contains one member of type `SHITEMID`. This structure looks like so:

```
typedef struct _SHITEMID {
    USHORT cb;
    BYTE abID[1];
} SHITEMID, * LPSHITEMID;
```

The first member of `SHITEMID`, *cb*, contains the number of bytes of the `SHITEMID` structure. `SHITEMID` is a variable-length structure, and *cb* contains two bytes specifying its size. For those of you who have never done any C programming, you probably have never seen this technique before: the first member of a structure is used to define the total length of a variable-length structure. The *abID* parameter is not a pointer, of course, because it is only 1 byte. It is a placeholder. It marks the first byte of an unknown number of bytes. One member of a variable length structure contains the number of bytes that begins at the location `abID[0]`. This is an efficient way to maintain a collection (a linked list perhaps) of like structures that are of different sizes. Without this technique, you would have to reallocate memory like this:

```
typedef struct _SHITEMID {
    USHORT cb;
    BYTE abID[1024];
} SHITEMID, * LPSHITEMID;
```

This is very inefficient, because you may have one instance of this structure that contains 1024 bytes of data and several hundred that contain only 10 bytes. Also, you are limited as to how large your structure can be. Because SHITEMID is of variable length, it can be as large or as small as needed.

Anyway, the data that follows can be in any format that is required by the namespace extension. Well, almost, but we'll talk about that in a second. This format allows IEnumIDList to enumerate a list of PIDLs in a generic fashion.

A PIDL is just a pointer to one or more ITEMIDLISTs that is terminated by an empty ITEMIDLIST (two 0s). Some PIDLs point to only one ITEMIDLIST, followed by an empty ITEMIDLIST. These are called *simple* PIDLs. A PIDL that points to more than one ITEMIDLIST is called a *complex* PIDL. Regardless of the type, the last ITEMIDLIST must contain all NULL values. This is shown in Figure 11-5.

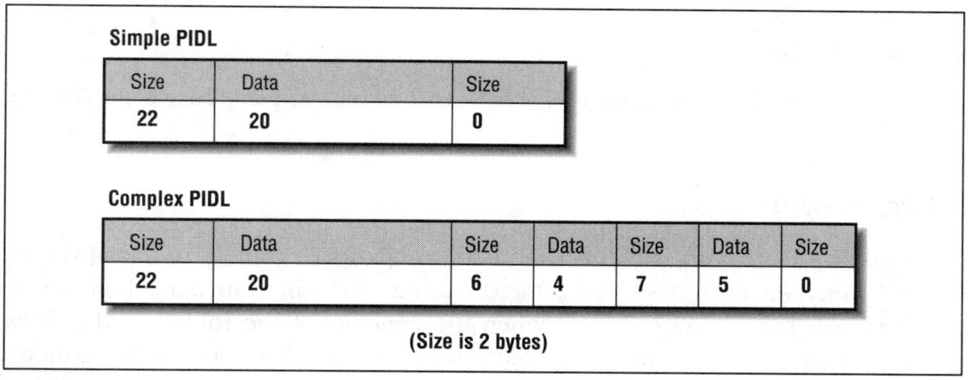

Simple PIDL

Size	Data	Size
22	20	0

Complex PIDL

Size	Data	Size	Data	Size	Data	Size
22	20	6	4	7	5	0

(Size is 2 bytes)

Figure 11-5. Simple and complex PIDLs

A PIDL always points to at least two ITEMIDLISTs (remember, there's always an empty ITEMIDLIST at the end). In other words, it's an array. So if you read something like "the last item in the PIDL," this means the last ITEMIDLIST in the array. So don't just think of a PIDL as a pointer to an ITEMIDLIST. It's easier to think about it in terms of an array, because that's what it really is. There is *never* just one ITEMIDLIST. Also, not to make things more confusing, but, by convention, the term PIDL is often used when referring to the underlying ITEMIDLIST structure. For instance, you'll never hear someone say, "What is the format of your ITEMIDLIST?" They'll just call it a PIDL. So when you read about the "format of a PIDL," you now know that what is being discussed is the ITEMIDLIST itself. With that said, let's talk about the format of a PIDL.

There is an important rule that must be followed when creating a PIDL. The data contained in your PIDLs (ITEMIDLISTs) *cannot contain pointers*. This is because PIDLs can be persisted (saved to disk) and then read back into memory at some point in the future (shortcut files are persisted ID lists). ITEMIDLISTs can also be copied into another memory block before they are used by Explorer. So a PIDL cannot contain a handle to an icon, for example; it must contain all the actual bits that make up the icon. A PIDL can't contain a pointer to a path, it must contain the actual path itself. Everything a PIDL needs to describe itself must be contained within it.

Namespace Interfaces

There are four primary interfaces that must be implemented when working with a namespace extension. These are:

- IPersistFolder
- IShellFolder
- IShellView
- IEnumIDList

Let's briefly discuss these interfaces. We'll go into more detail as we implement each one.

IPersistFolder

This interface is used to initialize shell folder objects. This interface contains one method inherited from IPersist, GetClassID, and one native method called Initialize. Initialize is used when the contents of the folder need a fully qualified PIDL in relation to the junction point of the extension. These methods are described in Table 11-1.

Table 11-1. IPersistFolder Methods

Method	Description
GetClassID	Returns the CLSID of the object implementing IPersistFolder.
Initialize	Instructs the object to initialize itself based on the PIDL that is passed in by the shell.

The IDL for IPersistFolder is shown in Example 11-1.

Example 11-1. IPersistFolder

```
typedef [public] long CLSID;
typedef [public] long LPCITEMIDLIST;

[
    uuid(000214ea-0000-0000-c000-000000000046),
    helpstring("IPersistFolder Interface"),
```

Example 11-1. IPersistFolder (continued)

```
    odl
]
interface IPersistFolder : IUnknown
{
    // IPersist methods
    HRESULT GetClassID([in, out] CLSID *lpClassID);

    // IPersistFolder methods
    HRESULT Initialize([in] LPCITEMIDLIST pidl);
}
```

GetClassID

This method returns the CLSID of the object implementing `IPersistFolder`. This method is inherited from `IPersist`, and its syntax is as follows:

```
    HRESULT GetClassID( CLSID *pClassID);
```

Its single parameter is:

pClassID

This is an [in, out] parameter that should contain the class identifier of the object that is implementing `IPersistFolder`.

Initialize

This tells the object to initialize itself based on the PIDL that is passed in. Its syntax is:

```
    HRESULT Initialize(LPCITEMIDLIST pidl);
```

with the following parameter:

pidl

Address of an `ITEMIDLIST` structure that contains the location of the folder.

When a folder's location in the namespace does not matter, this function can simply return S_OK.

IShellFolder

`IShellFolder` contains ten methods that are used to manage shell folders. This is really considered the primary interface of the namespace extension, because the shell uses this interface to communicate all of its requests to the extension object.

`IShellFolder` is responsible for creating references to `IShellView` for managing the view and to `IEnumIDList` for enumerating the folder's contents. In addition, `IShellFolder` provides references to `IExtractIcon` (so the shell can display icons for each item in the namespace) and to `IContextMenu` for any context menu support the namespace might need. The methods of `IShellFolder` are described in Table 11-2. Note that the methods that require vtable swapping are in boldface. Methods marked with an asterisk (*) do not need to be implemented for namespace extensions. Because we already have enough things to remember, we will focus only on the methods that require implementation.

Table 11-2. IShellFolder Methods

Method	Description
BindToObject	Returns the `IShellFolder` interface for the specified subfolder.
BindToStorage *	Not currently implemented.
CompareIDs	Determines the relative order of two file objects or folders, given their item identifier lists.
CreateViewObject	Creates a view object of the folder. This method is responsible for creating an instance of an object that implements the `IShellView` interface.
EnumObjects	Creates an instance of an object that implements the `IEnumIDList` interface. The primary function of this object is to enumerate the contents of a folder.
GetAttributesOf	Returns the attributes of the specified file object or subfolder. This method informs the shell whether an item is folder, has subfolders, etc.
GetDisplayNameOf	Returns the display name of a file object or subfolder.
GetUIObjectOf	Creates an interface that can be used to carry out operations on a file object or subfolder. Interfaces returned by this method include `IExtractIcon` and `IContextMenu`.
ParseDisplayName *	Translates a display name into an item identifier list.
SetNameOf *	Sets the display name of the specified file object or subfolder.

The IDL for `IShellFolder` is shown in Example 11-2.

Example 11-2. IShellFolder

```
// IShellFolder::GetDisplayNameOf/SetNameOf uFlags
typedef enum {
    SHGDN_NORMAL                = 0,
    SHGDN_INFOLDER              = 1,
    SHGDN_INCLUDE_NONFILESYS    = 0x2000,
    SHGDN_FORADDRESSBAR         = 0x4000,
    SHGDN_FORPARSING            = 0x8000,
} SHGNO;

// IShellFolder::EnumObjects
typedef enum {
    SHCONTF_FOLDERS             = 32,
    SHCONTF_NONFOLDERS          = 64,
    SHCONTF_INCLUDEHIDDEN       = 128,
} SHCONTF;
```

Example 11-2. IShellFolder (continued)

```
// IShellFolder::GetAttributesOf flags
typedef enum {
    SFGAO_CANCOPY           = 0x00000001,
    SFGAO_CANMOVE           = 0x00000002,
    SFGAO_CANLINK           = 0x00000004,
    SFGAO_CANRENAME         = 0x00000010,
    SFGAO_CANDELETE         = 0x00000020,
    SFGAO_HASPROPSHEET      = 0x00000040,
    SFGAO_DROPTARGET        = 0x00000100,
    SFGAO_CAPABILITYMASK    = 0x00000177,
    SFGAO_LINK              = 0x00010000,
    SFGAO_SHARE             = 0x00020000,
    SFGAO_READONLY          = 0x00040000,
    SFGAO_GHOSTED           = 0x00080000,
    SFGAO_HIDDEN            = 0x00080000,
    SFGAO_DISPLAYATTRMASK   = 0x000F0000,
    SFGAO_FILESYSANCESTOR   = 0x10000000,
    SFGAO_FOLDER            = 0x20000000,
    SFGAO_FILESYSTEM        = 0x40000000,
    SFGAO_HASSUBFOLDER      = 0x80000000,
    SFGAO_CONTENTSMASK      = 0x80000000,
    SFGAO_VALIDATE          = 0x01000000,
    SFGAO_REMOVABLE         = 0x02000000,
    SFGAO_COMPRESSED        = 0x04000000,
    SFGAO_BROWSABLE         = 0x08000000,
    SFGAO_NONENUMERATED     = 0x00100000,
    SFGAO_NEWCONTENT        = 0x00200000,
}SFGAO;

[
    uuid(000214e6-0000-0000-c000-000000000046),
    helpstring("IShellFolder Interface"),
    odl
]
interface IShellFolder : IUnknown
{
    HRESULT ParseDisplayName([in] HWND hwndOwner,
                             [in] LPBC pbcReserved,
                             [in] LPOLESTR lpszDisplayName,
                             [in] ULONG * pchEaten,
                             [in, out] LPITEMIDLIST * ppidl,
                             [in, out] ULONG *pdwAttributes);
    HRESULT EnumObjects([in] HWND hwndOwner,
                        [in] DWORD grfFlags,
                        [in, out] LPENUMIDLIST * ppenumIDList);
    HRESULT BindToObject([in] LPCITEMIDLIST pidl,
                         [in] LPBC pbcReserved,
                         [in] REFIID riid,
                         [in, out] LPVOID * ppvOut);
    HRESULT BindToStorage([in] LPCITEMIDLIST pidl,
                          [in] LPBC pbcReserved,
```

Example 11-2. IShellFolder (continued)

```
                            [in] REFIID riid,
                            [in,out] LPVOID * ppvObj);
    HRESULT CompareIDs([in] LPARAM lParam,
                       [in] LPCITEMIDLIST pidl1,
                       [in] LPCITEMIDLIST pidl2);
    HRESULT CreateViewObject([in] HWND hwndOwner,
                             [in] REFIID riid,
                             [in,out] LPVOID * ppvOut);
    HRESULT GetAttributesOf([in] UINT cidl,
                            [in,out] LPCITEMIDLIST * apidl,
                            [in,out] ULONG * rgfInOut);
    HRESULT GetUIObjectOf([in] HWND hwndOwner,
                          [in] UINT cidl,
                          [in,out] LPCITEMIDLIST * apidl,
                          [in] REFIID riid,
                          [in,out] UINT * prgfInOut,
                          [in,out] LPVOID * ppvOut);
    HRESULT GetDisplayNameOf([in] LPCITEMIDLIST pidl,
                             [in] DWORD uFlags,
                             [in] LPSTRRET lpName);
    HRESULT SetNameOf([in] HWND hwndOwner,
                      [in] LPCITEMIDLIST pidl,
                      [in] LPCOLESTR lpszName,
                      [in] DWORD uFlags,
                      [in,out] LPITEMIDLIST * ppidlOut);
}
```

BindToObject

This function retrieves the **IShellFolder** interface for a subfolder. *BindToObject* is called by the shell whenever a folder is opened. The major responsibility of this function is to provide the shell with an interface pointer to **IShellFolder** (for the subfolder). It is defined like so:

```
    HRESULT BindToObject(LPCITEMIDLIST pidl,
                         LPBC pbcReserved,
                         REFIID riid,
                         LPVOID *ppvOut);
```

with the following parameters:

pidl
> [in] Is the PIDL of the parent folder.

pbcReserved
> [in] Reserved; will be **NULL**.

riid
> [in] Points to the interface identifier for **IShellFolder**.

ppvOut
> [in, out] Gives the shell the **IShellFolder** interface for the subfolder.

CompareIDs

This function determines the display order of two folders or items. Its definition is as follows:

```
HRESULT CompareIDs(LPARAM lParam,
                   LPCITEMIDLIST pidl1,
                   LPCITEMIDLIST pidl2);
```

with the following parameters:

lParam

[in] This value will always be 0 when this function is called by the shell.

pidl1/pidl2

[in] These two PIDLs uniquely identify items or folders for comparison.

The method of comparison performed by this function is entirely up to the implementer. It will be different for every namespace extension, because the PIDL will most likely have a different format across extensions.

The function must return one of the following values:

< 0

The first PIDL should be displayed first (*pidl1* < *pidl2*).

> 0

The second PIDL should be displayed first (*pidl1* > *pidl2*).

= 0

The two items are the same (*pidl1* = *pidl2*).

CreateViewObject

This method is responsible for creating the view object for a shell folder. Its syntax is:

```
HRESULT CreateViewObject(HWND hwndOwner, REFIID riid, LPVOID *ppvOut);
```

It has the following parameters:

hwndOwner

[in] The handle of the window that is the parent to the view object.

riid

[in] The IShellView interface identifier.

ppvOut

[in, out] The address of the view object that will be returned to the shell.

The important thing to remember when implementing this method is that the object implementing IShellView must be different than the object that is implementing IShellFolder. This is to accommodate support for multiple views.

EnumObjects

This method creates an enumeration object (an object that implements `IEnumIDList`) that the shell will use to enumerate, and consequently display, the contents of a folder. It is defined as:

```
HRESULT EnumObjects(HWND hwndOwner, DWORD grfFlags,
                    LPENUMIDLIST *ppenumIDList);
```

with the following parameters:

hwndOwner

[in] Handle to the owner window a client should use to display a dialog or message box. The VB *MsgBox* function does not have an *hWnd* parameter (unlike the *MessageBox* API function), so this parameter can be ignored.

grfFlags

[in] Items that should be included in the enumeration. This value can be one or more of the following values:

Constant	Description
SHCONTF_FOLDERS	Include folders.
SHCONTF_NONFOLDERS	Include non-folders (items).
SHCONTF_INCLUDEHIDDEN	Include hidden items.

ppenumIDList

[out, retval] Address that receives a pointer to the `IEnumIDList` interface of the enumeration object.

As is the case with the view object, the enumeration object needs to be implemented in a separate object.

GetAttributesOf

This function retrieves the attributes of one or more folders or items. In terms of namespace extensions, the primary purpose of this method is to determine if a given item is a folder and, if so, whether it has subfolders. Its definition is:

```
HRESULT GetAttributesOf(UINT cidl, LPCITEMIDLIST *apidl, ULONG *rgfInOut);
```

with the following parameters:

cidl

[in] The number of PIDLs that are being pointed to by *apidl*.

apidl

[in, out] A pointer to an array of PIDLs.

rgfInOut

[in, out] One or more constants from the `SFGAO` enumeration (see Appendix A, *VBShell Library Listing*), shown upon returning from this method.

When implementing namespace extensions, however, the primary values of concern for this flag are:

Constant	Description
SFGAO_FOLDER	The item is a folder.
SFGAO_HASSUBFOLDER	The item contains subfolders.

If the SFGAO_HASSUBFOLDER bit has been set, the shell will draw a "+" node next to the folder.

GetDisplayNameOf

Provides a display name for a given PIDL. Its syntax is:

```
HRESULT GetDisplayNameOf(LPCITEMIDLIST pidl, DWORD uFlags, LPSTRRET lpName);
```

Its parameters are:

pidl

[in] The PIDL for which a display name is being requested.

uFlags

[in] Flags indicating the type of display name being requested. These values come from the SHGNO enumeration, which contains the following values:

Constant	Description
SHGDN_NORMAL	The full path of the PIDL from the root.
SHGDN_INFOLDER	The name is relative to the folder that is processing the name.
SHGDN_FORADDRESSBAR	The name will be used for display in the address bar combo box.
SHGDN_FORPARSING	This flag can be ignored for this discussion.
SHGDN_INCLUDE_ NONFILESYS	This flag can be ignored for this discussion.

lpName

[in] The address of an STRRET structure, which is defined like this:

```
typedef struct _STRRET {
    UINT uType;
    union {
        LPWSTR pOleStr;
        LPSTR pStr;
        UINT uOffset;
        char cStr[MAX_PATH];
    } DUMMYUNIONNAME;
} STRRET, *LPSTRRET;
```

As you can see, this structure contains a union, which has no analogue in Visual Basic. If you consider that, internally, all strings in VB are in Unicode, then the following redefinition makes sense (regardless of your platform):

```
Public Type STRRET
    uType As UINT
    pOLESTR As Long
End Type
```

The *uType* member can be one of the following values, although it should always equal STRRET_WSTR (in terms of the above definition of STRRET):

Constant	Description
STRRET_CSTR	The string is returned in the *cStr* member of the structure.
STRRET_OFFSET	The *uOffset* member value indicates the number of bytes from the beginning of the item identifier list where the string is located.
STRRET_WSTR	The string is at the address pointed to in the *pOleStr* member. This is a pointer to a Unicode string.

pOLESTR will point to a string that contains the display name.

GetUIObjectOf

The shell will call this method for any additional interfaces it might need to complete its functionality. For instance, the icons that are displayed for the namespace extension are managed by an object that implements IExtractIcon. When the shell is ready to display icons, it will call this method for the object. If the namespace has a context menu, the shell will call this method, asking for an object that implements IContextMenu. Maybe your extension provides InfoTips. If that is the case, the shell would call this method requesting an object that supports IQueryInfo.

GetUIObjectOf has the following definition:

```
HRESULT GetUIObjectOf(
    HWND hwndOwner,
    UINT cidl,
    LPCITEMIDLIST *apidl,
    REFIID riid,
    UINT *prgfInOut,
    LPVOID *ppvOut);
```

Its parameters are:

hwndOwner

[in] Handle to the owner window that a client should use to display a dialog or message box. The VB *MsgBox* function does not have an *hWnd* parameter (unlike the *MessageBox* API function), so this parameter can be ignored.

cidl
> [in] The number of PIDLs that are being pointed to by *apidl*.

apidl
> [in, out] A pointer to an array of PIDLs.

riid
> [in] A pointer to the GUID of the interface being requested.

prgfInOut
> [in, out] Reserved.

ppvOut
> [in] The address that receives the interface pointer.

The most common interfaces requested by the shell are shown in the following table:

Interface Identifier	Allowed cidl Value
IContextMenu	>=1
IContextMenu2	>=1
IDataObject	>=1
IDropTarget	=1
IExtractIcon	=1
IQueryInfo	=1

The only interface on this list that we have not discussed is `IContextMenu2`. This interface provides additional methods that allow the context menu to contain owner-drawn items.

IShellView

`IShellView`, which is derived from `IOleWindow`, is responsible for creating the view object and maintaining communication between the view and Explorer's frame window. This communication involves translating window messages, adding menu items and toolbar buttons, providing help text in the status bar, and maintaining the state of the view window. `IShellView` is composed of 12 methods, which are listed in Table 11-3. Methods marked with an asterisk do not need to be implemented.

Table 11-3. IShellView Methods

Method	Description
AddPropertySheetPages*	Adds pages to the Options property sheet.
CreateViewWindow	Creates the view window.

Table 11-3. IShellView Methods (continued)

Method	Description
ContextSensitiveHelp*	Determines whether context-sensitive help mode should be entered during an in-place activation session.
DestroyViewWindow	Destroys the view window.
EnableModeless*	Is not currently in use by Explorer.
EnableModelessSV*	Is not currently in use.
GetCurrentInfo	Returns the current folder settings. This is basically the type of view currently in use: Large Icons, Small Icons, List, or Details. This is how view state is maintained between the different namespace extensions that are grouped by the shell.
GetItemObject*	Is not used by namespace extensions.
GetWindow	Is inherited from IOleWindow. It should return the handle to the view object.
Refresh	Refreshes the display in response to a View → Refresh menu selection or to pressing F5.
SaveViewState*	Saves the shell's view settings so the current state can be restored during a future session.
SelectItem*	Changes the selection state of items within the shell view window.
TranslateAccelerator*	Translates accelerator keystrokes when a namespace extension's view has the focus.
UIActivate	Called whenever the activation state of the view window is changed by an event external to the view object itself.

The IDL for **IShellView** is contained in Example 11-3.

Example 11-3. IShellView

```
// shellview select item flags
typedef enum {
    SVSI_DESELECT        = 0x0000,
    SVSI_SELECT          = 0x0001,
    SVSI_EDIT            = 0x0003,
    SVSI_DESELECTOTHERS  = 0x0004,
    SVSI_ENSUREVISIBLE   = 0x0008,
    SVSI_FOCUSED         = 0x0010,
    SVSI_TRANSLATEPT     = 0x0020,
} SVSI;

// shellview get item object flags
typedef enum {
    SVGIO_BACKGROUND     = 0x00000000,
    SVGIO_SELECTION      = 0x00000001,
    SVGIO_ALLVIEW        = 0x00000002,
} SVGIO;
```

Example 11-3. IShellView (continued)

```
// uState values for IShellView::UIActivate
typedef enum {
    SVUIA_DEACTIVATE        = 0,
    SVUIA_ACTIVATE_NOFOCUS  = 1,
    SVUIA_ACTIVATE_FOCUS    = 2,
    SVUIA_INPLACEACTIVATE   = 3
} SVUIA_STATUS;

[
    uuid(000214e3-0000-0000-c000-000000000046),
    helpstring("IShellView Interface"),
    odl
]
interface IShellView: IUnknown
{
    // IOleWindow
    HRESULT GetWindow([out, retval] HWND * lphwnd);
    HRESULT ContextSensitiveHelp([in] BOOL fEnterMode);

    // IShellView
    HRESULT TranslateAccelerator([in] LPMSG lpmsg);
    HRESULT EnableModeless([in] BOOL fEnable);
    HRESULT UIActivate([in] UINT uState);
    HRESULT Refresh();
    HRESULT CreateViewWindow([in,out] IShellView  *lpPrevView,
                             [in] LPCFOLDERSETTINGS lpfs,
                             [in,out] IShellBrowser *psb,
                             [in] LPRECT prcView,
                             [in,out] HWND   *phWnd);
    HRESULT DestroyViewWindow();
    HRESULT GetCurrentInfo([in] LPFOLDERSETTINGS lpfs);
    HRESULT AddPropertySheetPages([in] DWORD dwReserved,
                                  [in] LPFNADDPROPSHEETPAGE lpfn,
                                  [in] LPARAM lparam);
    HRESULT SaveViewState();
    HRESULT SelectItem([in] LPCITEMIDLIST pidlItem,
                       [in] UINT uFlags);
    HRESULT GetItemObject([in] UINT uItem,
                          [in] REFIID riid,
                          [out, retval] IUnknown **ppv);
}
```

Of the methods shown in Table 11-3, the six discussed in the following sections must be implemented.

CreateViewWindow

This method is responsible for creating the view window. It is defined as follows in the Platform SDK:

```
HRESULT CreateViewWindow(
    ISHELLLINK *lpPrevView,
```

```
        LPFOLDERSETTINGS lpfs,
        IShellBrowser *psb,
        RECT *prcView,
        HWND *phWnd);
```

But the documentation is in error. The first parameter should be a pointer to an
`IShellView` interface:

```
HRESULT CreateViewWindow(
    IShellView *lpPrevView,
    LPFOLDERSETTINGS lpfs,
    IShellBrowser *psb,
    RECT *prcView,
    HWND *phWnd);
```

The parameters of the correct version of the method prototype are:

lpPrevView

[in, out] A pointer to the `IShellView` interface of the view object that is
being closed. This value can also be **NULL**.

lpfs

[in] Address of a **FOLDERSETTINGS** structure, which is defined as:

```
typedef struct {
    UINT ViewMode;
    UINT fFlags;
}FOLDERSETTINGS;
```

This structure is not used by the namespace directly, so a discussion is not in
order. The shell will use this structure to communicate the current view to the
namespace extension (Large Icons, Details, List, etc.). The namespace extension should cache this structure, so it can return it when the shell calls
`GetCurrentInfo`.

psb

[in, out] Address of the current instance of the `IShellBrowser` interface.
The view should call **AddRef** on this interface and keep the interface pointer
to allow communication with Explorer's frame window.

prcView

[in] Dimension of the view window in client coordinates.

phWnd

[in, out] Address of the window handle being created.

DestroyViewWindow

This method is called when the view window (or Explorer) is being closed. Its
syntax is simply:

```
HRESULT DestroyViewWindow();
```

GetCurrentInfo

This method is called by the shell to retrieve the current folder settings. The folder settings that were passed to `CreateViewWindow` can be returned to the shell via this method. Its syntax is:

```
HRESULT GetCurrentInfo(LPFOLDERSETTINGS lpfs);
```

It has a single parameter:

lpfs

[in] The address of a `FOLDERSETTINGS` structure. For information on the `FOLDERSETTINGS` structure, see the description of the `CreateViewWindow` method.

GetWindow

This method, which is inherited from `IOleWindow`, should return the window handle of the view object. Its syntax is:

```
HRESULT GetWindow(HWND *phwnd);
```

Its single parameter is:

phwnd

[out, retval] The address of the view object's window handle.

Refresh

This method refreshes the view object when the Refresh menu item is selected from Explorer's menu (or F5 is pressed). Its syntax is simply:

```
HRESULT Refresh();
```

UIActivate

This method is called when the activation state of the view window is changed by an event outside of the shell. For example, if the Tab key is pressed when the tree has the focus, the view window should be given the focus. The syntax of `UIActivate` is:

```
HRESULT UIActivate(UINT uState);
```

The method has the following parameters:

uState

[in] Contains flags specifying the activation state of the window. This can be one of the following values:

Constant	Description
SVUIA_ACTIVATE_FOCUS	The view window has the input focus.
SVUIA_ACTIVATE_NOFOCUS	The view is losing the input focus.

Constant	Description
SVUIA_DEACTIVATE	Explorer is about to destroy the view window.
SVUIA_INPLACEACTIVATE	This is not used for this interface.

IEnumIDList

IEnumIDList enumerates the contents of a shell folder. The methods that compose this interface are listed in Table 11-4.

Table 11-4. IEnumIDList Methods

Method	Description
Clone	Creates a clone of the current enumeration object.
Next	Retrieves the specified number of item identifiers.
Reset	Returns to the beginning of the enumeration.
Skip	Skips the specified number of items.

The primary method of this interface is **Next**. The namespace object is responsible for creating PIDLs that identify the contents of the currently selected folder. When the shell is ready for these PIDLs, it repeatedly calls **Next**. This method simply returns the next PIDL in an internal list of PIDLs that is maintained by the namespace extension. The complete IDL listing for IEnumIDList can be found in Example 11-4.

Example 11-4. IEnumIDList

```
[
    uuid(000214f2-0000-0000-c000-000000000046),
    helpstring("IEnumIDList Interface"),
    odl
]
interface IEnumIDList: IUnknown
{
    HRESULT Next([in] ULONG celt,
                 [in,out] LPITEMIDLIST *rgelt,
                 [in,out] ULONG *pceltFetched);
    HRESULT Skip([in] ULONG celt);
    HRESULT Reset();
    HRESULT Clone([in,out] IEnumIDList **ppenum);
}
```

Additional Interfaces

There are two additional interfaces that you will use (as opposed to implement) when you create a namespace extension: IShellBrowser and IMalloc. IShellBrowser is derived from IOleWindow and is used to add menu items and toolbar buttons to the Explorer frame window, as well as to display text in the status bar (among other things).

IMalloc is used to allocate and manage memory associated with PIDLs. For those of you who program in C/C++, you can think of this interface as the COM version of *malloc* and *realloc*.

We will not get into the gory details of these two interfaces except where necessary. Tables 11-5 and 11-6 summarize these two interfaces.

Table 11-5. IMalloc Interface

Method	Description
Alloc	Allocates a block of memory.
Realloc	Reallocates a block of memory.
Free	Frees an allocated block of memory.
GetSize	Returns the size of a block of allocated memory.
DidAlloc	Determines whether **IMalloc** was used to allocate the specified block of memory.
HeapMinimize	Minimizes the heap by releasing unused blocks of memory.

Table 11-6. IShellBrowser Interface

Method	Description
BrowseObject	Tells Explorer to browse in another folder.
EnableModelessSB	Enables or disables Explorer's modeless windows.
GetControlWindow	Gets the window handle to an Explorer control such as the tree view or status bar.
GetViewStateStream	Returns a stream that can be used to read and write the persistent data for a view.
InsertMenusSB	Inserts Explorer's menu items to an empty menu created by the view.
OnViewWindowActive	Notifies Explorer that the view was activated.
QueryActiveShellView	Returns the currently activated view object.
RemoveMenusSB	Notifies the container to remove its items from Explorer's menu. This is in contrast to **InsertMenusSB**.
SendControlMsg	Sends messages to Explorer controls such as the tree view or status bar.
SetMenuSB	Installs a composite menu in Explorer.
SetStatusTextSB	Sets and displays status bar text.
SetToolbarItems	Adds toolbar items to Explorer's toolbar.
TranslateAcceleratorSB	Translates accelerator keystrokes while the view is active.

Example 11-5 contains the IDL for both interfaces.

Example 11-5. IMalloc and IShellBrowser

```
[
    uuid(00000002-0000-0000-C000-000000000046),
    helpstring("IMalloc Interface"),
    odl
]
interface IMalloc : IUnknown
{
    long Alloc([in] ULONG cb);
    long Realloc ([in] VOID *pv, [in] ULONG cb);
    void Free([in] VOID *pv);
    ULONG GetSize([in] VOID *pv);
    int DidAlloc([in] VOID *pv);
    void HeapMinimize();
}


    //------------------------------------------------------------
    // IShellBrowser
    //
    // (this interface is actually derived from IOleWindow)
    //------------------------------------------------------------
    typedef enum {
        SBSP_DEFBROWSER             = 0x0000,
        SBSP_SAMEBROWSER            = 0x0001,
        SBSP_NEWBROWSER             = 0x0002,
        SBSP_DEFMODE                = 0x0000,
        SBSP_OPENMODE               = 0x0010,
        SBSP_EXPLOREMODE            = 0x0020,
        SBSP_ABSOLUTE               = 0x0000,
        SBSP_RELATIVE               = 0x1000,
        SBSP_PARENT                 = 0x2000,
        SBSP_NAVIGATEBACK           = 0x4000,
        SBSP_NAVIGATEFORWARD        = 0x8000,
        SBSP_ALLOW_AUTONAVIGATE     = 0x10000,
        SBSP_INITIATEDBYHLINKFRAME  = 0x80000000,
        SBSP_REDIRECT               = 0x40000000,
        SBSP_WRITENOHISTORY         = 0x08000000,
        SBSP_NOAUTOSELECT           = 0x04000000
    } SBSP_BROWSER;


    [
        uuid(000214e2-0000-0000-c000-000000000046),
        helpstring("IShellBrowser Interface"),
        odl
    ]
    interface IShellBrowser : IUnknown
    {
        // IOleWindow
        HRESULT GetWindow([out, retval] HWND * lphwnd);
        HRESULT ContextSensitiveHelp([in] BOOL fEnterMode);

        // IShellBrowser
        HRESULT InsertMenusSB(
```

Example 11-5. IMalloc and IShellBrowser (continued)

```
                    [in] HMENU hmenuShared,
                    [in] LPOLEMENUGROUPWIDTHS lpMenuWidths);

    HRESULT SetMenuSB([in] HMENU hmenuShared,
                    [in] HOLEMENU holemenuReserved,
                    [in] HWND hwndActiveObject);

    HRESULT RemoveMenusSB([in] HMENU hmenuShared);

    HRESULT SetStatusTextSB([in] LPCOLESTR lpszStatusText);

    HRESULT EnableModelessSB([in] BOOL fEnable);

    HRESULT TranslateAcceleratorSB([in] LPMSG lpmsg,
                    [in] WORD wID);

    HRESULT BrowseObject([in] LPCITEMIDLIST pidl,
                    [in] SBSP_BROWSER wFlags);

    HRESULT GetViewStateStream([in] DWORD grfMode,
                    [in, out] LPSTREAM  *ppStrm);

    HRESULT GetControlWindow([in] UINT id,
                    [out, retval] HWND * lphwnd);

    HRESULT SendControlMsg([in] UINT id,
                    [in] UINT uMsg,
                    [in] WPARAM wParam,
                    [in] LPARAM lParam,
                    [out, retval] LRESULT * pret);

    HRESULT QueryActiveShellView(
                    [out, retval] IShellView ** ppshv);

    HRESULT OnViewWindowActive([in] IShellView * ppshv);

    HRESULT SetToolbarItems([in] LPTBBUTTON lpButtons,
                    [in] UINT nButtons,
                    [in] UINT uFlags);
}
```

Creating the Namespace Extension

The extension we will build in this chapter is far more contrived than the previous examples. It does absolutely nothing. The point of this project is to learn how to build a namespace extension. Because most of the code in a namespace extension can be of a proprietary nature, it is best that we use an example that is fairly easy to implement yet covers all of the major features of a namespace extension.

Our project, which we'll call DemoSpace, begins with a junction point under *My Computer* called *Root*. *Root* will contain five "folders" numbered 0 through 4. Each folder will contain "items" numbered 0 through the current folder number. Demo-Space is shown in Figure 11-6.

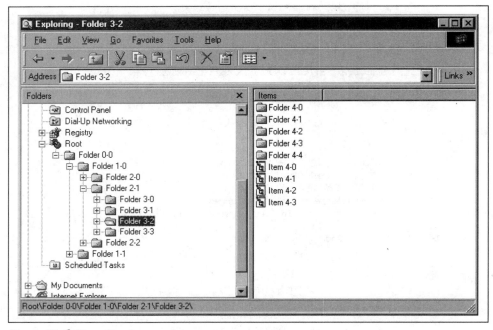

Figure 11-6. DemoSpace

When we wrote shell extensions, each extension mapped to one object. That object implemented all the interfaces that were required by the extension. But in this case, things work a little differently. Folders operate independently of the view. It is perfectly legal for a namespace extension to provide several views. So theoretically, folders and views represent a one-to-many relationship.

Namespace extensions will contain several objects, not just one. One object will implement IShellFolder and IPersistFolder. This object can be associated with the action that takes place in the tree view. Another object will implement IShellView, which of course, represents the content or view pane on the right side of Explorer. A third will implement IEnumIDList and is responsible for main-taining and providing the "items" in both the tree view and the content pane.

We will also add a few more classes when the time is right, but for now, let's create a new ActiveX DLL project called DemoSpace. We'll begin by adding three classes. Table 11-7 describes the classes and the interfaces they will implement. Add these to the project.

Table 11-7. Required Namespace Classes

Class	Implemented Interfaces
ShellFolder	IShellFolder, IPersistFolder
ShellView	IShellView
EnumIDList	IEnumIDList

We're going to have to write more than just a few lines of code to "wire" up this namespace extension. Previously, we were able to discuss one class at a time, write the code for it, enter in a few registry entries, and we were done. Not so in this case. Things won't make sense if we do it that way. A namespace extension has a certain flow, and we need to follow that flow to make the best sense of it all. Therefore, we will be doing some jumping around between these (and other) classes. Also, as mentioned previously, there is some code in a namespace extension that is generic, and there is more of it that is not. This distinction will be noted whenever applicable.

ShellFolder

As you might expect, we have some vtable swaps for this class. In this case, there are two methods that need to be swapped: **CompareIDs** and **GetUIObjectOf**. But this time we have a variation of the swap. Remember, each of these objects operates independently of the others. There might be a case in which two instances of ShellFolder exist at one time. This presents a little problem, which, fortunately, has a simple solution.

If you remember, vtables are *shared* between every instance of a class. All addresses of the methods that comprise a class are the *same* for each instance. What does this mean to us? Well, if you haven't noticed, we have been swapping these functions in the Initialize and Terminate events of the class. When a second instance of ShellFolder is instantiated, the functions will be swapped again. Consider this call:

```
m_pOldCompareIDs = SwapVtableEntry(ObjPtr(pFolder), _
                        8, _
                        AddressOf CompareIDsX)
```

The first time this function is called, the address of the **CompareIDs** method is swapped out with the *CompareIDsX* function defined in *Demospace.bas*. Now, if a second instance of ShellFolder is instantiated before the first instance terminates, this call will be made again. But remember, vtables are global for *every* instance of a class. So, on the second call, the vtable for the class already contains the address of *CompareIDsX*. Basically, all that happens in this case is that the same address is copied into the vtable. So our address swapping in the Initialize event is not a problem.

The problem lies in the Terminate event, when we swap the addresses back. If the first instance terminates, swapping the functions back, the second instance is no longer bound to the proper methods. A crash is sure to result.

We will get around this by actually reference counting ShellFolder ourselves. We will maintain a public counter declared in the *Demospace.bas* code module that is incremented every time Initialize is called and is decremented every time Terminate is called. If the counter is 0 when we terminate, we'll know it's safe to swap the methods back. There are four methods that need to be swapped: `BindToObject`, `CompareIDs`, `CreateViewObject`, and `GetUIObjectOf`. Let's look at the code for Class_Initialize and Class_Terminate, which is shown in Example 11-6.

Example 11-6. ShellFolder Class_Initialize/Class_Terminate

```
'Declared in Demospace.bas
Public g_FolderSwapRef As Long

'ShellFolder.cls
Private m_pOldBindToObject As Long
Private m_pOldCompareIDs As Long
Private m_pOldCreateViewObj As Long
Private m_pOldGetUIObjectOf As Long

Private Sub Class_Initialize()

    Set m_pMalloc = GetMalloc

    If g_FolderSwapRef = 0 Then
        Dim pFolder As IShellFolder
        Set pFolder = Me
        m_pOldBindToObject = SwapVtableEntry(ObjPtr(pFolder), _
            6, AddressOf BindToObjectX)
        m_pOldCompareIDs = SwapVtableEntry(ObjPtr(pFolder), _
            8, AddressOf CompareIDsX)
        m_pOldCreateViewObj = SwapVtableEntry(ObjPtr(pFolder), _
            9, AddressOf CreateViewObjectX)
        m_pOldGetUIObjectOf = SwapVtableEntry(ObjPtr(pFolder), _
            11, AddressOf GetUIObjectOfX)
    End If

    g_FolderSwapRef = g_FolderSwapRef + 1

End Sub

Private Sub Class_Terminate()

    g_FolderSwapRef = g_FolderSwapRef - 1

    If (g_FolderSwapRef = 0) Then
        Dim pFolder As IShellFolder
        Set pFolder = Me
        m_pOldBindToObject = SwapVtableEntry(ObjPtr(pFolder), _
```

Example 11-6. ShellFolder Class_Initialize/Class_Terminate (continued)

```
            6, m_pOldBindToObject)
        m_pOldCompareIDs = SwapVtableEntry(ObjPtr(pFolder), _
            8, m_pOldCompareIDs)
        m_pOldCreateViewObj = SwapVtableEntry(ObjPtr(pFolder), _
            9, m_pOldCreateViewObj)
        m_pOldGetUIObjectOf = SwapVtableEntry(ObjPtr(pFolder), _
            11, m_pOldGetUIObjectOf)
    End If

    Set m_pMalloc = Nothing

End Sub
```

We will use this same reference counting technique for ShellView and Enum-IDList, as well. Each of the Class_Initialize and Class_Terminate events for both of these classes will increment and decrement a counter. Class_Terminate will only swap back the methods in the vtable when the counter is equal to zero.

We will come back to **BindToObject**, **CompareIDs**, **CreateViewObject** and **GetUIObjectOf** later, since they are significant methods in the grand scheme of things.

For now, take note of the private member variable *m_pMalloc*. All of the primary classes in the namespace extension will use **IMalloc** to allocate memory for PIDLs. In the Class_Initialize event, we call *GetMalloc* to retrieve a reference to this interface. *GetMalloc* is shown in Example 11-7.

Example 11-7. GetMalloc

```
Public Function GetMalloc() As IMalloc

    Dim pMalloc As IMalloc
    Dim lpMalloc As Long
    Dim hr As Long

    hr = SHGetMalloc(lpMalloc)
    If (hr = S_OK) Then

        CopyMemory pMalloc, lpMalloc, 4

        Set GetMalloc = pMalloc

    End If

End Function
```

GetMalloc primarily wraps the function *SHGetMalloc*, which returns the **IMalloc** reference to us. *SHGetMalloc* is found in *shell32.dll* and is defined like so:

```
Public Declare Function SHGetMalloc Lib "shell32.dll" _
    (lpMalloc As Long) As Long
```

We used *CopyMemory* before when we had to deal with raw interface addresses. The difference here is that an AddRef is actually being performed when the function returns using **Set**. So it is safe to set the interface equal to **Nothing** when we are finished with it.

Now that we have laid the groundwork for ShellFolder, let's continue with implementing the methods the object will need to support. We'll start with GetClassID, only because it stands in the way of more important matters, and then move on from there.

GetClassID

The action (albeit there's not much of it) begins with **IPersistFolder**.

IPersistFolder contains one method, **Initialize**, that will *not* be implemented. But the method must return **S_OK**, or the whole works come tumbling down. In order to return **S_OK**, we can just leave the method empty. VB handles the rest:

```
Private Sub IPersistFolder_Initialize( _
    ByVal pidl As VBShellLib.LPCITEMIDLIST)
    'Must return S_OK
End Sub
```

Because **IPersistFolder** is "derived" from **IPersist**, it also contains **GetClassID**. We've seen this method more than a few times now (see the "Implementing IPersistFile" section in Chapter 5, *Icon Handlers*), but we've never actually implemented it. Let's do that now. Example 11-8 contains the implementation.

Example 11-8. IPersistFolder::GetClassID

```
Private Sub IPersistFolder_GetClassID(lpClassID As VBShellLib.clsid)

    Dim clsid As GUID
    Dim sProgID As String
    sProgID = "DemoSpace.ShellFolder"

    CLSIDFromProgID StrPtr(sProgID), clsid

    lpClassID = VarPtr(clsid)

End Sub
```

This method is quite simple. It is just required to return the CLSID for the object implementing **IShellFolder**. Not a string representation of the CLSID, mind you, but the actual 128-bit number. This is accomplished by calling *CLSIDFromProgID*, which is declared as follows:

```
Public Declare Function CLSIDFromProgID Lib "ole32.dll" _
    (ByVal lpszProgID As Long, pClsid As GUID) As Long
```

This method takes a pointer to a program identifier and to a GUID structure, which, as you might recall, is defined like so:

```
Public Type GUID
    Data1 As Long
    Data2 As Integer
    Data3 As Integer
    Data4(7) As Byte
End Type
```

With that out of the way, we are ready to create the view object.

CreateViewObject

This function is responsible for creating the object that will manage the view. For the most part, this function is generic. Example 11-9 shows the function in its entirety. The most exciting thing about this method is that it is one of the few times we actually have to call IUnknown::QueryInterface ourselves. It has that "I just got my hands dirty" feel to it, doesn't it? This method, like BindToObject, is also passed a reference to an IID. Under Windows 9x and NT, this IID always appears to be IShellView. However, under Windows 2000, the shell sometimes asks for IShellLink. We haven't discussed this latter interface, and we're not going to. But the gist of the IShellLink interface is that it is used for shortcuts. Specifically, this is used to accommodate distributed link tracking, which is a feature of Windows 2000 that enables client applications to track link sources that have moved. CreateViewObject needs to return E_OUTOFMEMORY in the event the shell requests an interface other than IShellView. Therefore, this method is swapped in the vtable with a replacement function.

Example 11-9. CreateViewObject

```
'Demospace.bas

Public Const IID_IShellView = "{000214E3-0000-0000-C000-000000000046}"

Public Function CreateViewObjectX(ByVal this As IShellFolder, _
                                  ByVal hwndOwner As hWnd, _
                                  ByVal riid As REFIID, _
                                  ppvOut As LPVOID) As Long

    CreateViewObjectX = E_OUTOFMEMORY

    Dim iid As String

    iid = GetIID(riid)

    If iid = IID_IShellView Then

        'Get reference to current shell folder.
        Dim pShellFolder As ShellFolder
```

Example 11-9. CreateViewObject (continued)

```
        Set pShellFolder = this

        'Create new view.
        Dim pShellView As ShellView
        Set pShellView = New ShellView

        'Pass folder info to view.
        pShellView.Initialize pShellFolder, pShellFolder.pidl

        'Query view for IShellFolder.
        Dim pUnk As IUnknownVB
        Set pUnk = pShellView
        pUnk.QueryInterface riid, ppvOut

        Set pUnk = Nothing
        Set pShellView = Nothing
        Set pShellFolder = Nothing

        CreateViewObjectX = S_OK

    End If

End Function
```

This quite possibly could be a generic implementation, but look at the call to ShellView.Initialize (not to be confused with Class_Initialize). This call is the equivalent of a C++ constructor. Note, though, that Initialize is not a method defined by the `IShellView` interface; we've implemented it purely to pass information to the view object class right when it is created. So in this case, we pass an object reference to ShellFolder and a PIDL. PIDLs should contain everything needed to describe the items they represent, so this implementation might suffice (it does for all three example extensions). But there might be times when your own Initialize event will require something a little more exotic. It's up to you. Whatever your view object might need, this is the place to pass it. Anyway, this version passes a PIDL to the view. The view object will use this PIDL to populate its list view control with folders and items.

After we have created an instance of ShellView, we get a reference to `IUnknownVB` (our no-holds-barred version of `IUnknown` which is discussed in detail in Chapter 6, *Property Sheet Handlers*), and we call `QueryInterface` with the *riid* and *ppvOut* parameters given to us by the shell. With this done, the shell now has a reference to our view object and will call `IShellView::CreateViewWindow`, which is the method that actually creates the view window and places it in the content pane.

Creating the View

We need to add the `Initialize` method to ShellView so that the view object can receive the object reference to ShellFolder and the PIDL that represents that folder. We'll do that first, then we will implement CreateViewWindow. Initialize is shown at the bottom of Example 11-10.

Example 11-10. ShellView Initialize

```
'ShellView.cls
Private m_pidl As LPITEMIDLIST
Private m_parentFolder As ShellFolder
Private m_pidlMgr As pidlMgr

Private Sub Class_Initialize()

    Set m_pidlMgr = New pidlMgr

End Sub


Private Sub Class_Terminate()

    Set m_pidlMgr = Nothing

End Sub

Public Sub Initialize(f As ShellFolder, ByVal pidl As LPITEMIDLIST)
    Set m_parentFolder = f
    m_pidl = m_pidlMgr.Copy(pidl)
End Sub
```

Don't worry about the code pertaining to pidlMgr. For now, just know that it is a class we will use to help us work with PIDLs. We'll get to the pidlMgr class when I talk about EnumIDList.

CreateViewWindow

The purpose of this function could not be clearer. Its name gives it away. *CreateViewWindow* is responsible for creating the view window and returning the handle of that window back to the shell. The function is fairly easy to implement, but there is quite a bit going on. The syntax of this method is as follows:

```
HRESULT CreateViewWindow(
    IShellView *lpPrevView,
    LPFOLDERSETTINGS lpfs,
    IShellBrowser *psb,
    RECT *prcView,
    HWND *phWnd
);
```

The first parameter, *lpPrevView*, is a pointer to the view window that was exited before our view object was created. This could be any view window, depending on where we were in the namespace before our extension was activated. This could also be a previous instance of our view object. The Platform SDK also says that this value could be NULL. In any case, we will not use the value. But it could come in handy if you want to communicate with the previous view in your own extension, possibly as an optimization.

The second parameter, *lpfs*, is very important. It's the address of a FOLDERSETTINGS structure. We don't need to go into details with this structure, but it is important. We will cache this value for later and give it right back to the shell. This parameter is how the shell maintains the state of the view—which, in this case, means one of the views (Web Page, Large Icons, Small Icons, List, and Details) defined by Explorer—when jumping between namespace extensions.

The third parameter, *psb*, is a reference to IShellBrowser. We will cache this value, as well. Later, we'll use it for a variety of tasks, such as adding menu items and displaying text in Explorer's status bar. The view object will also make use of this parameter to handle browsing into folders from the view pane side of things (versus the tree view side).

The fourth parameter, *prcView*, is the address of a RECT structure that contains the coordinates of the view pane. We'll create a local instance of this structure using *CopyMemory* and size our view window to these values.

Last, but not least, we have an HWND, which is an [in, out] parameter. So, when the view window has been created, we will use this parameter to pass the handle back to the shell.

CreateViewWindow is shown in Example 11-11. Take a look, and then we'll discuss the details.

Example 11-11. CreateViewWindow

```
'ShellFolder.cls

Private m_folderSettings As FOLDERSETTINGS

Private Sub IShellView_CreateViewWindow( _
    ByVal lpPrevView As VBShellLib.IShellView, _
    ByVal lpfs As VBShellLib.LPCFOLDERSETTINGS, _
    ByVal psb As VBShellLib.IShellBrowser, _
    ByVal prcView As VBShellLib.LPRECT, phWnd As VBShellLib.hWnd)

    Dim dwStyle As DWORD
    Dim parentWnd As hWnd
    Dim rc As RECT
```

Example 11-11. CreateViewWindow (continued)

```
'Save folder settings
CopyMemory m_folderSettings, ByVal lpfs, Len(m_folderSettings)

'Get window rect
CopyMemory rc, ByVal prcView, Len(rc)

Set m_frmView = New frmView

parentWnd = psb.GetWindow

dwStyle = GetWindowLong(m_frmView.hWnd, GWL_STYLE)
dwStyle = dwStyle Or WS_CHILD Or WS_CLIPSIBLINGS
SetWindowLong m_frmView.hWnd, GWL_STYLE, dwStyle
SetParent m_frmView.hWnd, parentWnd

MoveWindow m_frmView.hWnd, rc.Left, rc.Top, _
           rc.Right - rc.Left, rc.bottom - rc.Top, True

ShowWindow m_frmView.hWnd, SW_SHOW

phWnd = m_frmView.hWnd

Set m_pShellBrowser = psb
Set m_frmView.ShellBrowser = m_pShellBrowser

FillList

End Sub
```

After the FOLDERSETTINGS have been saved and the view window has been created and sized to the RECT structure, things get a little interesting.

First, we call IShellBrowser::GetWindow (IShellBrowser is actually derived from IOleWindow) to get the handle to the content pane window in Explorer. Once we have that, we can use *GetWindowLong* and *SetWindowLong* Win32 API functions to actually change the style bits of our window and transform it into a child window. The *SetParent* API function allows us to set the parent of our newly born child to the window given to us by IShellBrowser. Once this has all been accomplished, we can position our view according to prcView using *MoveWindow* and then use *ShowWindow* to display our view.

But we are not quite done. Before we exit the method, we need to give the handle to our view back to the shell. We will also save a private copy of IShellBrowser and give another copy to the view window. Finally, we call *FillList* to populate our view with items (we'll come back to this function in the "FillList" section later in this chapter). *FillList* is a function we will create to handle populating of the list view.

The View window

Of course, for any of the code in Example 11-12 actually to work, we need a view window. This is easy enough. Add a Form to the project called *frmView* and do the following:

1. Set its BorderStyle property equal to "None."
2. Add a list view control called "ListView."
3. Add a column header to the list view called "Items."
4. Add an ImageList control.

Now, we need to add a ShellBrowser property to the form, which *CreateViewWindow* will use to provide the form with a reference to IShellBrowser. The list view also needs to be resized to the form whenever Explorer is resized, so we'll use the *MoveWindow* API in a resize event to handle the job. Also, the form will eventually need to work with PIDLs, so we'll add a private instance of the mysterious pidlMgr class to the form as well (we'll talk about this class in "The PIDL Manager" later in this chapter). The code for frmView is shown in Example 11-12.

Example 11-12. frmView

```
Option Explicit

Private m_pidlMgr As pidlMgr
Private m_pShellBrowser As IShellBrowser

Private Sub Form_Load()
    Set m_pidlMgr = New pidlMgr
End Sub

Private Sub Form_Resize()
    MoveWindow ListView.hWnd, 0, 0, Me.Width, Me.Height, 1
End Sub

Private Sub Form_Unload(Cancel As Integer)
    Set m_pidlMgr = Nothing
    Set m_pShellBrowser = Nothing
End Sub

Public Property Set ShellBrowser(sb As IShellBrowser)
    Set m_pShellBrowser = sb
End Property
```

Back to ShellView

The remaining methods of IShellView, with the exception of UIActivate, can now be implemented. UIActivate, though, will have to remain until later, because it will be different for every namespace that you create.

The last of the `IShellView` methods are very simple to implement. Each requires a few lines of code. Let's get them out of the way, then we can get to the Enum-List class.

DestroyWindow

This method is called when Explorer wants to terminate the view window. When this happens we simply unload the form:

```
Private Sub IShellView_DestroyViewWindow()
    Unload m_frmView
    Set m_frmView = Nothing
End Sub
```

GetCurrentInfo

This method is called when the shell wants the current folder settings. These folder settings were cached in `IShellView::CreateViewWindow` (Example 11-12), so all we have to do is pass them back to the shell:

```
Private Sub IShellView_GetCurrentInfo( _
    ByVal lpfs As VBShellLib.LPFOLDERSETTINGS)
    CopyMemory ByVal lpfs, m_folderSettings, Len(m_folderSettings)
End Sub
```

GetWindow

The only responsibility of this method is to return the handle to the view object:

```
Private Function IShellView_GetWindow() As VBShellLib.hWnd
    IShellView_GetWindow = m_frmView.hWnd
End Function
```

Refresh

This method is called whenever the view is refreshed (i.e., View → Refresh is selected from Explorer's menu, or F5 is pressed). This method is fairly generic, but it is possible your needs could be greater. This implementation merely clears the list view and repopulates it:

```
Private Sub IShellView_Refresh()
    SendMessage m_frmView.ListView.hWnd, LVM_DELETEALLITEMS, 0, 0&
    FillList
End Sub
```

The remaining methods (with the exception of **UIActivate**) are not implemented.

Enumerating Shell Items

The shell tells the namespace extension to prepare the data that it wants displayed by calling `IShellFolder::EnumObjects`. The primary responsibility of this method is to create an object that implements `IEnumIDList`, which it will pass back to the shell. This object, in our case EnumIDList, is responsible for maintaining the list of PIDLs that represent the items the shell will display in either the tree view or the list view. Let's implement `IShellFolder::EnumObjects`; then we will move on to the EnumIDList class and see how that works. Enum-Objects is shown in Example 11-13.

Example 11-13. IShellFolder::EnumObjects

```
'ShellFolder.class

Private m_iLevel As Integer

Private Function IShellFolder_EnumObjects( _
    ByVal hwndOwner As VBShellLib.hWnd, _
    ByVal grfFlags As VBShellLib.DWORD) As VBShellLib.IEnumIDList

    Dim e As New EnumIDList
    e.CreateEnumList m_iLevel, grfFlags

    Set IShellFolder_EnumObjects = e

End Function
```

To implement EnumObjects, all we have to do is create an instance of Enum-IDList, which is our class that implements `IEnumIDList`. Then we pass this object back to Explorer.

Look at the call to `EnumIDList::CreateEnumList`. Before we give EnumIDList over to the shell, we need to actually create the list of items that it will wrap. *CreateEnumList* is not a method of `IEnumIDList`, it is a public function we'll add to EnumIDList for the purpose of creating the list of items.

It works like this: *CreateEnumList* will build a linked list of PIDLs that will be maintained internally by the EnumIDList class. This list of PIDLs contains one or more folders or items for a particular level of the namespace hierarchy. When the shell is ready for these items, it will call `IEnumIDList::Next` for a PIDL. Our implementation of `IEnumIDList::Next` will give the shell a PIDL from this internally maintained linked list. This happens repeatedly until there are no more PIDLs left in the list.

The two parameters to *CreateEnumList* require some explanation. *m_iLevel* is the current "level" where we are in the hierarchy. Look back at Figure 11-6 for a moment. The folders and items are in the following format: Type/Level/Index. The *m_iLevel* parameter represents this level. The second parameter, *grfFlags*, which is given to us by the shell, is quite important. This will be a value from the following `SHCONTF` enumeration:

```
typedef enum tagSHCONTF{
    SHCONTF_FOLDERS = 32,
    SHCONTF_NONFOLDERS = 64,
    SHCONTF_INCLUDEHIDDEN = 128,
} SHCONTF;
```

This flag lets us know whether the shell wants "folders" or "items" when it asks us to build the PIDL list. We will use this information to make sure we comply with the shell's request.

CreateEnumList

Before we actually implement *CreateEnumList*, let's get the Class_Initialize and Class_Terminate events out of the way. They are shown in Example 11-14. Once again, ignore the references to the pidlMgr class and the **IMalloc** reference. We will discuss these two items momentarily.

Example 11-14. EnumIDList Class_Initialize/Terminate

```
'EnumIDList.cls
Implements IEnumIDList

Private m_pMalloc As IMalloc
Private m_pidlMgr As pidlMgr
Private m_pOldNext As Long

Private Sub Class_Initialize()

    Set m_pMalloc = GetMalloc
    Set m_pidlMgr = New pidlMgr

    'Swap
    If (g_EnumSwapRef = 0) Then

        Dim pEnumIDList As IEnumIDList
        Set pEnumIDList = Me

        m_pOldNext = SwapVtableEntry(ObjPtr(pEnumIDList), 4, _
            AddressOf NextX)

    End If

    g_EnumSwapRef = g_EnumSwapRef + 1

End Sub

Private Sub Class_Terminate()

    DeleteList

    Set m_pidlMgr = Nothing
    Set m_pMalloc = Nothing
```

Example 11-14. EnumIDList Class_Initialize/Terminate (continued)

```
    g_EnumSwapRef = g_EnumSwapRef - 1

    If (g_EnumSwapRef = 0) Then
        Dim pEnumIDList As IEnumIDList
        Set pEnumIDList = Me

        m_pOldNext = SwapVtableEntry(ObjPtr(pEnumIDList), 4, _
            m_pOldNext)
    End If

End Sub
```

Notice the call to DeleteList in the Class_Terminate event. We'll talk about this function in the "Enumerating Shell Items" section later in this chapter, but for now, just know that it is a function that will be called to free the linked list we will create for the PIDLs.

Now on to CreateEnumList. This function will be different for every namespace extension. But its purpose is always the same: to build a list of PIDLs that will be used by IEnumIDList::Next. Let's look at the function, which is shown in Example 11-15; then we'll discuss its nuances.

Example 11-15. CreateEnumList

```
'DemoSpace.bas
Public Const g_nMaxLevels = 5


'EnumIDList.class
Public Function CreateEnumList(ByVal iLevel As LPITEMIDLIST, _
    ByVal dwFlags As DWORD) As Boolean

    Dim i As Integer
    Dim pidlNew As LPITEMIDLIST

    CreateEnumList = False

    If iLevel < g_nMaxLevels Then

        For i = 0 To iLevel
            pidlNew = m_pidlMgr.Create(PT_FOLDER, iLevel, i)
            If (pidlNew) Then
                AddToEnumList pidlNew
            End If
            CreateEnumList = True
        Next i

    End If

    'Enumerate the non-folder items (values)
    If (dwFlags And SHCONTF_NONFOLDERS) Then
```

Example 11-15. CreateEnumList (continued)

```
    iLevel = iLevel - 1

    If iLevel <= g_nMaxLevels Then
        For i = 0 To iLevel - 1
            pidlNew = m_pidlMgr.Create(PT_ITEM, iLevel, i)
            If (pidlNew) Then
                AddToEnumList pidlNew
            End If
        Next i
        CreateEnumList = True
    End If

  End If

End Function
```

First, the level is checked for validity. The hierarchy is restricted to five levels in this example by the constant **g_nMaxLevels**. If you look at Figure 11-6, you will see that the hierarchy contains folders with the levels 0–4.

We will use a **For...Next** loop to create the folders and items based on this level number that was passed in to the function. But keep this in mind: the implementation of this function is completely arbitrary. If you look at the example code for the sample RegSpace application, this function is implemented in a totally different manner. It uses the registry enumeration API functions to build the list of PIDLs.

The PIDL itself is created with a call to **pidlMgr::Create**. We will talk about this method in detail in "The PIDL Manager" section later in this chapter. For now just look at the call itself. If you examine the parameters to this function, you will see three values: the PIDL type (folder or item), the level of the PIDL item, and the index of the PIDL item. This is the format of our PIDL. If you remember, the PIDL is nothing more than two bytes that specify the size of the PIDL's data, followed by whatever data we want (terminated by an empty **ITEMIDLIST**). Therefore, our PIDL format is the following:

```
    size/type/level/index
```

pidlMgr::Create will create a PIDL in this format for us. We determine whether we are creating folders or non-folders by the *dwFlags* parameter.

Once we have the PIDL, we need to maintain it in a list of some sort.

A linked list in VB?

We will use an internal linked list to maintain our PIDLs. To understand how it works, you need to look at the following structure:

```
Public Type PIDLLIST
    pNext As Long
    pidl As LPITEMIDLIST
End Type
```

The *pidl* member is easy to understand—it contains the PIDL we want to keep track of. The *pNext* member contains a pointer to another structure of type PIDLLIST, which is the next PIDL in the list. Using this method, we can chain a list of PIDLs together (see Figure 11-7). This is much more efficient than using ReDim Preserve to build a variable length array, so don't just limit the linked lists to a namespace extension. They are good any time you have a variable-length list of data that needs to be searched efficiently.

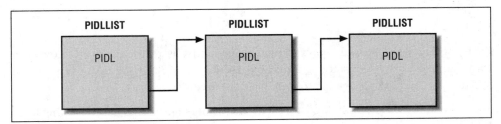

Figure 11-7. The linked list

AddToEnumList

Our EnumIDList class will contain three private member variables that correspond to the first member of the list, the current member of the list, and the last member of the list. *AddToEnumList* uses this information to determine where the next PIDL will go into the list and adjusts these list pointers accordingly. Let's examine the *AddToEnumList* function, which is shown in Example 11-16.

Example 11-16. AddToEnumList

```
'EnumIDList.cls

Public m_pFirst As Long
Public m_pCurrent As Long
Public m_pLast As Long

Public Function AddToEnumList(ByVal pidl As LPITEMIDLIST) As Boolean

    Dim aPidlList As PIDLLIST
    Dim pNewItem As Long

    AddToEnumList = False

    'Allocate memory for enum linked list item
    pNewItem = m_pMalloc.Alloc(Len(aPidlList))

    If (pNewItem > 0) Then
```

Example 11-16. AddToEnumList (continued)

```
        aPidlList.pNext = 0&
        aPidlList.pidl = pidl

        CopyMemory ByVal pNewItem, aPidlList, Len(aPidlList)

        If (m_pFirst = 0) Then
            m_pFirst = pNewItem
            m_pCurrent = m_pFirst
        End If

        If (m_pLast > 0) Then
            CopyMemory aPidlList, ByVal m_pLast, Len(aPidlList)
            aPidlList.pNext = pNewItem
            CopyMemory ByVal m_pLast, aPidlList, Len(aPidlList)
        End If

        m_pLast = pNewItem

        AddToEnumList = True

    End If

End Function
```

We'll use the shell's memory allocator for the first time to allocate the memory for the new linked list item.

The PIDL is assigned to the **PIDLLIST** structure, and *pNext* is set to 0&. Note that the ampersand in the assignment statement is important. This is a long value that is a **NULL** address. This marks the end of the list.

The first time *AddToEnumList* is called, *m_pFirst* and *m_pCurrent* are both assigned to the **PIDLLIST** link item. Thereafter, the *pNext* member of *m_pLast* is assigned to the new item, and the new item is added to the end of the list. When the shell starts calling **IEnumIDList::Next** for PIDLs, we will pass back whatever PIDL is pointed to by *m_pCurrent*. *m_pCurrent* will then be adjusted to point to the next item in the linked list.

Because we have allocated the memory for the linked list ourselves, when Enum-IDList terminates, we free the list using a call to DeleteList (see Example 11-14). DeleteList is shown in Example 11-17.

Example 11-17. DeleteList

```
Private Sub DeleteList()

    Dim aPidlList As PIDLLIST

    Do While (m_pFirst > 0)
```

Example 11-17. DeleteList (continued)

```
    CopyMemory aPidlList, ByVal m_pFirst, Len(aPidlList)
    m_pFirst = aPidlList.pNext

    If (aPidlList.pidl > 0) Then
        m_pidlMgr.Delete aPidlList.pidl
    End If

  Loop

  m_pFirst = 0
  m_pCurrent = 0
  m_pLast = 0

End Sub
```

Starting with *m_pFirst*, DeleteList merely copies the PIDL into a local instance of
PIDLLIST, adjusts *m_pFirst* to point to the next PIDL in the list, then frees the
current PIDL (which is now in *aPidlList*) by calling `pidlMgr::Delete`. This
function merely wraps a call to `IMalloc::Free`.

Next

Shortly after we have built our linked list of PIDLs, the shell begins to call several
functions repeatedly in an effort to display the PIDL appropriately. It will call
`IEnumIDList::Next` for the PIDL itself. It will call `IShellFolder::`
`GetAttributesOf` to find out whether this PIDL is a folder or an item. It will call
`IShellFolder::GetDisplayNameOf` for the display text of the PIDL. And it will
call `IShellFolder::CompareIDs` to determine in which order it should display
the PIDLs. Then it will call `IEnumIDList::Next` again. This process repeats until
there are no more PIDLs. The process looks like this:

1. Get PIDL.

2. Determine attributes: is it a "File" or a "Folder?"

3. Get the display name of the PIDL.

4. Compare this PIDL to a previous PIDL to determine the display order.

5. Start over.

As we mentioned earlier, when the shell calls the **Next** method, we will give it
the next PIDL in our linked list via the *rgelt* parameter; this is whatever is
pointed to by *m_pCurrent*. *m_pCurrent* is then adjusted to point to the next
item in the list. If *m_pCurrent* is equal to 0, we know that we are at the end of
the list, so we return *S_FALSE*. The shell will also expect us to tell it how many
PIDLs we are returning. Although we will not do this, this method can be written

to accommodate returning several PIDLs at once. This process is demonstrated in Example 11-18. Remember, this method has undergone a vtable swap; therefore, it exists in a code module.

Example 11-18. NextX

```
'DemoSpace.bas

Public Function NextX(ByVal this As IEnumIDList, _
                      ByVal celt As ULONG, _
                      rgelt As LPITEMIDLIST, _
                      pceltFetched As ULONG) As Long

    Dim cEnumIDList As EnumIDList
    Set cEnumIDList = this

    NextX = S_FALSE
    pceltFetched = 0
    rgelt = 0

    If cEnumIDList.m_pCurrent = 0 Then
        Exit Function
    End If

    Dim aPidlList As PIDLLIST
    CopyMemory aPidlList, _
               ByVal cEnumIDList.m_pCurrent, _
               Len(aPidlList)

    rgelt = aPidlList.pidl

    cEnumIDList.m_pCurrent = aPidlList.pNext
    pceltFetched = 1

    NextX = S_OK

End Function
```

The PIDL Manager

Before we continue, we really need to discuss *pidlMgr.cls*. This class is a helper class that we will use to manage functions involving PIDLs. These helper functions include things like creating, copying, and deleting PIDLs, getting the last PIDL in a list of PIDLs, getting the next PIDL in a list of PIDLs, as well as additional functions that are more specific to our particular namespace extension.

So add a new class to the project called *pidlMgr.cls*, and let's start implementing some of the functionality of this class.

Delete

We have used three functions from this class so far: *Delete*, *Copy*, and *Create*. *Delete* is by far the easiest of the functions to implement. It just wraps a call to `IMalloc::Free`. *Delete* looks like this:

```
'pidlMgr.cls

Private m_pMalloc As IMalloc

Private Sub Class_Initialize()
    Set m_pMalloc = GetMalloc
End Sub

Private Sub Class_Terminate()
    Set m_pMalloc = Nothing
End Sub

Public Sub Delete(ByVal pidl As LPITEMIDLIST)
    m_pMalloc.Free pidl
End Sub
```

Copy

Copy is used to make a copy of the PIDL:

```
Public Function Copy(ByVal pidlSource As LPITEMIDLIST) As LPITEMIDLIST
    Dim pidlTarget As LPITEMIDLIST
    Dim cbSource As UINT

    Copy = 0

    If (pidlSource = 0) Then
        Exit Function
    End If

    cbSource = GetSize(pidlSource)

    pidlTarget = m_pMalloc.Alloc(cbSource)
    If (pidlTarget > 0) Then
        CopyMemory ByVal pidlTarget, ByVal pidlSource, cbSource
        Copy = pidlTarget
    End If

End Function
```

Create

This method is a little more involved, but the reason for this requires some background information. We have already discussed the format of the PIDL with which we will be dealing in this example. It looks like this:

```
size/type/level/index
```

Therefore, you might expect to create a UDT to represent this PIDL. Perhaps something like the following:

```
Type PIDL
    iSize As Integer
    pType As Long
    iLevel As Integer
    iIndex As Integer
End Type
```

Unfortunately, we cannot do this. The data that comprises the PIDL must be sequential. That is, the PIDL data must immediately follow the two bytes indicating the size of the PIDL itself. The UDT that has been described will not work, because VB aligns UDTs on 4-byte boundaries (Long values). What does this mean exactly? Well, look at the UDT for a moment. The first member, *iSize*, is an Integer. In VB, for backward-compatibility reasons, that is a 2-byte value. When we talk about aligning data on 4-byte boundaries, this means VB will place two empty bytes immediately after *iSize* to pad the member to 4-bytes. The same is done with *iLevel* and *iIndex*. So, rather than having sequential data, we have data with holes in it, as Figure 11-8 illustrates.

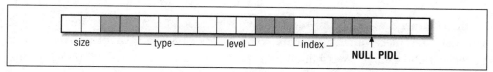

Figure 11-8. PIDL aligned on 4-byte boundaries

The simple solution to this problem is to use *CopyMemory* and to build our PIDL in memory as if it were a 0-byte aligned structure. Let's step through **Create** a few lines at a time, starting with the beginning of the method in Example 11-19, and discuss the function.

Example 11-19. Create from pidlMgr

```
Public Enum PIDLTYPE
    PT_FOLDER = 0
    PT_ITEM = 1
End Enum

Public Function Create(ByVal pt As PIDLTYPE, ByVal iLevel As Integer, ByVal iIndex As
Integer) As LPITEMIDLIST

    Dim iSize As Integer
    Dim pidl As LPITEMIDLIST

    'pidl size bytes (2) + pt(4) + iLevel(2) + iIndex(2)
    iSize = 10

    'Allocate memory for PIDL + a NULL ITEMIDLIST entry.
    pidl = m_pMalloc.Alloc(iSize + 2)
```

The first thing that happens is that the memory for the PIDL is allocated. The size of our PIDL is 10 bytes. That's 2 bytes for the size, 4 bytes for the type, 2 bytes for the "level," and 2 bytes for the "index." Therefore, we use **IMalloc** to allocate 10 bytes for our **PIDL**:

```
If (pidl > 0) Then

    CopyMemory ByVal pidl, iSize, 2
```

If the memory was allocated successfully (it is always prudent to check for this), then the size of the PIDL is copied into the first 2 bytes (the size) of the memory that will hold the PIDL. We can then use pointer arithmetic to copy the remaining values into the proper locations. Since we know our PIDL size is 2 bytes, we can skip 2 bytes forward in memory (PIDL + 2) and get the address for the **PIDLTYPE**. **PIDLTYPE** is 4 bytes, so jumping forward 6 bytes (PIDL + 6) will give us the address of the PIDLs level, and so on:

```
'Copy data into pidl
CopyMemory ByVal pidl + 2, pt, 4      'PIDLTYPE
CopyMemory ByVal pidl + 6, iLevel, 2 'PIDL level
CopyMemory ByVal pidl + 8, iIndex, 2 'PIDL index
```

Finally, we need to terminate the PIDL with a **NULL**, **ITEMIDLIST**. We could just terminate the PIDL with 2 bytes containing 0s, specifying a PIDL of no size. But to be technically accurate, we will end the PIDL with 2 **NULL** bytes (refer back to the **SHITEMID** structure). We then return the PIDL back to the caller:

```
'Add empty ITEMIDLIST to end of PIDL
CopyMemory ByVal pidl + iSize, 0, 2

    End If

    Create = pidl

End Function
```

Because we have created the PIDL in this manner, we will write several helper functions in PidlMgr to help us extract these values: *GetPidlSize*, *GetPidlType*, *GetPidlLevel*, and *GetPidlIndex*. Of the four functions, only one, *GetPidlSize*, can ever be used again. After all, the PIDL's size will always be the first 2 bytes of the structure. Even so, when you write your own namespace extensions, you will have to write similar functions to retrieve information from the PIDL. The rest are specific to the extension. These functions are shown in Example 11-20. They are self-explanatory.

Example 11-20. pidlMgr Helper Functions

'pidlMgr.cls

```
Public Function GetPidlSize(ByVal pidl As LPITEMIDLIST) As Integer
    Dim iSize As Integer
    GetPidlSize = 0
    If (pidl = 0) Then
        Exit Function
    End If
    'Size is the first 2 bytes of the pidl
    CopyMemory iSize, ByVal pidl, 2
    GetPidlSize = iSize
End Function

Public Function GetPidlType(ByVal pidl As LPITEMIDLIST) As PIDLTYPE
    Dim pt As Integer
    GetPidlType = 0
    If (pidl = 0) Then
        Exit Function
    End If
    'The "level" of the pidl is stored in bytes 3-6
    CopyMemory pt, ByVal pidl + 2, 4
    GetPidlType = pt
End Function

Public Function GetPidlLevel(ByVal pidl As LPITEMIDLIST) As Integer
    Dim iLevel As Integer
    GetPidlLevel = 0
    If (pidl = 0) Then
        Exit Function
    End If
    'The "level" of the pidl is stored in bytes 7-8.
    CopyMemory iLevel, ByVal pidl + 6, 2
    GetPidlLevel = iLevel
End Function

Public Function GetPidlIndex(ByVal pidl As LPITEMIDLIST) As Integer
    Dim iIndex As Integer
    GetPidlIndex = 0
    If (pidl = 0) Then
        Exit Function
    End If
    'The "index" of the pidl is stored in bytes 9-10.
    CopyMemory iIndex, ByVal pidl + 8, 2
    GetPidlIndex = iIndex
End Function
```

We will add new functions to PidlMgr as needed. But for now let's see what happens after our list has been built and the shell has called **IEnumIDList::Next**.

GetAttributesOf

Now that the shell has one of our PIDLs (as a result of calling `IEnumIDList::Next`) it needs to determine whether that PIDL is a folder or not. It does this by asking us, by way of a call to `IShellFolder::GetAttributesOf`. This method is defined as follows:

```
HRESULT GetAttributesOf(UINT cidl, LPCITEMIDLIST *apidl, ULONG *rgfInOut);
```

The first parameter, *cidl*, is the length of the PIDL array that is being pointed to by the second parameter. This is important. We are not getting a PIDL here. We are getting a pointer to an array of PIDLs. This method should be coded to handle more than one PIDL, even though it will not come into play in the example. It merely provides us the opportunity to write some really dangerous code involving pointer arithmetic. The second parameter, *rgfInOut*, is an [in, out] parameter that will be assigned one or more values from the `SFGAO` enumeration. We are only concerned with two of these values, `SFGAO_FOLDER` and `SFGAO_HASSUBFOLDER`. Let's look at the implementation, which begins at Example 11-21.

Example 11-21. IShellFolder::GetAttributesOf

```
Private Sub IShellFolder_GetAttributesOf( _
    ByVal cidl As VBShellLib.UINT, _
    aPidl As VBShellLib.LPCITEMIDLIST, _
    rgfInOut As VBShellLib.ULONG)

    Dim i As UINT
    Dim dwAttribs As DWORD
    Dim pidl As LPITEMIDLIST

    dwAttribs = dwAttribs Or 0
    rgfInOut = -1

    For i = 0 To cidl - 1
        CopyMemory pidl, aPidl + (i * 4), 4
```

Everything here is fairly straightforward until we get to the call to *CopyMemory*. This just increments the address of *aPidl* by 4 (the size of a pointer to an `ITEMIDLIST` which is a PIDL) every time we iterate the loop. This will happen *cidl* times:

```
        If m_pidlMgr.GetPidlType(pidl) = PT_FOLDER Then
            dwAttribs = dwAttribs Or SFGAO_FOLDER
```

Now that we have the PIDL, we can call `PidlMgr::GetPidlType` to retrieve the type of the PIDL. If it is a folder, then we add `SFGAO_FOLDER` to our attributes `DWORD`:

```
        If m_pidlMgr.GetPidlLevel(pidl) < g_nMaxLevels Then
            dwAttribs = dwAttribs Or SFGAO_HASSUBFOLDER
```

```
              End If

          End If

      Next i

      rgfInOut = rgfInOut And dwAttribs

  End Sub
```

Next, we'll get the PIDL level. If it's less than *g_nMaxLevels*, we know that is has subfolders beneath it. Therefore, we turn on the **SFGAO_HASSUBFOLDER** bits in the attributes **DWORD**. This will cause Explorer to draw the "+" node next to the folder.

When all is said and done, we return the PIDL attributes by way of *rgfInOut*.

Of course, this is all very specific to the example for the chapter. When you write your own namespace extensions, the format that you decide to create for your PIDL needs to take functions like *GetAttributesOf* into consideration. A good rule of thumb is that a PIDL should be able to describe its name and location. Go through the additional sample code that is provided with this chapter and see how this method is implemented in those examples. This should give you a better feel for writing extensions of your own.

GetDisplayNameOf

The shell also needs a way to determine the text to display for a PIDL. It does this by calling **IShellFolder::GetDisplayNameOf**. Its syntax is as follows:

```
HRESULT GetDisplayNameOf(LPCITEMIDLIST pidl, DWORD uFlags,
    LPSTRRET lpName);
```

The first parameter, *pidl*, is the PIDL for which the shell wants display information.

The second parameter, *uFlags*, is a value from the **SHGDN** enumeration. This value tells us how the shell is trying to display the name. Table 11-8 describes the values from this enumeration. Our chapter example does not use these values, but the additional examples do. If you want more details, check them out. Here, we're just going to return the same string no matter what the circumstances.

Table 11-8. SHGDN Enumeration

Constant	Description
SHGDN_NORMAL	The name is a full name relative to the desktop and not to any specific folder.
SHGDN_INFOLDER	The name is relative to the folder that is processing the name.
SHGDN_NORMAL	The name will be used for generic display.

Table 11-8. SHGDN Enumeration (continued)

Constant	Description
SHGDN_FORADDRESSBAR	The name will be used for display in the address bar combo box.
SHGDN_FORPARSING	The name will be used for parsing. It can be passed to ParseDisplayName.

The last parameter, *lpName*, is the address of an STRRET structure, which is defined as follows:

```
Public Const STRRET_WSTR = &H0

Public Type STRRET
    uType As UINT
    pOLESTR As Long
End Type
```

This parameter is how we'll return the display name to the shell.

Let's examine the implementation for *GetDisplayNameOf*, which is shown in Example 11-22.

Example 11-22. IShellFolder::GetDisplayNameOf

```
Private Sub IShellFolder_GetDisplayNameOf( _
    ByVal pidl As VBShellLib.LPCITEMIDLIST, _
    ByVal uFlags As VBShellLib.DWORD, _
    ByVal lpName As VBShellLib.LPSTRRET)

    Dim pString As Long
    Dim szText As String
    Dim szID As String
    Dim dwFlags As DWORD
        dwFlags = uFlags And &HFF00

    szText = m_pidlMgr.GetPidlName(pidl) & vbNullChar


    pString = m_pMalloc.Alloc(LenB(szText))
    If (pString) Then
        CopyMemory ByVal pString, ByVal StrPtr(szText), LenB(szText)
    End If

    Dim sret As STRRET
    sret.uType = STRRET_WSTR
    sret.pOLESTR = pString

    CopyMemory ByVal lpName, sret, Len(sret)

End Sub
```

The first interesting thing that happens is that we call `PidlMgr::GetPidlName` to build the display name of the PIDL. This function merely uses the helper functions we talked about earlier (*GetPidlType, GetPidlLevel, GetPidlLevel,* and *GetPidlIndex*) to build a string in the following format:

```
Folder/Item Level-Index.
```

Next, memory for the string is allocated using **IMalloc**, and the contents of the string are copied into that location. This makes it "global" to the shell's address space. If we didn't do this, *szText* would go out of scope as soon as the method terminated.

Finally, we populate the **STRRET** structure. The first member is set to **STRRET_WSTR** to inform the shell that the pointer we are giving it is to a wide character string. Then the second member is assigned a string pointer.

There is something very important worth mentioning at this point. The *lpName* parameter is being used to return information back to the shell, yet the parameter is defined as [in] in the type library. This is done with a purpose in mind. If we had defined this as an [in, out] parameter, we could have coded the last part of this method like so:

```
Dim sret As STRRET
sret.uType = STRRET_WSTR
sret.pOLESTR = pString

lpName = VarPtr(sret)
```

This sure looks better than the *CopyMemory* call, doesn't it? The problem is that the shell now has a pointer to a structure that is about to go out of scope. So the information contained in this structure is literally destroyed moments later. We could kludge this by declaring the structure as a private member to the shell folder class; then it would stay in scope for as long as the class was alive. But if we do this for every structure we need to pass back to the shell, things start to get confusing (as if they aren't confusing enough with us hacking the vtables of all these classes).

By defining this parameter as [in], VB declares it as **ByVal**, which forces us to actually copy the contents of the structure to the address specified by *lpName*. Therefore, every time we have a pointer to a structure, we will always define it as [in].

CompareIDs

`IShellFolder::CompareIDs` is called by the shell to give the namespace an opportunity to sort the PIDLs that are about to be displayed. If you look at a directory in Explorer, the Details view contains four columns: Name, Size, Type, and Modified. Explorer sorts the list based on the column you select. This is CompareIDs at work.

When CompareIDs is called, the shell passes us two PIDLs, and our implementation needs to determine which one should be displayed first:

- If PIDL #1 is displayed first, we return −1.

- If PIDL #2 is displayed first, we return a number > 0.

- If the PIDLs are the same, we return 0.

Our implementation is simple. First, we make sure folders are displayed first, then we sort on the level, and finally we sort on the index (see Figure 11-6). Before we jump into the code, here is an important concept to remember. The PIDLs we will be getting here will not always contain one item. The PIDL really does represent a path back to the root of the extension. We will get PIDLs that look like this:

```
Folder 1-1/Folder 2-2/Folder 3-1/Folder 4-1/Item 1-1
```

This list contains five **ITEMIDLIST**s. The PIDL is the pointer to this list. This is an important concept (which is why we're going over it again and again). A PIDL is not one thing. It is a pointer to a list such as this.

What the shell will give us here is a pointer to the first item in the array of **ITEMIDLIST**s—Folder 1-1. The value we want for sorting purposes, however, is Item 1-1. Therefore, CompareIDs will use a method in the PidlMgr class called **GetLastItem** to get this value. This method is defined in Example 11-23.

Example 11-23. The GetLastItem Method

```
Public Function GetLastItem(ByVal pidl As LPITEMIDLIST) _
    As LPITEMIDLIST

    Dim pidlLast As LPITEMIDLIST
    Dim pidlTemp As LPITEMIDLIST
        pidlTemp = pidl
    Dim iSize As Integer

    iSize = GetPidlSize(pidlTemp)

    Do While (iSize > 0)
        pidlLast = pidlTemp
        pidlTemp = GetNextItem(pidlTemp)
        iSize = GetPidlSize(pidlTemp)
    Loop

    GetLastItem = pidlLast

End Function
```

`PidlMgr::GetLastItem` makes use of a helper function, *GetNextItem*, which retrieves the next shell identifier in a PIDL. This function is defined in Example 11-24.

Example 11-24. The GetNextItem Method

```
Public Function GetNextItem(ByVal pidl As LPITEMIDLIST) _
    As LPITEMIDLIST

    GetNextItem = 0

    If (pidl > 0) Then

        Dim iSize As Integer
        iSize = GetPidlSize(pidl)

        'Pointer arithmetic in BASIC (scary, huh?)
        GetNextItem = pidl + iSize

    End If

End Function
```

And finally, here we get to CompareIDs. It has been swapped in the vtable because we need to return specialized values. Example 11-25 contains the implementation.

Example 11-25. CompareIDsX

```
'DemoSpace.bas

Public Function CompareIDsX(ByVal this As IShellFolder, _
                    ByVal lParam As lParam, _
                    ByVal pidl1 As LPCITEMIDLIST, _
                    ByVal pidl2 As LPCITEMIDLIST) As Long

    Dim pidlMgr As pidlMgr
    Set pidlMgr = New pidlMgr

    Dim pidlTemp1 As LPITEMIDLIST
    Dim pidlTemp2 As LPITEMIDLIST

    Dim pt1 As PIDLTYPE
    Dim pt2 As PIDLTYPE
    Dim iLvl1 As Integer
    Dim iLvl2 As Integer
    Dim iIndex1 As Integer
    Dim iIndex2 As Integer

    'Default - pidls are equal
    CompareIDsX = 0

    pidlTemp1 = pidlMgr.GetLastItem(pidl1)
```

Example 11-25. CompareIDsX (continued)

```
    pidlTemp2 = pidlMgr.GetLastItem(pidl2)

    pt1 = pidlMgr.GetPidlType(pidlTemp1)
    pt2 = pidlMgr.GetPidlType(pidlTemp2)
    If (pt1 <> pt2) Then
        CompareIDsX = pt1 - pt2
        Exit Function
    End If

    iLvl1 = pidlMgr.GetPidlLevel(pidlTemp1)
    iLvl2 = pidlMgr.GetPidlLevel(pidlTemp2)

    If (iLvl1 <> iLvl2) Then
        CompareIDsX = iLvl1 - iLvl2
        Exit Function
    End If

    iIndex1 = pidlMgr.GetPidlIndex(pidlTemp1)
    iIndex2 = pidlMgr.GetPidlIndex(pidlTemp2)
    CompareIDsX = iIndex1 - iIndex2

End Function
```

This is the first function to check if you write a namespace extension and items are not getting displayed in the proper order or the behavior of the extension seems odd.

This is one of the most crucial functions you must write when implementing a namespace. If this function does not work, nothing will.

GetUIObjectOf

When the shell requires additional interfaces to carry out tasks for the namespace extension, it calls `IShellFolder::GetUIObjectOf`. For instance, when the shell needs to display icons for the namespace extension, it calls GetUIObjectOf and asks for an `IExtractIcon` interface. If the shell wants to display a context menu, it will ask for an `IContextMenu` interface. In this way, GetUIObjectOf is sort of a specialized QueryInterface. Its syntax is:

```
HRESULT GetUIObjectOf(HWND hwndOwner, UINT cidl,
                      LPCITEMIDLIST *apidl, REFIID riid,
                      UINT *prgfInOut, LPVOID *ppvOut);
```

The first parameter, *hwndOwner*, is the parent window to use if the extension needs to display a message box. This is of no consequence to the VB programmer, because the *MsgBox* function supplied by Visual Basic does not allow one to specify the parent.

The second parameter, `cidl`, is the count of the PIDLs in the third parameter, `apidl`. This method can be coded similarly to `IShellFolder::GetAttributesOf` to handle more than one PIDL if that functionality is needed. It is usually not, however.

The third parameter, `apidl`, is a pointer to a GUID that represents the interface the shell is interested in acquiring from us. We will write a function that will take this pointer and convert it into a string that represents this interface. This will allow us to use simple comparisons to figure out which interface the shell is asking for.

The fourth parameter, `prgfInOut`, is reserved and is not used.

The fifth parameter, `ppvOut`, is the address that will receive the interface pointer.

To implement this method, we will rely heavily on a function that we will write called *GetIID*. This function takes a pointer to a GUID and returns a string representation of the GUID. This function is shown Example 11-26.

Example 11-26. GetIID Function

```
Public Function GetIID(ByVal riid As REFIID) As String

    Dim aGuid As GUID
    CopyMemory aGuid, ByVal riid, Len(aGuid)

    Dim pClsid As Long
    StringFromCLSID aGuid, pClsid

    Dim strOut As String * 255
    StrFromPtrW pClsid, strOut

    Dim iid As String
    GetIID = Left(strOut, InStr(strOut, vbNullChar) - 1)

End Function
```

GetIID makes use of a function called *StringFromCLSID*, which is found in *ole32.dll*. The function is declared as follows:

```
Public Declare Function StringFromCLSID Lib "ole32.dll" _
    (pClsid As GUID, lpszProgID As Long) As Long
```

The function doesn't return an actual string that can be used by VB, but rather a pointer to a string. Therefore, we need a function that will take this pointer and return us a string. This function is called *StringFromPointer*, and it is shown in Example 11-27.

Example 11-27. StringFromPointer Function

```
Public Sub StringFromPointer(pOLESTR As Long, strOut As String)

    Dim b(255) As Byte
    Dim iTemp As Integer
    Dim iCount As Integer
    Dim i As Integer

    iTemp = 1

    'Walk the string and retrieve the first byte of each WORD.
    While iTemp <> 0
        CopyMemory iTemp, ByVal pOLESTR + i, 2
        b(iCount) = iTemp
        iCount = iCount + 1
        i = i + 2
    Wend

    'Copy the byte array to our string.
    CopyMemory ByVal strOut, b(0), iCount

End Sub
```

Working with a CLSID

There are four helper functions found in *ole32.dll* that can be very helpful when working with a CLSID. They are declared as follows:

```
Public Declare Function CLSIDFromProgID Lib "ole32.dll" (ByVal lpszProgID As
Long, pClsid As GUID) As Long

Public Declare Function CLSIDFromString Lib "ole32.dll" (ByVal lpszProgID As
Long, pClsid As GUID) As Long

Private Declare Function ProgIDFromCLSID Lib "ole32.dll" (pCLSID As GUID,
lpszProgID As Long) As Long

Public Declare Function StringFromCLSID Lib "ole32.dll" (pClsid As GUID,
lpszProgID As Long) As Long
```

These four functions allow you to use CLSIDs in almost any circumstance. The functions all take pointers to strings as parameters, so you will have to use *StrPtr* to provide these values. For the functions that return pointers to strings, use the *StrFromPtrW* function shown in this chapter.

Now we're ready to discuss `GetUIObjectOf`. The address for this method has been swapped in the vtable for a function called *GetUIObjectOfX*. This is done because we need to be able to return `E_NOINTERFACE` if the shell asks us for an interface that we cannot provide. Example 11-28 shows our implementation of *GetUIObjectOfX*.

Example 11-28. GetUIObjectOfX

```
'DemoSpace.bas

Public Const IID_IExtractIconA = _
    "{000214EB-0000-0000-C000-000000000046}"
Public Const IID_IExtractIconW = _
    "{000214FA-0000-0000-C000-000000000046}"

Public Function GetUIObjectOfX(ByVal this As IShellFolder, _
    ByVal hwndOwner As hWnd, ByVal cidl As UINT, _
    aPidl As LPCITEMIDLIST, _
    ByVal riid As REFIID, _
    prgfInOut As UINT, ByVal ppvOut As LPVOID) As Long

    GetUIObjectOfX = E_NOINTERFACE

    Dim pUnk As IUnknownVB
    Dim pidl As LPITEMIDLIST
    Dim clsShellFolder As ShellFolder

    Dim szIID As String
        szIID = GetIID(riid)
```

The first thing we need to do is figure out which interface the shell is asking for by calling GetIID with the *riid* parameter. Next, we will check to see if the interface is **IExtractIconA** (Windows 98) or **IExtractIconW** (NT). All other requests will be ignored:

```
        If (szIID = IID_IExtractIconA) Then

            Set clsShellFolder = this
            Dim extIconA As ExtractIcon
            Set extIconA = New ExtractIcon

            extIconA.pidl = aPidl

            Dim iExtIconA As IExtractIconA
            Set iExtIconA = extIconA
            Set pUnk = iExtIconA
            pUnk.AddRef

            CopyMemory ByVal ppvOut, iExtIconA, 4

            GetUIObjectOfX = S_OK

        ElseIf (szIID = IID_IExtractIconW) Then
```

Once it has been determined that the shell is asking for **IExtractIcon**, we can declare an instance of our ExtractIcon class (which implements both

IExtractIconA and IExtractIconW) and pass it the PIDL that was given to us by the shell through the *aPidl* parameter:

```
Set clsShellFolder = this
Dim extIconW As ExtractIcon
Set extIconW = New ExtractIcon

'Pass pidl to IExtractIcon.
extIconW.pidl = aPidl
```

Next, we'll query our ExtractIcon class for the IExtractIcon itself. But before we pass the interface back to the shell, we need to do an AddRef so the interface will still be valid once this method terminates. We'll do that using IUnknownVB. Once this has been accomplished, the interface is copied to the address *ppvOut*:

```
Dim iExtIconW As IExtractIconW
Set iExtIconW = extIconW
Set pUnk = iExtIconW
pUnk.AddRef

CopyMemory ByVal ppvOut, iExtIconW, 4

GetUIObjectOfX = S_OK

    End If

  End Function
```

If all is well, the method should return S_OK.

ExtractIcon

ExtractIcon is a class we will use to provide the shell with icons for our namespace extension. You should already be familiar with IExtractIcon (see Chapter 5), so we will not discuss these interfaces again. But we will implement the interface a little bit differently than we did in Chapter 5. For one thing, our icons are not located in a file this time around. They will be stored in an image list. Therefore, we will implement Extract to provide the icons from an image list. GetIconLocation will only be used to specify the index of the icon in the image list.

If you recall from Example 11-28, we passed a PIDL to ExtractIcon. This is done through a property in the class called PIDL. This is shown in Example 11-29.

Example 11-29. ExtractIcon

```
Implements IExtractIconA
Implements IExtractIconW

Private m_pidl As LPITEMIDLIST
Private m_pidlMgr As pidlMgr
```

Example 11-29. ExtractIcon (continued)

```
Private m_pMalloc As IMalloc
Private m_hWnd As Long

Private Const ILD_TRANSPARENT = 1

Private Sub Class_Initialize()
    Set m_pMalloc = GetMalloc
    Set m_pidlMgr = New pidlMgr
End Sub

Private Sub Class_Terminate()
If (m_pidl > 0) Then
        m_pidlMgr.Delete m_pidl
    End If
Set m_pidlMgr = Nothing
End Sub

Public Property Let pidl(ByVal p As LPITEMIDLIST)
    m_pidl = m_pidlMgr.Copy(p)
End Property
```

GetIconLocation

GetIconLocation will only provide the index for the icon, not its location. Because of this, the shell will expect **Extract** to provide the actual location of the icon. Let's take a peek at **GetIconLocation**, which is shown in Example 11-30. We'll implement this method first, and then we'll tackle **Extract**. We'll only look at the **IExtractIconW** functions, but this should not be a problem. If you remember from Chapter 5, the difference between **IExtractIconW** and **IExtractIconA** is how the string containing the path to the icon must be handled. We will not be providing the shell a path for the icon location, so both interfaces can be implemented with the same code.

Example 11-30. IExtract::GetIconLocation

```
Private Sub IExtractIconW_GetIconLocation( _
    ByVal uFlags As VBShellLib.UINT, _
    ByVal szIconFile As VBShellLib.LPWSTRVB, _
    ByVal cchMax As VBShellLib.UINT, _
    piIndex As Long, pwFlags As VBShellLib.GETICONLOCATIONRETURN)

    pwFlags = GIL_NOTFILENAME

    'pidl is either a value or a folder
    Dim pidlTemp As LPITEMIDLIST

    pidlTemp = m_pidlMgr.GetLastItem(m_pidl)

    If m_pidlMgr.GetPidlType(pidlTemp) = PT_ITEM Then
```

Example 11-30. IExtract::GetIconLocation (continued)

```
        piIndex = ICON_ITEM

    Else
        If (uFlags And GIL_OPENICON) Then
            piIndex = ICON_OPEN
        Else
            piIndex = ICON_CLOSED
        End If
    End If
End Sub
```

The first thing we need to do is get the last item in the PIDL. This makes sense if you think of the PIDL as a file path. You want to display an icon for the item at the end of the "path," not the beginning, right? Once we have the last item in the PIDL, we determine its type by calling `PidlMgr::GetPidlType`. Then we will know whether it is a "folder" or an "item."

If we have a folder, we need to check the *uFlags* parameter for `GIL_OPENICON`. This will tell us whether the folder is opened or closed.

The values denoted by `ICON_` are merely constants describing the index of a particular icon in the image list that is located on *frmView*. They are simply:

```
    Public Const ICON_OPEN = 0
    Public Const ICON_CLOSED = 1
    Public Const ICON_ITEM = 2
```

Extract

Extract is short and sweet. It is shown in Example 11-31.

Example 11-31. IExtractIcon::Extract

```
Private Sub IExtractIconW_Extract( _
    ByVal pszFile As VBShellLib.LPWSTRVB, _
    ByVal nIconIndex As VBShellLib.UINT, _
    phiconLarge As VBShellLib.HICON, _
    phiconSmall As VBShellLib.HICON, _
    ByVal nIconSize As VBShellLib.UINT)

    Dim hImgList As Long
    hImgList = frmView.ImageList.hImageList

    phiconSmall = ImageList_GetIcon( _
        hImgList, nIconIndex, ILD_TRANSPARENT)

    phiconLarge = ImageList_GetIcon( _
        hImgList, nIconIndex, ILD_TRANSPARENT)

End Sub
```

Since our view will never change, we only need to provide small icons to the shell. Therefore, *phiconSmall* and *phiconLarge* can both point to the same icons. The function *ImageList_GetIcon*, which actually returns the handle to the icons, is located in *comctl32.dll* and is declared as follows:

```
Public Declare Function ImageList_GetIcon Lib "comctl32.dll" _
    (ByVal himl As Long, ByVal i As Integer, ByVal flags As UINT) _
    As HICON
```

FillList

We need to get back to ShellView and finish it up. We have one function left that handles populating the view object with items, called *FillList*. Every namespace extension you write will have a *FillList* function, but as you can probably imagine, the implementation of this function is highly dependent on the format of the PIDL being used.

Here's how the function works. If you remember, we wrote a function called *Initialize* in ShellView which we used to pass in an instance of ShellFolder and a PIDL to the class. *FillList* relies on this instance of ShellFolder for calling Enum-Objects. It will call EnumObjects, which will return an `IEnumIDList` interface. Once *FillList* has the `IEnumIDList` interface, it calls `IEnumIDList::Next` repeatedly in a loop until no more PIDLs are returned. As each PIDL is returned, we determine if the PIDL is a folder or an item and populate the list view accordingly. *FillList* is shown in Example 11-32. Let's go through it slowly.

Example 11-32. FillList

```
Public Sub FillList()

    Dim pEnumIDList As IEnumIDList
    Dim pShellFolder As IShellFolder
    Dim pidl As LPITEMIDLIST
    Dim dwFetched As DWORD
    Dim szPidlName As String
    Dim lIconIndex As Long

    Dim lv As ListView
    Set lv = m_frmView.ListView

    SendMessage lv.hWnd, LVM_DELETEALLITEMS, 0, 0
```

The first significant thing that happens is that all the items in the list view are cleared. This is done using *SendMessage* in this example, but it doesn't have to be done this way. You could also call `lv.ListItems.Clear`. It's just a matter of personal preference:

```
    Dim hr As Long
    Set pShellFolder = m_parentFolder
```

```
Set pEnumIDList = pShellFolder.EnumObjects _
    (m_frmView.hWnd, SHCONTF_NONFOLDERS)
```

Then we call `IShellFolder::EnumObjects` to get an `IEnumIDList` interface. This call is a little misleading here. It looks like we are asking for only non-folders (items), but this is not the case. If you examine *CreateEnumList* (Example 11-14), which is the function that builds the list for us, you will see that folders will *always* be added to the list (this is an implementation decision, not something that has to be done this way). By specifying `SHCONTF_NONFOLDERS`, we are asking for items *in addition to* folders:

```
If (ObjPtr(pEnumIDList) > 0) Then

    'Turn off listview redraw
    SendMessage lv.hWnd, WM_SETREDRAW, 0, 0

    pEnumIDList.Next 1, pidl, dwFetched
```

After we have checked to make sure that our `IEnumIDList` interface is valid, *SendMessage* is used to turn off the drawing on the list view. This minimizes flickering when the list view is being populated with items. Once the drawing is off, we call `IEnumIDList::Next` for the first PIDL. `IEnumIDList` is interesting in this example, because it is the first (and only) time that we directly use an interface that has been implemented by us:

```
Do While (dwFetched > 0)

    Dim li As ListItem
    Dim pidlTemp As LPITEMIDLIST

    szPidlName = m_pidlMgr.GetPidlName(pidl)

    If (m_pidlMgr.GetPidlType(pidl) = PT_FOLDER) Then
        lIconIndex = 2
    ElseIf (m_pidlMgr.GetPidlType(pidl) = PT_ITEM) Then
        lIconIndex = 3
    End If
```

When a PIDL has been returned to us, we get its display name and type. We could have called `IShellFolder::GetDisplayNameOf` for the name, but this would have been overkill. `GetDisplayNameOf` calls `PidlMgr::GetPidlName`, so we can just get to the point and call it ourselves.

The icon index is determined by the type. An interesting point to make here is that we ourselves are determining which icon should be displayed. Technically, we could call `IShellFolder::GetUIObjectOf` to get an `IExtractIcon` interface, and call `GetIconLocation` for this index value. Our implementation is so simple in this example, though, that it's easier just to do it this way.

Another reason that we do this ourselves is that we would have to write additional code to determine under which version of Windows we are running so we could return the appropriate interface (**IExtactIconA** or **IExtractIconW**):

```
        Set li = lv.ListItems.Add(, , szPidlName, , lIconIndex)
        li.Tag = Str(pidl)

        pEnumIDList.Next 1, pidl, dwFetched

    Loop
```

After the item is added to the list, we store the PIDL in the Tag property of the list item. This is done for one reason only. Our example will allow folder browsing from the view object. This means that when a folder item is double-clicked in the list view, navigation will take place. We need this PIDL so that we can determine whether a "folder" or an "item" was selected.

This happens repeatedly until there are no more PIDLs:

```
        'Turn on listview redraw
        SendMessage lv.hWnd, WM_SETREDRAW, 1, 0

    End If

    Set pEnumIDList = Nothing

End Sub
```

After the list view has been filled, drawing is turned back on, and our **IEnumIDList** interface is released.

Finishing the View Object

We have one more detail left on the view object. We need to allow for the browsing of folders. When a folder is double-clicked in the list view, we should navigate to that folder. Fortunately for us, this is a simple process. Everything is handled by **IShellBrowser**. To add this functionality, we add code for the DblClick event in list view. This code is shown in Example 11-33.

Example 11-33. ListView_DblClick

```
Private Sub ListView_DblClick()

    Dim pidl As LPITEMIDLIST
    Dim li As ListItem
    Set li = ListView.SelectedItem

    pidl = CLng(li.Tag)

    If (m_pidlMgr.GetPidlType(pidl) = PT_FOLDER) Then
        m_pShellBrowser.BrowseObject pidl, SBSP_DEFBROWSER Or _
```

Example 11-33. ListView_DblClick (continued)

```
                    SBSP_RELATIVE
    End If


    Set li = Nothing

End Sub
```

The PIDL is extracted from the Tag property of the list item that was double-clicked and converted back to a Long. Its type is then determined. If the list item is a folder, `IShellBrowser::BrowseObject` is called. This has the same effect as if we were to double-click on the item in the tree view ourselves.

BindToObject

We have one more method left in `IShellFolder` that we need to implement. This method, `BindToObject`, is called when a folder is opened in the tree view. Its syntax is as follows:

```
    HRESULT BindToObject(LPCITEMIDLIST pidl, LPBC pbcReserved,
                    REFIID riid,LPVOID *ppvOut);
```

`BindToObject` acts similarly to QueryInterface. The shell will ask for an interface via the *riid* parameter, and it will be our job to provide the interface through *ppvOut*. In fact, we'll just forward this request to `IUnknownVB::QueryInterface`. Under Windows 9x and Windows NT, the shell will always ask for `IShellFolder`. But not so for Windows 2000. In the event that the shell asks for another interface, we need to be prepared to return E_OUTOFMEMORY—which is why this method has been swapped in the vtable with a replacement function. The remaining code for the ShellFolder class in shown in Example 11-34.

Example 11-34. IShellFolder::BindToObject

```
'Demospace.bas

Public Const IID_IShellFolder = _
            "{000214E6-0000-0000-C000-000000000046}"

Public Function BindToObjectX(ByVal this As IShellFolder, _
                    ByVal pidl As LPCITEMIDLIST, _
                    ByVal pbcReserved As LPBC, _
                    ByVal riid As REFIID, _
                    ppvOut As LPVOID) As Long

    BindToObjectX = E_OUTOFMEMORY

    Dim iid As String
        iid = GetIID(riid)

    If iid = IID_IShellFolder Then
```

Example 11-34. IShellFolder::BindToObject (continued)

```
                'Current shell folder.
                Dim pParentShellFolder As ShellFolder
                Set pParentShellFolder = this

                'New child shell folder.
                Dim pShellFolder As ShellFolder
                Set pShellFolder = New ShellFolder

                'Pass current pidl and folder reference.
                'to child folder
                Set pShellFolder.Parent = pParentShellFolder
                pShellFolder.pidl = pidl

                'Give new shell folder back to the shell.
                Dim pUnk As IUnknownVB
                Set pUnk = pShellFolder

                pUnk.QueryInterface riid, ppvOut

                Set pUnk = Nothing
                Set pShellFolder = Nothing
                Set pParentShellFolder = Nothing

                BindToObjectX = S_OK

        End If

End Function

'ShellFolder.cls
Public Property Set Parent(p As ShellFolder)
        Set m_parentFolder = p
End Property

Public Property Let pidl(ByVal p As LPITEMIDLIST)

        m_pidl = m_pidlMgr.Copy(p)

        Dim pidlTemp As LPITEMIDLIST
            pidlTemp = m_pidlMgr.GetLastItem(m_pidl)

        m_iLevel = m_pidlMgr.GetPidlLevel(pidlTemp) + 1

End Property
```

 When BindToObject terminates, the IShellFolder interface that we have passed back to the shell is still valid even though we have not called AddRef implicitly. This is because QueryInterface calls AddRef for us. In fact, this behavior is a rule for properly implementing QueryInterface.

Basically, opening another folder repeats the entire process we have just walked through. When `BindToObject` is called, we create an instance of ShellFolder ourselves, passing it a reference to the current ShellFolder and the current PIDL. The `IShellFolder` interface is then given back to the shell, and the process begins again.

Registering DemoSpace

The last thing we need to do is register the namespace extension. The registry information shown in Example 11-35 will insert our namespace extension under My Computer. Remember, if you type this listing in, everything inside of the square brackets must be on the same line.

Example 11-35. DemoSpace.reg

```
REGEDIT4

[HKEY_CLASSES_ROOT\CLSID\{DAE49F45-660D-11D3-BB7C-444553540000}]
@="Root"

[HKEY_CLASSES_ROOT\CLSID\{DAE49F45-660D-11D3-BB7C-444553540000}\ShellFolder\]
"Attributes"=dword:a0000000

[HKEY_CLASSES_ROOT\CLSID\{DAE49F45-660D-11D3-BB7C-444553540000}\DefaultIcon\]
@="shell32.dll,46"

[HKEY_LOCAL_MACHINE\Software\Microsoft\Windows\CurrentVersion\Explorer
\MyComputer\Namespace\{DAE49F45-660D-11D3-BB7C-444553540000}\]
@ = "Nothing Special Namespace Extension"

HKEY_LOCAL_MACHINE\SOFTWARE\Microsoft\WindowsNT\CurrentVersion\
ShellExtensions\Approved\]
"{DAE49F45-660D-11D3-BB7C-444553540000}"="Demo namespace in VB"
```

The CLSID in the listing is the same CLSID you would find under the `HKEY_ CLASSES_ROOT\DemoSpace.ShellFolder` key. This is important. Everything starts with `IShellFolder`.

Also, notice the `Attributes` setting. This value is created by ORing the `SFGAO` constants (See Example 11-2). The value A0000000 is a result of `SFGAO_FOLDER` ORed with `SFGAO_HASSUBFOLDERS`. This attribute is for the junction point of our namespace extension. Without this key, we wouldn't be able to open our namespace extension at all.

You might also decide that you would like to insert this example under the Desktop. This is as simple as changing My Computer to Desktop in the registry script. If you do this, you might also want to change the attributes to A0000020. This value is the result of ORing together `SFGAO_FOLDER`, `SFGAO_HASSUBFOLDERS`, and

SFGAO_CANDELETE. When you add a namespace extension under the Desktop, an icon is added to the Desktop. By adding the SFGAO_CANDELETE attribute, the Delete command is available from the context menu of the namespace extension. Otherwise, it would be impossible to remove the icon from the Desktop.

Practical Coding Examples

Writing a namespace extension is a pretty big undertaking, and most of the code in a namespace extension is specific to the extension itself. This is due to the fact that PIDLs are different for every extension. As it turns out, a majority of the code in a practical namespace extension involves managing a PIDL in one way or another. Therefore, we did things a little differently in this chapter: the example code for this chapter was not designed to be practical in any sense of the word. Rather, it was designed to be simple so we could focus on how to implement a namespace rather than have to wade through large volumes of proprietary code.

However, once you've worked through this generic example of implementing a namespace extension, you'll want to take a careful look at the downloadable code samples, which contain two "real world" namespace extensions: RegSpace, which allows you to browse the keys and value entries of the registry as if they were part of the filesystem, and ROTSpace, which similarly presents the Running Object Table (ROT) as a part of the shell namespace.

RegSpace

The first is based on the RegView example (a namespace extension implemented in C++) in the MSDN library. As you might be able to guess from the name, this extension provides a view of the registry from within Explorer. The VB version of RegView, which we'll call RegSpace, can be seen in action in Figure 11-9. RegSpace is an example of a namespace extension with a fairly complex hierarchy.

ROTSpace

The second extension, ROTSpace, is a view of the ROT. The ROT is a globally accessible table that keeps track of all running COM objects that can be identified with a moniker. A *moniker* acts like a name that uniquely identifies a COM object much in the same way that a path identifies a file in the filesystem. IMoniker is what makes a moniker a moniker, and the interesting thing about monikers is that they support what is known as binding. Binding means locating an object named by the moniker, activating it, and returning a pointer to a requested interface on the object. What's even more interesting is that if the moniker is already running, you can attach to the running instance (but we're not going to talk about that). ROTSpace is shown in Figure 11-10.

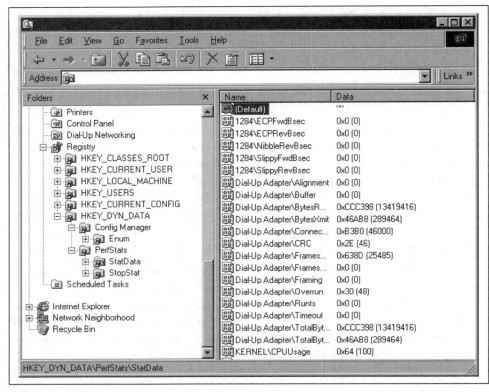

Figure 11-9. RegSpace

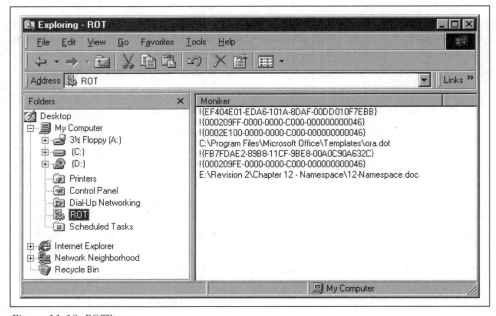

Figure 11-10. ROTSpace

IV

Browser Extensions

12

Browser Extensions

Remember when VB 5.0 came out? It was the first appearance of the Microsoft Internet Control. A great control, really, that basically represented an instance of Internet Explorer. At the time, it seemed like there were articles everywhere exclaiming, "Write a browser in FOUR lines of code!" or "Write Your Own Internet Applications Now!" Yes, it's true, you can write a browser with just a few lines of code or create a host of other standalone Internet applications very quickly with this control. But standalone? Wouldn't it be cooler to write an Internet application that was integrated with Explorer automatically? Yes, it would, and this is where browser helper objects come in. Browser helper objects, or BHOs, are very similar to shell extensions. They run in-process to Explorer and are loaded every time a new instance of Explorer is started. But unlike shell extensions, they can perform a wide variety of tasks. You are limited only by your imagination in what you can do with BHOs. Why? Because once loaded, the BHO has full access to IE's event sink. This means that, as you surf the Internet, the browser helper is right there every step of the way. BHOs can log on to your favorite web-based email site automatically as soon as you navigate to the URL, or they can automatically retrieve information from your online brokerage account. They can do just about whatever you want them to do, because BHOs have complete access to every piece of HTML that passes through your browser. They can access it before you see it or before you leave it.

You might have seen a BHO in action if you frequently visit Yahoo! They have a toolbar that can be added to Internet Explorer called Yahoo! Companion, which provides quick access to many of the features at their web site. This component is a BHO.

We'll discuss Browser Extensions in this chapter as well. They are implemented just like BHOs, but are specific to Internet Explorer 5.0. The advantage of using browser extensions is that you can add menu items and toolbar buttons for the extension to Explorer.

Speaking of Explorer, let's clarify something at the outset: in this chapter, Explorer and Internet Explorer are the same, as far as we're concerned. Sure, there are differences between the two programs, but don't sweat the small stuff. We'll use the term Explorer to mean both programs. We can do that because browser helper objects are loaded by both of these programs. You see, the term "browser" here doesn't necessarily mean a web browser. Explorer proper is also a browser. Its tree view allows you to *browse* the Windows namespace. So, even though we will be discussing BHOs in the context of the Internet (and Internet Explorer) in this chapter, keep in mind that they can be written for Explorer as well.

Browser Helper Objects

Before looking at developing Browser Extensions for IE 5.0, we'll look at developing BHOs.

How BHOs Work

Browser helper objects are simple components, really. Once you know what you are doing, you could probably build one in about five minutes (minus any functionality, of course).

When Explorer first loads, it examines the following key for any browser helper objects that might be registered:

```
HKEY_LOCAL_MACHINE\
    Software\
        Microsoft\
            Windows\
                CurrentVersion\
                    Explorer\
                        Browser Helper Objects
```

Chances are, if you look in your registry right now, this key is not there, or if it does exist, it is empty. That's because Internet Explorer does not install a default set of browser helpers.

When BHOs are loaded, Explorer passes to the component what is known as a *site pointer*, which is actually an **IUnknown** interface pointer that the BHO can use to communicate with Explorer. Beyond this point, everything a BHO does is application-dependent. Typically, though, the BHO will be used to gain access to the current instance of Internet Explorer by querying the site pointer for **IWebBrowser2**. Once it has this interface, it has access to all of IE's events, as well as full access to Microsoft's Dynamic HTML Object Model. This means that whatever is being displayed in the browser is fully accessible to the BHO. So, as you might guess, BHOs can evolve from a very simple components into complex entities rather quickly.

Browser Helper Interfaces

Browser helper objects are only required to implement one interface: `IObjectWithSite`. `IObjectWithSite` consists of two methods, `SetSite` and `GetSite`, as Table 12-1 shows.

Table 12-1. IObjectWithSite

Method	Description
GetSite	Returns the last site set with `SetSite`.
SetSite	Provides the `IUnknown` site pointer of Explorer.

GetSite

This function returns the last site set with `SetSite`. Its syntax is:

```
HRESULT GetSite(REFIID riid, void** ppvSite);
```

with the following parameters:

riid
>   [in] The interface identifier whose pointer should be returned in *ppvSite*.

ppvSite
>   [in, out] Address of the interface pointer described by *riid*

The job of `GetSite` is simply to return the site pointer passed in by Explorer via `SetSite`. It is provided as a means for additional objects to gain access to the site pointer; it is a hooking mechanism.

The interesting thing about this method is that its arguments look very much like those of *QueryInterface*. This is no coincidence. The only thing this method needs to do is forward the *riid* and *ppvSite* parameters to a *QueryInterface* call and return the result.

SetSite

When an instance of Explorer is fired up, the BHO is loaded and Explorer calls `SetSite`, passing in an `IUnknown` interface pointer. This is known as a *site pointer*. The syntax of the `SetSite` method is:

```
HRESULT SetSite(IUnknown* pUnkSite);
```

Its single parameter is:

pUnkSite
>   [in] Site pointer.

A BHO typically will query the site pointer for the IWebBrowser2 interface. When you declare a variable as type Internet Explorer, this is really a reference to IWebBrowser2 (but we'll talk about that soon enough). This gives the browser helper access to the current instance of the web browser, including IE's event sink.

The IDL to define the IObjectWithSite interface is shown in Example 12-1. Notice that the IUnknown pointer has been replaced with IUnknownVB in the IDL definition. Here, this is done "just in case" for flexibility. Later, you might want to call *QueryInterface*, AddRef, or even Release on the site pointer. Who knows? Here, though, it's not really necessary. When we implement SetSite, we'll cache a copy of the site pointer in a private member that will be declared as IUnknownVB. Our private member will give us access to all of IUnknown's methods (which is necessary to properly implement GetSite).

Example 12-1. IDL for the IObjectWithSite Interface

```
[
    uuid(FC4801A3-2BA9-11CF-A229-00AA003D7352),
    helpstring("IObjectWithSite Interface"),
    odl
]
interface IObjectWithSite : IUnknown
{
    HRESULT SetSite([in] IUnknownVB* pSite);
    HRESULT GetSite([in] REFIID priid,
                    [in, out] VOID * ppvObj);
}
```

The Project

We begin by creating a new ActiveX DLL project called BHO and adding three references to our project:

- Our type library
- Microsoft Internet Controls
- Microsoft HTML Object Library

The Microsoft HTML Object Library will most likely have to be added manually. It is in the system directory in a DLL named *mshtml.dll.*

We will call our class clsInetSpeak for reasons that will be apparent later, and the first thing we will do is implement IObjectWithSite:

```
'clsInetSpeak
Implements IObjectWithSite
```

Next we implement SetSite. First, we add two private member variables to the class. The first is of type IUnknownVB. This is used to save the site pointer passed into us by Explorer. The second is of type Internet Explorer. This is used to manipulate the current running instance of Explorer. This is demonstrated in Example 12-2.

Example 12-2. SetSite Implementation

```
'clsInetSpeak

Implements IObjectWithSite

Private m_pUnkSite As IUnknownVB
Private WithEvents m_ie As InternetExplorer

Private Sub IObjectWithSite_SetSite( _
    ByVal pSite As VBShellLib.IUnknownVB)

    If ObjPtr(pSite) = 0 Then
        CopyMemory m_ie, 0&, 4
        Exit Sub
    End If

    Set m_pUnkSite = pSite   'Save the site pointer for GetSite
    Set m_ie = pSite         'QueryInterface for IWebBrowser2

End Sub
```

SetSite is also called when Explorer is closed, and the value of the *pSite* argument, instead of containing the site pointer, contains a null pointer. When this happens, we need to overwrite the address of *m_ie* with 0 and exit the sub. We *do not* set *m_ie* equal to Nothing. This is speculation, but it appears that setting *m_ie* equal to Nothing here does not immediately release the component. Explorer thinks that it still has a valid reference and crashes. Overwriting the address with a 0 prevents this from happening.

Notice in Example 12-2 that *m_ie* is declared WithEvents. This gives us access to a wide variety of events that are fired by Explorer. We'll talk about that shortly, but let's implement GetSite first. It's one line of code, so let's get it out of the way. Example 12-3 contains the code.

Example 12-3. GetSite

```
Private Sub IObjectWithSite_GetSite(
    ByVal priid As VBShellLib.REFIID,
    ppvObj As VBShellLib.VOID)

    m_pUnkSite.QueryInterface priid, ppvObj

End Sub
```

Can life get simpler than this? All we need to do here is call *QueryInterface* on the site pointer with the parameters passed in by the shell. We are done.

If we stop right here, the code we have so far is the minimal skeleton required to implement any BHO. You might want to save this somewhere as a template for creating future BHOs.

Registration

Registering browser helper objects is quite easy. Figure 12-1 shows the appropriate entry. `{xxxxxxxx-xxxx-xxxx-xxxx-xxxxxxxxxxxx}` represents the CLSID of the BHO.

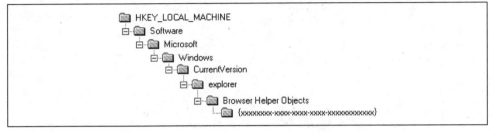

Figure 12-1. Registering BHOs

Example 12-4 shows the registry script for the BHO that will be created in this chapter. It only contains one entry. You can modify this script easily for your own helper objects.

Example 12-4. Registry Script for BHO

```
REGEDIT4

[HKEY_LOCAL_MACHINE\Software\Microsoft\Windows
\CurrentVersion\Explorer\Browser Helper Objects\
{D6862A22-1DD6-11D3-BB7C-444553540000}\]
```

IWebBrowser2

We are actually going to do something with this BHO we are building, but first we need to discuss this Internet Explorer reference we have and all the things we can do with it. This should give you a better idea of the types of projects you can create with BHOs.

That reference we're holding to Internet Explorer is actually an **IWebBrowser2** interface. Why is it important that you know this? Well, for one thing, the documentation for **IWebBrowser2** is much better than for the Microsoft Internet Control, and the methods of the **IWebBrowser2** interface correspond to the methods and properties of Internet Explorer. This is important because the interfaces we will be working with contain so many methods (over 70 of them) that it would be impractical to list them all here. But since the documentation for this interface is good, you should be able to figure out what most of the methods are for. These interfaces are all documented in the Platform SDK and are listed as **IHTMLxxxx**. You can access them and view their type information in the Object Browser by adding a reference to the Microsoft HTML Object Library (*MSHTML.TLB*) to your project.

Most of the methods of **IWebBrowser2** deal with explicit settings of the Explorer program itself: status bar text, menu visibility, view mode, current URL, etc. But there is one property that is especially important to us: Document. This property returns a reference to an **IHTMLDocument2** interface. From this interface, we can navigate the entire Dynamic HTML object model, which is depicted in Figure 12-2. This means that our BHO has access to any element on a given web page. If we want to change the **href** property of an anchor tag that is nested four frames deep inside the third form on the page, no problem. If we want to execute JavaScript against the currently loaded page, we can do that too. In fact, we can programmatically change any element we want or strip information from any page we desire.

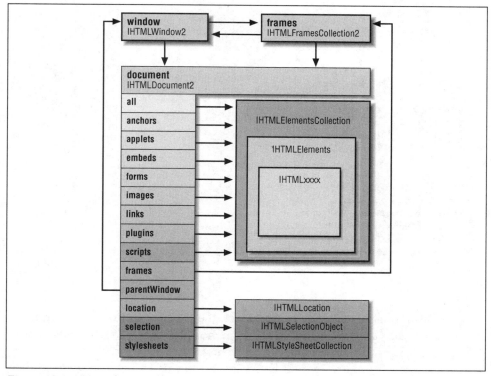

Figure 12-2. HTML object model

Let's take some of the confusion out of navigating the object model. We start by retrieving the value of the Document property of **IWebBrowser2**, which gives us an `IHTMLDocument2` interface. From here, we can get the parent window of the document, the collection of frames inside of a document, or an object that is a part of the current document itself. Think about it in terms of a web page. A web page contains a main window. This window contains the document. The document can contain a collection of frames. Each one of these frames contains a window. Taking this frame window as a Window object brings us back to the top of the hierarchy.

Once we have an `IHTMLDocument2` interface, we can get to any element (<BODY>, <A>, <TABLE>, etc.) on a page. Each of these elements has a corresponding interface that is in the format `IHTMLxxxx`. As Figure 12-1 illustrates, there are several collections available to us. Let's take the "all" collection for example. The all property returns an `IHTMLElementsCollection` interface that will allow us to iterate through every element on a web page. Once we have a specific element, we can then get any number of the `IHTMLxxxx` interfaces. The code fragment in Example 12-5 demonstrates this.

Example 12-5. Traversing an HTML Document

```
Private WithEvents m_ie As InternetExplorer
.
.
.
Dim pDocument as IHTMLDocument2
Dim pElements as IHTMLElementsCollection
Dim pElement as IHTMLElement

Set pDocument = m_ie.Document
Set pElements = pDocument.all

'Loop through each element
For i = 0 to pElements.length - 1
    Set pElement = pElements.item(i)
    if pElement.tagName = "a" Then
        Dim pAnchor as IHTMLAnchorElement
        Set pAnchor = pElement
        pAnchor.href = "http://www.oreilly.com"
        .
        .
        .
```

As we loop through each element, we check the tag name. If the tag is equal to "a," then we can *QueryInterface* for `IHTMLAnchorElement`. The code fragment in Example 12-5 would actually change the `href` of each anchor it came across to *http://www.oreilly.com*. You would be redirected to this URL if you were to then click on the link.

There are over 100 `IHTMLxxxx` interfaces documented in the Platform SDK, and each has methods specific to its function. It is well beyond the scope of this book to document them all. A good place to start is `IHTMLWindow2` and `IHTMLDocument2`. You can navigate the entire Dynamic HTML Object Library from these two interfaces. Oddly enough, if you are running IE 4.0, these two interfaces are marked [`hidden`] in the library. If you have installed IE 5.0, all of the interfaces are visible.

Events

The Microsoft Internet Control provides 18 events for which we can add our code. Table 12-2 contains a complete list of the events provided by Internet Explorer. These events seemingly cover just about every situation you might envision. The events typically used in a browser extension are marked with an asterisk.

 There is no event for a refresh. But the flexibility is there for you to handle this situation yourself. The NavigateComplete2 event is passed a parameter, *URL*, that identifies the resource to which the browser has navigated. You can store the value of this argument to a Private member variable. Then you can check the *URL* argument in the BeforeNavigate2 event against the stored value. If they are the same, a refresh has occurred.

Table 12-2. DWebBrowserEvents2 Methods

Method	Fired When . . .
StatusTextChange	The status bar text has changed.
ProgressChange	Information on the progress of a download is updated.
CommandStateChange	The enabled state of a menu command changes.
DownloadBegin*	A navigation operation is starting, shortly after the BeforeNavigate2 event, unless the navigation is canceled.
DownloadComplete*	A navigation operation finishes, is stopped, or has failed.
TitleChange	The title of a document in the Web Browser control becomes available or has changed.
PropertyChange	The `IWebBrowser2::PutProperty` method changes the value of a property.
BeforeNavigate2*	The Web Browser control is about to navigate to a new URL.
NewWindow2	A new window is created for displaying a resource.
NavigateComplete2*	The browser has completed navigation to a new location.
DocumentComplete*	The document being navigated to has finished loading.
OnQuit	The Internet Explorer application is ready to quit.
OnVisible	The window for the WebBrowser should be shown or hidden.
OnToolBar	The ToolBar property has changed.

Table 12-2. DWebBrowserEvents2 Methods (continued)

Method	Fired When . . .
OnMenuBar	The MenuBar property has changed.
OnStatusBar	The StatusBar property has changed.
OnFullScreen	The FullScreen property has changed.
OnTheaterMode	The TheaterMode property has changed.

Okay, let's add some code to our BHO skeleton. This is going to be temporary code that we will rip out later. The purpose is just to show you some object model navigation techniques. This exercise will also demonstrate how one task can be accomplished several different ways.

If you have IE 5.0, undoubtedly you have seen the new feature that remembers values that have been entered previously. Say you go to log in to your Hotmail account. IE 5.0 will ask you if you would like to save the password information. If you say "yes," the next time you come to Hotmail, your previously entered information is available, and then you can log in automatically.

We're not going to do anything *that* fancy, but this example could be the foundation for such a component. All this component will do is fill in our login name when we go to Hotmail. Everything is hardcoded. This is just a beta, after all!

The first thing we need to do is to add a private member variable to our class, called *m_bGoingToHotmail*. Then we add some code to the BeforeNavigate2 event, as Example 12-6 shows.

Example 12-6. BeforeNavigate2 Example

```
Private Sub m_ie_BeforeNavigate2(ByVal pDisp As Object, _
                                 URL As Variant, _
                                 Flags As Variant, _
                                 TargetFrameName As Variant, _
                                 PostData As Variant, _
                                 Headers As Variant, _
                                 Cancel As Boolean)

    If URL = "http://www.hotmail.com/" Then
        m_bGoingToHotmail = True
    Else
        m_bGoingToHotmail = False
    End If

End Sub
```

The reason we are testing for this URL in the BeforeNavigate2 event is that at the time of this writing, when you go to Hotmail, you are immediately redirected to another URL. BeforeNavigate2 will allow us to capture the URL *http://www.hotmail.com* before the redirection, so we'll know we're at the right place. The result of this event procedure is that when you navigate to Hotmail, a flag indicating this fact is set. Hotmail can redirect us to wherever, and we still know we are heading there.

Now we just have to implement one more event, DocumentComplete. This event is called when the page has finished loading and the document is available. The HTML source for the Hotmail login page indicates that there is one form on the page, and that the login text box we are interested in is on the form. Example 12-7 shows one possible way of navigating to the text box and setting its value.

Example 12-7. DocumentComplete Event Procedure

```
Private Sub m_ie_DocumentComplete(ByVal pDisp As Object, _
                            URL As Variant)

    If (m_bGoingToHotmail = True) Then

        Dim i As Long

        Dim pDoc As IHTMLDocument2
        Set pDoc = m_ie.Document

        Dim pForms As IHTMLElementCollection
        Set pForms = pDoc.Forms

        Dim pForm As IHTMLFormElement
        Set pForm = pForms.Item(0)

        Dim pElements As Object
        Set pElements = pForm.elements

        Dim pElement As IHTMLElement
        Set pElement = pElements.Item("login")

        Dim pInput As IHTMLInputTextElement
        Set pInput = pElement
        pInput.Value = "oreilly"

    End If

End Sub
```

Wow, that's a bunch of code for one simple task! Don't worry, we'll trim it down to size in a little while, but for now let's walk through it.

First, we get the current document by calling the Document property of *m_ie* and assigning the resulting object reference to *pDoc*. Then we get the collection of all the forms on the page and assign it to *pForms*. Since we have looked at the source to the page, we know there is only one form, so we can get the form directly without looping through the collection by calling:

```
Set pForm = pForms.Item(0)
```

Now we get to an inconsistency in the model. We want to grab a collection of all the elements on the form, so we call the elements property of `IHTMLFormElement`. You might expect this to return an `IHTMLElementsCollection` reference, but it does not. It returns an `IDispatch` interface.

Once we have all the elements on the form, we can get the element we are looking for by name with the call:

```
Set pElement = pElements.Item("login")
```

We can then query *pElement* for `IHTMLInputTextElement` and set the value of the text box with the call:

```
Dim pInput As IHTMLInputTextElement
Set pInput = pElement
pInput.Value = "oreilly"
```

Wait, don't run away. That was the convoluted, horribly inefficient way to achieve this task. Achieving this goal is really is much easier than Example 12-7 shows.

Okay, delete the DocumentComplete code, and we'll try this again. Let's look at Example 12-8.

Example 12-8. Easier DocumentCompleteevent Procedure

```
Private Sub m_ie_DocumentComplete(ByVal pDisp As Object, _
                            URL As Variant)

   If (m_bGoingToHotmail = True) Then

       Dim pDoc As IHTMLDocument2
       Set pDoc = m_ie.Document

       Dim pElements As IHTMLElementCollection
       Set pElements = pDoc.All

       Dim pInput As IHTMLInputTextElement
       Set pInput = pElements.Item("login")

       pInput.Value = "oreilly"

   End If

End Sub
```

Once again, we get the current document by calling the Document property. But this time, instead of getting the elements of a form, we just grab the whole page by calling All. Once we have all the elements, we can get the element we are interested in directly by name.

We can also use JavaScript to achieve our goal. Example 12-9 illustrates this point.

Example 12-9. Yet Another DocumentComplete Event Procedure

```
Private Sub m_ie_DocumentComplete(ByVal pDisp As Object, _
                                  URL As Variant)

    If (m_bGoingToHotmail = True) Then

        Dim pDoc As IHTMLDocument2
        Set pDoc = m_ie.Document

        Dim pWnd As IHTMLWindow2
        Set pWnd = pDoc.parentWindow

        Dim strJava As String
        strJava = "document.passwordform.login.value = 'oreilly';"

        pWnd.execScript strJava

    End If

End Sub
```

That's kind of slick, isn't it? We get the current document as before. Then we get the current window by calling parentWindow. This returns an **IHTMLWindow2** interface. **IHTMLWindow2** is [hidden], by the way, if you're still running IE 4.0. Once we have that, we can execute JavaScript directly against the page by calling *execScript. execScript* takes a string that contains either JavaScript or VBScript, which can be specified by a second, optional parameter to the method.

You can execute two whole pages of JavaScript if you want. As long as each statement is delimited by a semicolon, the whole two pages could be shoved into a string and sent to *execScript*. But that's a little unwieldy. The easy way would be to chop up the string into manageable chunks and execute them one at a time:

```
strJava = "document.passwordform.login.value = 'oreilly';"
pWnd.execScript strJava
strJave = "document.submit();"
pWnd.execScript strJava
    .
    .
    .
```

Before we continue, delete the code for BeginNavigate2 and DocumentComplete, so we can have a fresh start. Ahhh, that's better.

Browser Extensions

We can take the code we have so far a step further . . . but only if you have Internet Explorer 5.0 installed on your box. IE 5.0 provides us with the means to add a menu item and toolbar button for our component. There is some grunt work involved, but it's not too bad. Basically, we have to add a bunch of settings to the registry, and our component needs to implement an additional interface, `IOleCommandTarget`.

We are also going to become somewhat familiar what another new interface called `IServiceProvider`. This is because we cannot query the site pointer for `IWebBrowser2` like we did for BHOs. We will get access to an `IServiceProvider` interface that we can use to request the `IWebBrowser2`. As you will see in "Browser Extension Interfaces" later in this chapter, we will have to jump through a few hoops to do this.

Just to keep things a little suspenseful, we'll wait until the component is wired up and ready to go before we actually discuss its purpose. Exciting, huh?

How Browser Extensions Work

For the most part, browser extensions work just like browser helper objects. But there are some minor differences. For one thing, they are registered differently. When Explorer loads a browser extension, it looks under the following key:

```
HKEY_LOCAL_MACHINE\
    SOFTWARE\
        Microsoft\
            InternetExplorer\
                Extensions\
```

There are also some additional registry entries that will provide the toolbar icons and the menu item text, but we'll discuss them later.

Browser Extension Interfaces

Like BHOs, browser extensions implement `IObjectWithSite`. They are also required to implement another interface called `IOleCommandTarget`. This interface is used to execute menu and toolbar commands. In addition to `IOleCommandTarget`, browser extensions must be aware of another interface called `IServiceProvider`. Browser extension are a little different than BHOs in that they cannot query for IE directly from the site pointer. Rather, they are given a pointer to an `IServiceProvider` interface. `IServiceProvider`, in turn, supplies the browser extension with a reference to `IWebBrowser2`.

We've already discussed `IObjectWithSite` in the section on BHOs. In the following sections, we'll discuss the `IOleCommandTarget` and `IServiceProvider` interfaces.

IOleCommandTarget

In terms of browser extensions, `IOleCommandTarget` allows us to process menu and toolbar commands that we have added to Explorer. This interface contains two methods, which are described in Table 12-3.

Table 12-3. IOleCommandTarget

Method	Description
QueryStatus	Returns the status of one or more commands generated by user-interface events.
Exec	Executes a command from the menu or the toolbar.

QueryStatus. The shell calls this method to determine which commands are supported by the BHO and which commands are enabled or disabled, and to provide the name or status of a command:

```
HRESULT QueryStatus(GUID *pguidCmdGroup, ULONG cCmds,
                    OLECMD *prgCmds, OLECMDTEXT *pCmdText);
```

Its parameters are:

pguidCmdGroup

[in] A NULL for browser extensions.

cCmds

[in] The number of commands in the *prgCmds* array.

prgCmds

[in] An array of OLECMD structures that indicate the commands for which Explorer needs information. OLECMD is defined as follows:

```
typedef struct _tagOLECMD {
    ULONG cmdID;
    DWORD cmdf;
} OLECMD;
```

Its members are as follows:

cmdID

This is the ID of one of Explorer's commands, which is taken from the following enumeration:

```
typedef enum
{
    OLECMDID_OPEN               = 1,
    OLECMDID_NEW                = 2,
    OLECMDID_SAVE               = 3,
    OLECMDID_SAVEAS             = 4,
    OLECMDID_SAVECOPYAS         = 5,
    OLECMDID_PRINT              = 6,
    OLECMDID_PRINTPREVIEW       = 7,
    OLECMDID_PAGESETUP          = 8,
    OLECMDID_SPELL              = 9,
    OLECMDID_PROPERTIES         = 10,
    OLECMDID_CUT                = 11,
    OLECMDID_COPY               = 12,
    OLECMDID_PASTE              = 13,
    OLECMDID_PASTESPECIAL       = 14,
```

```
                   OLECMDID_UNDO                    = 15,
                   OLECMDID_REDO                    = 16,
                   OLECMDID_SELECTALL               = 17,
                   OLECMDID_CLEARSELECTION          = 18,
                   OLECMDID_ZOOM                    = 19,
                   OLECMDID_GETZOOMRANGE            = 20
                   OLECMDID_UPDATECOMMANDS          = 21
                   OLECMDID_REFRESH                 = 22
                   OLECMDID_STOP                    = 23
                   OLECMDID_HIDETOOLBARS            = 24
                   OLECMDID_SETPROGRESSMAX          = 25
                   OLECMDID_SETPROGRESSPOS          = 26
                   OLECMDID_SETPROGRESSTEXT         = 27
                   OLECMDID_SETTITLE                = 28
                   OLECMDID_SETDOWNLOADSTATE        = 29
                   OLECMDID_STOPDOWNLOAD            = 30
                   OLECMDID_ONTOOLBARACTIVATED      = 31,
                   OLECMDID_FIND                    = 32,
                   OLECMDID_DELETE                  = 33,
                   OLECMDID_HTTPEQUIV               = 34,
                   OLECMDID_HTTPEQUIV_DONE          = 35,
                   OLECMDID_ENABLE_INTERACTION      = 36,
                   OLECMDID_ONUNLOAD                = 37
               } OLECMDID;
```

cmdf

This is the type of support provided by the BHO for the command that is specified by *cmdID*. It can be one value from the following enumeration:

```
typedef enum
{
    OLECMDF_SUPPORTED    = 1,
    OLECMDF_ENABLED      = 2,
    OLECMDF_LATCHED      = 4,
    OLECMDF_NINCHED      = 8
} OLECMDF;
```

The OME_CMDF_SUPPORTED and OLECMDF_ENABLED items are fairly obvious. OLECMDF_LATCHED means the command is an on-off toggle that is currently on. The meaning of OLECMD_NINCHED is somewhat mysterious. The Platform SDK says that the value is reserved for future use. However, the value supposedly represents the undefined state of a three-state control.

pCmdTest

[in] Pointer to an OLECMDTEXT structure that is used to return name/status information to Explorer for one command. This value can be NULL, indicating that the caller does not need the information. The structure is defined as follows:

```
typedef struct _tagOLECMDTEXT
{
    DWORD cmdtextf;
    ULONG cwActual;
```

```
        ULONG cwBuf;
        wchar_t rgwz[1];
    }OLECMDTEXT;
```

The members of OLECMDTEXT are:

cmdtextf

> Value that determines whether the *rgwz* member contains status text or a command name. This value is defined in the OLECMDTEXTF enumeration:

```
typedef enum
{
    OLECMDTEXTF_NONE   = 0,
    OLECMDTEXTF_NAME   = 1,
    OLECMDTEXTF_STATUS = 2
} OLECMDTEXTF;
```

cwActual

> The number of characters actually written to the *rgwz* buffer before *QueryStatus* returns.

cwBuf

> The number of elements in the *rgwz* buffer.

rgwz

> A wide-character buffer (two bytes per character) that receives the status text or command name.

Exec. This method is used to execute a command. It can also be used to display help for a command. Its syntax is:

```
HRESULT Exec(GUID *pguidCmdGroup, DWORD nCmdID, DWORD nCmdExecOpt,
        VARIANTARG *pvaIn, VARIANTARG *pvaOut);
```

with the following parameters:

pguidCmdGroup

> [in] A NULL for browser extensions.

nCmdID

> [in] Command to be executed.

nCmdExecOpt

> [in] One or more values from the OLECMDEXECOPT enumeration that describe how the command should be executed. This parameter should be ignored for browser extensions.

pvaIn

> [in] Pointer to a VARIANTARG (same as a Variant) structure that contains input arguments. This parameter can also be NULL.

pvaOut

> [in, out] Pointer to a VARIANTARG structure that returns command output. This parameter can also be NULL.

Example 12-10 contains the interface definition for `IOleCommandTarget`.

Example 12-10. IOleCommandTarget Interface

```
[
    uuid(B722BCCB-4E68-101B-A2BC-00AA00404770),
    helpstring("IOleCommandTarget Interface"),
    odl
]
interface IOleCommandTarget : IUnknown
{

    typedef enum OLECMDF {
        OLECMDF_SUPPORTED       = 0x00000001,
        OLECMDF_ENABLED         = 0x00000002,
        OLECMDF_LATCHED         = 0x00000004,
        OLECMDF_NINCHED         = 0x00000008,
    } OLECMDF;

    typedef struct _tagOLECMD {
        ULONG   cmdID;
        DWORD   cmdf;
    } OLECMD;

    typedef struct _tagOLECMDTEXT{
            DWORD cmdtextf;
            ULONG cwActual;
            ULONG cwBuf;
            wchar_t *rgwz;
    } OLECMDTEXT;

    typedef enum OLECMDID {
        OLECMDID_OPEN                   = 1,
        OLECMDID_NEW                    = 2,
        OLECMDID_SAVE                   = 3,
        OLECMDID_SAVEAS                 = 4,
        OLECMDID_SAVECOPYAS             = 5,
        OLECMDID_PRINT                  = 6,
        OLECMDID_PRINTPREVIEW           = 7,
        OLECMDID_PAGESETUP              = 8,
        OLECMDID_SPELL                  = 9,
        OLECMDID_PROPERTIES             = 10,
        OLECMDID_CUT                    = 11,
        OLECMDID_COPY                   = 12,
        OLECMDID_PASTE                  = 13,
        OLECMDID_PASTESPECIAL           = 14,
        OLECMDID_UNDO                   = 15,
        OLECMDID_REDO                   = 16,
        OLECMDID_SELECTALL              = 17,
        OLECMDID_CLEARSELECTION         = 18,
        OLECMDID_ZOOM                   = 19,
        OLECMDID_GETZOOMRANGE           = 20,
        OLECMDID_UPDATECOMMANDS         = 21,
        OLECMDID_REFRESH                = 22,
```

Example 12-10. IOleCommandTarget Interface (continued)

```
        OLECMDID_STOP                           = 23,
        OLECMDID_HIDETOOLBARS                   = 24,
        OLECMDID_SETPROGRESSMAX                 = 25,
        OLECMDID_SETPROGRESSPOS                 = 26,
        OLECMDID_SETPROGRESSTEXT                = 27,
        OLECMDID_SETTITLE                       = 28,
        OLECMDID_SETDOWNLOADSTATE               = 29,
        OLECMDID_STOPDOWNLOAD                   = 30,
        OLECMDID_ONTOOLBARACTIVATED             = 31,
        OLECMDID_FIND                           = 32,
        OLECMDID_DELETE                         = 33,
        OLECMDID_HTTPEQUIV                      = 34,
        OLECMDID_HTTPEQUIV_DONE                 = 35,
        OLECMDID_ENABLE_INTERACTION             = 36,
        OLECMDID_ONUNLOAD                       = 37,
        OLECMDID_PROPERTYBAG2                   = 38,
        OLECMDID_PREREFRESH                     = 39,
    } OLECMDID;

    typedef enum OLECMDTEXTF {
        OLECMDTEXTF_NONE            = 0,
        OLECMDTEXTF_NAME            = 1,
        OLECMDTEXTF_STATUS          = 2,
    } OLECMDTEXTF;

    typedef enum OLECMDEXECOPT {
        OLECMDEXECOPT_DODEFAULT         = 0,
        OLECMDEXECOPT_PROMPTUSER        = 1,
        OLECMDEXECOPT_DONTPROMPTUSER    = 2,
        OLECMDEXECOPT_SHOWHELP          = 3
    } OLECMDEXECOPT;

    HRESULT QueryStatus([in] LPGUID pguidCmdGroup,
                        [in] ULONG cCmds,
                        [in,out] LPOLECMD *prgCmds,
                        [in,out] LPOLECMDTEXT *pCmdText);

    HRESULT Exec([in] LPGUID pguidCmdGroup,
                [in] DWORD nCmdID,
                [in] DWORD nCmdExecOpt,
                [in] VARIANT *pvaIn,
                [in,out] VARIANT *pvaOut);
}
```

IServiceProvider

IServiceProvider contains one method (which is very much like QueryInterface) called QueryService, as the following table shows:

Method	Description
QueryService	Creates or accesses the specified service and returns an interface pointer to it.

QueryService. This method is very similar to `QueryInterface` in form and function. It takes a pointer to the GUID of the service we are looking for, namely IWebBrowserApp, and a pointer to the interface we want from that service (in our case, IWebBrowser2). It returns the interface we have requested (hopefully). Its syntax is:

```
HRESULT QueryService(REFGUID guidService, REFIID riid, void** ppvOut);
```

Its parameters are as follows:

guidService
> [in] Identifier for the requested service.

riid
> [in] Identifier for the interface on the request service.

ppvOut
> [out, retval] Address that receives the interface pointer requested by *riid.*

Example 12-11 contains the complete listing for `IServiceProvider`.

Example 12-11. IServiceProvider Interface

```
[
    uuid(6d5140c1-7436-11ce-8034-00aa006009fa),
    helpstring("IServiceProvider Interface"),
    odl
]
interface IServiceProvider : IUnknown
{
    HRESULT QueryService([in]  LPGUID guidService,
                         [in]  REFIID riid,
                         [out, retval] IDispatch **ppvObject);
}
```

SetSite Revisited

As stated earlier, we are going to have to implement `SetSite` a little bit differently. Let's take the code piece by piece. The following code fragment should look familiar. It's the same code you would implement for a BHO:

```
Private Sub IObjectWithSite_SetSite(_
    ByVal pSite As VBShellLib.IUnknownVB)

    If ObjPtr(pSite) = 0 Then
        CopyMemory m_ie, 0&, 4
        Exit Sub
    End If

    Set m_pUnkSite = pSite    'Save the site pointer for GetSite
```

Here's where things get a little different. Instead of asking for IWebBrowser2, we need to get IServiceProvider. So, we'll query the site pointer for this interface:

```
Dim pServiceProvider As IServiceProvider
Set pServiceProvider = m_pUnkSite
```

Now, QueryService takes a pointer to a GUID for both of its arguments. To get these GUIDs, we need to declare a couple of constants in *clsInetSpeak* that represent the string values of the GUIDs we are interested in. They are as follows:

```
Private Const IID_IWebBrowserApp = _
    "{0002DF05-0000-0000-C000-000000000046}"
Private Const IID_IWebBrowser2 = _
    "{D30C1661-CDAF-11D0-8A3E-00C04FC9E26E}"
```

We are going to use an API function found in *ole32.dll* to map these string values to an actual GUID. This function is called *CLSIDFromString*, and it is declared as follows:

```
Public Declare Function CLSIDFromString Lib "ole32.dll" _
    (ByVal lpszProgID As Long, pCLSID As GUID) As Long
```

Its parameters are:

lpszProgId

This is a pointer to the string representation of a CLSID.

pCLSID

This is a pointer to a GUID structure defined as so:

```
Public Type GUID
    Data1 As Long
    Data2 As Integer
    Data3 As Integer
    Data4(7) As Byte
End Type
```

Now, back to SetSite. Continuing on with our implementation, we declare two variables to hold the IIDs, *clsidWebApp* and *clsidWebBrowser2*, and then we call *CLSIDFromString* to populate those structures:

```
Dim clsidWebApp As GUID
Dim clsidWebBrowser2 As GUID

CLSIDFromString StrPtr(IID_IWebBrowserApp), clsidWebApp
CLSIDFromString StrPtr(IID_IWebBrowser2), clsidWebBrowser2
```

Now all we have to do is call QueryService and release IServiceProvider. We have to use *VarPtr*, because QueryService needs the *pointer* to the GUID:

```
Set m_ie = pServiceProvider.QueryService( _
    VarPtr(clsidWebApp), VarPtr(clsidWebBrowser2))

Set pServiceProvider = Nothing
```

We now have our IWebBrowser2 interface. The good news here is that GetSite is the same, so we don't have to worry about it at all. The complete listing for SetSite can be found in Example 12-12.

Example 12-12. SetSite for Browser Extension

```
Private Sub IObjectWithSite_SetSite(ByVal pSite As IUnknownVB)

    If ObjPtr(pSite) = 0 Then
        CopyMemory m_ie, 0&, 4
        Exit Sub
    End If

    Set m_pUnkSite = pSite      'Save the site pointer for GetSite

    Dim pServiceProvider As IServiceProvider
    Set pServiceProvider = m_pUnkSite

    Dim clsidWebApp As GUID
    Dim clsidWebBrowser2 As GUID

    'Query service provider to get IWebBrowser2 (Internet Explorer)
    CLSIDFromString StrPtr(IID_IWebBrowserApp), clsidWebApp
    CLSIDFromString StrPtr(IID_IWebBrowser2), clsidWebBrowser2

    Set m_ie = pServiceProvider.QueryService(_
        VarPtr(clsidWebApp), VarPtr(clsidWebBrowser2))

    Set pServiceProvider = Nothing


End Sub
```

Adding the Menu Item

To add a menu item for our component, we need to add several values to the registry. They all reside under the key shown in Figure 12-3. Take a look, then we'll talk about it.

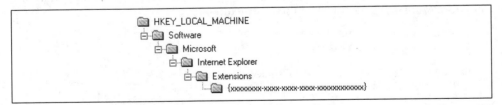

Figure 12-3. Browser extension key

All values for our browser extension will go under the HKEY_LOCAL_MACHINE\ Software\Microsoft\Internet Explorer\Extension\<*GUID*> key. This is important. The GUID denoted by the xes in Figure 12-3 is *not* the CLSID of our component. It is just a randomly generated GUID that uniquely identifies this key. This value exists nowhere else in the registry. So, use GUIDGEN to create this key.

Once you have added this key to the registry, we need to add several values, which are shown in Figure 12-4.

Figure 12-4. Browser extension menu values

The CLSID {1FBA04EE-3024-11d2-8F1F-0000F87ABD16} is a fixed value. Every browser extension you write needs that exact `clsid` value; it's not some made up value. If you search the registry for the value, you will find the entry, "Toolbar Extension for Executable."

`ClsidExtension`, however, is the registry value that points to our browser extension. `MenuStatusBar` contains the text that will be displayed in the status bar when our menu item is selected, and `MenuText` contains the text of our menu item.

You cannot use an ampersand (&) to define hotkeys for this menu because there is nothing in place to prevent conflicts with other menu items.

Browser extension commands are located under the Tools menu in Internet Explorer 5.0. They are also available from Explorer, but only when browsing the Web.

Finally, there is another optional value you can add called `MenuCustomize`. If you create a string value with this name and set it equal to "help" (case doesn't matter), your menu item will appear under the Help menu instead of the Tools menu. If the `MenuCustomize` key does not exist or its value is set to anything other than "help," the menu item will appear under the Tools menu.

Adding the Toolbar Button

Adding a toolbar button is as simple as adding three more string values to the registry and creating a couple of icons. See Figure 12-5 for the additional registry values. You must create four icons for the button. These include a 20×20 icon and a 16×16 icon that represent the default state of the button, and two more icons of the same dimensions that represent the "hot" image that is displayed when the mouse is over the button.

The icon values in the registry can point to an *.ico* file or, as you can see in Figure 12-5, a resource in a Windows executable. The format for the latter option is:

```
Executable, Resource ID
```

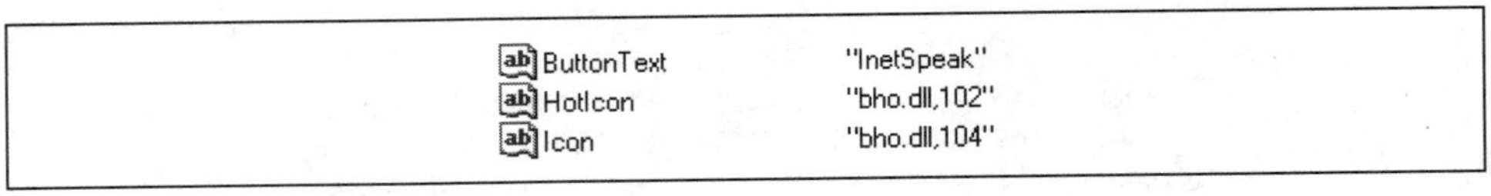

ab	ButtonText	"InetSpeak"
ab	HotIcon	"bho.dll,102"
ab	Icon	"bho.dll,104"

Figure 12-5. Registry settings for a toolbar button

If you opt to store the icons in a DLL, you should probably register your components in the system directory. This will free you from having to map a path for these entries.

After you have added these entries, you will need to select View → Toolbars → Customize from Internet Explorer's main menu. A dialog will present you with the opportunity to add the button to the toolbar.

QueryStatus

The shell calls `IOleCommandTarget::QueryStatus` to inquire about the status of a menu or toolbar command (i.e., whether the command is enabled or disabled). The funny thing is, if we do not supply the status information, Explorer will disable any toolbar buttons we may have added (this does not affect menu items) after we use them for the first time. So, to keep things working properly, we will need to implement this method.

Actually, this behavior is interesting because after our browser extension has been called once, `QueryStatus` will be called every time *any* command is issued. It will also be called when the user just clicks on a web page! This means you can write code to enable or disable your extension based on existing Explorer commands like Refresh, Home, or Print.

`QueryStatus` is defined as follows:

```
HRESULT QueryStatus( const GUID *pguidCmdGroup, ULONG cCmds,
    OLECMD *prgCmds, OLECMDTEXT *pCmdText);
```

The first parameter, *pguidCmdGroup*, is a pointer to the GUID that represents the command group. In terms of our extension, we do not care about this value; it is going to be NULL.

The second parameter, *cCmds*, is the count of OLECMD structures in the array pointed to by the third parameter, *prgCmds*. These two parameters are the ones that concern us most. Our implementation of `QueryStatus` will loop through these commands and merely tell the shell that the commands are supported and enabled.

The last parameter, *pCmdText*, is a pointer to an OLECMDTEXT structure that is used to return command name and status information back to the shell. We do not need to worry about this parameter for browser extensions.

The code for `QueryStatus` is shown in Example 12-13.

Example 12-13. QueryStatus

```
Private Sub IOleCommandTarget_QueryStatus( _
    ByVal pguidCmdGroup As VBShellLib.LPGUID, _
    ByVal cCmds As VBShellLib.ULONG, _
    ByVal prgCmds As VBShellLib.LPOLECMD, _
    ByVal pCmdText As VBShellLib.LPOLECMDTEXT)

    Dim i As Integer

    For i = 0 To cCmds - 1
        Dim cmd As OLECMD

        CopyMemory cmd, ByVal prgCmds + (Len(cmd) * i), Len(cmd)
        cmd.cmdf = OLECMDF_SUPPORTED Or OLECMDF_ENABLED
        CopyMemory ByVal prgCmds + (Len(cmd) * i), cmd, Len(cmd)

    Next i

End Sub
```

In the case of our example, when `QueryStatus` is called, *cCmds* will always be 1, since our extension only adds a single command to the Explorer menu. Regardless, the method has been coded to demonstrate how you would handle more than one command. Since *prgCmds* is a pointer to an array, pointer arithmetic is used to calculate the offset of the command structure in memory. A local copy of the structure is created, and the appropriate values are added to the structure. The local instance of the command is then copied back into the array.

Exec

Yes, it's time to actually accomplish something with this component. The extension in this chapter performs an important service. It translates Internet-speak into plain English. Remember the first time you got on the Web and saw a sentence like this: "Well, IMHO, I think this book rocks!" IMHO? What the heck is IMHO? Well, with our handy translator installed, you will be able to highlight these bizarre acronyms and watch as IMHO is translated into, "In my honest/humble opinion," right on the page. That's sort of practical, right?

The code to accomplish this amazing feat goes into `IOleCommandTarget::Exec`, which is shown in Example 12-14. Once we get the `IHTMLDocument2` interface, its Selection property will give us the text that is selected on the current page in the form of an `IHTMLSelectionObject` interface pointer. A method of this interface gives us the text range of the current selection, and from there we are able to get to the text itself. Then we are free to modify it in any way we see fit. The translation is accomplished with a humongous `Select...Case` block. If any of your favorite goofy acronyms have been left out, go ahead and add them.

Example 12-14. Exec Implementation

```
Private Sub IOleCommandTarget_Exec(_
    ByVal pguidCmdGroup As VBShellLib.LPGUID, _
    ByVal nCmdID As VBShellLib.DWORD, _
    ByVal nCmdExecOpt As VBShellLib.DWORD, _
    pvaIn As Variant, _
    pvaOut As Variant)

    Translate

End Sub

Private Sub Translate()

    Dim pDoc As IHTMLDocument2
    Dim pTextRange As IHTMLTxtRange
    Dim sDef As String

    Set pDoc = m_ie.Document
    Set pTextRange = pDoc.selection.createRange

    Select Case Trim(pTextRange.Text)
        Case "IMHO"
            sDef = "[In My Honest/Humble Opinion]"
        Case "FYI"
            sDef = "[For Your Information]"
        Case "AFAIK"
            sDef = "[As Far As I Know]"
        Case "LOL"
            sDef = "[Laughing Out Loud/Lots Of Laughs]"
        Case "BTW"
            sDef = "[By The Way]"
        Case "TIA"
            sDef = "[Thanks In Advance]"
        Case "RTM"
            sDef = "Read The Manual"
        Case "RTFM"
            sDef = "Read The Fine Manual"
        Case ":)", ":-)"
            sDef = "[Smile]"
        Case ";)", ";-)"
            sDef = "[Wink]"
        Case ":(", ":-("
            sDef = "[Boo-hoo]"
        Case Else
            sDef = pTextRange.Text
    End Select

    pTextRange.Text = sDef

    Set pTextRange = Nothing
    Set pDoc = Nothing

End Sub
```

If you followed along with the chapter, the browser extension should already have the appropriate entries in the registry. But you will need to move the extension into your system directory if you want the icons for the toolbar button to be displayed properly. After you move the extension, register it using *regsvr32.exe*. Also, don't forget that in order for the toolbar button to show up, you will have to add it to the toolbar yourself by selecting View → Toolbars → Customize from IE 5.0's menu.

13

Band Objects

If you need to extend the shell and a GUI is a must, band objects are the way to go. Band objects are only available with shell versions 4.71 and later. This means that to use them, you need to have installed Internet Explorer 4.0 or later *with the shell integration option selected* (this is built into Windows 2000 by default). Well, actually, that isn't entirely true. If you haven't installed shell integration, you are limited to using band objects with Internet Explorer. In other words, you're restricted to Internet-only applications. But, hey, that might not be so bad, right? The Internet is a big place. Just be aware that with the shell integration installed, you have the ability to write band objects that take advantage of your "local" needs as well.

Band objects come in several flavors: Explorer bands (also called Explorer bars), Communication bands, and Desk bands. There is also an additional band type called a Tool band. All four bands are implemented in exactly the same way. The distinction between them lies in where the bands are displayed. Explorer bars are displayed vertically on the left side of Explorer. Examples of system-defined Explorer bands include the Search, Favorites, History, and Folders bands. These can be accessed by selecting View → Explorer Bar in Explorer's main menu. The remaining band objects are:

Communication bands
> An example of a Communication band is the Tip of the Day band, which is accessed from the same menu.

Desk bands
> These are not displayed in Explorer proper, but rather in the task bar (actually, the desktop is a running instance of Explorer).

Tool bands

These were introduced with Internet Explorer Version 5.0. The radio band is an example of such a band (yes, IE 5.0 has a radio). This band type is basically an addition to Explorer's toolbar.

Illustrations of all four band types can be seen in Figures 13-1 through 13-4.

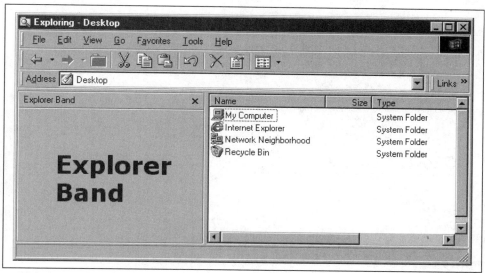

Figure 13-1. Explorer band

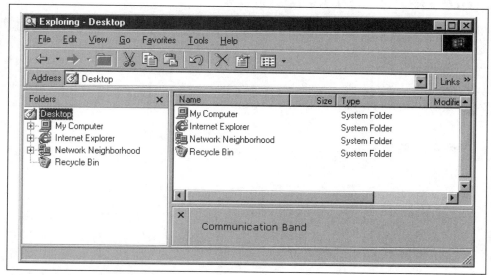

Figure 13-2. Communication band

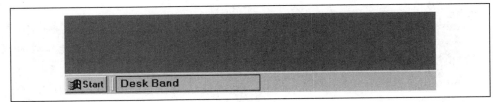

Figure 13-3. Desk band

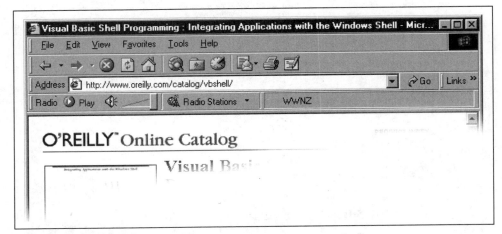

Figure 13-4. Tool band

How Band Objects Work

Talking about band objects can get a little confusing, so let's get some terminology straight before we continue. *Band object* refers to the component that is implementing the band.

Each registered band object has a corresponding menu item under the View → Explorer Bar menu on Explorer's frame window. Band objects are registered under the CLSID key in the registry like so:

```
HKEY_CLASSES_ROOT\
    CLSID\
        {CLSID}\      Default = Menu Name
            Implemented Categories\
                {CATID}
```

{*CLSID*}, in this instance, is the CLSID of the band object. {*CATID*}, on the other hand, is a component category identifier that designates the band as either a Desk Band, an Explorer band, or a Communication band.

When the menu item specified by the default value of {*CLSID*} is selected, Explorer loads the band object and initializes it through IObjectWithSite by passing a site pointer to the band object (see Chapter 12, *Browser Extensions*).

The site pointer allows the band object to communicate with the site in the container (the container being the actual band Explorer will create for the band object window).

The band object's first priority, after it has grabbed its own copy of the site pointer, is to obtain the window handle for the container in which it will live. Explorer creates the container for the band object automatically (thus saving us much toil), so all the band object needs to do is query the site pointer for IOleWindow. This interface contains a method, GetWindow, that will provide the band object with a handle to the container window. Armed with the window handle, the band object merely needs to create an instance of its window (this is a normal VB form without a border). Once this has been accomplished, it can use the Windows API to make it a child window of the window returned by GetWindow.

Explorer will begin calling methods on the band object's primary interface, IDeskBand. It will determine the dimensions of the band by calling IDeskBand::GetBandInfo, which it will use in order to construct a band that is the proper size ("proper size" most likely meaning the size of the VB form).

It will also call IDeskBand::GetWindow, which is kind of interesting, because this is the same method the band object calls to get Explorer's container window handle. (IDeskBand is derived from IOleWindow.) Explorer is now turning around and asking the band object for its window. The band object then passes the handle to its window (i.e., to the VB form).

When Explorer is ready to show or hide the window, it will call IDeskBand::ShowDW, and when it is ready to destroy the window, it will call IDeskBand::CloseDW. In case you're wondering, the "DW" at the end of these two methods stands for "docking window."

Band Object Interfaces

Band objects are required to implement IDeskband and IObjectWithSite. The Platform SDK says that they must also implement IPersist and IPersistStream, but this is not the case. Optionally, if the band accepts user input, it needs to implement IInputObject. Bands can also provide context menus by implementing IContextMenu. We have already discussed IObjectWithSite and IContextMenu, so basically all we need to do is get up to speed with IDeskband and IInputObject. So, let's get to it.

IDeskband

IDeskband, the primary interface of the band object, is derived from IDockingWindow, which, in turn, is derived from IOleWindow.

IDeskband contains only one native method: GetBandInfo. There are three methods that are inherited from IDockingWindow, and two that have been inherited from IOleWindow. We have already seen IOleWindow while discussing IShellBrowser in Chapter 11, *Namespace Extensions*, so we will forego another discussion. Table 13-1 describes all the methods of the IDeskband interface. The methods that have been marked with an asterisk do not have to be implemented.

Table 13-1. IDeskband Methods

IOleWindow	
GetWindow	Returns the window handle to one of the windows participating in in-place activation (frame, document, parent, or in-place object window).
ContextSensitiveHelp*	Determines whether context-sensitive help mode should be entered during an in-place activation session.
IDockingWindow	
ShowDW	Called when the docking window is supposed to be shown or hidden.
CloseDW	Called when the docking window is about to be closed.
ResizeBorderDW*	Notifies the docking window object that the frame's border space has changed. This method is never called for any band object.
IDeskband	
GetBandInfo	Gets information for a band object.

ShowDW

Tells the band object to show or hide itself. Its syntax is:

```
HRESULT ShowDW(BOOL bShow);
```

Its single parameter is:

bShow
> [in] If this value is 0, the band object should be hidden; otherwise, it should be displayed.

CloseDW

Called when the band object is about to be closed. The band object should use this method to save persistent information (if necessary). Its syntax is:

```
HRESULT CloseDW(DWORD dwReserved);
```

Its single parameter is:

dwReserved
> [in] This is reserved and should always be zero.

GetBandInfo

This method retrieves band object information that includes the view mode and size of the band. Its syntax is:

```
HRESULT GetBandInfo(DWORD dwBandID, DWORD dwViewMode, DESKBANDINFO* pdbi);
```

with the following parameters:

dwBandID

[in] The identifier of the band. This value is assigned by the shell.

dwViewMode

[in] The view mode of the band object, which is one of the following values:

DBIF_VIEWMODE_NORMAL

The band is being displayed horizontally.

DBIF_VIEWMODE_VERTICAL

The band is being displayed vertically.

DBIF_VIEWMODE_FLOATING

The band is floating.

DBIF_VIEWMODE_TRANSPARENT

The band is being displayed transparently.

pdbi

[in] This is a pointer to a **DESKBANDINFO** structure. This structure contains everything a band object will need to display itself. Its definition is:

```
typedef struct {
    DWORD dwMask;
    POINTL ptMinSize;
    POINTL ptMaxSize;
    POINTL ptIntegral;
    POINTL ptActual;
    WCHAR wszTitle[256];
    DWORD dwModeFlags;
    COLORREF crBkgnd;
} DESKBANDINFO;
```

dwMask

Contains flags that determine which members of the structure are being requested. This can be one or more of the following values:

DBIM_MINSIZE

ptMinSize is being requested.

DBIM_MAXSIZE

ptMaxSize is being requested.

DBIM_INTEGRAL

ptIntegral is being requested.

DBIM_ACTUAL

ptActual is being requested.

DBIM_TITLE
> *wszTitle* is being requested.

DBIM_MODEFLAGS
> *dwModeFlags* is being requested.

DBIM_BKCOLOR
> *crBkgnd* is being requested.

ptMinSize
> This is a POINTL structure (same as POINTAPI with Long members) containing the minimum size of the band object.

ptMaxSize
> This is the maximum size of the band object. Like *ptMinSize*, this is also a POINTL structure. If there is no limit for either the *x* or *y* values, −1& should be used.

ptIntegral
> This is a POINTL structure containing the sizing step of the band object. This member is only valid if *dwModeFlags* contains DBIMF_VARIABLEHEIGHT.

ptActual
> This is a POINTL structure that contains the *ideal* size of the band object. This size is not guaranteed.

wszTitle
> This is the title of the band object.

dwModeFlags
> These flags determine the mode of operation for a band object. They can be one or more of the following values:

DBIMF_NORMAL
> The band is normal and the other mode flags modify this flag.

DBIMF_VARIABLEHEIGHT
> The height of the band object can be modified, and the *ptIntegral* member defines the increment by which the band object can be resized.

DBIMF_DEBOSSED
> The band object is displayed with a sunken look.

DBIMF_BKCOLOR
> The band will be displayed with the background color *crBkgnd.*

crBkgnd
> This is the background color of the band object. This is only valid if *dwModeFlags* contains DBIMF_BKCOLOR.

Example 13-1 contains the IDL listing for `IDeskband`.

Example 13-1. IDeskband Interface

```
typedef [public] long DESKBANDINFO;

[
    uuid(eb0fe172-1a3a-11d0-89b3-00a0c90a90ac),
    helpstring("IDeskband Interface"),
    odl
]
interface IDeskBand : IUnknown
{
    //IOleWindow
    HRESULT GetWindow([out, retval] long *phWnd);
    HRESULT ContextSensitiveHelp([in] boolean fEnterMode);

    //IDockingWindow
    HRESULT ShowDW([in] boolean fShow);
    HRESULT CloseDW([in] long dwReserved);
    HRESULT ResizeBorderDW([in] long prcBorder,
                           [in] long punkToolbarSite,
                           [in] boolean fReserved);

    //IDeskBand
    HRESULT GetBandInfo ([in] long dwBandID,
                         [in] long dwViewMode,
                         [in] LPDESKBANDINFO pdbi);
}
```

Notice that the DESKBANDINFO pointer in the GetBandInfo method has been redefined as a long. That's because the structure contains members that are not automation compatible. To access this parameter from VB when we implement this method, we'll have to use *CopyMemory* to get a local instance before we can do anything with the structure.

IInputObject

IInputObject is used to process accelerators and change UI activation for a band object. It contains three methods which are summarized in Table 13-2. Note that the methods marked with an asterisk more often than not do not need to be implemented.

Table 13-2. IInputObject

Method	Description
HasFocusIO*	Determines if one of the object's windows has the keyboard focus.
TranslateAcceleratorIO*	Passes keyboard accelerators to the object.
UIActivateIO	Activates or deactivates the object.

HasFocusIO

The syntax of `HasFocusIO` is very simple:

```
HRESULT HasFocusIO();
```

If the band object has keyboard focus this method should return S_OK; otherwise, it should return S_FALSE.

TranslateAcceleratorIO

This method should return S_OK if the accelerator was translated; otherwise, it should return S_FALSE. Its syntax is:

```
HRESULT TranslateAcceleratorIO(LPMSG lpMsg);
```

Its single parameter is:

lpMsg

[in] A pointer to a MSG structure, which is defined like so:

```
typedef struct tagMSG {
    HWND hwnd;
    UINT message;
    WPARAM wParam;
    LPARAM lParam;
    DWORD time;
    POINT pt;
} MSG;
```

This structure will contain the keyboard message that is being translated. Its members are defined like so:

hwnd

The handle of the window receiving the message.

message

The message number.

wParam and lParam

These parameters specify additional information about a message and are different depending on the message number.

time

The time the message was posted.

pt

A POINT structure containing the cursor position in screen coordinates at the time the message was posted.

UIActivateIO

This method is called when the band is being activated or deactivated. Its syntax is:

```
HRESULT UIActivateIO(BOOL fActivate, LPMSG lpMsg);
```

Its parameters are:

fActivate

[in] This value is nonzero if the band is being activated; otherwise, it is zero.

lpMsg

[in] This is a pointer to a MSG structure that contains the message that caused the change in activation states.

The IDL for IInputObject is defined in Example 13-2.

Example 13-2. IInputObject Interface

```
typedef [public] long LPMSG;

[
    uuid(68284faa-6a48-11d0-8c78-00c04fd918b4),
    helpstring(("IInputObject Interface"),
    odl
]
interface IInputObject : IUnknown
{
    HRESULT UIActivateIO([in] boolean fActivate, [in] LPMSG lpMsg);
    HRESULT HasFocusIO();
    HRESULT TranslateAcceleratorIO([in] LPMSG lpMsg);
```

The Project: FileSpider

In this chapter, we are actually going to build a very useful band object. Believe it or not, you might end up using this band object all the time. It's that cool. So what does it do?

Okay, imagine this scenario: you are surfing the Web and you come across a page that has several files you wish to download. Normally, you would have to download one file at a time. Once the file is downloaded, you click on the next file, wait, click on the next file, and so on. Of course, you would also have to wait on this page or bookmark it if you wanted to continue surfing while the files were downloading. Pretty lame, right? Well, FileSpider fixes all of that.

FileSpider "crawls" a web page and makes a list of all files that are available for downloading. You select the files you want to download, and FileSpider downloads them one at a time in the background, freeing you up to surf to your heart's content. You can also build your list of files from several pages. There are no limits here. The file list is persistent, which means that you can download the files at a later time should you wish to do so. Everything is automatically saved in the registry. All of FileSpider's commands can be accessed from a toolbar in the band window. We'll also throw in a context menu just to say we did. This should give you an idea how context menus are handled outside of context menu handlers (see Chapter 4, *Context Menu Handlers*). Figure 13-5 shows FileSpider in action.

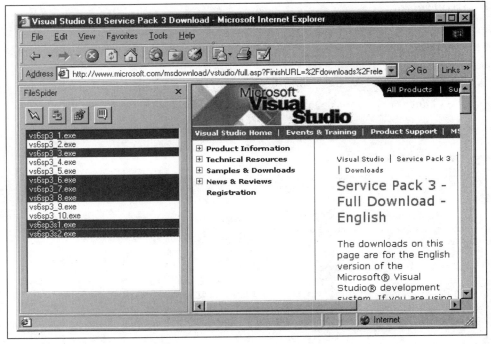

Figure 13-5. FileSpider band object

We are ready to begin the project. We need to create a new ActiveX DLL project named FileSpider. Once this is done we need to do several things:

1. Add a class module to project called *SpiderBand.cls*.

2. Add two modules named *BandObject.bas* and *ContextMenu.bas*. Code relevant to the Band Object will go in the first module. Context menu-specific code will go in the second.

3. Add a reference to our shell library, as well as to *MSHTML.DLL* (the HTML Object Model).

FileSpider will additionally contain five forms, but we'll discuss those as we get to them. For now, though, let's concentrate on getting the code together for a minimal band object.

We'll start in *SpiderBand.cls* by implementing the interfaces we need:

```
'SpiderBand.cls

Implements IDeskBand
Implements IInputObject
Implements IObjectWithSite
Implements IContextMenu
```

We now have some serious work ahead of us because we need to implement all of these interfaces. We'll do everything in order of familiarity. So let's start with `IContextMenu` (which we've known about since Chapter 4), and take it from there. To implement this interface properly, we'll need to swap out the vtable entry for `QueryContextMenu`, so there is a little busy work up front. Then we'll implement the method, which involves simply adding menu items using the Windows API. This is really no different from the last time we implemented it. We will also implement `InvokeCommand`, the method that actually carries out the menu commands, by forwarding all calls from the context menu to the band form. We do this so the context menu and the toolbar can use the same code. `IContextMenu::GetCommandString` is not implemented, so we'll just ignore it and pretend it doesn't exist.

Class_Initialize/Class_Terminate

The Initialize and Terminate events for the class should look very familiar. All we are going to use them for is to swap out vtable entries for `IContextMenu::QueryContextMenu` (see Chapter 4). A Private member variable named *m_pOldQueryContextMenu* is added to the class to store the original function address of `QueryContextMenu`. The Initialize and Terminate events are shown in Example 13-3.

Example 13-3. Initialize and Terminate

```
Private m_pOldQueryContextMenu As Long

Private Sub Class_Initialize()

    Dim pContextMenu As IContextMenu
    Set pContextMenu = Me

    m_pOldQueryContextMenu = SwapVtableEntry( _
                        ObjPtr(pContextMenu), _
                        4, _
                        AddressOf QueryContextMenuX)

End Sub

Private Sub Class_Terminate()

    Dim pContextMenu As IContextMenu
    Set pContextMenu = Me

    m_pOldQueryContextMenu = SwapVtableEntry(_
                        ObjPtr(pContextMenu), _
                        4, _
                        m_pOldQueryContextMenu)

End Sub
```

The replacement function, *QueryContextMenuX*, is fairly straightforward compared to the last time we visited this function in Chapter 4. *QueryContextMenuX* is located in *ContextMenu.bas*. This function provides context menu support for the four commands that FileSpider will need: Crawl, Download, Preferences, and About. These commands will accomplish the following:

Command	Description
Crawl	Crawls a web page and makes a list of files that were found.
Download	Starts downloading (one file at time) all of the files that have been selected in the band's main window.
Preferences	Displays the Preferences dialog, which allows configuration information for the band to be entered.
About	Displays an about box.

The entire listing for this module is shown in Example 13-4.

Example 13-4. ContextMenu.bas

```
Public Declare Function InsertMenu Lib "user32" _
            Alias "InsertMenuA" (ByVal HMENU As Long, _
            ByVal nPosition As Long, ByVal wFlags As Long, _
            ByVal wIDNewItem As Long, _
            ByVal lpNewItem As String) As Long

'Menu Constants
Public Const MF_BYPOSITION = &H400&
Public Const MF_STRING = &H0&
Public Const MF_SEPARATOR = &H800&

Public Function QueryContextMenuX(_
            ByVal This As IContextMenu, _
            ByVal HMENU As Long, _
            ByVal indexMenu As Long, _
            ByVal idCmdFirst As Long, _
            ByVal idCmdLast As Long, _
            ByVal uFlags As Long) As Long

    Dim sMenuItem As String
    Dim idCmd As Long

    idCmd = idCmdFirst

    sMenuItem = "&Crawl"
    Call InsertMenu(HMENU, indexMenu, MF_STRING Or MF_BYPOSITION, _
                idCmd, sMenuItem)
    idCmd = idCmd + 1
    indexMenu = indexMenu + 1

    sMenuItem = "&Download"
    Call InsertMenu(HMENU, indexMenu, MF_STRING Or MF_BYPOSITION, _
```

Example 13-4. ContextMenu.bas (continued)

```
                    idCmd, sMenuItem)
    idCmd = idCmd + 1
    indexMenu = indexMenu + 1

    sMenuItem = "&Preferences"
    Call InsertMenu(HMENU, indexMenu, MF_STRING Or MF_BYPOSITION, _
                    idCmd, sMenuItem)
    idCmd = idCmd + 1
    indexMenu = indexMenu + 1

    sMenuItem = "&About"
    Call InsertMenu(HMENU, indexMenu, MF_STRING Or MF_BYPOSITION, _
                    idCmd, sMenuItem)
    idCmd = idCmd + 1
    indexMenu = indexMenu + 1

    'Always return number of items added to the menu
    'indexMenu will equal that in this instance, but not
    'others....like adding to an existing context menu
    QueryContextMenuX = indexMenu

End Function
```

Just for a refresher, let's briefly discuss **QueryContextMenu**. This is a method of **IContextMenu** that adds items to the context menu. It is defined like so:

```
HRESULT QueryContextMenu(
    HMENU hmenu,
    UINT indexMenu,
    UINT idCmdFirst,
    UINT idCmdLast,
    UINT uFlags
    );
```

Its parameters are:

hmenu

[in] The handle of the context menu to which we will be adding items.

indexMenu

[in] The zero-based position at which the first menu item is to be inserted.

idCmdFirst

[in] The minimum value that can be specified as a menu identifier, or simply a number that uniquely identifies the menu item.

idCmdLast

[in] The maximum value that can be specified as a menu identifier.

uFlags

[in] This value can be ignored. For a description, see the discussion of **QueryContextMenu** in Chapter 4.

The parameters we are concerned with in this instance are *hMenu*, *indexMenu*, and *idCmdFirst*.

As you can see from the listing, each of these relevant items go hand in hand with the parameters that we need to call the *InsertMenu* API, which is defined like so:

```
Public Declare Function InsertMenu Lib "user32" _
    Alias "InsertMenuA" (ByVal HMENU As Long, _
                         ByVal nPosition As Long, _
                         ByVal wFlags As Long, _
                         ByVal wIDNewItem As Long, _
                         ByVal lpNewItem As String) As Long
```

As each item is added to the context menu, the command ID and the menu index are both incremented. Also, it should be mentioned that the command identifier is *not* incremented if a separator is being added.

Next, we need to implement the `InvokeCommand` method. If you recall from Chapter 4, this method is called when an item is selected from a context menu. Our implementation is very simple. All we are going to do is to forward the `InvokeCommand` calls to the band object form. We do this because each context menu item corresponds to a toolbar item on the band form. If we put all the command code in the band form, we can keep *SpiderBand.cls* generic enough to use in our future band object projects. Example 13-5 details our implementation of `InvokeCommand` and also shows the handler that is found in our band form, *frmBand.frm*.

Example 13-5. InvokeCommand

```
'SpiderBand.cls

Private Sub IContextMenu_InvokeCommand(_
            ByVal lpcmi As VBShellLib.LPCMINVOKECOMMANDINFO)

    'Let the band handle the menu implementation
    frmBand.MenuHandler lpcmi

End Sub


'frmBand.frm

Public Sub MenuHandler(lpcmi As Long)

    Dim cmi As CMINVOKECOMMANDINFO
    CopyMemory cmi, ByVal lpcmi, Len(cmi)

    Select Case cmi.lpVerb
        Case 0  'Crawl
            cmdCrawl = True
        Case 1  'Download
```

Example 13-5. InvokeCommand (continued)

```
            cmdDL = True
      Case 2  'Preferences
          cmdPrefs = True
      Case 3  'About
          cmdAbout = True
  End Select

End Sub
```

Once *MenuHandler* is called, *CopyMemory* is used to get a local instance of **CMINVOKECOMMANDINFO** from *lpcmi*, the pointer passed to the function. We can then check the *lpVerb* member of the structure to determine the index of the context menu item that has been selected. As you can see from the listing, we are not using a toolbar control for the band object, but rather four individual buttons. Setting a command equal to **True** is just like clicking on the button with the mouse. Routing the commands to one place keeps us from having to duplicate code.

IObjectWithSite

Our **IObjectWithSite::SetSite** implementation is very similar to a browser extension (see Chapter 12). Once again, we need to use **IServiceProvider** to get the current instance of Internet Explorer. This will be passed on to our band form and made available to the Crawl command (the command that actually crawls a web page looking for downloadable files). But there are a few additional actions that must be performed. Let's go through Example 13-6, which contains the code that implements the **SetSite** method, now.

Example 13-6. SetSite

```
Private m_pSite As IUnknownVB
Private m_ContainerWnd As Long
Private m_bandWnd As Long
Private m_pOldQueryContextMenu As Long

Private Const IID_IWebBrowserApp = _
    "{0002DF05-0000-0000-C000-000000000046}"
Private Const IID_IWebBrowser2 = _
    "{D30C1661-CDAF-11D0-8A3E-00C04FC9E26E}"

Private Sub IObjectWithSite_SetSite(ByVal pUnkSite As IUnknownVB)

    Dim isp As IServiceProvider
    Dim oleWnd As IOleWindow

    Dim wba As GUID 'IWebBrowserApp
    Dim wb2 As GUID 'IWebBrowser2
```

Example 13-6. SetSite (continued)

```
Dim dwStyle As Long

If Not (pUnkSite Is Nothing) Then

    If Not (m_pSite Is Nothing) Then
        Set m_pSite = Nothing
    End If

    Set m_pSite = pUnkSite
    Set oleWnd = pUnkSite          ' QueryInterface for IOleWindow

    'QueryInterface for IServiceProvider
    Set isp = pUnkSite

    'Query service provider to get IWebBrowser2 (InternetExplorer)
    CLSIDFromString StrPtr(IID_IWebBrowserApp), wba
    CLSIDFromString StrPtr(IID_IWebBrowser2), wb2

    'Get IWebBrowser2
    Set frmBand.InternetExplorer = _
    isp.QueryService(VarPtr(wba), VarPtr(wb2))

    Set isp = Nothing

    If Not (oleWnd Is Nothing) Then

        m_ContainerWnd = oleWnd.GetWindow
        m_bandWnd = frmBand.hwnd

      dwStyle = GetWindowLong(m_bandWnd, GWL_STYLE)
      dwStyle = dwStyle Or WS_CHILD Or WS_CLIPSIBLINGS
      SetWindowLong m_bandWnd, GWL_STYLE, dwStyle
      SetParent m_bandWnd, m_ContainerWnd

    End If

    Set oleWnd = Nothing

Else
    Set m_pSite = Nothing
End If

End Sub
```

If the site pointer passed in by the shell is valid, we do two things. First, we save the site pointer in a private member variable named *m_pSite*. This will be used later when we implement `GetSite`. As you can see, we have declared a local instance of `IOleWindow`. We also need to query the site pointer for `IOleWindow`. This will allow us to get the container window for our band object. We can also query the site pointer to get `IServiceProvider`. Once we have `IServiceProvider`, we can get `IWebBrowser2` and pass this directly to our band form.

If our `IOleWindow` interface is valid, then we can get the container window. We are also going to store the handle of our band form in a private member variable. Instead of using VB commands like Show and Hide, we will use the API to manipulate the form through its handle.

What's all the business with *GetWindowLong* and *SetWindowLong*? Well, our band form needs to be a child window, so we need to get the window's style information and add `WS_CHILD` and `WS_CLIPSIBLINGS`. We use *GetWindowLong* to reapply the style to the window. These two functions are declared like this:

```
Public Declare Function GetWindowLong Lib "user32" Alias _
    "GetWindowLongA" (ByVal hwnd As Long, _
                    ByVal nIndex As Long) As Long

Public Declare Function SetWindowLong Lib "user32" Alias _
    "SetWindowLongA" (ByVal hwnd As Long, _
                    ByVal nIndex As Long, _
                    ByVal dwNewLong As Long) As Long
```

Once we have done that, we can call `SetParent` to actually make our band form a child of the container window. If we did not do this extra step, the band object would still work, but Explorer would lose focus when we click on the band object. By doing this, the band object will appear to be a contiguous part of Explorer.

Our `GetSite` implementation is the same as always, as shown in Example 13-7.

Example 13-7. GetSite

```
Private Sub IObjectWithSite_GetSite(_
    ByVal priid As LPGUID, _
    ppvSite As LPVOID)

    m_pSite.QueryInterface priid, ppvSite

End Sub
```

IInputObject

We only need to implement one method for `IInputObject`, and that is `UIActivateIO`. All we need to do with this method is give focus to our band form when the shell tells us. We do not need to discuss this interface in any more detail, because we are not going to use accelerators. The `UIActivate` implementation is shown in Example 13-8.

Example 13-8. UIActivate

```
Private Sub IInputObject_UIActivateIO(_
    ByVal fActivate As Boolean, _
    ByVal lpMsg As lpMsg)
```

Example 13-8. UIActivate (continued)

```
    If (fActivate) Then
        SetFocus m_bandWnd
    End If

End Sub
```

IDeskBand

Implementing `IDeskBand` is a simple and straightforward process. We already have everything we need to implement this interface in place, and most of the methods require only a line of code. Let's implement these one-liners first. We'll start with `CloseDW`:

```
Private Sub IDeskBand_CloseDW(ByVal dwReserved As Long)

    Unload frmBand

End Sub
```

Could things be simpler? It should be noted that you do not even have to implement this method. We do because our band form has code in its Unload event. If we do not close the form here, Unload will not be called.

`GetWindow` is equally as simple:

```
Private Function IDeskBand_GetWindow() As Long

    IDeskBand_GetWindow = m_bandWnd

End Function
```

That's it. All we need to do is return the handle to our band form.

ShowDW is not exactly a one-liner, but it is just as easy to implement. The shell passes in a Boolean value. If this value is **True**, we show the window; if not, we hide it. We will use the *ShowWindow* API to achieve the desired results:

```
Private Sub IDeskBand_ShowDW(ByVal fShow As Boolean)
    If (fShow) Then
        ShowWindow m_bandWnd, SW_SHOW
    Else
        ShowWindow m_bandWnd, SW_HIDE
    End If
End Sub
```

The only method with any substance, really, is `GetBandInfo`. `GetBandInfo` is where we get a chance to tell Explorer some band-specific information, such as the minimum, maximum, and ideal size of our band, and the title of our band. This method is shown in Example 13-9.

Example 13-9. GetBandInfo

```vb
Private Sub IDeskBand_GetBandInfo(_
    ByVal dwBandID As Long, _
    ByVal dwViewMode As Long, _
    ByVal pdbi As VBShellLib.DESKBANDINFO)

    Dim dbi As DESKBANDINFO

    If pdbi = 0 Then
        Exit Sub
    End If

    CopyMemory dbi, ByVal pdbi, Len(dbi)

    If (dbi.dwMask And DBIM_MINSIZE) Then
        dbi.ptMinSize.x = 10&
        dbi.ptMinSize.y = 50&
    End If

    If (dbi.dwMask And DBIM_MAXSIZE) Then
        dbi.ptMaxSize.x = -1&
        dbi.ptMaxSize.y = -1&
    End If

    If (dbi.dwMask And DBIM_INTEGRAL) Then
        dbi.ptIntegral.x = 1&
        dbi.ptIntegral.y = 1&
    End If

    If (dbi.dwMask And DBIM_ACTUAL) Then
        dbi.ptActual.x = 0&
        dbi.ptActual.y = 0&
    End If

    If (dbi.dwMask And DBIM_TITLE) Then
        Dim title() As Byte
        title = "FileSpider" & vbNullChar
        CopyMemory dbi.wszTitle(0), title(0), UBound(title) + 1
    End If

    If (dbi.dwMask And DBIM_MODEFLAGS) Then
        dbi.dwModeFlags = DBIMF_VARIABLEHEIGHT
    End If

    If (dbi.dwMask And DBIM_BKCOLOR) Then
        'Use the default background color by removing
        'DBIM_BKCOLOR flag and setting crBkgnd
    End If

    CopyMemory ByVal pdbi, dbi, Len(dbi)

End Sub
```

The Band Form

Now that the band object is wired up, the remainder of the action either starts or ends in the band form. The band form is shown in Figure 13-6.

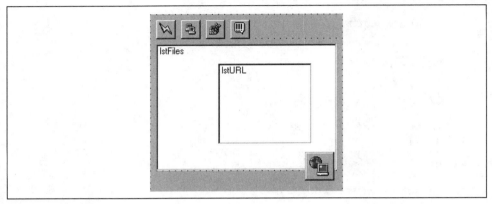

Figure 13-6. Band object form

If we discuss every single line of code in *frmBand* and the other forms, we are going to get way off track. And besides, nothing is more lame than a computer book with a bunch of pages of GUI settings. Just look at the downloadable code provided for this chapter. We'll discuss the good stuff, but much of the code remaining involves saving settings and URL information to the registry and retrieving that information.

The code we are most interested in at this point (and the code most open for improvement by you) is the *Crawl* function. Let's take a look:

```
'frmBand.frm

Private m_ie As InternetExplorer

Private Sub Crawl()

    Dim i As Long
    Dim pDoc As IHTMLDocument2
    Dim pRootWnd As IHTMLWindow2
    Dim pWnd As IHTMLWindow2
    Dim pFrames As IHTMLFramesCollection2
    Dim nFrames As Long

    Set pDoc = m_ie.Document
    Set pWnd = pDoc.parentWindow
    Set pRootWnd = pWnd.top
    Set pFrames = pRootWnd.frames
```

```
        'Get number of frames on page
        nFrames = pFrames.length
```

Here's what's going on. First, we grab the current document from our private instance of Internet Explorer. The problem is that the current document might not be the top-level document. It might be a document embedded in a frame somewhere deep in the document. So, we need to get the parent window of the document. Once we have that, we can get the top-level window. When we get the top-level window, we can get a collection of all the frames on the page. (Confused? There is a picture of the object model in Figure 12-2). This is important, because we want the *Crawl* function to work across frames. With the frames collection in hand, we can loop through each frame and search the corresponding document for files. If there are no frames, our job is even easier:

```
    If (nFrames > 1) Then

        For i = 0 To nFrames - 1

            Dim pFrameDoc As IHTMLDocument2
            Dim pFrameWnd As IHTMLWindow2

            Set pFrameWnd = pFrames.Item(i)
            Set pFrameDoc = pFrameWnd.Document

            Call FindFiles(pFrameDoc)

            Set pFrameDoc = Nothing
            Set pFrameWnd = Nothing

        Next i

    Else

        Call FindFiles(pDoc)

    End If

    Set pFrames = Nothing
    Set pRootWnd = Nothing
    Set pWnd = Nothing
    Set pDoc = Nothing

End Sub
```

Crawl delegates to a function called *FindFiles*. It is *FindFile*'s job to search a document for files. How does it know which files to look for? *WAV? EXE? JPG?* That is left entirely up to the user and is determined by the settings in the Preferences dialog. Some background information that you'll need to know when we discuss *FindFiles* is that there is a private variable that contains an array of types in which we are interested (*.exe, .wav, .jpg,* etc.). This variable is called *m_sTypes*. There is also another member variable that contains the number of types, called *m_nTypes*.

FindFiles is quite a beast, so rather than dump a gargantuan listing on you, we'll step through it slowly:

```
Private Sub FindFiles(doc As IHTMLDocument2)

    On Error GoTo FindFiles_Err

    Dim i, j, nElements As Long
    Dim pElements As IHTMLElementCollection
    Dim pElement As IHTMLElement
    Dim nPos As Integer
    Dim sUrl As String

    'Get all the BODY elements of the current page
    Set pElement = doc.body
    Set pElements = pElement.All

    'Get number of elements on the current page
    nElements = pElements.length
```

This block of code retrieves the <BODY> element, then gets all the elements that are part of the body (which could really be quite a few). Now, we know the number of elements in the collection, so we can loop through each individual element in the collection looking for <A> tags. If we have an anchor, then we can get the href portion of the tag, which will contain the filename:

```
    For i = 0 To nElements - 1

        Dim sTag As String

        Set pElement = pElements.Item(i)

        'Check every "anchor" for file type
        sTag = UCase(pElement.tagName)

        If sTag = "A" Then
            Dim pAnchor As IHTMLAnchorElement
            Dim sHref As String

            Set pAnchor = pElement
            sHref = LCase(pAnchor.href)
```

Now that we have a filename, we need to check to see if we are interested in its type. To accomplish this, we loop through the *m_sTypes* array, which contains all of the file extensions for which we are looking. If so, we pass the URL to a function called *ParseURL*. We will not discuss this function, but here is what it does: it merely separates the address portion of the URL from the filename. The URL is stored in an invisible list box on the band form, and the filename is added to the main list box. A list of filenames in the main window just looks better than the full URL, and it's easier to read:

```
          For j = 0 To m_nTypes - 1
              nPos = InStr(sHref, m_sTypes(j))
              If nPos Then
                  sUrl = ParseURL(sHref)
                  'Just show file name in list box, but store
                  'the rest of the URL in a hidden list box
                  nPos = InStrRev(sUrl, "/")
                  If (nPos) Then
                      lstURL.AddItem Left(sUrl, nPos)
                      lstFiles.AddItem Right(sUrl, Len(sUrl) - nPos)
                  Else
                      lstFiles.AddItem sUrl
                  End If
              End If
          Next j

          Set pAnchor = Nothing

      End If

   Next i

   Set pElement = Nothing
   Set pElements = Nothing

End Sub
```

The Preferences Dialog

The Preferences dialog, which is shown in Figure 13-7, is used mainly to configure the FileSpider band object. Most of the code only sets and retrieves registry
settings. But there is one interesting aspect of this form that is worth discussing,
and that is the directory dialog. FileSpider requires that a download directory be
specified. This, of course, is the directory where FileSpider will dump all downloaded files.

Figure 13-7. Preferences dialog

To specify a directory accurately, we need a way to navigate directories. Fortunately, the shell itself provides us with a ready-made dialog that will allow us to navigate directories. This dialog is shown in Figure 13-8.

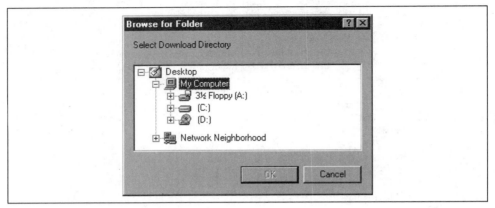

Figure 13-8. Directory browser

First things first. We need two functions from the Shell API and one from the Windows API before we can get started. They are declared as follows:

```
' Displays a dialog box that allows you to select a directory
Private Declare Function SHBrowseForFolder Lib "shell32" _
    (lpbi As BROWSEINFO) As Long

' Converts a PIDL into a readable path string
Private Declare Function SHGetPathFromIDList Lib "shell32" _
    (ByVal pidList As Long, ByVal lpBuffer As String) As Long

' Copies a string
Private Declare Function lstrcat Lib "kernel32" Alias "lstrcatA" _
    (ByVal lpString1 As String, ByVal lpString2 As String) As Long
```

As you can see, *SHBrowseForFolder* takes a **BROWSEINFO** structure, so we'll need one of those. Here's the declaration:

```
Private Type BROWSEINFO
    hWndOwner       As Long    ' Handle to the owner of the dialog
    pIDLRoot        As Long    ' Location of the root folder
    pszDisplayName  As Long    ' Pointer to a buffer for display name
    lpszTitle       As Long    ' Text above tree control in the dialog
    ulFlags         As Long    ' Should contain BIF_RETURNONLYFSDIRS,
                               ' BIF_DONTGOBELOWDOMAIN
    lpfnCallback    As Long    ' Address of a callback (not needed)
    lParam          As Long    ' Value passed to callback (not needed)
    iImage          As Long    ' Image associated with selected folder
End Type
```

Now we are ready to implement the function. In the FileSpider band, the code lies in the cmdDir_Click event, which is shown in Example 13-10. A more efficient way is to wrap this code into a class to make it more portable. But if the book did everything for you, you would have nothing to do on those lonely, rainy nights, right?

Example 13-10. The cmdDir_Click Event Procedure

```
Private Sub cmdDir_Click()

    Dim pidl As LPITEMIDLIST
    Dim tBrowseInfo As BROWSEINFO
    Dim sBuffer As String
    Dim szTitle As String

    szTitle = "Select Download Directory"
    With tBrowseInfo
        .hWndOwner = Me.hwnd
        .lpszTitle = lstrcat(szTitle, "")
        .ulFlags = BIF_RETURNONLYFSDIRS + BIF_DONTGOBELOWDOMAIN
    End With

    pidl = SHBrowseForFolder(tBrowseInfo)

    If (pidl) Then
        sBuffer = Space(MAX_PATH)
        SHGetPathFromIDList pidl, sBuffer
        sBuffer = Left(sBuffer, InStr(sBuffer, vbNullChar) - 1)
        txtDir = sBuffer
    End If

End Sub
```

We sure know what PIDLs are at this point in the game, don't we? (If not, you must have totally skipped Chapter 11!) This function looks fairly simple. BROWSEINFO contains the handle to the parent responsible for the directory dialog and the title of the directory. When it is passed to *SHBrowseForFolder*, the directory dialog is displayed appropriately. When a directory is selected, we are returned a PIDL. We can pass the PIDL to *SHGetPathFromIDList* to get the path. With our knowledge of PIDLs, it's possible that we could write our own *SHGetPathFromIDList* function (if we were so inclined).

Registry

Here's the big question. How do we distinguish our band object as an Explorer band versus a Communication band or a Desk band? We do this by assigning our component to the Explorer Band *component category*. Component categories are used to group functionality. For instance, when you create an ActiveX DLL component in Visual Basic, a registry setting is added that specifies the component to be in the category "Automation Objects." Verify this for yourself. Look up any of the

CLSIDs for the components we have created in this book under its `HKEY_`
`CLASSES_ROOT\CLSID` entry. You will find a subkey named `Implemented`
`Categories`. Here you will find the following key:

    {40FC6ED5-2438-11CF-A3DB-080036F12502}

Now, search for this key under the following key:

    HKEY_CLASSES_ROOT\Component Categories

You will find that this CLSID represents a category called "Automation Objects."
OLE View groups components by category. Take a look. If you ever work on a
project containing several components that implement common interfaces, you
might want to create your own component category. It's as simple as creating a
GUID with *GUIDGEN.EXE* and adding it to:

    HKEY_CLASSES_ROOT\Component Categories

This mechanism allows the shell to quickly find the components it requires, in our
case, Explorer Bands. Table 13-3 lists the CLSIDs for the three types of band
objects.

Table 13-3. CLSIDs of Band Categories

Band Category	CLSID
Desk Band	{00021492-0000-0000-C000-000000000046}
Explorer Band	{00021493-0000-0000-C000-000000000046}
Communication Band	{00021494-0000-0000-C000-000000000046}

So, in order to implement our component as an Explorer Band, we need to implement the category {00021493-0000-0000-C000-000000000046}. The default value for
the `HKEY_CLASSES_ROOT\CLSID` key becomes the name that will be displayed in
Explorer's menu for the band object. These settings are shown in Figure 13-9.

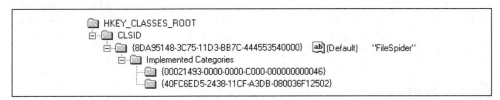

Figure 13-9. FileSpider registry settings

Now that the band object is compiled and registered, it can be activated by selecting it from Explorer's View menu, as shown in Figure 13-10.

The complete listing for the FileSpider registry script is shown in Example 13-11.

Something to Know About Desk Bands

When implementing a desk band, there is something you need to know if you happen to be running Windows 2000 (also Windows 98 Second Edition).

It seems Windows 2000 keeps a category cache that updates itself only if it has determined that an installation has been run or if the cache location in the registry is not present. Restarting the shell will do nothing in terms of getting the shell to recognize the band.

The solution is to delete the following key from the registry:

```
HKEY_CLASSES_ROOT\
    Component Categories\
        {00021492-0000-0000-C000-000000000046}\
            Enum
```

The CLSID under *Component Categories* is the category for desk bands (see Table 13-3).

You can read more about this feature in KnowledgeBase article Q214842.

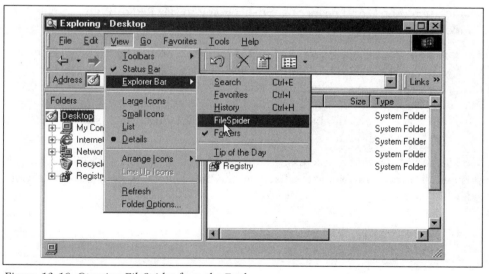

Figure 13-10. Opening FileSpider from the Explorer menu

Example 13-11. FileSpider Registry Script

```
REGEDIT4

[HKEY_CLASSES_ROOT\CLSID\{8DA95148-3C75-11D3-BB7C-444553540000}]
@ = "FileSpider"
```

Example 13-11. FileSpider Registry Script (continued)

```
[HKEY_CLASSES_ROOT\CLSID\{8DA95148-3C75-11D3-BB7C-444553540000}\Implemented
Categories\{00021493-0000-0000-C000-000000000046}]
```

Tool Bands

Before signing off, we really need to discuss tool bands. There is an additional registry setting you must be aware of in order to implement this band properly:

```
HKEY_LOCAL_MACHINE\
    Software\
        Microsoft\
            Internet Explorer\
                Toolbar = '{CLSID}'
```

Other than that, tool bands are registered just as you would an Explorer band.

Unfortunately, at the time of this writing, tool bands are not really ready for prime time; there are some problems.

For one (see Knowledge Base article Q23161), the shell seems to ignore your menu title for the tool band. It'll just use the same name as whatever tool band was registered first. And chances are that's going to be "Radio" if you installed the Windows Media Player with IE 5.0.

The problems don't stop there, either. It seems that somewhere between turning your tool band on and off and opening and closing Explorer, the Radio band will disappear from the menu altogether; you will have to reinstall from the IE 5.0 CD. This is a real bummer if you happen to like this Radio band. No tunes! But guess what? Even after the Radio band is gone, you're tool band *might* still be there; it'll be called "Radio," though.

We all know how fast problems get addressed in this business, so it'll be no surprise at all if these problems are fixed by the time this book comes to print. Consider this a heads up.

14

Docking Windows

Like band objects, docking windows provide a way for you to add your own user interface elements to Explorer. They share another similarity with band objects in that they can exist in several locations—either at the top or bottom of Explorer's client area as a horizontal window (see Figure 14-1) or to the left or right of the client area as a vertical window. Unlike band objects, however, you do not have to have Active Desktop installed in order to use them from both Explorer and Internet Explorer.

But there are a few drawbacks. They're not too bad, but worth mentioning. Docking windows have no associated menu item or toolbar button. So turning them on and off will require you to write some custom code, which could possibly be a problem. This gets trickier because docking window forms must be borderless. Borderless windows cannot have menus. If you define one, VB will add a title bar to the window. So you will not even be able to define a pop-up menu. Also, docking windows don't have the innate ability to be resized like Explorer and Communication bands. If you remember (think way back to the last chapter), a band object's container is automatically sized in response to Explorer being resized. Docking windows have no such luxury. While Explorer does provide size information to the docking window, the docking window itself must take responsibility for positioning itself. In fact, a majority of a docking window's time is spent figuring out its own position in Explorer's frame.

Something else you should know is that docking windows are not standalone components. That is, you don't create a "docking window component" that must be configured in the registry. Docking windows are created by existing components that wish to have a user interface. We have already discussed many of these components: namespace extensions, browser helper objects, browser extensions, and, yes, even band objects. Figure 14-1 shows a docking window that is docked at the bottom of the browser; this is the browser helper object from Chapter 12, *Browser Extensions*, which now has a user interface.

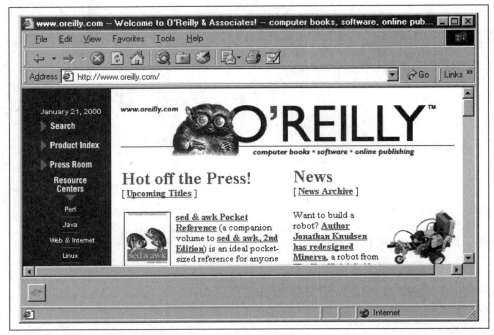

Figure 14-1. Docking window

How Docking Windows Work

It takes a least two objects to create a functional docking window. The first is the primary object—the object that wants to display a docking window (a namespace extension, BHO, band, etc.). The second object is the docking window itself. It contains all of the implementation code specific to docking windows. In this way, the relationship between the primary object and the docking window is similar to the one between a shell folder and a view; it allows the *possibility* of a one-to-many relationship.

The docking window object is very much like a band object in that it implements `IObjectWithSite` and `IDockingWindow`. `IDeskband`, which is the primary interface for band objects, is derived from `IDockingWindow`. So essentially, a docking window must implement the same core functionality as a band object; it must be able to respond to the shell's requests to show, close, and resize the window. Additionally, it must also be able to provide a window handle (of the docking window) to Explorer. This behavior is no different from that of band objects. Well, actually, there is one difference, which we've already talked about: band objects do not have to provide resize information to the shell. Docking windows do.

In order for the primary object to create a docking window, it must first get its hands on an `IServiceProvider` interface. Depending on the circumstances, this is done in one of two ways. If the component implements `IObjectWithSite`, as is the case with BHOs, browser extensions, or band objects, all it has to do is query the site pointer passed in by the shell. (See the discussion of site pointers in Chapter 12.) If the component is a namespace extension, it can get to `IServiceProvider` by means of the `IShellBrowser` interface that is passed to the component in the `IShellView::CreateViewWindow` method.

Once the primary object has an `IServiceProvider` interface pointer, it can then call the `QueryService` method to get `IDockingWindowFrame`; this contains a method called `AddToolbar`. `AddToolbar` is the method that is used to add a docking window to Explorer. When the component calls `AddToolBar`, it passes a reference to an object that implements `IDockingWindow` (and `IObjectWithSite`). This object, of course, is the docking window. From this point, control is transferred from the primary component to the docking window.

Once the shell has access to the docking window object, it calls `IObjectWithSite::SetSite`. The docking window object uses the site pointer in order to obtain a reference to `IDockingWindowSite`. This interface will help the docking window negotiate its border space within the client area of Explorer.

After the docking window determines its position, it is displayed.

Docking Window Interfaces

Docking windows require the use of four interfaces: `IObjectWithSite`, `IDockingWindow`, `IDockingWindowFrame`, and `IDockingWindowSite`. In the remainder of this section, we'll discuss the four interfaces and their members that are relevant to developing docking windows.

IObjectWithSite

The shell provides a site pointer to the docking window via the `IObjectWithSite` interface in a manner similar to browser helper objects or band objects. The primary object—that is, the object that will create the docking window—uses `IObjectWithSite` to obtain references to `IServiceProvider` and, optionally, `IWebBrowser2`. The secondary component, which is the actual docking window implementation, uses `IObjectWithSite` to obtain `IDockingWindowFrame`. `IObjectWithSite` is summarized in Table 14-2, but for a more complete discussion, please refer to Chapter 12.

Table 14-1. IObjectWithSite Methods

Method	Description
GetSite	Returns the last site set with SetSite.
SetSite	Provides the IUnknown site pointer of Explorer.

IDockingWindow

We have already discussed IDockingWindow. If you remember our discussion of band objects, the IDeskband interface is derived from IDockingWindow. There is nothing new that we need to discuss concerning this interface. Table 14-1 provides a refresher course on the interface and on IOleWindow, the interface from which it is derived, but if you would like more detail, see Chapter 13, *Band Objects*. Methods marked with an asterisk are not implemented.

Table 14-2. IDockingWindow Methods

IOleWindow	
GetWindow	Returns the window handle to one of the windows participating in in-place activation (frame, document, parent, or in-place object window).
ContextSensitiveHelp*	Determines whether context-sensitive help mode should be entered during an in-place activation session.
IDockingWindow	
ShowDW	Called when the docking window is supposed to be shown or hidden.
CloseDW	Called when the docking window is about to be closed.
ResizeBorderDW	Notifies the docking window object that the frame's border space has changed. This method is not implemented for band objects, but for docking windows it is a must.

IDockingWindowFrame

This interface is implemented by Explorer and provides all the methods necessary to add docking windows to a frame (see Table 14-3). It too is derived from IOleWindow.

Table 14-3. IDockingWindowFrame Methods

IOleWindow	
(See Table 14-1 for IOleWindow methods)	
IDockingWindowFrame	
AddToolbar	Used to add a docking window to the frame.
FindToolbar*	Finds the specified docking window in the frame and returns a reference to it.
RemoveToolbar*	Removes a docking window from the frame.

AddToolbar

Adds a docking window to Explorer or Internet Explorer's frame. The docking window must implement `IDockingWindow`. The component that creates the docking window calls this method once it has retrieved a pointer to the `IDockingWindowFrame` interface by calling `IServiceProvider::QueryService`. The syntax of `AddToolbar` is as follows:

```
HRESULT AddToolbar(IUnknown* punkSrc, LPCWSTR pwszItem,
    DWORD dwAddFlags);
```

with the following parameters:

punkSrc

[in] A reference to the object implementing `IDockingWindow` (i.e., a reference to the docking window).

pwszItem

[in] The address of a null-terminated UNICODE string that will be used to identify the docking window. This string can be used later, if necessary, to locate a docking window by calling *FindToolbar*.

dwAddFlags

[in] A flag that defines the visibility of the docking window being added. This should either be zero, which specifies that the docking window should be visible, or `DWFAF_HIDDEN`.

FindToolbar

Finds a docking window in the frame. The method is declared as follows:

```
HRESULT FindToolbar(LPCWSTR pwszItem, REFIID riid,
                    LPVOID* ppvObj);
```

Its parameters are:

pwszItem

[in] This is a pointer to the same string that was passed to `AddToolbar`.

riid

[in] This is a pointer to the GUID that identifies `IDockingWindow`.

ppvOut

[in, out] If the call is successful, this will contain the `IDockingWindow` interface of the requested docking window.

This method is not necessary for implementing docking windows. The primary component should keep all references to docking windows cached as private member variables; it would never need to call this method in that circumstance. Presumably, an object that implements a docking window might provide the name of the window (as specified in the call to `AddToolbar`) by means of a Public property. Additional components having an interest in the docking window could then locate it in the frame by calling `FindToolbar`.

RemoveToolbar

Removes the specified docking window from the frame. Its syntax is as follows:

```
HRESULT RemoveToolbar(IUnknown* punkSrc, DWORD dwRemoveFlags);
```

Its parameters are as follows:

punkSrc

[in] This is the address of the docking window object. The shell will call `IDockingWindow::CloseDW` in response to this call.

dwRemoveFlags

[in] Option flags for removing the docking window object. These flags have no meaning in terms of implementing a docking window. Because the Platform SDK does not document the meaning of these flags, it is assumed they are used by internal Microsoft implementations of the interface. This parameter can be one or more of the following values:

Constant	Description
DWFRF_NORMAL	The default delete processing is performed.
DWFRF_DELETECONFIGDATA	In addition to deleting the toolbar, any configuration data is removed as well.

Most likely, this method would not be called under normal circumstances. That's because the docking window itself should have access to the information that the primary component does; it should be able to remove itself. This method is used when the docking window is not your own (well, most likely).

IDockingWindowSite

This interface, which is implemented by Explorer, is used to manage the border space for one or more docking windows. A docking window component can use this interface to obtain its real estate within Explorer's client area. `IDockingWindowSite` is derived from `IOleWindow`; its members are listed in Table 14-4.

Table 14-4. IDockingWindowSite

IOleWindow	
(See Table 14-1 for IOleWindow methods)	
IDockingWindowSite	
GetBorderDW	Gets the border space that has been allocated for the docking window. Note, that this method is in no way tied to SetBorderSpaceDW. The two methods operate independently of each other. The only requirement is that this method is only valid after an initial call to RequestBorderSpaceDW.

Table 14-4. IDockingWindowSite (continued)

RequestBorderSpaceDW	Requests border space for the docking window. The space is not actually allocated until SetBorderSpaceDW is called. The space returned might be different from the requested amount. The request can also be refused altogether. After calling this method, GetBorderDW should be called to get the *actual* space that was allocated.
SetBorderSpaceDW	Allocates space for the docking window. Usually, this method is called immediately after RequestBorderSpaceDW to finalize the request for space.

GetBorderDW

Retrieves the border space that has been requested by the docking window. RequestBorderSpaceDW must be called first. After a request is made, this method gets the actual space allotted to the docking window. It is important to note that the space requested may be different than the space that is actually reserved. The syntax of GetBorderDW is:

```
HRESULT GetBorderDW(IUnknown* punkSrc, LPRECT prcBorder);
```

with the following parameters:

punkSrc

[in] Address of the docking window interface for the object that has requested space (that is, for the docking window).

prcBorder

[in] Address of a RECT structure that will contain border coordinates to be used by the docking window upon the successful return of this method.

RequestBorderSpaceDW

This method is called to request border space for the docking window; it is either approved, denied, or adjusted to accommodate the shell. If the request is approved or modified the method will return zero. Otherwise, an OLE error will be raised.

The actual space is not allocated until SetBorderSpaceDW is called. Here is the syntax for this method:

```
HRESULT RequestBorderSpaceDW(IUnknown* punkSrc, LPCBORDERWIDTHS pbw);
```

with the following parameters:

punkSrc

[in] The address of the docking window interface for the object that is requesting space.

pbw

[in] A pointer to a BORDERWIDTHS structure (which is the same thing as a RECT structure) that contains the requested border space.

SetBorderSpaceDW

Allocates border space for the docking window. Its syntax is:

```
HRESULT SetBorderSpaceDW(IUnknown* punkSrc, LPCBORDERWIDTHS pbw);
```

with the following parameters:

punkSrc

> [in] Address of the docking window interface for which border space is being assigned.

pbw

> [in] Address of a BORDERWITHS (RECT) structure containing the coordinates for the space that is being allocated.

The Project

The project for this chapter is fairly straightforward. We are going to start with the browser helper object that we built in Chapter 12 and give it a user interface. Not too creative, but that's not really the point. The point is to show you how you can take a simple component like a BHO and give it a user interface. Coming up with a creative way to use this knowledge will be your job. Now, how's that for passing the buck? You might be saying to yourself, "The component in Chapter 12 already has a user interface." True, but browser extensions (as opposed to BHOs) are for IE 5.0 and up. A BHO with a docking window is backwards compatible to IE 4.0.

Primary Component

Let's start with the IObjectWithSite::SetSite method of the component we built in Example 12-2. We'll add the code necessary for the docking window and then discuss the details. We only need to add a few new lines of code, which appear in boldface in Example 14-1.

Example 14-1. SetSite in Primary Object

```
Private Const IID_IShellBrowser = _
    "{000214e2-0000-0000-c000-000000000046}"

Private Const IID_IDockingWindowFrame = _
    "{47d2657a-7b27-11d0-8ca9-00a0c92dbfe8}"

Private szToolbar As String

Private Sub Class_Initialize()
    szToolbar = "IEDockingWindow"
End Sub
```

Example 14-1. SetSite in Primary Object (continued)

```
Private Sub IObjectWithSite_SetSite(ByVal pSite As IUnknownVB)

    If ObjPtr(pSite) = 0 Then
        CopyMemory m_ie, 0&, 4
        Exit Sub
    End If

    Set m_pUnkSite = pSite      'Save the site pointer for GetSite

    Dim pServiceProvider As IServiceProvider
    Set pServiceProvider = m_pUnkSite

    Dim clsidWebApp As GUID
    Dim clsidWebBrowser2 As GUID
    Dim clsidShellBrowser As GUID
    Dim clsidDockWndFrame As GUID

    'Query service provider to get IWebBrowser2 (InternetExplorer)
    CLSIDFromString StrPtr(IID_IWebBrowserApp), clsidWebApp
    CLSIDFromString StrPtr(IID_IWebBrowser2), clsidWebBrowser2
    CLSIDFromString StrPtr(IID_IShellBrowser), _
        clsidShellBrowser
    CLSIDFromString StrPtr(IID_IDockingWindowFrame), _
        clsidDockWndFrame

    Set m_ie = pServiceProvider.QueryService(_
        VarPtr(clsidWebApp), VarPtr(clsidWebBrowser2),

    Set m_pDockingWindowFrame = _
        pServiceProvider.QueryService _
                        (VarPtr(clsidShellBrowser), _
                        VarPtr(clsidDockWndFrame))


    Dim pDockWnd As clsDockWindow
    Set pDockWnd = New clsDockWindow

    pDockWnd.Initialize DW_BOTTOM

    Set pDockWnd.InternetExplorer = m_ie
    Set pDockWnd.InetSpeak = Me

    m_pDockingWindowFrame.AddToolbar pDockWnd, _
                        ByVal StrPtr(szToolbar), _
                        0

    Set pServiceProvider = Nothing

End Sub
```

The first thing that is added are two new constants that contain the string repre-
sentations of the CLSIDs for IShellBrowser and IDockingWindowFrame. We

will use them in conjunction with the *CLSIDFromString* API to obtain their actual numerical equivalents. After we have the CLSIDs, we can then query the "Shell Browser Service" to obtain a pointer to `IDockingWindowFrame`.

 If you have been wondering what other "services" are provided by the shell through `IServiceProvider`, you are not alone. This information does not seem to exist in the Platform SDK.

Now that we have access to `IDockingWindowFrame`, we can create an instance of clsDockWindow. This is our class that will implement all the specifics of the docking window; it implements `IObjectWithSite` and `IDockingWindow`. But before we pass the object to `AddToolbar`, we'll need to do some initialization work first. This includes telling the docking window where it will be displayed and providing it with references to Internet Explorer and our InetSpeak object.

The first thing we do is call the `Initialize` method of clsDockWindow (not to be confused with Class_Initialize, which is, of course, called automatically). This is a method of the class itself, created for our own convenience. It takes a location parameter; either `DW_TOP`, `DW_BOTTOM`, `DW_LEFT`, or `DW_RIGHT`. The docking window will use this information in order to position itself in the proper location within Explorer's frame window. Basically, this function sets a Private member variable in clsDockWindow. The `IDockingWindow::ResizeBorderDW` will make use of this parameter when it requests border space for the window. Ignore the implementation details of `Initialize` for now; we'll look at the actual method in the next section.

Next, we pass the docking window a reference to Internet Explorer and to clsInetSpeak, our BHO. This gives the docking window access to all those Internet goodies as well as access back to the primary component, which it will need to execute commands.

Finally, we call `IDockingWindowFrame::AddToolbar` to display the docking window. At this point the shell calls `IObjectWithSite::SetSite` on the docking window, transferring control away from the primary component.

Docking Window Component

The first thing we need to do in order to create our docking window component is to add a new class module to the project called clsDockWindow and make sure that it is implementing the appropriate interfaces:

```
Implements IDockingWindow
Implements IObjectWithSite
```

Before we start implementing any interfaces, let's get our class methods out of the way. If you remember from Example 14-1, we have three such methods: `Initialize`, `InternetExplorer`, and `InetSpeak`.

The first method, `Initialize`, which we've already discussed in the previous section, is just used to pass position and size information to the docking window. This information will be used when the docking window negotiates its border space within Explorer's client area. This function is simply:

```
Public Enum DW_LOCATION
    DW_TOP = 1
    DW_LEFT = 2
    DW_BOTTOM = 3
    DW_RIGHT = 4
End Enum

Private m_location As DW_LOCATION
Private m_nSize As Integer

Public Sub Initialize(ByVal Location As DW_LOCATION)
    m_location = Location
    m_nSize = size
End Sub
```

The class is also going to need a subroutine that the docking window form can call in order to specify its dimensions. That function looks like so:

```
Private m_nWidth As Integer
Private m_nHeight As Integer

Friend Sub SetSize(ByVal x As Integer, ByVal y As Integer)
    m_nWidth = x
    m_nHeight = y
End Sub
```

The next two functions are used to pass object references to the docking window. These two functions are self-explanatory and are defined like so:

```
Public Property Set InternetExplorer(ie As InternetExplorer)
    Set m_ie = ie
    Set frmDock.InternetExplorer = m_ie
End Property

Public Property Set InetSpeak(ins As clsInetSpeak)
    Set m_iis = ins
    Set frmDock.InetSpeak = m_iis
End Property
```

As you can see, these properties are also mirrored within the docking window form. This will give the form access to these objects as well.

With the exception of the InetSpeak property, clsDockWindow is
generic. There are no other specific references used in the class.
Should you want to reuse the class, you could merely replace the
InetSpeak property with one that accepts objects of your own type.

SetSite

Now, the easiest thing to do is get the **IObjectWithSite** implementation out of
the way. The docking window's version of **SetSite** is much simpler than our
other implementations. All we need to do is query the site pointer for the
IDockingWindowSite interface. We'll cache it away in a private member variable. Later, the docking window will use it to negotiate its border space.

Another thing we need to be aware of is that **SetSite** will be called again when
Explorer shuts down. This is no different than any other time we have implemented **IObjectWithSite**, so just consider this a reminder. It's easy enough to
determine whether Explorer has been shut down. All we need to do is examine
the cached site pointer. If its address is not zero, then we know **SetSite** has
already been called. If that's the case, we'll need to exit. Example 14-2 contains
the details.

Example 14-2. The Docking Window's SetSite Method

```
Private m_pDockSite As IDockingWindowSite

Private Sub IObjectWithSite_SetSite( _
    ByVal pSite As VBShellLib.IUnknownVB)

    If (ObjPtr(m_pDockSite)) Then
        Set m_pDockSite = Nothing
        Exit Sub
    End If

    If ObjPtr(pSite) Then
        Set m_pDockSite = pSite
    End If

End Sub
```

GetSite

There is nothing new to **GetSite**. It is implemented like we have always done
before:

```
Private Sub IObjectWithSite_GetSite( _
        ByVal priid As VBShellLib.REFIID, _
        ppvObj As VBShellLib.VOID)
```

```
        Dim pUnknown As IUnknownVB

        Set pUnknown = m_pDockSite
        pUnknown.QueryInterface priid, ppvObj

    End Sub
```

The docking window form

Now before we continue, let's actually design the docking window. We need to add a new form to the project called *frmDock*. As with all docking windows you write, it needs to be borderless. Also, you want to size the form approximately to the size you want it be when it is displayed. The band has a height of 600. 600/15 = 40, which is the height in pixels that we want for display.

After adding the form, you can add a command button called cmdInetSpeak to the form. This button will carry out our command. The band is shown in Figure 14-2.

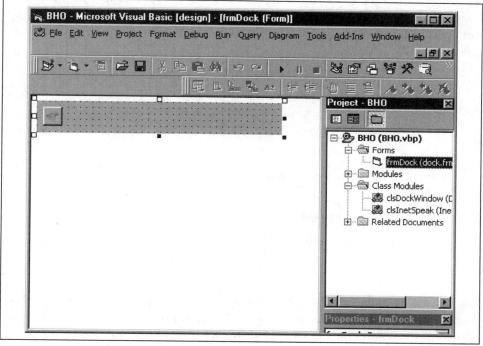

Figure 14-2. Docking window design

We need to add a few properties to the docking window that will allow the component to pass references into the form for **IWebBrowser2**, *clsInetSpeak*, and **IDockingWindow**. These properties look like this:

```
    Private m_dw As clsDockWindow
    Private WithEvents m_ie As InternetExplorer
    Private m_iis As clsInetSpeak
```

```
Friend Property Set InternetExplorer(ie As InternetExplorer)
    Set m_ie = ie
End Property

Friend Property Set InetSpeak(iis As clsInetSpeak)
    Set m_iis = iis
End Property

Friend Property Set DockingWindow(dw As clsDockWindow)
    Set m_dw = dw
End Property
```

Now that the form has a valid reference to clsInetSpeak, we can add code to the command button that actually fires the command. This is simply:

```
Private Sub cmdInetSpeak_Click()
    m_iis.Translate
End Sub
```

Also, this is an Internet-specific component. It doesn't really apply to file objects. So we need a way to disable the browser when we are not browsing the Web. We can capture the BeforeNavigate2 event from our IE reference to accomplish the task. The code looks like this:

```
Private Sub m_ie_BeforeNavigate2(ByVal pDisp As Object, _
                        URL As Variant, _
                        Flags As Variant, _
                        TargetFrameName As Variant, _
                        PostData As Variant, _
                        Headers As Variant, _
                        Cancel As Boolean)

    'Need to make sure command does not get
    'executed against non-HTML
    If InStr(URL, "http") Then
        cmdInetSpeak.Enabled = True
    Else
        cmdInetSpeak.Enabled = False
    End If

End Sub
```

Last but not least, we need to add some code to the Form_Load and Form_Unload events. When the form is loaded, its size information becomes valid. We'll use this opportunity to inform the docking window class about the form's size:

```
Private Sub Form_Load()
    m_dw.SetSize Me.Width / Screen.TwipsPerPixelX, _
                Me.Height / Screen.TwipsPerPixelY
End Sub
```

The Form_Unload event will merely be used to clean up after ourselves; we'll free up our object references here:

```
Private Sub Form_Unload(Cancel As Integer)
    Set m_dw = Nothing
    Set m_ie = Nothing
    Set m_iis = Nothing
End Sub
```

Okay, we have the docking window designed, so let's get back to clsDockWindow and our `IDockingWindow` implementation. The big action happens in `IDockingWindow::ResizeBorderDW` and `IDockingWindow::ShowDW`, so we'll save those methods for last. For now, we'll get the easier methods out of the way.

CloseDW

Some things never change. Just as was the case with band objects, this method's only responsibility is to unload the docking window:

```
Private Sub IDockingWindow_CloseDW(ByVal dwReserved As Long)
    Unload frmDock
End Sub
```

GetWindow

This method also performs the same duty that it did when we were discussing band objects. All it needs to do is return with a window handle for our docking window:

```
Private Function IDockingWindow_GetWindow() As Long
    IDockingWindow_GetWindow = frmDock.hwnd
End Function
```

ResizeBorderDW

Okay, now we're ready to get down to business. We need to implement `ResizeBorderDW`, which we have not done before. All we had to do for bands was capture the Resize event and perform any resizing that might be necessary. The container was able to handle itself as far as size and position. This is not the case here. Whenever Explorer is resized, the docking window has to renegotiate its border space and resize itself accordingly. Let's take a peek at the implementation for this method (see Example 14-3).

Example 14-3. ResizeBorderDW Implementation

```
Private Sub IDockingWindow_ResizeBorderDW( _
    ByVal prcBorder As Long, _
    ByVal punkToolbarSite As VBShellLib.IUnknownVB, _
    ByVal fReserved As Boolean)

    If NegotiateBorderSpace Then
        IDockingWindow_ShowDW True
    End If

End Sub
```

Well, that looks innocuous, doesn't it? That's because all the work is being done by a private helper function called *NegotiateBorderSpace*. If the border space is obtained successfully, the function then calls *ShowDW* to display the docking window. We'll talk about *ShowDW* soon, but now, let's get into *NegotiateBorderSpace*, which is shown in Example 14-4.

Example 14-4. NegotiateBorderSpace

```
Private m_rcDisplay As RECT

Private Function NegotiateBorderSpace() As Boolean

    NegotiateBorderSpace = False

    Dim pDockingWindow As IDockingWindow
    Dim bw As RECT  'BORDERWIDTHS
    Dim rcBorder As RECT
    Dim rcTemp As RECT
    Dim nSize As Integer

    Select Case m_location
        Case DW_TOP
            nSize = m_nHeight
            bw.Top = nSize
        Case DW_LEFT
            nSize = m_nWidth
            bw.Left = nSize
        Case DW_BOTTOM
            nSize = m_nHeight
            bw.bottom = nSize
        Case DW_RIGHT
            nSize = m_nWidth
            bw.Right = nSize
    End Select

    Set pDockingWindow = Me
    m_pDockSite.RequestBorderSpaceDW pDockingWindow, _
        ByVal VarPtr(bw)

    m_pDockSite.SetBorderSpaceDW pDockingWindow, _
        ByVal VarPtr(bw)

    m_pDockSite.GetBorderDW pDockingWindow, ByVal VarPtr(rcBorder)

    Select Case m_location
        Case DW_RIGHT
            m_rcDisplay.Left = rcBorder.Right - m_nSize
            m_rcDisplay.Top = rcBorder.Top
            m_rcDisplay.Right = rcBorder.Right
            'Accomodate Status Bar
            m_rcDisplay.bottom = rcBorder.bottom - 82

        Case DW_LEFT
```

Example 14-4. NegotiateBorderSpace (continued)

```
            m_rcDisplay.Left = rcBorder.Left
            m_rcDisplay.Top = rcBorder.Top
            m_rcDisplay.Right = rcBorder.Left + m_nSize
            'Accomodate Status Bar
            m_rcDisplay.bottom = rcBorder.bottom - 82

        Case DW_TOP
            m_rcDisplay.Left = rcBorder.Left
            m_rcDisplay.Top = rcBorder.Top
            m_rcDisplay.Right = rcBorder.Right - rcBorder.Left
            m_rcDisplay.bottom = m_nSize

        Case DW_BOTTOM
            m_rcDisplay.Left = rcBorder.Left
            m_rcDisplay.Top = rcBorder.bottom - m_nSize
            m_rcDisplay.Right = rcBorder.Right - rcBorder.Left
            ' -1 leaves beveled edge on Status Bar
            m_rcDisplay.bottom = m_nSize - 1

    End Select

    NegotiateBorderSpace = True

End Function
```

Let's step through this nice and easy; it's actually much easier than it looks. The first thing that happens is that a RECT structure, *bw*, is filled out based on the parameters we passed to the Initialize function of the class. In terms of the chapter example, we asked for a docking window on the bottom of Explorer's frame window. Earlier, when our window was loaded, its size (converted from twips to pixels) was passed back to *clsDockWindow*. Since the form's height is 600, and 600 divided by Screen.TwipsPerPixelY (15) equals 40, we will end up with a RECT structure whose *bottom* member is set to 40. All the other values of the RECT will contain 0.

Next, we get a reference to our own IDockingWindow interface pointer. This is passed to IDockingWindowSite::RequestBorderSpaceDW along with a pointer to *bw*. Translation: *allocate border space that is 40 pixels tall at the bottom of your client area. This object is going to need it.*

Next, we finalize the request by calling SetBorderSpaceDW. This actually allocates and reserves the space for our docking window.

Now, things get a little confusing. We call GetBorderDW, which returns to us another RECT structure, *rcBorder*, that *supposedly* contains the dimensions of the space that has been allocated for our docking window. In practice, the method seems to return the dimensions of the entire client area. So the rest of this function is dedicated to determining the actual location of the docking window based on the size of the client area and the location and size that we have asked for. When all is said and done, we have a private member variable, *m_rcDisplay*, that contains the actual coordinates of the window.

ShowDW

The last thing on our list for clsDockWindow is **ShowDW**. As you might remember from Chapter 13, this method is called when the window is about to be either displayed or destroyed. Example 14-5 contains the code listing.

Example 14-5. ShowDW

```
Private m_hwnd As hwnd

Private Sub IDockingWindow_ShowDW(ByVal fShow As Boolean)

    Dim pDockingWindow As IDockingWindow
    Dim rcBorderWidths As RECT
    Dim dwStyle As DWORD

    If Not m_hwnd Then
        m_hwnd = frmDock.hwnd
        dwStyle = GetWindowLong(m_hwnd, GWL_STYLE)
        dwStyle = dwStyle Or WS_CHILD Or WS_CLIPSIBLINGS
        SetWindowLong m_hwnd, GWL_STYLE, dwStyle
        SetParent frmDock.hwnd, m_pDockSite.GetWindow
    End If

    If (fShow) Then

        ShowWindow frmDock.hwnd, SW_SHOW
        MoveWindow frmDock.hwnd, m_rcDisplay.Left, _
                    m_rcDisplay.Top, m_rcDisplay.Right, _
                    m_rcDisplay.bottom, True

    Else

        ShowWindow frmDock.hwnd, SW_HIDE
        Set pDockingWindow = Me

        'Release border space - rcBorderWidths is empty
        m_pDockSite.SetBorderSpaceDW pDockingWindow, _
        ByVal VarPtr(rcBorderWidths)

    End If

End Sub
```

The docking window, like the band object, also needs to have some style bits changed and have its parent window set to the container window. Remember, we do this so that when the docking window gets the focus, Explorer will not *lose* the focus. The idea here is that the docking window is fully integrated, right? But since

ShowDW will be called many times throughout the docking window's life, we need to make sure this does not happen more than once.

If *fShow* is True, we simply show the window and move its position to coordinates specified by the RECT *m_rcDisplay* (the coordinates were determined in NegotiateBorderSpace).

If *fShow* is False, we hide the window and release the border space. To release the border space, IDockingWindowSite::SetBorderSpaceDW is called with the address of an empty RECT.

That's it; we have done everything we need in order to implement a docking window.

Registration

Good news! There is nothing you have to do registry-wise in order to implement a docking window. Registry entries are specific to the types of components that implement them. To register the component for this chapter, just run the registry script for Chapter 12.

V

Appendixes

A

VBShell Library Listing

This appendix lists the IDL source code for the VB Shell Library—the type library used in developing the examples for this book—which you can use when developing your own shell extensions:

```
[
    uuid(39898EB0-DE1B-11d2-9FD6-00550076E06F),
    version(1.0),
    helpstring("VB Shell Library")
]
library VBShellLib
{

    importlib("stdole2.tlb");

    //-----------------------------------------------------------
    // Forward declaration of interfaces
    //-----------------------------------------------------------
    interface IContextMenu;
    interface ICopyHookA;
    interface ICopyHookW;
    interface IDataObject;
    interface IDeskband;
    interface IDockingWindow;
    interface IDockingWindowFrame;
    interface IDockingWindowSite;
    interface IDropTarget;
    interface IEnumFORMATETC;
    interface IEnumIDList;
    interface IExtractIconA;
    interface IExtractIconW;
    interface IFileViewerA;
    interface IFileViewerSite;
    interface IFileViewerW;
    interface IInputObject;
    interface IMalloc;
```

```
interface IObjectWithSite;
interface IOleCommandTarget;
interface IOleWindow;
interface IPersist;
interface IPersistFile;
interface IPersistFolder;
interface IQueryInfo;
interface IServiceProvider;
interface IShellBrowser;
interface IShellExtInit;
interface IShellFolder;
interface IShellLinkA;
interface IShellLinkW;
interface IShellPropSheetExt;
interface IShellView;
interface IStream;
interface IUnknownVB;


//-----------------------------------------------------------
// Types
//-----------------------------------------------------------
typedef [public] long BOOL;
typedef [public] unsigned char BYTE;
typedef [public] long CLSID;
typedef [public] long COLORREF;
typedef [public] long DESKBANDINFO;
typedef [public] long DLGPROC;
typedef [public] long DWORD;
typedef [public] long HANDLE;
typedef [public] long HBITMAP;
typedef [public] long HGLOBAL;
typedef [public] long HICON;
typedef [public] long HINSTANCE;
typedef [public] long HKEY;
typedef [public] long HMENU;
typedef [public] long HOLEMENU;
typedef [public] long HWND;
typedef [public] double LARGE_INTEGER;
typedef [public] long LPBC;
typedef [public] long LPARAM;
typedef [public] long LPCBORDERWIDTHS;
typedef [public] long LPCFOLDERSETTINGS;
typedef [public] long LPCITEMIDLIST;
typedef [public] long LPCMINVOKECOMMANDINFO;
typedef [public] long LPCOLESTR;
typedef [public] long LPDESKBANDINFO;
typedef [public] long LPFNADDPROPSHEETPAGE;
typedef [public] long LPFNPSPCALLBACK;
typedef [public] long LPFOLDERSETTINGS;
typedef [public] long LPFORMATETC;
typedef [public] long LPGUID;
typedef [public] long LPITEMIDLIST;
typedef [public] long LPOLECMD;
typedef [public] long LPOLECMDTEXT;
```

```
typedef [public] long LPOLEMENUGROUPWIDTHS;
typedef [public] long LPOLESTR;
typedef [public] long LPPROPSHEETPAGE;
typedef [public] long LPRECT;
typedef [public] long LPSTRVB;
typedef [public] long LPTSTRVB;
typedef [public] long LPCSTRVB;
typedef [public] long LPCTSTRVB;
typedef [public] long LPFVSHOWINFO;
typedef [public] long LPMSG;
typedef [public] long LPWSTRVB;
typedef [public] long LPCWSTRVB;
typedef [public] long LPSHITEMID;
typedef [public] long LPSTGMEDIUM;
typedef [public] long LPSTREAM;
typedef [public] long LPSTRRET;
typedef [public] long LPTBBUTTON;
typedef [public] long LPTSTR;
typedef [public] long LPUNKNOWN;
typedef [public] long LPVARIANTARG;
typedef [public] long LPWIN32_FIND_DATA;
typedef [public] long LPVOID;
typedef [public] long LRESULT;
typedef [public] long REFGUID;
typedef [public] long REFIID;
typedef [public] long UINT;
typedef [public] double ULARGE_INTEGER;
typedef [public] long ULONG;
typedef [public] long VOID;
typedef [public] long WPARAM;
typedef [public] short WORD;


//------------------------------------------------------------
// C O M M O N   T Y P E S
//------------------------------------------------------------

//typedef struct {
//    DWORD data1;
//    short data2;
//    short data3;
//    BYTE  data4[8];
//} GUID;

typedef enum {
    FCIDM_SHVIEWFIRST    = 0x0000,
    FCIDM_SHVIEWLAST     = 0x7fff,
    FCIDM_BROWSERFIRST   = 0xa000,
    FCIDM_BROWSERLAST    = 0xbf00,
    FCIDM_GLOBALFIRST    = 0x8000,
    FCIDM_GLOBALLAST     = 0x9fff,
} FCIDM;

//#define FCIDM_GLOBALLAST 0x9fff
typedef enum {
```

```
        FCIDM_MENU_FILE              = (0x9fff+0x0000),
        FCIDM_MENU_EDIT              = (0x9fff+0x0040),
        FCIDM_MENU_VIEW              = (0x9fff+0x0080),
        FCIDM_MENU_VIEW_SEP_OPTIONS  = (0x9fff+0x0081),
        FCIDM_MENU_TOOLS             = (0x9fff+0x00c0),
        FCIDM_MENU_TOOLS_SEP_GOTO    = (0x9fff+0x00c1),
        FCIDM_MENU_HELP              = (0x9fff+0x0100),
        FCIDM_MENU_FIND              = (0x9fff+0x0140),
        FCIDM_MENU_EXPLORE           = (0x9fff+0x0150),
        FCIDM_MENU_FAVORITES         = (0x9fff+0x0170),
    } FCIDM_MENU;

    typedef struct tagFILETIME {
        DWORD   dwLowDateTime;
        DWORD   dwHighDateTime;
    } FILETIME;

    typedef enum {
        MK_LBUTTON = 0x0001,
        MK_RBUTTON = 0x0002,
        MK_SHIFT   = 0x0004,
        MK_CONTROL = 0x0008,
        MK_MBUTTON = 0x0010,
        MK_ALT     = 0x0020
    } KEYSTATES;

    typedef enum {
        MIIM_STATE       = 0x00000001,
        MIIM_ID          = 0x00000002,
        MIIM_SUBMENU     = 0x00000004,
        MIIM_CHECKMARKS  = 0x00000008,
        MIIM_TYPE        = 0x00000010,
        MIIM_DATA        = 0x00000020,
    } MIIM;

    typedef struct {
        UINT     cbSize;
        MIIM     fMask;
        UINT     fType;
        UINT     fState;
        UINT     wID;
        HMENU    hSubMenu;
        HBITMAP  hbmpChecked;
        HBITMAP  hbmpUnchecked;
        DWORD    dwItemData;
        LPTSTR   dwTypeData;
        UINT     cch;
    } MENUITEMINFO;

    typedef struct {
        long width[6];
    } OLEMENUGROUPWIDTHS;
```

```
typedef struct {
    long x;
    long y;
} POINT;

typedef [public] POINT POINTL;

typedef struct {
    long left;
    long top;
    long right;
    long bottom;
} RECT;

//-----------------------------------------------------------
// I N T E R F A C E S
//-----------------------------------------------------------


//-----------------------------------------------------------
//
// IContextMenu
//
//-----------------------------------------------------------
typedef enum {
    CF_TEXT             = 1,
    CF_BITMAP           = 2,
    CF_METAFILEPICT     = 3,
    CF_SYLK             = 4,
    CF_DIF              = 5,
    CF_TIFF             = 6,
    CF_OEMTEXT          = 7,
    CF_DIB              = 8,
    CF_PALETTE          = 9,
    CF_PENDATA          = 10,
    CF_RIFF             = 11,
    CF_WAVE             = 12,
    CF_UNICODETEXT      = 13,
    CF_ENHMETAFILE      = 14,
    CF_HDROP            = 15,
    CF_LOCALE           = 16,
    CF_MAX              = 17,
    CF_OWNERDISPLAY     = 0x0080,
    CF_DSPTEXT          = 0x0081,
    CF_DSPBITMAP        = 0x0082,
    CF_DSPMETAFILEPICT  = 0x0083,
    CF_DSPENHMETAFILE   = 0x008E
} CLIPFORMAT;

typedef struct {
    DWORD    cbSize;
    DWORD    fMask;
    HWND     hwnd;
```

```
        LPCSTRVB  lpVerb;
        LPCSTRVB  lpParameters;
        LPCSTRVB  lpDirectory;
        int       nShow;
        DWORD     dwHotKey;
        HANDLE    hIcon;
} CMINVOKECOMMANDINFO;

typedef enum {
        DVASPECT_CONTENT   = 1,
        DVASPECT_THUMBNAIL = 2,
        DVASPECT_ICON      = 4,
        DVASPECT_DOCPRINT  = 8
} DVASPECT;

typedef enum {
        GCS_VERBA     = 0x00000000,
        GCS_HELPTEXTA = 0x00000001,
        GCS_VALIDATEA = 0x00000002,
        GCS_VERBW     = 0x00000004,
        GCS_HELPTEXTW = 0x00000005,
        GCS_VALIDATEW = 0x00000006,
        GCS_UNICODE   = 0x00000004,
} GETCOMMANDSTRINGFLAGS;

typedef enum {
        MF_INSERT          = 0x00000000,
        MF_CHANGE          = 0x00000080,
        MF_APPEND          = 0x00000100,
        MF_DELETE          = 0x00000200,
        MF_REMOVE          = 0x00001000,
        MF_BYCOMMAND       = 0x00000000,
        MF_BYPOSITION      = 0x00000400,
        MF_SEPARATOR       = 0x00000800,
        MF_ENABLED         = 0x00000000,
        MF_GRAYED          = 0x00000001,
        MF_DISABLED        = 0x00000002,
        MF_UNCHECKED       = 0x00000000,
        MF_CHECKED         = 0x00000008,
        MF_USECHECKBITMAPS = 0x00000200,
        MF_STRING          = 0x00000000,
        MF_BITMAP          = 0x00000004,
        MF_OWNERDRAW       = 0x00000100,
        MF_POPUP           = 0x00000010,
        MF_MENUBARBREAK    = 0x00000020,
        MF_MENUBREAK       = 0x00000040,
        MF_UNHILITE        = 0x00000000,
        MF_HILITE          = 0x00000080,
        MF_DEFAULT         = 0x00001000,
        MF_SYSMENU         = 0x00002000,
        MF_HELP            = 0x00004000,
        MF_RIGHTJUSTIFY    = 0x00004000,
        MF_MOUSESELECT     = 0x00008000,
        MF_END             = 0x00000080
} MENUFLAGS;
```

```
typedef enum {
    TYMED_HGLOBAL      = 1,
    TYMED_FILE         = 2,
    TYMED_ISTREAM      = 4,
    TYMED_ISTORAGE     = 8,
    TYMED_GDI          = 16,
    TYMED_MFPICT       = 32,
    TYMED_ENHMF        = 64,
    TYMED_NULL         = 0
} TYMED;

typedef struct {
    long   cfFormat;
    long   ptd;
    DWORD  dwAspect;
    long   lindex;
    TYMED  tymed;
} FORMATETC;

// This is really a union
// This is a generic definition
typedef struct {
    TYMED      tymed;
    long       pData;
    IUnknown  *pUnkForRelease;
} STGMEDIUM;


typedef enum {
    CMF_NORMAL        = 0x00000000,
    CMF_DEFAULTONLY   = 0x00000001,
    CMF_VERBSONLY     = 0x00000002,
    CMF_EXPLORE       = 0x00000004,
    CMF_NOVERBS       = 0x00000008,
    CMF_CANRENAME     = 0x00000010,
    CMF_NODEFAULT     = 0x00000020,
    CMF_INCLUDESTATIC = 0x00000040,
    CMF_RESERVED      = 0xffff0000
} QUERYCONTEXTMENUFLAGS;



[
    uuid(000214e4-0000-0000-c000-000000000046),
    helpstring("IContextMenu Interface"),
    odl
]
interface IContextMenu : IUnknown
{
    HRESULT QueryContextMenu(
                [in] HMENU hmenu,
                [in] UINT indexMenu,
                [in] UINT idCmdFirst,
                [in] UINT idCmdLast,
                [in] QueryContextMenuFlags uFlags);
```

```
        HRESULT InvokeCommand([in] LPCMINVOKECOMMANDINFO lpcmi);

        HRESULT GetCommandString([in] UINT    idCmd,
                                 [in] UINT    uType,
                                 [in] UINT    pwReserved,
                                 [in] LPSTRVB pszName,
                                 [in] UINT    cchMax);
    }


    //------------------------------------------------------------
    // ICopyHook
    //------------------------------------------------------------

    typedef enum {
        FO_MOVE   = 0x0001,
        FO_COPY   = 0x0002,
        FO_DELETE = 0x0003,
        FO_RENAME = 0x0004
    } FO;

    [
        uuid(000214EF-0000-0000-C000-000000000046),
        helpstring("ICopyHookA Interface"),
        odl
    ]
    interface ICopyHookA : IUnknown
    {
        HRESULT CopyCallback([in] HWND hwnd,
                             [in] UINT wFunc,
                             [in] UINT wFlags,
                             [in] LPCSTRVB pszSrcFile,
                             [in] DWORD dwSrcAttribs,
                             [in] LPCSTRVB pszDestFile,
                             [in] DWORD dwDestAttribs);
    }


    [
        uuid(000214FC-0000-0000-C000-000000000046),
        helpstring("ICopyHookW Interface"),
        odl
    ]
    interface ICopyHookW : IUnknown
    {
        HRESULT CopyCallback([in] HWND hwnd,
                             [in] UINT wFunc,
                             [in] UINT wFlags,
                             [in] LPCWSTRVB pszSrcFile,
                             [in] DWORD dwSrcAttribs,
                             [in] LPCWSTRVB pszDestFile,
                             [in] DWORD dwDestAttribs);
    }

    //------------------------------------------------------------
    // IDataObject
    //------------------------------------------------------------
```

```
typedef enum {
    DV_E_FORMATETC              = 0x80040064,
    DV_E_DVTARGETDEVICE         = 0x80040065,
    DV_E_STGMEDIUM              = 0x80040066,
    DV_E_STATDATA               = 0x80040067,
    DV_E_LINDEX                 = 0x80040068,
    DV_E_TYMED                  = 0x80040069,
    DV_E_CLIPFORMAT             = 0x8004006A,
    DV_E_DVASPECT               = 0x8004006B,
    DV_E_DVTARGETDEVICE_SIZE    = 0x8004006C,
    DV_E_NOIVIEWOBJECT          = 0x8004006D
} DV_ERROR;

typedef enum tagDATADIR
{
    DATADIR_GET = 1,
    DATADIR_SET = 2
} DATADIR;


[
    uuid(0000010e-0000-0000-C000-000000000046),
    helpstring("IDataObject Interface"),
    odl
]
interface IDataObject : IUnknown
{
    HRESULT GetData(
                [in] FORMATETC *pformatetcIn,
                [in,out] STGMEDIUM *pmedium);

    HRESULT GetDataHere(
                [in] FORMATETC *pformatetc,
                [in,out] STGMEDIUM *pmedium);

    HRESULT QueryGetData(
                [in] FORMATETC *pformatetc);

    HRESULT GetCanonicalFormatEtc(
                [in] FORMATETC *pformatectIn,
                [in,out] FORMATETC *pformatetcOut);

    HRESULT SetData(
                [in] FORMATETC *pformatetc,
                [in] STGMEDIUM *pmedium,
                [in] BOOL fRelease);

    HRESULT EnumFormatEtc(
                [in] long dwDirection,
                [in,out] IEnumFORMATETC **ppenumFormatEtc);

    HRESULT DAdvise(
                [in] FORMATETC *pformatetc,
                [in] long advf,
```

```
                            [in] long pAdvSink,
                            [in] long pdwConnection);

        HRESULT DUnadvise(
                            [in] long dwConnection);

        HRESULT EnumDAdvise(
                            [in] long ppenumAdvise);
    }


    //---------------------------------------------------------
    // IDockingWindow (derived from IOleWindow)
    //---------------------------------------------------------
    [
        uuid(012dd920-7b26-11d0-8ca9-00a0c92dbfe8),
        helpstring("IDockingWindow Interface"),
        odl
    ]
    interface IDockingWindow : IUnknown
    {

        //IOleWindow
        HRESULT GetWindow([out, retval] long *phWnd);
        HRESULT ContextSensitiveHelp([in] boolean fEnterMode);

        //IDockingWindow
        HRESULT ShowDW([in] boolean fShow);
        HRESULT CloseDW([in] long dwReserved);
        HRESULT ResizeBorderDW([in] long prcBorder,
                            [in] IUnknownVB *punkToolbarSite,
                            [in] boolean fReserved);
    }


    //---------------------------------------------------------
    // IDockingWindowFrame (derived from IOleWindow)
    //---------------------------------------------------------
    [
        uuid(47d2657a-7b27-11d0-8ca9-00a0c92dbfe8),
        helpstring("IDockingWindowFrame Interface"),
        odl
    ]
    interface IDockingWindowFrame : IUnknown
    {

        //IOleWindow
        HRESULT GetWindow([out, retval] long *phWnd);
        HRESULT ContextSensitiveHelp([in] boolean fEnterMode);

        //IDockingWindowFrame
        HRESULT AddToolbar([in] IUnknown *punkSrc,
                        [in] LPCWSTRVB pwszItem,
                        [in] DWORD dwAddFlags);

        HRESULT RemoveToolbar([in] IUnknown *punkSrc,
                            [in] DWORD dwRemoveFlags);
```

```
             HRESULT FindToolbar([in] LPCWSTRVB pwszItem,
                                 [in] REFIID riid,
                                 [in,out] LPVOID* ppvObj);

}


//-----------------------------------------------------------
// IDockingWindowSite (derived from IOleWindow)
//-----------------------------------------------------------
[
    uuid(2a342fc2-7b26-11d0-8ca9-00a0c92dbfe8),
    helpstring("IDockingWindowSite Interface"),
    odl
]
interface IDockingWindowSite : IUnknown
{

    //IOleWindow
    HRESULT GetWindow([out, retval] long *phWnd);
    HRESULT ContextSensitiveHelp([in] boolean fEnterMode);

    //IDockingWindowSite
    HRESULT GetBorderDW([in] IUnknown* punkObj,
                        [in] LPRECT prcBorder);

    HRESULT RequestBorderSpaceDW([in] IUnknown* punkObj,
                                 [in] LPCBORDERWIDTHS pbw);

    HRESULT SetBorderSpaceDW([in] IUnknown* punkObj,
                             [in] LPCBORDERWIDTHS pbw);

}



//-----------------------------------------------------------
// IDeskband (derived from IDockingWindow)
//-----------------------------------------------------------
typedef enum {
    DBIM_MINSIZE   = 0x0001,
    DBIM_MAXSIZE   = 0x0002,
    DBIM_INTEGRAL  = 0x0004,
    DBIM_ACTUAL    = 0x0008,
    DBIM_TITLE     = 0x0010,
    DBIM_MODEFLAGS = 0x0020,
    DBIM_BKCOLOR   = 0x0040
} DBIM;

// DESKBANDINFO dwModeFlags values
typedef enum {
    DBIMF_NORMAL         = 0x0000,
    DBIMF_VARIABLEHEIGHT = 0x0008,
    DBIMF_DEBOSSED       = 0x0020,
    DBIMF_BKCOLOR        = 0x0040
} DBIMF;
```

```
// GetBandInfo view mode values
typedef enum {
    DBIF_VIEWMODE_NORMAL        =   0x0000,
    DBIF_VIEWMODE_VERTICAL      =   0x0001,
    DBIF_VIEWMODE_FLOATING      =   0x0002,
    DBIF_VIEWMODE_TRANSPARENT   =   0x0004
} DBIF;

[
    uuid(eb0fe172-1a3a-11d0-89b3-00a0c90a90ac),
    helpstring("IDeskBand Interface"),
    odl
]
interface IDeskBand : IUnknown
{

    //IOleWindow
    HRESULT GetWindow([out, retval] long *phWnd);
    HRESULT ContextSensitiveHelp([in] boolean fEnterMode);

    //IDockingWindow
    HRESULT ShowDW([in] boolean fShow);
    HRESULT CloseDW([in] long dwReserved);
    HRESULT ResizeBorderDW([in] long prcBorder,
                           [in] long punkToolbarSite,
                           [in] boolean fReserved);

    //IDeskBand
    HRESULT GetBandInfo([in] long dwBandID,
                        [in] long dwViewMode,
                        [in] LPDESKBANDINFO pdbi);
}


//-----------------------------------------------------------
// IDropTarget
//-----------------------------------------------------------

typedef enum {
    DROPEFFECT_NONE = 0,
    DROPEFFECT_COPY = 1,
    DROPEFFECT_MOVE = 2,
    DROPEFFECT_LINK = 4,
    DROPEFFECT_SCROLL = 0x80000000
} DROPEFFECT;
[
    uuid(00000122-0000-0000-C000-000000000046),
    helpstring("IDropTarget Interface"),
    odl
]
interface IDropTarget : IUnknown
{

    typedef IDropTarget *LPDROPTARGET;
```

```
    HRESULT DragEnter
    (
        [in] IDataObject *pDataObj,
        [in] KEYSTATES grfKeyState,
        [in] long x,
        [in] long y,
        [in, out] DROPEFFECT *pdwEffect
    );

    HRESULT DragOver
    (
        [in] KEYSTATES grfKeyState,
        [in] long x,
        [in] long y,
        [in, out] DROPEFFECT *pdwEffect
    );

    HRESULT DragLeave(void);

    HRESULT Drop
    (
        [in] IDataObject *pDataObj,
        [in] KEYSTATES grfKeyState,
        [in] long x,
        [in] long y,
        [in, out] DROPEFFECT *pdwEffect
    );
}


//-----------------------------------------------------------
// IEnumFORMATETC
//-----------------------------------------------------------
[
    uuid(00000103-0000-0000-C000-000000000046),
    helpstring("IEnumFORMATETC Interface"),
    odl
]
interface IEnumFORMATETC : IUnknown
{
    HRESULT Next([in] ULONG celt,
                 [in, out] FORMATETC *rgelt,
                 [in, out] ULONG *pceltFetched);
    HRESULT Skip([in] ULONG celt);
    HRESULT Reset();
    HRESULT Clone([in, out] IEnumFORMATETC **ppenum);
}


//-----------------------------------------------------------
// IEnumIDList
//-----------------------------------------------------------
[
    uuid(000214f2-0000-0000-c000-000000000046),
    helpstring("IEnumIDList Interface"),
    odl
]
```

```
interface IEnumIDList : IUnknown
{
    HRESULT Next([in] ULONG celt,
                [in, out] LPITEMIDLIST *rgelt,
                [in, out] ULONG *pceltFetched);
    HRESULT Skip([in] ULONG celt);
    HRESULT Reset();
    HRESULT Clone([in, out] IEnumIDList **ppenum);
}


//-------------------------------------------------------------
// IExtractIcon
//-------------------------------------------------------------

// GetIconLocation input flags
typedef enum {
    GIL_OPENICON = 0x0001,
    GIL_FORSHELL = 0x0002,
    GIL_ASYNC    = 0x0020
} GETICONLOCATIONINPUT;

// GetIconLocation return flags
typedef enum {
    GIL_SIMULATEDOC  = 0x0001,
    GIL_PERINSTANCE  = 0x0002,
    GIL_PERCLASS     = 0x0004,
    GIL_NOTFILENAME  = 0x0008,
    GIL_DONTCACHE    = 0x0010
} GETICONLOCATIONRETURN;

[
    uuid(000214eb-0000-0000-c000-000000000046),
    helpstring("IExtractIconA Interface"),
    odl
]
interface IExtractIconA : IUnknown
{

    HRESULT GetIconLocation(
                [in] UINT uFlags,
                [in] LPSTRVB szIconFile,
                [in] UINT cchMax,
                [in, out] long *piIndex,
                [in, out] GETICONLOCATIONRETURN *pwFlags);


    HRESULT Extract([in] LPCSTRVB pszFile,
                [in] UINT nIconIndex,
                [in, out] HICON *phiconLarge,
                [in, out] HICON *phiconSmall,
                [in] UINT nIconSize);
}
```

```
[
    uuid(000214fa-0000-0000-c000-000000000046),
    helpstring("IExtractIconW"),
    odl
]
interface IExtractIconW : IUnknown
{
    HRESULT GetIconLocation(
                [in] UINT uFlags,
                [in] LPWSTRVB szIconFile,
                [in] UINT cchMax,
                [in, out] long *piIndex,
                [in, out] GETICONLOCATIONRETURN *pwFlags);

    HRESULT Extract([in] LPWSTRVB pszFile,
                [in] UINT nIconIndex,
                [in, out] HICON *phiconLarge,
                [in, out] HICON *phiconSmall,
                [in] UINT nIconSize);
}


//-----------------------------------------------------------
// IFileViewer
//-----------------------------------------------------------
typedef enum {
    FVSIF_RECT      = 0x00000001,
    FVSIF_PINNED    = 0x00000002,
    FVSIF_NEWFAILED = 0x08000000,
    FVSIF_NEWFILE   = 0x80000000,
    FVSIF_CANVIEWIT = 0x40000000
}FVSIF;


[
    uuid(000214f0-0000-0000-c000-000000000046),
    helpstring("IFileViewerA Interface"),
    odl
]
interface IFileViewerA : IUnknown
{
    HRESULT ShowInitialize([in] IFileViewerSite *lpfsi);
    HRESULT Show([in] LPFVSHOWINFO pvsi);
    HRESULT PrintTo([in] LPSTRVB pszDriver,
                [in] BOOL fSuppressUI);
}


[
    uuid(000214f8-0000-0000-c000-000000000046),
    helpstring("IFileViewerW Interface"),
    odl
]
interface IFileViewerW : IUnknown
{
    HRESULT ShowInitialize([in] IFileViewerSite *lpfsi);
    HRESULT Show([in] LPFVSHOWINFO pvsi);
```

```
        HRESULT PrintTo([in] LPWSTRVB pszDriver,
                        [in] BOOL fSuppressUI);
}


//-----------------------------------------------------------
// IFileViewerSite
//-----------------------------------------------------------
[
    uuid(000214f3-0000-0000-c000-000000000046),
    helpstring("IFileViewerSite Interface"),
    odl
]
interface IFileViewerSite : IUnknown
{
    HRESULT SetPinnedWindow([in] HWND hwnd);
    HRESULT GetPinnedWindow([out, retval] HWND *phwnd);
}


//-----------------------------------------------------------
//IInputObject
//-----------------------------------------------------------
[
    uuid(68284faa-6a48-11d0-8c78-00c04fd918b4),
    helpstring("IInputObject Interface"),
    odl
]
interface IInputObject : IUnknown
{
    HRESULT UIActivateIO([in] boolean fActivate,
                         [in] LPMSG lpMsg);
    HRESULT HasFocusIO();
    HRESULT TranslateAcceleratorIO([in] LPMSG lpMsg);
}


//-----------------------------------------------------------
//IMalloc
//-----------------------------------------------------------
[
    uuid(00000002-0000-0000-C000-000000000046),
    helpstring("IMalloc Interface"),
    odl
]

interface IMalloc : IUnknown
{

    //void *Alloc([in] ULONG cb);
    long Alloc([in] ULONG cb);

    //void *Realloc ([in] void *pv,
    //               [in] ULONG cb);
    long Realloc ([in] VOID *pv, [in] ULONG cb);

    void Free([in] VOID *pv);
```

```
        ULONG GetSize([in] VOID *pv);

        int DidAlloc([in] VOID *pv);

        void HeapMinimize();
    }


//------------------------------------------------------------
//IObjectWithSite
//------------------------------------------------------------
[
    uuid(FC4801A3-2BA9-11CF-A229-00AA003D7352),
    helpstring("IObjectWithSite Interface"),
    odl
]
interface IObjectWithSite : IUnknown
{
    HRESULT SetSite([in] IUnknownVB* pSite);
    HRESULT GetSite([in] REFIID priid,
                    [in, out] VOID * ppvObj);
}


//------------------------------------------------------------
//IOleCommandTarget
//------------------------------------------------------------

[
    uuid(B722BCCB-4E68-101B-A2BC-00AA00404770),
    helpstring("IOleCommandTarget Interface"),
    odl
]
interface IOleCommandTarget : IUnknown
{

    typedef enum OLECMDF {
        OLECMDF_SUPPORTED      = 0x00000001,
        OLECMDF_ENABLED        = 0x00000002,
        OLECMDF_LATCHED        = 0x00000004,
        OLECMDF_NINCHED        = 0x00000008,
    } OLECMDF;

    typedef struct _tagOLECMD {
        ULONG   cmdID;
        DWORD   cmdf;
    } OLECMD;

    typedef struct _tagOLECMDTEXT{
            DWORD cmdtextf;
            ULONG cwActual;
            ULONG cwBuf;
            long  rgwz;
    } OLECMDTEXT;
```

```
typedef enum OLECMDID {
    OLECMDID_OPEN                        = 1,
    OLECMDID_NEW                         = 2,
    OLECMDID_SAVE                        = 3,
    OLECMDID_SAVEAS                      = 4,
    OLECMDID_SAVECOPYAS                  = 5,
    OLECMDID_PRINT                       = 6,
    OLECMDID_PRINTPREVIEW               = 7,
    OLECMDID_PAGESETUP                   = 8,
    OLECMDID_SPELL                       = 9,
    OLECMDID_PROPERTIES                  = 10,
    OLECMDID_CUT                         = 11,
    OLECMDID_COPY                        = 12,
    OLECMDID_PASTE                       = 13,
    OLECMDID_PASTESPECIAL                = 14,
    OLECMDID_UNDO                        = 15,
    OLECMDID_REDO                        = 16,
    OLECMDID_SELECTALL                   = 17,
    OLECMDID_CLEARSELECTION              = 18,
    OLECMDID_ZOOM                        = 19,
    OLECMDID_GETZOOMRANGE                = 20,
    OLECMDID_UPDATECOMMANDS              = 21,
    OLECMDID_REFRESH                     = 22,
    OLECMDID_STOP                        = 23,
    OLECMDID_HIDETOOLBARS                = 24,
    OLECMDID_SETPROGRESSMAX              = 25,
    OLECMDID_SETPROGRESSPOS              = 26,
    OLECMDID_SETPROGRESSTEXT             = 27,
    OLECMDID_SETTITLE                    = 28,
    OLECMDID_SETDOWNLOADSTATE            = 29,
    OLECMDID_STOPDOWNLOAD                = 30,
    OLECMDID_ONTOOLBARACTIVATED          = 31,
    OLECMDID_FIND                        = 32,
    OLECMDID_DELETE                      = 33,
    OLECMDID_HTTPEQUIV                   = 34,
    OLECMDID_HTTPEQUIV_DONE              = 35,
    OLECMDID_ENABLE_INTERACTION          = 36,
    OLECMDID_ONUNLOAD                    = 37,
    OLECMDID_PROPERTYBAG2                = 38,
    OLECMDID_PREREFRESH                  = 39,
} OLECMDID;

typedef enum OLECMDTEXTF {
    OLECMDTEXTF_NONE        = 0,
    OLECMDTEXTF_NAME        = 1,
    OLECMDTEXTF_STATUS      = 2,
} OLECMDTEXTF;

typedef enum OLECMDEXECOPT {
    OLECMDEXECOPT_DODEFAULT         = 0,
    OLECMDEXECOPT_PROMPTUSER        = 1,
    OLECMDEXECOPT_DONTPROMPTUSER    = 2,
    OLECMDEXECOPT_SHOWHELP          = 3
} OLECMDEXECOPT;
```

```
        HRESULT QueryStatus([in] LPGUID pguidCmdGroup,
                            [in] ULONG cCmds,
                            [in] LPOLECMD prgCmds,
                            [in] LPOLECMDTEXT pCmdText);

        HRESULT Exec([in] LPGUID pguidCmdGroup,
                     [in] DWORD nCmdID,
                     [in] DWORD nCmdExecOpt,
                     [in] VARIANT *pvaIn,
                     [in, out] VARIANT *pvaOut);

}


//-----------------------------------------------------------
//IOleWindow
//-----------------------------------------------------------
[
    uuid(00000114-0000-0000-C000-000000000046),
    helpstring("IOleWindow Interface"),
    odl
]
interface IOleWindow : IUnknown
{
    HRESULT GetWindow([out, retval] long *phwnd);
    HRESULT ContextSensitiveHelp([in] boolean fEnterMode);
};


//-----------------------------------------------------------
//IPersist
//-----------------------------------------------------------
[
    uuid(0000010c-0000-0000-C000-000000000046),
    helpstring("IPersist Interface"),
    odl
]
interface IPersist : IUnknown
{
    HRESULT GetClassID([in, out] CLSID *lpClassID);
}


//-----------------------------------------------------------
//
// IPersistFile
//
// (this interface is actually derived from
//  IPersist not IUnknown)
//-----------------------------------------------------------

[
    uuid(0000010b-0000-0000-C000-000000000046),
    helpstring("IPersistFile Interface"),
    odl
]
interface IPersistFile : IUnknown
```

```
{

    //IPersist
    HRESULT GetClassID([in, out] CLSID *lpClassID);

    //IPersistFile
    HRESULT IsDirty();

    HRESULT Load([in] LPCOLESTR pszFileName,
                 [in] DWORD dwMode);

    HRESULT Save([in] LPCOLESTR pszFileName,
                 [in] BOOL fRemember);

    HRESULT SaveCompleted([in] LPCOLESTR pszFileName);

    HRESULT GetCurFile([in, out] LPOLESTR *ppszFileName);

}


//-----------------------------------------------------------
// IPersistFolder
//
// (this interface is actually derived from
//   IPersist not IUnknown)
//-----------------------------------------------------------
[
    uuid(000214ea-0000-0000-c000-000000000046),
    helpstring("IPersistFolder Interface"),
    odl
]
interface IPersistFolder : IUnknown
{
    // IPersist methods
    HRESULT GetClassID([in, out] CLSID *lpClassID);

    // IPersistFolder methods
    HRESULT Initialize([in] LPCITEMIDLIST pidl);
}

//-----------------------------------------------------------
// IQueryInfo
//-----------------------------------------------------------
[
    uuid(00021500-0000-0000-C000-000000000046),
    helpstring("IQueryInfo Interface"),
    odl
]
interface IQueryInfo : IUnknown
{
    HRESULT GetInfoTip([in] DWORD dwFlags,
                       [in, out] LPWSTRVB *ppwszTip);
    HRESULT GetInfoFlags([in, out] DWORD *pdwFlags);
}
```

```
[
    uuid(6d5140c1-7436-11ce-8034-00aa006009fa),
    helpstring("IServiceProvider Interface"),
    odl
]


//------------------------------------------------------------
// IServiceProvider
//------------------------------------------------------------
interface IServiceProvider : IUnknown
{

    HRESULT QueryService(
        [in] REFGUID guidService,
        [in] REFIID riid,
        [out, retval] IUnknown** ppvObject);
}


//------------------------------------------------------------
// IShellBrowser
//
// (this interface is actually derived from
//   IOleWindow)
//------------------------------------------------------------
typedef enum {
    SBSP_DEFBROWSER           = 0x0000,
    SBSP_SAMEBROWSER          = 0x0001,
    SBSP_NEWBROWSER           = 0x0002,
    SBSP_DEFMODE              = 0x0000,
    SBSP_OPENMODE             = 0x0010,
    SBSP_EXPLOREMODE          = 0x0020,
    SBSP_ABSOLUTE             = 0x0000,
    SBSP_RELATIVE             = 0x1000,
    SBSP_PARENT               = 0x2000,
    SBSP_NAVIGATEBACK         = 0x4000,
    SBSP_NAVIGATEFORWARD      = 0x8000,
    SBSP_ALLOW_AUTONAVIGATE   = 0x10000,
    SBSP_INITIATEDBYHLINKFRAME = 0x80000000,
    SBSP_REDIRECT             = 0x40000000,
    SBSP_WRITENOHISTORY       = 0x08000000,
    SBSP_NOAUTOSELECT         = 0x04000000
} SBSP_BROWSER;


[
    uuid(000214e2-0000-0000-c000-000000000046),
    helpstring("IShellBrowser Interface"),
    odl
]
interface IShellBrowser : IUnknown
{
    // IOleWindow
    HRESULT GetWindow([out, retval] HWND * lphwnd);
    HRESULT ContextSensitiveHelp([in] BOOL fEnterMode);
```

```
// IShellBrowser
HRESULT InsertMenusSB(
            [in] HMENU hmenuShared,
            [in] LPOLEMENUGROUPWIDTHS lpMenuWidths);

HRESULT SetMenuSB([in] HMENU hmenuShared,
                  [in] HOLEMENU holemenuReserved,
                  [in] HWND hwndActiveObject);

HRESULT RemoveMenusSB([in] HMENU hmenuShared);

HRESULT SetStatusTextSB([in] LPCOLESTR lpszStatusText);

HRESULT EnableModelessSB([in] BOOL fEnable);

HRESULT TranslateAcceleratorSB([in] LPMSG lpmsg,
                               [in] WORD wID);

HRESULT BrowseObject([in] LPCITEMIDLIST pidl,
                     [in] SBSP_BROWSER wFlags);

HRESULT GetViewStateStream([in] DWORD grfMode,
                           [in, out] LPSTREAM *ppStrm);

HRESULT GetControlWindow([in] UINT id,
                         [out, retval] HWND * lphwnd);

HRESULT SendControlMsg([in] UINT id,
                       [in] UINT uMsg,
                       [in] WPARAM wParam,
                       [in] LPARAM lParam,
                       [out, retval] LRESULT * pret);

HRESULT QueryActiveShellView(
                    [out, retval] IShellView ** ppshv);

HRESULT OnViewWindowActive([in] IShellView * ppshv);

HRESULT SetToolbarItems([in] LPTBBUTTON lpButtons,
                        [in] UINT nButtons,
                        [in] UINT uFlags);
}

//----------------------------------------------------------
// IShellExtInit
//----------------------------------------------------------

[
    uuid(000214E8-0000-0000-C000-000000000046),
    helpstring("IShellExtInit Interface"),
    odl
]
interface IShellExtInit : IUnknown
{
```

```
        HRESULT Initialize(
                      [in] LPCITEMIDLIST pidlFolder,
                      [in] IDataObject   *pDataObj,
                      [in] HKEY          hKeyProgID);
}



//----------------------------------------------------------
// IShellFolder
//----------------------------------------------------------

// IShellFolder::GetDisplayNameOf/SetNameOf uFlags
typedef enum {
    SHGDN_NORMAL            = 0,
    SHGDN_INFOLDER          = 1,
    SHGDN_INCLUDE_NONFILESYS = 0x2000,
    SHGDN_FORADDRESSBAR     = 0x4000,
    SHGDN_FORPARSING        = 0x8000,
} SHGNO;

// IShellFolder::EnumObjects
typedef enum {
    SHCONTF_FOLDERS         = 32,
    SHCONTF_NONFOLDERS      = 64,
    SHCONTF_INCLUDEHIDDEN   = 128,
} SHCONTF;

// IShellFolder::GetAttributesOf flags
typedef enum {
    SFGAO_CANCOPY           = 0x00000001, // DROPEFFECT_COPY
    SFGAO_CANMOVE           = 0x00000002, // DROPEFFECT_MOVE
    SFGAO_CANLINK           = 0x00000004, // DROPEFFECT_LINK
    SFGAO_CANRENAME         = 0x00000010,
    SFGAO_CANDELETE         = 0x00000020,
    SFGAO_HASPROPSHEET      = 0x00000040,
    SFGAO_DROPTARGET        = 0x00000100,
    SFGAO_CAPABILITYMASK    = 0x00000177,
    SFGAO_LINK              = 0x00010000,
    SFGAO_SHARE             = 0x00020000,
    SFGAO_READONLY          = 0x00040000,
    SFGAO_GHOSTED           = 0x00080000,
    SFGAO_HIDDEN            = 0x00080000,
    SFGAO_DISPLAYATTRMASK   = 0x000F0000,
    SFGAO_FILESYSANCESTOR   = 0x10000000,
    SFGAO_FOLDER            = 0x20000000,
    SFGAO_FILESYSTEM        = 0x40000000,
    SFGAO_HASSUBFOLDER      = 0x80000000,
    SFGAO_CONTENTSMASK      = 0x80000000,
    SFGAO_VALIDATE          = 0x01000000,
    SFGAO_REMOVABLE         = 0x02000000,
    SFGAO_COMPRESSED        = 0x04000000,
    SFGAO_BROWSABLE         = 0x08000000,
    SFGAO_NONENUMERATED     = 0x00100000,
    SFGAO_NEWCONTENT        = 0x00200000,
}SFGAO;
```

```
typedef struct _SHITEMID {
    short cb;
    BYTE  abID[1];
} SHITEMID;

typedef struct _ITEMIDLIST {
    SHITEMID mkid;
} ITEMIDLIST;

[
    uuid(000214e6-0000-0000-c000-000000000046),
    helpstring("IShellFolder Interface"),
    odl
]
interface IShellFolder : IUnknown
{
    HRESULT ParseDisplayName([in] HWND hwndOwner,
                             [in] LPBC pbcReserved,
                             [in] LPOLESTR lpszDisplayName,
                             [in] ULONG * pchEaten,
                             [in, out] LPITEMIDLIST * ppidl,
                             [in, out] ULONG *pdwAttributes);

    HRESULT EnumObjects(
                [in] HWND hwndOwner,
                [in] DWORD grfFlags,
                [out, retval] IEnumIDList ** ppenumIDList);

    HRESULT BindToObject([in] LPCITEMIDLIST pidl,
                         [in] LPBC pbcReserved,
                         [in] REFIID riid,
                         [in, out] LPVOID *ppvOut);

    HRESULT BindToStorage([in] LPCITEMIDLIST pidl,
                          [in] LPBC pbcReserved,
                          [in] REFIID riid,
                          [in, out] LPVOID * ppvObj);

    HRESULT CompareIDs([in] LPARAM lParam,
                       [in] LPCITEMIDLIST pidl1,
                       [in] LPCITEMIDLIST pidl2);

    HRESULT CreateViewObject([in] HWND hwndOwner,
                             [in] REFIID riid,
                             [in, out] LPVOID * ppvOut);

    HRESULT GetAttributesOf([in] UINT cidl,
                            [in, out] LPCITEMIDLIST * apidl,
                            [in, out] ULONG * rgfInOut);

    HRESULT GetUIObjectOf([in] HWND hwndOwner,
                          [in] UINT cidl,
                          [in, out] LPCITEMIDLIST * apidl,
                          [in] REFIID riid,
```

```
                              [in, out] UINT * prgfInOut,
                              [in] LPVOID ppvOut);

    HRESULT GetDisplayNameOf([in] LPCITEMIDLIST pidl,
                             [in] DWORD uFlags,
                             [in] LPSTRRET lpName);

    HRESULT SetNameOf([in] HWND hwndOwner,
                      [in] LPCITEMIDLIST pidl,
                      [in] LPCOLESTR lpszName,
                      [in] DWORD uFlags,
                      [in, out] LPITEMIDLIST * ppidlOut);
}


//------------------------------------------------------------
// IShellLinkA
//------------------------------------------------------------
[
    uuid(000214EE-0000-0000-C000-000000000046),
    helpstring("IShellLinkA Interface"),
    odl
]
interface IShellLinkA : IUnknown {

    HRESULT GetPath([in] LPSTRVB pszFile,
                    [in] int cchMaxPath,
                    [in] LPWIN32_FIND_DATA pfd,
                    [in] DWORD fFlags);

    HRESULT GetIDList([out, retval] LPITEMIDLIST * ppidl);

    HRESULT SetIDList([in] LPCITEMIDLIST pidl);

    HRESULT GetDescription([in] LPCSTRVB pszName,
                           [in] int cchMaxName);

    HRESULT SetDescription([in] LPCSTRVB pszName);

    HRESULT GetWorkingDirectory([in] LPCSTRVB pszDir,
                                [in] int cchMaxPath);

    HRESULT SetWorkingDirectory([in] LPCSTRVB pszDir);

    HRESULT GetArguments([in] LPSTRVB pszArgs,
                         [in] int cchMaxPath);

    HRESULT SetArguments([in] LPCSTRVB pszArgs);

    HRESULT GetHotkey([out, retval] WORD *pwHotkey);

    HRESULT SetHotkey([in] WORD wHotkey);

    HRESULT GetShowCmd([out, retval] int *piShowCmd);
```

```
    HRESULT SetShowCmd([in] int iShowCmd);

    HRESULT GetIconLocation([in] LPSTRVB pszIconPath,
                            [in] int cchIconPath,
                            [out, retval] int *piIcon);

    HRESULT SetIconLocation([in] LPCSTRVB pszIconPath,
                            [in] int iIcon);

    HRESULT SetRelativePath([in] LPCSTRVB pszPathRel,
                            [in] DWORD dwReserved);

    HRESULT Resolve([in] HWND hwnd, [in] DWORD fFlags);

    HRESULT SetPath([in] LPCSTRVB pszFile);
}

//--------------------------------------------------------
// IShellLinkW
//--------------------------------------------------------
[

    uuid(000214F9-0000-0000-C000-000000000046),
    helpstring("IShellLinkW Interface"),
    odl
]
interface IShellLinkW : IUnknown {

    HRESULT GetPath([in] LPWSTRVB pszFile,
                    [in] int cchMaxPath,
                    [in] LPWIN32_FIND_DATA pfd,
                    [in] DWORD fFlags);

    HRESULT GetIDList([out, retval] LPITEMIDLIST * ppidl);

    HRESULT SetIDList([in] LPCITEMIDLIST pidl);

    HRESULT GetDescription([in] LPCWSTRVB pszName,
                           [in] int cchMaxName);

    HRESULT SetDescription([in] LPCWSTRVB pszName);

    HRESULT GetWorkingDirectory([in] LPCWSTRVB pszDir,
                                [in] int cchMaxPath);

    HRESULT SetWorkingDirectory([in] LPCWSTRVB pszDir);

    HRESULT GetArguments([in] LPCWSTRVB pszArgs,
                         [in] int cchMaxPath);

    HRESULT SetArguments([in] LPCWSTRVB pszArgs);

    HRESULT GetHotkey([out, retval] WORD *pwHotkey);
```

```
        HRESULT SetHotkey([in] WORD wHotkey);

        HRESULT GetShowCmd([out, retval] int *piShowCmd);

        HRESULT SetShowCmd([in] int iShowCmd);

        HRESULT GetIconLocation([in] LPCWSTRVB pszIconPath,
                                [in] int cchIconPath,
                                [out, retval] int *piIcon);

        HRESULT SetIconLocation([in] LPCWSTRVB pszIconPath,
                                [in] int iIcon);

        HRESULT SetRelativePath([in] LPCSTRVB pszPathRel,
                                [in] DWORD dwReserved);

        HRESULT Resolve([in] HWND hwnd, [in] DWORD fFlags);

        HRESULT SetPath([in] LPCWSTRVB pszFile);
}

//------------------------------------------------------------
// IShellPropSheetExt
//------------------------------------------------------------

typedef struct MSG {
    HWND    hwnd;
    UINT    message;
    WPARAM  wParam;
    LPARAM  lParam;
    DWORD   time;
    POINT   pt;
} MSG;

typedef struct {
    HWND hwndFrom;
    UINT idFrom;
    UINT code;
} NMHDR;

typedef enum {
    PSPCB_RELEASE = 1,
    PSPCB_CREATE  = 2
} PROPSHEETCALLBACKMSG;

typedef enum {
    PSP_DEFAULT         = 0x00000000,
    PSP_DLGINDIRECT     = 0x00000001,
    PSP_USEHICON        = 0x00000002,
    PSP_USEICONID       = 0x00000004,
    PSP_USETITLE        = 0x00000008,
    PSP_RTLREADING      = 0x00000010,
    PSP_HASHELP         = 0x00000020,
    PSP_USEREFPARENT    = 0x00000040,
```

```
        PSP_USECALLBACK       = 0x00000080,
        PSP_PREMATURE         = 0x00000400,
        PSP_HIDEHEADER        = 0x00000800,
        PSP_USEHEADERTITLE    = 0x00001000,
        PSP_USEHEADERSUBTITLE = 0x00002000
} PROPERTYSHEETFLAG;

typedef enum {
        PSN_SETACTIVE  = -200,
        PSN_KILLACTIVE = -201,
        PSN_APPLY = -202,
        PSN_RESET = -203,
        PSN_QUERYCANCEL = -209
} PROPSHEETNOTIFYMSG;

typedef struct {
        DWORD dwSize;
        DWORD dwFlags;
        HINSTANCE hInstance;
        LPCSTRVB pszTemplate;
        HICON hIcon;
        LPCSTRVB pszTitle;
        DLGPROC pfnDlgProc;
        LPARAM lParam;
        LPFNPSPCALLBACK pfnCallback;
        long pcRefParent;
        LPCTSTRVB pszHeaderTitle;
        LPCTSTRVB pszHeaderSubTitle;
} PROPSHEETPAGE;


[
        uuid(000214e9-0000-0000-c000-000000000046),
        helpstring("IShellPropSheetExt Interface"),
        odl
]
interface IShellPropSheetExt : IUnknown
{
        HRESULT AddPages([in] LPFNADDPROPSHEETPAGE lpfnAddPage,
                         [in] LPARAM lParam);

        HRESULT ReplacePage(
                [in] UINT uPageID,
                [in] LPFNADDPROPSHEETPAGE lpfnReplaceWith,
                [in] LPARAM lParam);
}


//------------------------------------------------------------
// IShellView
//
// (this interface is actually derived from
//  IOleWindow not IUnknown)
//------------------------------------------------------------
```

```
typedef enum {
    FCW_STATUS      = 0x0001,
    FCW_TOOLBAR     = 0x0002,
    FCW_TREE        = 0x0003,
    FCW_INTERNETBAR = 0x0006,
    FCW_PROGRESS    = 0x0008,
} FCW;

typedef struct {
    UINT    ViewMode;
    UINT    fFlags;
}FOLDERSETTINGS;

typedef struct _LVITEM {
    UINT    mask;
    int     iItem;
    int     iSubItem;
    UINT    state;
    UINT    stateMask;
    LPTSTR  pszText;
    int     cchTextMax;
    int     iImage;
    LPARAM  lParam;
    int     iIndent;
} LVITEM;


// shellview select item flags
typedef enum {
    SVSI_DESELECT       = 0x0000,
    SVSI_SELECT         = 0x0001,
    SVSI_EDIT           = 0x0003,
    SVSI_DESELECTOTHERS = 0x0004,
    SVSI_ENSUREVISIBLE  = 0x0008,
    SVSI_FOCUSED        = 0x0010,
    SVSI_TRANSLATEPT    = 0x0020,
} SVSI;

// shellview get item object flags
typedef enum {
    SVGIO_BACKGROUND    = 0x00000000,
    SVGIO_SELECTION     = 0x00000001,
    SVGIO_ALLVIEW       = 0x00000002,
} SVGIO;

// uState values for IShellView::UIActivate
typedef enum {
    SVUIA_DEACTIVATE        = 0,
    SVUIA_ACTIVATE_NOFOCUS  = 1,
    SVUIA_ACTIVATE_FOCUS    = 2,
    SVUIA_INPLACEACTIVATE   = 3
} SVUIA_STATUS;
```

```
[
    uuid(000214e3-0000-0000-c000-000000000046),
    helpstring("IShellView Interface"),
    odl
]
interface IShellView : IUnknown
{
    // IOleWindow
    HRESULT GetWindow([out, retval] HWND * lphwnd);
    HRESULT ContextSensitiveHelp([in] BOOL fEnterMode);

    // IShellView
    HRESULT TranslateAccelerator([in] LPMSG lpmsg);

    HRESULT EnableModeless([in] BOOL fEnable);

    HRESULT UIActivate([in] SVUIA_STATUS uState);

    HRESULT Refresh();

    HRESULT CreateViewWindow(
                [in, out]  IShellView *lpPrevView,
                [in] LPCFOLDERSETTINGS lpfs,
                [in, out] IShellBrowser  * psb,
                [in] LPRECT prcView,
                [in, out] HWND   *phWnd);

    HRESULT DestroyViewWindow();

    HRESULT GetCurrentInfo([in] LPFOLDERSETTINGS lpfs);

    HRESULT AddPropertySheetPages(
                [in] DWORD dwReserved,
                [in] LPFNADDPROPSHEETPAGE lpfn,
                [in] LPARAM lparam);

    HRESULT SaveViewState();

    HRESULT SelectItem([in] LPCITEMIDLIST pidlItem,
                    [in] UINT uFlags);

    HRESULT GetItemObject([in] UINT uItem,
                    [in] REFIID riid,
                    [in] LPVOID *ppv);

}


//---------------------------------------------------------
// IStream
//
// (this interface is actually derived from
//   ISequentialStream)
//---------------------------------------------------------
```

```
[
    uuid(0000000c-0000-0000-C000-000000000046),
    helpstring("IStream Interface"),
    odl
]
interface IStream : IUnknown
{

    // ISequentialStream Methods
    HRESULT Read([in, out] void *pv,
                 [in] ULONG cb,
                 [out, retval] ULONG *pcbRead);

    HRESULT Write([in] LPVOID *pv,
                  [in] ULONG cb,
                  [out, retval] ULONG *pcbWritten);

    //IStream

    typedef struct tagSTATSTG
    {
        LPOLESTR pwcsName;
        DWORD type;
        ULARGE_INTEGER cbSize;
        FILETIME mtime;
        FILETIME ctime;
        FILETIME atime;
        DWORD grfMode;
        DWORD grfLocksSupported;
        CLSID clsid;
        DWORD grfStateBits;
        DWORD reserved;
    } STATSTG;

    typedef enum tagSTGTY
    {
        STGTY_STORAGE    = 1,
        STGTY_STREAM     = 2,
        STGTY_LOCKBYTES  = 3,
        STGTY_PROPERTY   = 4
    } STGTY;

    typedef enum tagSTREAM_SEEK
    {
        STREAM_SEEK_SET = 0,
        STREAM_SEEK_CUR = 1,
        STREAM_SEEK_END = 2
    } STREAM_SEEK;

    typedef enum tagLOCKTYPE
    {
        LOCK_WRITE       = 1,
        LOCK_EXCLUSIVE   = 2,
        LOCK_ONLYONCE    = 4
    } LOCKTYPE;
```

```
            HRESULT Seek(
                [in] LARGE_INTEGER dlibMove,
                [in] DWORD dwOrigin,
                [out, retval] ULARGE_INTEGER *plibNewPosition);

            HRESULT SetSize([in] ULARGE_INTEGER libNewSize);

            HRESULT CopyTo([in] IStream *pstm,
                           [in] ULARGE_INTEGER cb,
                           [in, out] ULARGE_INTEGER *pcbRead,
                           [in, out] ULARGE_INTEGER *pcbWritten);

            HRESULT Commit([in] DWORD grfCommitFlags);

            HRESULT Revert();

            HRESULT LockRegion(
                [in] ULARGE_INTEGER libOffset,
                [in] ULARGE_INTEGER cb,
                [in] DWORD dwLockType);

            HRESULT UnlockRegion(
                [in] ULARGE_INTEGER libOffset,
                [in] ULARGE_INTEGER cb,
                [in] DWORD dwLockType);

            HRESULT Stat(
                [in, out] STATSTG *pstatstg,
                [in] DWORD grfStatFlag);

            HRESULT Clone(
                [out, retval] IStream **ppstm);

    }


    // IUnknown implementation
    [
        uuid(00000000-0000-0000-C000-000000000046),
        helpstring("IUnknownVB Interface"),
        odl
    ]
    interface IUnknownVB
    {
        HRESULT QueryInterface([in] REFIID priid,
                               [in, out] VOID *ppvObject);

        long AddRef();

        long Release();

    };



}
```

B

Pointers

CopyMemory is used a great deal throughout the course of this book to copy memory from one location to another. Without this function, it would be impossible to use pointers in Visual Basic. Since the function does exist, it is possible to write some very dangerous VB code. A short course on *CopyMemory* and pointers is definitely in order.

CopyMemory

There is really no function called *CopyMemory*. *CopyMemory* is merely an alias for the Win32 function *RtlMoveMemory*. Bruce McKinney, the author of *Hardcore Visual Basic* (Microsoft Press), was probably the first to use the alias *CopyMemory*. Now it is quite common to see *RtlMoveMemory* declared in this fashion. Its syntax (as reflected in a Visual Basic **Declare** statement) is:

```
Public Declare Sub CopyMemory Lib "kernel32" Alias "RtlMoveMemory" _
    (pDest As Any, pSource As Any, ByVal ByteLen As Long)
```

where *pDest* is a pointer to the starting target address to which data is to be copied, *pSource* is a pointer to the starting address from which data is to be copied, and *ByteLen* is the number of bytes to be copied.

The Undocumented VBA Functions

CopyMemory does not do the job alone. Without the help of three undocumented functions—*VarPtr*, *StrPtr*, and *ObjPtr*, this function would be useless. These functions return pointers to variables, strings, and objects, respectively. One or more of these functions usually gets the source or destination address that make up the arguments to *CopyMemory*. All three of these functions are located in the VB runt-ime DLL. Incidentally, all three functions are internally mapped to the same func-tion, *VarPtr*, but you should use each function as it was designed to be used or you will have some problems.

VarPtr

This function is used to return a pointer to a variable. Not only does this include variables of all native VB datatypes, but UDTs as well. The function returns a Long value, which is the address of the variable. Do not use this function to get point-ers to Strings; you will not get the value that you expect. Use *StrPtr* instead.

The following code fragment uses *VarPtr* to return the starting address of a user-defined type:

```
Dim ft As FILETIME
Dim pft As Long
pft = VarPtr(ft)
```

StrPtr

This function is used exclusively to return pointers to Strings. Never use *VarPtr* when you want the address of a String, since it returns a pointer to the ANSI buffer VB creates when passing Strings to API functions.

The following code fragment uses *StrPtr* to return the starting address of a Visual Basic string:

```
Dim str As String
    str = "Hello, Kara!"

Dim pstr As Long
    pstr = StrPtr(str)
```

ObjPtr

Use this function when you need to return the address of an Object. This is useful if you need to get at the vtable for a class (and quite dangerous, too). You can also use this function to determine whether an instance of a class is valid.

For example, the following code fragment determines whether **adoConnection** is a valid object reference and, if it is, calls its **Close** method and releases the object reference:

```
If ObjPtr(adoConnection) <> 0 Then
    adoConnection.Close
    Set adoConnection = Nothing
End If
```

Some CopyMemory Examples

When looking at the following examples, note the distinction between passing an argument by reference (**ByRef**) versus passing an argument by value (**ByVal**). Remember, when you pass an argument **ByVal**, you are passing the actual value. When you pass an argument **ByRef** (also designated by the absence of the **ByRef** keyword, since this is Visual Basic's default method of parameter passing), you are really passing a pointer to that value. Keep this in mind as you look at the following examples.

Example 1

```
Private Type SomeUDT
    Field1 As String * 256
    Field2 As String * 256
    Field3 As String * 256
End Type

Public Sub CopyUDT()

    Dim udtA As SomeUDT'This is a user-defined type
    Dim udtB As SomeUDT

    udtA.Field1 = "Bill Purvis"
    udtA.Field2 = "Chris Mercier"
    udtA.Field3 = "Kelly Christopher"

    CopyMemory udtB, udtA, Len(udtB)

End Sub
```

This example shows a nice way to a copy a user-defined type. This is much more efficient than doing the following:

```
udtB.Field1 = udtA.Field1
udtB.Field2 = udtA.Field2
udtB.Field3 = udtA.Field3
```

Examine the call to *CopyMemory* for a moment. Notice that both UDTs are passed by reference. In fact, UDTs will always be passed by reference. This is enforced by the compiler itself. So, essentially, there is nothing to remember here. If you forget that UDTs are always passed by reference, the compiler will remind you. Also, note that this example works because the members of the UDT are fixed-length strings. If they were not, chances are this code would cause a protection fault.

Example 2

In the previous example, we had direct access to both the source and destination variables (both UDTs were declared locally). But many times throughout the

course of this book, we have had only the raw address to some value. This was
the case in Chapter 8, *Data Handlers*, when we created a data handler. The shell
called the `IDataObject::GetData` method in our component and passed a
pointer to a `FORMATETC` structure and a pointer to a `STGMEDIUM` structure:

```
Public Sub IDataObject_GetData(ByVal pFmtEtc As FORMATETC, _
                               ByVal pmedium as STGMEDIUM)

    Dim fmtEtc As FORMATETC

    CopyMemory fmtEtc, ByVal pFmtEtc, Len(fmtEtc)
    .
    .
    .
```

In this example, we are copying a `FORMATETC` structure from the address `pFmtEtc`
into a local instance that we can directly address within the function. As you can
see, `fmtEtc`, our local instance of FORMATETC, is passed to *CopyMemory* by reference. Remember that all UDTs are always passed by reference, so this is why we
do this.

Our source parameter to *CopyMemory*, however, is being passed `ByVal`. Why?
Think about this—*CopyMemory* copies a specified amount of data from one
address to another address. Well, the value of `pFmtEtc` is an address itself. It is
the address from which we want to copy. So if we did this as:

```
'This is wrong
CopyMemory fmtEtc, pFmtEtc, Len(fmtEtc)
```

we would be passing the address of an address! In other words, a pointer to a
pointer. We want *CopyMemory* to copy data from the address specified by
pFmtEtc; therefore we pass it `ByVal`.

Example 3

This example is the exact opposite of Example 2 (as far as the direction of the
copy). In this example, a pointer to some address far, far away is being passed
into the function. The function then copies an Integer value to that address:

```
Public Function Foo(ByVal pInteger As Long)
    Dim nValue As Integer
    nValue = 1138
    CopyMemory ByVal pInteger, nValue, 2
End Function
```

There are several things to note in this example. The first is that the parameter to
the function is a pointer to an integer. Any address is always 4-bytes wide on a 32-
bit machine. An Integer is 2-bytes wide. The moral of this story? It's really stupid to
go around passing pointers to integers because they are bigger than the datatype
itself. So keep in mind that this is just an example, okay?

Our destination in this example is *pInteger*. It is an address, so it needs to be passed ByVal, as was stated in the "Example 2" section. But *nValue* is passed by reference. Why? Well, *nValue* equals 1138. If we passed *nValue* ByVal, this would tell *CopyMemory* to copy 2 bytes from the *address* 1138 to the location pointed to by *pInteger*. Who knows what value is at the address 1138? This is not what we want. We want to copy the *actual* value, 1138, to the location *pInteger*; therefore, it is passed by reference. This tells *CopyMemory* to copy 2 bytes of data from the address of *nValue* (which contains 1138) to the address pInteger.

Typically, though, you should not have to use any of the pointer functions when you are working with your day-to-day code. Consider, the *SetWindowText* API function:

```
BOOL SetWindowText( HWND hWnd, LPCTSTR lpString);
```

Parameter two is a pointer to a string, yet in Visual Basic this function is declared as follows:

```
Public Declare Function SetWindowText _
    Lib "user32" Alias "SetWindowTextA" (ByVal hwnd As Long, _
    ByVal lpString As String) As Long
```

Even though the function requires a pointer, we can pass a string to it directly from VB. This is because VB really handles passing the address of the string to the API function for us.

Even API calls that require UDTs, like *GetWindowRect*, allow us to pass a UDT directly to the function. This is because, once again, VB handles passing the address to the UDT for us. And this is the case for 99.9% of the coding you will do.

The point is, if you find yourself using these pointer functions, chances are, you are doing so unnecessarily. Nothing is worse for a developer than having to look at miles and miles of convoluted code. These pointer functions are only useful in the extreme cases where there is no other way to achieve the desired results. Consider the **PROPSHEETPAGE** structure (in IDL):

```
typedef [public] long LPCSTRVB;

typedef struct {
        DWORD dwSize;
        DWORD dwFlags;
        HINSTANCE hInstance;
        LPCSTRVB pszTemplate;
        HICON hIcon;
        LPCSTRVB pszTitle;
        DLGPROC pfnDlgProc;
        LPARAM lParam;
        LPFNPSPCALLBACK pfnCallback;
        long pcRefParent;
```

```
        LPCTSTRVB pszHeaderTitle;
        LPCTSTRVB pszHeaderSubTitle;
    } PROPSHEETPAGE;
```

The *pszTitle* member of this structure is really a Long value—an address. Without *StrPtr*, there is no way at all to provide the address of a string to populate this structure. This is a valid reason to use the function. This structure also contains a member called *lParam*, which is also a 4-byte value. By using *ObjPtr*, we can store the address of our object in this parameter. When this structure is passed back to us in a callback procedure, we are able to retrieve the reference and gain access back to our object. It's a very handy and very appropriate use of *ObjPtr*. And it's very rare, too, so you probably won't use it more than once or twice.

Index

About the Author

J. P. Hamilton is a software engineer who lives and works in Houston, Texas. At the age of eight, a serious addiction to Space Invaders and a lack of funds led him to his first PC, a 6502-based beast built by Ohio Scientific. He's been programming ever since. He has been dabbling in the black art of COM programming for several years and uses both the C++ and Visual Basic languages. From time to time, he leaves the realm of programming to pursue his other interests: skydiving, running marathons, yoga, and drinking coffee. His machine at home also doubles as a digital audio workstation where he composes electronic music of all kinds. He believes one should experience as much as possible in this life, and is currently scheming for a way to climb Mt. Everest.

Colophon

Our look is the result of reader comments, our own experimentation, and feedback from distribution channels. Distinctive covers complement our distinctive approach to technical topics, breathing personality and life into potentially dry subjects.

The animal on the cover of *Visual Basic Shell Programming* is a sea urchin (*globigerina foraminifer*). The name "sea urchin" is derived from an Old English word for the spiny hedgehog, a land animal similar to the American porcupine; they have been referred to as the "porcupines of the sea." Like a porcupine's quills, the sea urchin counts on its long spines to deter hungry predators.

The sea urchin's outer skeleton, called a test, is composed of ten fused plates that encircle the sea urchin's inner organs. Every other section has holes through which the sea urchin can extend its tubed feet. These feet are controlled by a water vascular system. By changing the amount of water inside, the animal can extend or contract its feet to move about. Sea urchins primarily use their feet to hang on to the bottom while feeding, but they can move quickly if necessary, moving on their feet, spines, or even their teeth. The sea urchin uses its teeth to scrape rocks clean of algae. Due to such wear, the animal's teeth frequently grow and replace worn ones.

The sea urchin is sought out as food for birds, sea stars, cod, lobsters, and humans. Sea urchin eggs, commonly known as roe, are considered a delicacy in Asia and the United States and are a main component of sushi.

Jeffrey Holcomb was the production editor for *Visual Basic Shell Programming*. Clairemarie Fisher O'Leary was the copyeditor. Mary Sheehan, Nancy Kotary, and

Madeleine Newell provided quality control. Mary Sheehan and Emily Quill provided production assistance. Nancy Crumpton wrote the index.

Ellie Volckhausen designed the cover of this book, based on a series design by Edie Freedman. The cover image is a 19th-century engraving from the Dover Pictorial Archive. Emma Colby produced the cover layout with QuarkXPress 4.1 using Adobe's ITC Garamond font.

Alicia Cech and David Futato designed the interior layout based on a series design by Nancy Priest. Mike Sierra implemented the design in FrameMaker 5.5.6. The text and heading fonts are ITC Garamond Light and Garamond Book. The illustrations that appear in the book were produced by Robert Romano and Rhon Porter using Macromedia FreeHand 8 and Adobe Photoshop 5. This colophon was written by Maureen Dempsey.

Whenever possible, our books use RepKover™, a durable and flexible lay-flat binding. If the page count exceeds RepKover's limit, perfect binding is used.

More Titles from O'Reilly
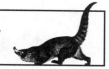

Visual Basic Programming

Developing Visual Basic Add-ins

By Steven Roman
1st Edition December 1998
186 pages, ISBN 1-56592-527-0

A tutorial and reference guide in one, this short book covers all the basics of creating customized VB add-ins to extend the IDE, allowing developers to work more productively with Visual Basic. Readers with even a modest acquaintance with VB will be developing add-ins in no time. Includes numerous simple code examples.

VB & VBA in a Nutshell: The Language

By Paul Lomax
1st Edition October 1998
656 pages, ISBN 1-56592-358-8

For Visual Basic and VBA programmers, this book boils down the essentials of the VB and VBA languages into a single volume, including undocumented and little-documented areas essential to everyday programming. The convenient alphabetical reference to all functions, procedures, statements, and keywords allows programmers to use this book both as a standard reference guide and as a tool for troubleshooting and identifying programming problems.

Access Database Design & Programming, 2nd Edition

By Steven Roman
2nd Edition July 1999
432 pages, ISBN 1-56592-626-9

This second edition of the bestselling *Access Database Design & Programming* covers Access' new VBA Integrated Development Environment used by Word, Excel, and PowerPoint; the VBA language itself; Microsoft's latest data access technology, Active Data Objects (ADO); plus Open Database Connectivity (ODBC).

Learning Word Programming

By Steven Roman
1st Edition October 1998
408 pages, ISBN 1-56592-524-6

This no-nonsense book delves into VBA programming and tells how you can use VBA to automate all the tedious, repetitive jobs you never thought you could do in Microsoft Word. It takes the reader step-by-step through writing VBA macros and programs, illustrating how to generate tables of a particular format, manage shortcut keys, create fax cover sheets, and reformat documents.

Visual Basic Controls in a Nutshell

By Evan S. Dictor
1st Edition July 1999
762 pages, ISBN 1-56592-294-8

To create professional applications, developers need extensive knowledge of Visual Basic controls and their numerous properties, methods, and events. This quick reference documents the steps involved in using each major VB control, the order in which their events are fired, and the unexpected ways in which their properties, methods, and events interact.

Learning VBScript

By Paul Lomax
1st Edition July 1997
616 pages, Includes CD-ROM
ISBN 1-56592-247-6

This definitive guide shows Web developers how to take full advantage of client-side scripting with the VBScript language. In addition to basic language features, it covers the Internet Explorer object model and discusses techniques for client-side scripting, like adding ActiveX controls to a Web page or validating data before sending it to the server. Includes CD-ROM with over 170 code samples.

O'REILLY®

TO ORDER: **800-998-9938** • *order@oreilly.com* • *http://www.oreilly.com/*
OUR PRODUCTS ARE AVAILABLE AT A BOOKSTORE OR SOFTWARE STORE NEAR YOU.
FOR INFORMATION: **800-998-9938** • **707-829-0515** • *info@oreilly.com*

Visual Basic Programming

ASP in a Nutshell

By A. Keyton Weissinger
1st Edition February 1999
426 pages, ISBN 1-56592-490-8

This detailed reference contains all the information Web developers need to create effective Active Server Pages (ASP) applications. It focuses on how features are used in a real application and highlights little-known or undocumented aspects, enabling even experienced developers to advance their ASP applications to new levels.

Developing ASP Components

By Shelley Powers
1st Edition April 1999
510 pages, ISBN 1-56592-446-0

Developing add-on controls and components is emerging as a multibillion dollar industry that is increasingly attracting the attention of developers. This book provides developers with the information and real-world examples they need to create custom ASP components using any of the three major development tools: Visual Basic, Visual C++, and J++.

ADO: The Definitive Guide

By Jason T. Roff
1st Edition November 2000 (est.)
450 pages (est.), ISBN 1-56592-415-0

The architecture of ADO, Microsoft's newest form of database communication, is simple, concise, and efficient. This indispensable reference takes a comprehensive look at every object, collection, method, and property of ADO for developers who want to get a leg up on this exciting new technology.

Writing Excel Macros

By Steven Roman
1st Edition May 1999
552 pages, ISBN 1-56592-587-4

Writing Excel Macros offers a solid introduction to writing VBA macros and programs in Excel and shows you how to get more power out of Excel at the programming level. Learn how to get the most out of this formidable application as you focus on programming languages, the Visual Basic Editor, handling code, and the Excel object model.

Win32 API Programming with Visual Basic

By Steve Roman
1st Edition November 1999
534 pages, Includes CD-ROM
ISBN 1-56592-631-5

This book provides the missing documentation for VB programmers who want to harness the power of accessing the Win32 API within Visual Basic. It shows how to create powerful and unique applications without needing a background in Visual C++ or Win32 API programming.

How to stay in touch with O'Reilly

1. Visit Our Award-Winning Web Site

http://www.oreilly.com/

★ "Top 100 Sites on the Web" —*PC Magazine*
★ "Top 5% Web sites" —*Point Communications*
★ "3-Star site" —*The McKinley Group*

Our web site contains a library of comprehensive product information (including book excerpts and tables of contents), downloadable software, background articles, interviews with technology leaders, links to relevant sites, book cover art, and more. File us in your Bookmarks or Hotlist!

2. Join Our Email Mailing Lists

New Product Releases

To receive automatic email with brief descriptions of all new O'Reilly products as they are released, send email to:
listproc@online.oreilly.com
Put the following information in the first line of your message (*not* in the Subject field):
subscribe oreilly-news

O'Reilly Events

If you'd also like us to send information about trade show events, special promotions, and other O'Reilly events, send email to:
listproc@online.oreilly.com
Put the following information in the first line of your message (*not* in the Subject field):
subscribe oreilly-events

3. Get Examples from Our Books via FTP

There are two ways to access an archive of example files from our books:

Regular FTP

- ftp to:
  ftp.oreilly.com
  (login: anonymous
  password: your email address)
- Point your web browser to:
  ftp://ftp.oreilly.com/

FTPMAIL

- Send an email message to:
  ftpmail@online.oreilly.com
  (Write "help" in the message body)

4. Contact Us via Email

order@oreilly.com
To place a book or software order online. Good for North American and international customers.

subscriptions@oreilly.com
To place an order for any of our newsletters or periodicals.

books@oreilly.com
General questions about any of our books.

software@oreilly.com
For general questions and product information about our software. Check out O'Reilly Software Online at **http://software.oreilly.com/** for software and technical support information. Registered O'Reilly software users send your questions to: **website-support@oreilly.com**

cs@oreilly.com
For answers to problems regarding your order or our products.

booktech@oreilly.com
For book content technical questions or corrections.

proposals@oreilly.com
To submit new book or software proposals to our editors and product managers.

international@oreilly.com
For information about our international distributors or translation queries. For a list of our distributors outside of North America check out:
http://www.oreilly.com/www/order/country.html

5. Work with Us

Check out our website for current employment opportunites:
www.jobs@oreilly.com
Click on "Work with Us"

O'Reilly & Associates, Inc.
101 Morris Street, Sebastopol, CA 95472 USA
TEL   707-829-0515 or 800-998-9938
         (6am to 5pm PST)
FAX   707-829-0104

O'REILLY®

International Distributors

UK, EUROPE, MIDDLE EAST AND AFRICA (EXCEPT FRANCE, GERMANY, AUSTRIA, SWITZERLAND, LUXEMBOURG, LIECHTENSTEIN, AND EASTERN EUROPE)

INQUIRIES
O'Reilly UK Limited
4 Castle Street
Farnham
Surrey, GU9 7HS
United Kingdom
Telephone: 44-1252-711776
Fax: 44-1252-734211
Email: information@oreilly.co.uk

ORDERS
Wiley Distribution Services Ltd.
1 Oldlands Way
Bognor Regis
West Sussex PO22 9SA
United Kingdom
Telephone: 44-1243-779777
Fax: 44-1243-820250
Email: cs-books@wiley.co.uk

FRANCE

INQUIRIES
Éditions O'Reilly
18 rue Séguier
75006 Paris, France
Tel: 33-1-40-51-52-30
Fax: 33-1-40-51-52-31
Email: france@editions-oreilly.fr

ORDERS
GEODIF
61, Bd Saint-Germain
75240 Paris Cedex 05, France
Tel: 33-1-44-41-46-16 (French books)
Tel: 33-1-44-41-11-87 (English books)
Fax: 33-1-44-41-11-44
Email: distribution@eyrolles.com

GERMANY, SWITZERLAND, AUSTRIA, EASTERN EUROPE, LUXEMBOURG, AND LIECHTENSTEIN

INQUIRIES & ORDERS
O'Reilly Verlag
Balthasarstr. 81
D-50670 Köln
Germany
Telephone: 49-221-973160-91
Fax: 49-221-973160-8
Email: anfragen@oreilly.de (inquiries)
Email: order@oreilly.de (orders)

CANADA (FRENCH LANGUAGE BOOKS)

Les Éditions Flammarion ltée
375, Avenue Laurier Ouest
Montréal (Québec) H2V 2K3
Tel: 00-1-514-277-8807
Fax: 00-1-514-278-2085
Email: info@flammarion.qc.ca

HONG KONG

City Discount Subscription Service, Ltd.
Unit D, 3rd Floor, Yan's Tower
27 Wong Chuk Hang Road
Aberdeen, Hong Kong
Tel: 852-2580-3539
Fax: 852-2580-6463
Email: citydis@ppn.com.hk

KOREA

Hanbit Media, Inc.
Chungmu Bldg. 201
Yonnam-dong 568-33
Mapo-gu
Seoul, Korea
Tel: 822-325-0397
Fax: 822-325-9697
Email: hant93@chollian.dacom.co.kr

PHILIPPINES

Global Publishing
G/F Benavides Garden
1186 Benavides Street
Manila, Philippines
Tel: 632-254-8949/637-252-2582
Fax: 632-734-5060/632-252-2733
Email: globalp@pacific.net.ph

TAIWAN

O'Reilly Taiwan
No. 3, Lane 131
Hang-Chow South Road
Section 1, Taipei, Taiwan
Tel: 886-2-23968990
Fax: 886-2-23968916
Email: taiwan@oreilly.com

CHINA

O'Reilly Beijing
Room 2410
160, FuXingMenNeiDaJie
XiCheng District
Beijing, China PR 100031
Tel: 86-10-66412305
Fax: 86-10-86631007
Email: beijing@oreilly.com

INDIA

Computer Bookshop (India) Pvt. Ltd.
190 Dr. D.N. Road, Fort
Bombay 400 001 India
Tel: 91-22-207-0989
Fax: 91-22-262-3551
Email: csbsbom@giasbm01.vsnl.net.in

JAPAN

O'Reilly Japan, Inc.
Yotsuya Y's Building
7 Banch 6, Honshio-cho
Shinjuku-ku
Tokyo 160-0003 Japan
Tel: 81-3-3356-5227
Fax: 81-3-3356-5261
Email: japan@oreilly.com

ALL OTHER ASIAN COUNTRIES

O'Reilly & Associates, Inc.
101 Morris Street
Sebastopol, CA 95472 USA
Tel: 707-829-0515
Fax: 707-829-0104
Email: order@oreilly.com

AUSTRALIA

Woodslane Pty., Ltd.
7/5 Vuko Place
Warriewood NSW 2102
Australia
Tel: 61-2-9970-5111
Fax: 61-2-9970-5002
Email: info@woodslane.com.au

NEW ZEALAND

Woodslane New Zealand, Ltd.
21 Cooks Street (P.O. Box 575)
Waganui, New Zealand
Tel: 64-6-347-6543
Fax: 64-6-345-4840
Email: info@woodslane.com.au

LATIN AMERICA

McGraw-Hill Interamericana
Editores, S.A. de C.V.
Cedro No. 512
Col. Atlampa
06450, Mexico, D.F.
Tel: 52-5-547-6777
Fax: 52-5-547-3336
Email: mcgraw-hill@infosel.net.mx